ISLAMIC REPUBLIC AND NATIONS

ISLAMIC REPUBLIC AND NATIONS

Dr. Akhlaque Ahmad

RANDOM PUBLICATIONS

NEW DELHI - 110 002 (INDIA)

Islamic Republic and Nations

ISBN 978-93-51117-29-2

Published in 2015 in India by

RANDOM PUBLICATIONS

4376-A/4B, Gali Murari Lal, Ansari Road
New Delhi-110 002
Phone: +9111-43580356, 23289044
E-mail: randomexports@gmail.com; sales@randompublications.com;
info@randompublications.com

Reprinted 2026

Type Setting by: Friends Media, Delhi-110089

Preface

Islamic republic is the name given to several states in countries ruled by Islamic laws, including the Islamic Republics of Pakistan, Iran, Afghanistan, and Mauritania. Pakistan first adopted the title under the constitution of 1956. Mauritania adopted it on 28 November 1958. Iran adopted it after the 1979 Iranian Revolution that overthrew the Pahlavi dynasty. Afghanistan adopted it after the 2001 overthrow of the Taliban. Despite the similar name the countries differ greatly in their governments and laws. The term Islamic republic has come to mean several different things, some contradictory to others. To some Muslim religious leaders in the Middle East and Africa who advocate it, an Islamic Republic is a state under a particular Islamic form of government. They see it as a compromise between a purely Islamic Caliphate, and secular nationalism and republicanism. In their conception of the Islamic republic, the penal code of the state is required to be compatible with some or all laws of Sharia, and the state may not be a monarchy as many Middle Eastern states are presently. Iran's Islamic republic is in contrast to the semi-secular state of the Islamic Republic of Pakistan, where Islamic laws are technically considered to override laws of the state, though in reality their relative hierarchy is ambiguous. The Islamic Republic of Iran came into existence following the Iranian Revolution and a national referendum held on 1 April 1979.

The Turkic Uyghur and Kirghiz controlled Turkish Islamic Republic of East Turkestan was declared in 1933 as an independent Islamic republic, by Sabit Damulla Abdulbaki and Muhammad Amin Bughra. However, the Chinese Muslim 36th Division of the National Revolutionary Army defeated their armies and destroyed the republic during the Battles of Kashgar, Yangi Hissar and Yarkand. The Chinese Muslim Generals Ma Fuyuan and Ma Zhancang declared the destruction of the rebel forces and the return of the area to the control of the Republic of China in 1934, followed by the executions of the Turkic Muslim Emirs Abdullah Bughra and Nur Ahmad Jan Bughra.

The Chinese Muslim General Ma Zhongying then entered the Id Kah Mosque in Kashgar, and lectured the Turkic Muslims on being loyal to the Central Government. Pakistan was the first country to adopt the adjective "Islamic" to modify its republican status under its otherwise secular constitution. Despite this definition the country did not have a state religion until 1973, when a new constitution, more democratic and less secular, was adopted. Pakistan only uses the "Islamic" name on its passports, visas and coins. Although Islamic Republic is specifically mentioned in the Constitution of 1973, all government documents are prepared under the name of the Government of Pakistan. The Constitution of Pakistan, part IX, article 227 says "All existing laws shall be brought in conformity with the Injunctions of Islam as laid down in the Quran and Sunnah, in this Part referred to as the Injunctions of Islam, and no law shall be enacted which is repugnant to such Injunctions" Today, many Muslim countries have incorporated Islamic law, wholly or in part, into their legal systems. Certain Muslim states have declared Islam to be their state religion in their constitutions, but do not apply Islamic law in their courts.

The present book is an effort to understand the social, political and legal aspects of the Muslim states and their relation to the out world.

I thank all members of my team who have helped in the preparation of the book. My special thanks go to "Random Publications" who have published the book.

— *Dr. Akhlaque Ahmad*

Contents

Chapter 1

Islamic Countries in South Asia

Introduction

An Islamic state is a type of government, in which the primary basis for government is Islamic religious law (*sharia*). From the early years of Islam, numerous governments have been founded as "Islamic", beginning most notably with the caliphate established by the Islamic prophet, Muhammad and including subsequent governments ruled under the direction of a caliph (meaning "successor" to Muhammad). However, the term "Islamic state" has taken on a more specific modern connotation since the 20th century. The concept of the modern Islamic state has been articulated and promoted by ideologues such as Abul A'la Maududi, Ayatollah Ruhollah Khomeini, Israr Ahmed, and Sayyid Qutb. Like the earlier notion of the caliphate, the modern Islamic state is rooted in Islamic law. It is modelled after the rule of Muhammad. However, unlike caliph-led governments which were imperial despotisms or monarchies (Arabic: *malik*), a modern Islamic state can incorporate modern political institutions such as elections, parliamentary rule, judicial review, and popular sovereignty. Today, many Muslim countries have incorporated Islamic law, wholly or in part, into their legal systems. Certain Muslim states have declared Islam to be their state religion in their constitutions, but do not apply Islamic law in their courts. Islamic states which are not Islamic monarchies are usually referred to as Islamic republics.

The Historical Islamic State

Early Islamic Governments

The term caliphate refers to the first system of government established by Muhammad in 622 CE, under the Constitution of

Medina. It represented the political unity of the Muslim *Ummah* (nation), although it did not always incorporate the full religious community of Muslims (for example, Khawarijites and Shia). It was subsequently led by Muhammad's disciples who were known as the Rightly Guided (*Rashidun*) Caliphs (632-661 CE).

The Arabian Empire significantly expanded under the Umayyad Caliphate (661-750) and the Abbasid Caliphate (750-1258).

The Essence of Islamic Governments

The essence or guiding principles of an Islamic government or Islamic state, is the concept of *Al-Shura.* Different scholars have different understandings or thoughts, with regard to the concept al-Shura, However, most Muslim scholars are of the opinion that Islamic al-Shura should consist of:

- Meeting or consultation, that follows the teachings of Islam.
- Consultation following the guidelines of the *Quran* and *Sunnah.*
- There is a leader elected among them to head the meeting.
- The discussion should be based on *mushawarah* and *mudhakarah.*
- All the members are given fair opportunity to voice out their opinions.
- The issue should be of *maslahah ammah* or public interest.
- The voices of the majority are accepted, provided that it does not violate with the teachings of the Quran or Sunnah.

Muhammad himself respected the decision of the shura members. He is the champion of the notion of al-shura, and this was illustrated in one of the many historical events, such as, in the Battle of Khandaq (Battle of the Trench), where Muhammad was faced with two decisions, i.e. to fight the invading pagan Arabs outside of Medina or wait till they enter the city.

After consultation with the *sahabah* (companions), it was suggested by Salman al-Farsi that it would be better if the Muslims fought the unbelievers within Medina by building a big ditch on the northern periphery of Medina to prevent the enemies from entering Medina. This idea was later supported by the majority of the sahabah, and thereafter Muhammad also approved it.

The reason why Muhammad placed great emphasis on the agreement of the decision of the shura, was because the majority of opinion (by the sahabah) is better than the decision made by one individual.

Revival and Abolition of the Ottoman Caliphate

The Ottoman Sultan, Selim I (1512–1520) reclaimed the title of caliph, which had been in dispute and asserted by a diversity of rulers and "shadow caliphs" in the centuries of the Abbasid-Mamluk Caliphate since the Mongols' sacking of Baghdad and the killing of the last Abbasid Caliph in Baghdad, Iraq 1258.

The Ottoman Caliphate as an office of the Ottoman Empire was abolished under Mustafa Kemal Atatürk in 1924 as part of Atatürk's Reforms. This move was most vigorously protested in India, as Gandhi and Indian Muslims united behind the *symbolism* of the Ottoman Caliph in the Khilafat (or "Caliphate") Movement, which sought to reinstate the Caliph deposed by Atatürk. The Khilafat Movement leveraged the Ottoman political resistance to the British Empire, and this international anti-imperial connection proved to be a galvanizing force during India's nascent nationalism movement of the early 1900s, for Hindus and Muslims alike, even though India was far from the seat of the Ottoman Caliphate in Istanbul.

The Modern Islamic State

Origins in 20th-century nationalist and anti-imperialist movements "The very term, 'Islamic State', was never used in the theory or practice of Muslim political science, before the twentieth century," a Pakistani scholar wrote, and western scholars of Islam agree. The modern conceptualization of the "Islamic state" is attributed to Abul A'la Maududi (1903–1979), a Pakistani Muslim theologian who founded the political party Jamaat-e-Islami and inspired other Islamic revolutionaries such as Ayatollah Ruhollah Khomeini. Abul A'la Maududi's early political career was influenced greatly by anti-colonial agitation in India, especially after the tumultuous abolition of the Ottoman Caliphate in 1924 stoked anti-British sentiment.

The Islamic state was perceived as a "third way" between the rival political systems of democracy and socialism. Maududi's seminal writings on Islamic economics argued as early as 1941 against free-market capitalism and socialist state intervention in the economy, similar to Mohammad Baqir al-Sadr's later *Our Economics* written in 1961. Maududi envisioned the ideal Islamic state as combining the democratic principles of electoral politics with the socialist principles of concern for the poor.

Islamic States Today

Today, many Muslim countries have incorporated Islamic law, wholly or in part, into their legal systems. Certain Muslim states have declared Islam to be their state religion in their constitutions, but do not apply Islamic law in their courts. Islamic states which are not Islamic monarchies are usually referred to as Islamic republics, including the Islamic Republics of Pakistan, Iran and Afghanistan. Pakistan adopted the title under the constitution of 1956. Mauritania adopted it on 28 November 1958. Iran adopted it after the 1979 Revolution that overthrew the Pahlavi dynasty. In Iran, the form of government is known as "Guardianship of the Islamic Jurists". Afghanistan was run as an Islamic state ("Islamic State of Afghanistan") in the post-communist era since 1992 but then de facto by the Taliban ("Islamic Emirate of Afghanistan") in areas controlled by them since 1996, and after the 2001 overthrow of the Taliban the country is still known as the "Islamic Republic of Afghanistan". Despite the similar name, the countries differ greatly in their governments and laws.

Pan-Islamism is a form of religious nationalism within political Islam which advocates the unification of the Muslim world under a single Islamic state, often described as a caliphate.

The Libyan interim Constitutional Declaration of 3 August 2011 declared Islam to be the official religion of Libya.

Iran

Leading up to the Iranian Revolution of 1979, many of the highest-ranking clergy in Shia Islam held to the standard doctrine of the Imamate, which allows political rule only by Muhammad or one of his true successors. They were opposed to creating an Islamic state, Ayatollah Borujerdi, Grand Ayatollah Shariatmadari, and Grand Ayatollah Abu al-Qasim al-Khoei). Contemporary theologians who were once part of the Iranian Revolution also became disenchanted and critical of the unity of religion and state in the Islamic Republic of Iran, are advocating secularization of the state to preserve the purity of the Islamic faith.

Pakistan

Pakistan was created as a separate state for Indian Muslims in British India in 1947, and followed the parliamentary form of democracy. In 1949, the first Constituent Assembly of Pakistan passed the Objectives Resolution which envisaged an official role for Islam as the state religion to make sure any future law should not violate its basic teachings. On the whole, the state retained most of the laws that were inherited from the British legal code that had been enforced by the British Raj since the 19th century. In 1956, the elected parliament formally adopted the name "Islamic Republic of Pakistan", declaring Islam as the official religion.

ISIL (Parts of Iraq and Syria)

The Islamic State of Iraq and the Levant (ISIL), alternately translated as the Islamic State of Iraq and Syria (ISIS) or the Islamic State of Iraq and al-Sham, also known by the Arabic acronym *DAISH*, now calling themselves the Islamic State (IS), is an unrecognised state and active jihadist militant group in Iraq and Syria. This Islamic State of Iraq and the Levant was declared on 29 June 2014 and was previously named Islamic State of Iraq. The group is not recognised as a state by any country.

Senior Muslim scholars from Iraq and Egypt, including the Grand Mufti, stated that the ISIL group does not represent Islam and is unislamic.

Afghanistan

Afghanistan, officially the Islamic Republic of Afghanistan, is a landlocked country located in Central Asia and South Asia. It has a population of approximately 31 million people, making it the 42nd most populous country in the world. It is bordered by Pakistan in the south and east; Iran in the west; Turkmenistan, Uzbekistan, and Tajikistan in the north; and China in the far northeast. Its territory covers 652,000 km^2 (252,000 sq mi), making it the 41st largest country in the world.

Flag Emblem

Human habitation in Afghanistan dates back to the Middle Paleolithic Era, and the country's strategic location along the Silk Road connected it to the cultures of the Middle East, Central Asia, and South Asia. Through the ages the land has been home to various peoples and witnessed many military campaigns, notably by Alexander the Great, Arab Muslims, Genghis Khan, and in the modern-era by Western powers. The land also served as a source from which the Kushans, Hephthalites, Samanids, Ghaznavids, Ghorids, Khiljis, Mughals, Durranis, and others have risen to form major empires.

The political history of the modern state of Afghanistan began with the Hotaki and Durrani dynasties in the 18th Century. In the late 19th century, Afghanistan became a buffer state in the "Great Game" between British India and the Russian Empire. Following the 1919 Anglo-Afghan War, King Amanullah and King Mohammed Zahir Shah attempted modernisation of the country. A series of coups in 1973, 1978, and 1979 was followed by a Soviet invasion and a series of civil wars that devastated much of the country.

History of Afganistan

Excavations of prehistoric sites by Louis Dupree and others suggest that humans were living in what is now Afghanistan at least 50,000 years ago, and that farming communities in the area were among the earliest in the world. An important site of early historical activities, many believe that Afghanistan compares to Egypt in terms of the historical value of its archaeological sites.

The country sits at a unique nexus point where numerous civilizations have interacted and often fought. It has been home to various peoples through the ages, among them the ancient Iranian peoples who established the dominant role of Indo-Iranian languages in the region. At multiple points, the land has been incorporated within large regional empires, among them the Achaemenid Empire, the Macedonian Empire, the Indian Maurya Empire, and the Islamic Empire. Many kingdoms have also risen to power in what is now Afghanistan, such as the Greco-Bactrians, Kushans, Hephthalites, Kabul Shahis, Saffarids, Samanids, Ghaznavids, Ghurids, Kartids, Timurids, Mughals, and finally the Hotaki and Durrani dynasties that marked the political origins of the modern state.

Pre-Islamic Period

Archaeological exploration done in the 20th century suggests that the geographical area of Afghanistan has been closely connected by culture and trade with its neighbours to the east, west, and north. Artifacts typical of the Paleolithic, Mesolithic, Neolithic, Bronze, and Iron ages have been found in Afghanistan. Urban civilization is believed to have begun as early as 3000 BCE, and the early city of Mundigak (near Kandahar in the south of the country) may have been a colony of the nearby Indus Valley Civilization.

After 2000 BCE, successive waves of semi-nomadic people from Central Asia began moving south into Afghanistan; among them were many Indo-European-speaking Indo-Iranians. These tribes later migrated further south to India, west to what is now Iran, and towards Europe via the area north of the Caspian Sea. The region as a whole was called Ariana.

The people shared similar culture with other Indo-Iranians. The ancient religion of Kafiristan survived here until the 19th century. Another religion, Zoroastrianism is believed by some to have originated in what is now Afghanistan between 1800 and 800 BCE, as its founder Zoroaster is thought to have lived and died in Balkh. Ancient Eastern Iranian languages may have been spoken in the region around the time of the rise of Zoroastrianism. By the middle of the 6th century

BCE, the Achaemenid Persians overthrew the Medes and incorporated Arachosia, Aria, and Bactria within its eastern boundaries. An inscription on the tombstone of King Darius I of Persia mentions the Kabul Valley in a list of the 29 countries that he had conquered.

Alexander the Great and his Macedonian forces arrived to the area of Afghanistan in 330 BCE after defeating Darius III of Persia a year earlier in the Battle of Gaugamela. Following Alexander's brief occupation, the successor state of the Seleucid Empire controlled the region as one of their easternmost territories until 305 BCE, when they gave much of it to the Indian Maurya Empire as part of an alliance treaty. The Mauryans introduced Buddhism and controlled the area south of the Hindu Kush until they were overthrown about 185 BCE. Their decline began 60 years after Ashoka's rule ended, leading to the Hellenistic reconquest of the region by the Greco-Bactrians. Much of it soon broke away from the Greco-Bactrians and became part of the Indo-Greek Kingdom. The Indo-Greeks were defeated and expelled by the Indo-Scythians in the late 2nd century BCE.

During the first century BCE, the Parthian Empire subjugated the region, but lost it to their Indo-Parthian vassals. In the mid-to-late first century CE the vast Kushan Empire, centred in modern Afghanistan, became great patrons of Buddhist culture, making Buddhism flourish throughout the region. The Kushans were defeated by the Sassanids in the 3rd century CE. Although the Indo-Sassanids continued to rule at least parts of the region. They were followed by the Kidarite Huns who, in turn, were replaced by the Hephthalites. By the 6th century CE, the successors to the Kushans and Hepthalites established a small dynasty called Kabul Shahi.

Islamization and Mongol Invasion

Between the 4th and 19th centuries, the northwestern area of modern Afghanistan was referred to by the regional name Khorasan. Two of the four capitals of Khorasan (Herat and Balkh) are now located in Afghanistan, while the regions of Kandahar, Zabulistan, Ghazni, Kabulistan, and Afghanistan formed the frontier between Khorasan and Hindustan. Arab Muslims brought Islam to Herat and Zaranj in 642 CE and began spreading eastward; some of the native inhabitants they encountered accepted it while others revolted. The land was collectively recognised by the Arabs as al-Hind due to its cultural connection with Greater India. Before Islam was introduced, people of the region were multi-religious, including Zoroastrians, Buddhists, Surya and Nana worshipers, Jews, and others. The Zunbils and Kabul Shahi were first conquered in 870 CE by the Saffarid Muslims of Zaranj.

Later, the Samanids extended their Islamic influence south of the Hindu Kush. It is reported that Muslims and non-Muslims still lived side by side in Kabul before the Ghaznavids rose to power in the 10th century.

Afghanistan became one of the main centres in the Muslim world during the Islamic Golden Age. By the 11th century, Sultan Mahmud of Ghazni defeated the remaining Hindu rulers and effectively Islamized the wider region, with the exception of Kafiristan. The Ghaznavid dynasty was defeated and became the Nasher Khans. They were replaced by the Ghurids, who expanded and advanced the already powerful Islamic empire. In 1219 AD, Genghis Khan and his Mongol army overran the region. His troops are said to have annihilated the Khorasanian cities of Herat and Balkh as well as Bamyan.

The destruction caused by the Mongols forced many locals to return to an agrarian rural society. Mongol rule continued with the Ilkhanate in the northwest while the Khilji dynasty administered the Afghan tribal areas south of the Hindu Kush until the invasion of Timur, who established the Timurid dynasty in 1370. During the Ghaznavid, Ghurid, and Timurid eras, the region produced many fine Islamic architectural monuments and numerous scientific and literary works.

Babur, a descendant of both Timur and Genghis Khan, arrived from Fergana and captured Kabul from the Arghun dynasty. From there he began dominating control of the central and eastern territories of Afghanistan. He remained in Kabulistan until 1526 when he invaded Delhi in India to replace the Lodi dynasty with the Mughal Empire. From the 16th century to the early 18th century, the region was contested between the Khanate of Bukhara, the Persian Safavid dynasty, and the Mughal Empire.

Hotaki Dynasty and Durrani Empire

Mir Wais Hotak, the chieftain of the Ghilzai tribe, successfully rebelled against the declining Safavids in 1709. Along with Ghaznavid Khan Nasher, he overthrew and killed Gurgin Khan, and made the Afghan region independent from Persia. By 1713, Mir Wais had decisively defeated two larger Persian armies, one led by Khusraw Khán and the other by Rustam Khán. The armies were sent by Sultan Husayn, the Shah of Persia, to re-take control of the Kandahar region. Mir Wais died of natural causes in 1715 and was succeeded by his brother Abdul Aziz, who was soon killed by Mir Wais' son Mahmud for treason. Mahmud led his Afghan army in 1722 to the Persian capital of Isfahan, captured the city after the Battle of Gulnabad and proclaimed himself King of Persia. The Persians rejected Mahmud, and after the massacre of thousands of religious scholars, nobles, and members of the Safavid family, the Hotaki dynasty was ousted and banished from Persia by Nader Shah after the 1729 Battle of Damghan.

***Figure:** Mir Wais Hotak, considered the Grandfather of the Nation*

***Figure:** Ahmad Shah Durrani, founder of the last Afghan empire and viewed as Father of the Nation*

In 1738, Nader Shah and his Afsharid forces captured Kandahar, the last Hotaki stronghold, from Shah Hussain Hotaki, at which point the incarcerated 16-year-old Ahmad Shah Durrani was freed and made the commander of Nader Shah's four thousand Abdali Afghans, joining him in his invasion of India. After the death of Nader Shah in 1747, the Afghans chose Durrani as their head of state. Durrani and his Afghan army conquered present-day Afghanistan, Pakistan, the Khorasan and Kohistan provinces of Iran, and Delhi in India. He defeated the Indian Maratha Empire, and one of his biggest victories was the 1761 Battle of Panipat.

In October 1772, Durrani died of natural causes and was buried at a site now adjacent to the Shrine of the Cloak in Kandahar. He was succeeded by his son, Timur Shah, who transferred the capital of Afghanistan from Kandahar to Kabul in 1776. After Timur's death in 1793, the Durrani throne passed down to his son Zaman Shah, followed by Mahmud Shah, Shuja Shah and others.

The Afghan Empire was under threat in the early 19th century by the Persians in the west and the British-backed Sikhs in the east. Fateh Khan, leader of the Barakzai tribe, had installed 21 of his brothers in positions of power throughout the empire. After his death, they rebelled and divided up the provinces of the empire between themselves. During this turbulent period, Afghanistan had many temporary rulers until Dost Mohammad Khan declared himself emir in 1826. The Punjab region was lost to Ranjit Singh, who invaded Khyber Pakhtunkhwa and in 1834 captured the city of Peshawar. In 1837, during the Battle of Jamrud near the Khyber Pass, Akbar Khan and the Afghan army killed Sikh Commander Hari Singh Nalwa. By this time the British were advancing from the east and the first major conflict during the "Great Game" was initiated.

Western Influence

Following the 1842 defeat of the British-Indian forces and victory of the Afghans, the British established diplomatic relations with the Afghan government and withdrew all forces from the country. They returned during the Second Anglo-Afghan War in the late 1870s for about two years to assist Abdur Rahman Khan defeat Ayub Khan. The United Kingdom began to exercise a great deal of influence after this and even controlled the state's foreign policy. In 1893, Mortimer Durand made Amir Abdur Rahman Khan sign a controversial agreement in which the ethnic Pashtun and Baloch territories were divided by the Durand Line. This was a standard divide and rule policy of the British and would lead to strained relations, especially with the later new state of Pakistan.

After the Third Anglo-Afghan War and the signing of the Treaty of Rawalpindi in 1919, King Amanullah Khan declared Afghanistan a sovereign and fully independent state. He moved to end his country's traditional isolation by establishing diplomatic relations with the international community and, following a 1927–28 tour of Europe and Turkey, introduced several reforms intended to modernise his nation.

A key force behind these reforms was Mahmud Tarzi, an ardent supporter of the education of women. He fought for Article 68 of Afghanistan's 1923 constitution, which made elementary education compulsory. The institution of slavery was abolished in 1923.

Some of the reforms that were actually put in place, such as the abolition of the traditional burqa for women and the opening of a number of co-educational schools, quickly alienated many tribal and religious leaders. Faced with overwhelming armed opposition, Amanullah Khan was forced to abdicate in January 1929 after Kabul fell to rebel forces led by Habibullah Kalakani. Prince Mohammed Nadir Shah, Amanullah's cousin, in turn defeated and killed Kalakani in November 1929, and was declared King Nadir Shah. He abandoned the reforms of Amanullah Khan in favour of a more gradual approach to modernisation but was assassinated in 1933 by Abdul Khaliq, a Hazara school student.

Mohammed Zahir Shah, Nadir Shah's 19-year-old son, succeeded to the throne and reigned from 1933 to 1973. Until 1946, Zahir Shah ruled with the assistance of his uncle, who held the post of Prime Minister and continued the policies of Nadir Shah. Another of Zahir Shah's uncles, Shah Mahmud Khan, became Prime Minister in 1946 and began an experiment allowing greater political freedom, but reversed the policy when it went further than he expected. He was replaced in 1953 by Mohammed Daoud Khan, the king's cousin and brother-in-law. Daoud Khan sought a closer relationship with the Soviet Union and a more distant one towards Pakistan. Afghanistan remained neutral and was neither a participant in World War II nor aligned with either power bloc in the Cold War. However, it was a beneficiary of the latter rivalry as both the Soviet Union and the United States vied for influence by building Afghanistan's main highways, airports, and other vital infrastructure. In 1973, while King Zahir Shah was on an official overseas visit, Daoud Khan launched a bloodless coup and became the first President of Afghanistan. In the meantime, Zulfikar Ali Bhutto got neighbouring Pakistan involved in Afghanistan. Some experts suggest that Bhutto paved the way for the April 1978 Saur Revolution.

Marxist Revolution and Soviet War

In April 1978, the communist People's Democratic Party of Afghanistan (PDPA) seized power in Afghanistan in the Saur Revolution. Within months, opponents of the communist government launched an uprising in eastern Afghanistan that quickly expanded into a civil war waged by guerrilla mujahideen against government forces countrywide. The Pakistani government provided these rebels with covert training centres, while the Soviet Union sent thousands of military advisers to support the PDPA government. Meanwhile, increasing friction between the competing factions of the PDPA — the dominant Khalq and the more moderate Parcham — resulted in the dismissal of Parchami cabinet members and the arrest of Parchami military officers under the pretext of a Parchami coup.

In September 1979, Nur Muhammad Taraki was assassinated in a coup within the PDPA orchestrated by fellow Khalq member Hafizullah Amin, who assumed the presidency. Distrusted by the Soviets, Amin was assassinated by Soviet special forces in December 1979. A Soviet-organised government, led by Parcham's Babrak Karmal but inclusive of both factions, filled the vacuum. Soviet troops were deployed to stabilize Afghanistan under Karmal in more substantial numbers, although the Soviet government did not expect to do most of the fighting in Afghanistan. As a result, however, the Soviets were now directly involved in what had been a domestic war in Afghanistan. The PDPA prohibited usury, declared equality of the sexes, and introducing women to political life.

The United States has been supporting anti-Soviet forces (mujahideen) as early as mid-1979. Billions in cash and weapons, which included over two thousand FIM-92 Stinger surface-to-air missiles, were provided by the United States and Saudi Arabia to Pakistan. The 10-year Soviet war in Afghanistan resulted in the deaths of over 1 million Afghans, mostly civilians, and the creation of about 6 million refugees who fled Afghanistan, mainly to Pakistan and Iran. Faced with mounting international pressure and numerous casualties, the Soviets withdrew in 1989 but continued to support Afghan President Mohammad Najibullah until 1992.

Civil War

From 1989 until 1992, Najibullah's government tried to solve the ongoing civil war without Soviet troops on the ground but with economic and military aid. Najibullah tried to build support for his government and tried to portray his government as Islamic, and in the 1990 constitution the country officially became an Islamic state and all references of communism were removed. Nevertheless, Najibullah did not win any significant support, and with the dissolution of the Soviet Union in December 1991, he was left without foreign aid. This, coupled with the internal collapse of his government, led to his ousting from power in April 1992.

After the fall of Najibullah's government in 1992, the post-communist Islamic State of Afghanistan was established by the

Peshawar Accord, a peace and power-sharing agreement under which all the Afghan parties were united in April 1992, except for the Pakistani supported Hezb-e Islami of Gulbuddin Hekmatyar. Hekmatyar started a bombardment campaign against the capital city Kabul, which marked the beginning of a new phase in the war.

Saudi Arabia and Iran supported different Afghan militias and instability quickly developed. The conflict between the two militias soon escalated into a full-scale war.

Due to the sudden initiation of the war, working government departments, police units, and a system of justice and accountability for the newly created Islamic State of Afghanistan did not have time to form. Atrocities were committed by individuals of the different armed factions while Kabul descended into lawlessness and chaos. Because of the chaos, some leaders increasingly had only nominal control over their (sub-)commanders. For civilians there was little security from murder, rape, and extortion. An estimated 25,000 people died during the most intense period of bombardment by Hekmatyar's Hezb-i Islami and the Junbish-i Milli forces of Abdul Rashid Dostum, who had created an alliance with Hekmatyar in 1994. Half a million people fled Afghanistan.

Southern and eastern Afghanistan were under the control of local commanders such as Gul Agha Sherzai and others. In 1994, the Taliban (a movement originating from Jamiat Ulema-e-Islam-run religious schools for Afghan refugees in Pakistan) also developed in Afghanistan as a political-religious force. The Taliban took control of Kabul and several provinces in southern and central Afghanistan in 1994 and forced the surrender of dozens of local Pashtun leaders.

In late 1994, forces of Ahmad Shah Massoud held on to Kabul and bombardment of the city came to a halt. The Islamic State government took steps to open courts, restore law and order, and initiate a nationwide political process with the goal of national consolidation and democratic elections. Massoud invited Taliban leaders to join the process but they refused.

Taliban Emirate and Northern Alliance

The Taliban's early victories in 1994 were followed by a series of defeats that resulted in heavy losses that led analysts to believe the Taliban movement had run its course. The Taliban started shelling Kabul in early 1995 but were repelled by forces under Massoud.

On 26 September 1996, as the Taliban, with military support from Pakistan and financial support from Saudi Arabia, prepared for another major offencive, Massoud ordered a full retreat from Kabul. The Taliban seized Kabul on 27 September 1996, and established the Islamic Emirate of Afghanistan. They imposed on the parts of Afghanistan under their control their political and judicial interpretation of Islam, issuing edicts especially targeting women. According to Physicians for Human Rights (PHR), "no other regime in the world has methodically and violently forced half of its population into virtual house arrest, prohibiting them on pain of physical punishment."

After the fall of Kabul to the Taliban, Massoud and Dostum created the United Front (Northern Alliance). The United Front included Massoud's predominantly Tajik forces, Dostum's Uzbek forces, and Hazara and Pashtun factions under leaders such as Haji Mohammad Mohaqiq, Abdul Haq, and Abdul Qadir. The Taliban defeated Dostum's forces during the Battles of Mazar-i-Sharif (1997–98). The Taliban committed systematic massacres against civilians in northern and western Afghanistan. Pakistan's Chief of Army Staff, Pervez Musharraf, was responsible for sending tens of thousands of Pakistanis to fight alongside the Taliban and bin Laden against Northern Alliance forces. In 2001 alone, there were believed to be 28,000 Pakistani nationals fighting inside Afghanistan. From 1996 to 2001, the al-Qaeda network of Osama bin Laden and Ayman al-Zawahiri was harbored by the Taliban in Afghanistan, and bin Laden sent thousands of Arab recruits to fight against the United Front.

Massoud remained the only leader of the United Front in Afghanistan. In the areas under his control, Massoud set up democratic institutions and signed the Women's Rights Declaration. The fighting also caused around 1 million people to flee Taliban controlled areas. From 1990 to September 2001, 400,000 Afghan civilians have reportedly died in the wars. On 9 September 2001, Massoud was assassinated by two French-speaking Arab suicide attackers inside Afghanistan, and two days later the September 11 attacks were carried out in the United States. The US government identified Osama bin Laden and al-Qaeda as the perpetrators of the attacks, and demanded that the Taliban hand over bin Laden. After refusing to comply with the US demand, the October 2001 Operation Enduring Freedom was launched. During the initial invasion, US and UK forces bombed parts of Afghanistan and worked with ground forces of the Northern Alliance to remove the Taliban from power and destroy al-Qaeda training camps.

Recent History (2002–Present)

In December 2001, after the Taliban government was toppled and the new Afghan government under Hamid Karzai was formed, the International Security Assistance Force (ISAF) was established by the

UN Security Council to help assist the Karzai administration and provide basic security. Taliban forces also began regrouping inside Pakistan, while more coalition troops entered Afghanistan and began rebuilding the war-torn country. Shortly after their fall from power, the Taliban began an insurgency to regain control of Afghanistan. Over the next decade, ISAF and Afghan troops led many offencives against the Taliban but failed to fully defeat them. Afghanistan remained one of the poorest countries in the world due to a lack of foreign investment, government corruption, and the Taliban insurgency.

Meanwhile, the Afghan government was able to build some democratic structures, and, on December 7, 2004, the country changed its name to the Islamic Republic of Afghanistan. Attempts were made, often with the support of foreign donor countries, to improve the country's economy, healthcare, education, transport, and agriculture. ISAF forces also began to train the Afghan armed forces and police. In the decade following 2002, over five million Afghan refugees were repatriated to the country, including many who were forcefully deported from Western countries.

By 2009, a Taliban-led shadow government began to form in many parts of the country. US President Barack Obama announced that the U.S. would deploy another 30,000 U.S. soldiers to the country in 2010 for a period of two years. In 2010, Karzai attempted to hold peace negotiations with the Taliban and other groups, but these groups refused to attend and bombings, assassinations, and ambushes intensified.

After the May 2011 death of Osama bin Laden in Pakistan, many prominent Afghan figures were assassinated, Afghanistan–Pakistan border skirmishes intensified, and many large scale attacks by the Pakistani-based Haqqani Network took place across Afghanistan. The United States warned the Pakistani government of possible military action within Pakistan if the government refused to attack these forces in the Federally Administered Tribal Areas, as the United States blamed rogue elements within the Pakistani government for the increased attacks. The Pakistani Army began to intensify their attacks against these groups as part of the War in North West Pakistan.

Following the 2014 presidential election President Hamid Karzai left power and Ashraf Ghani became President on 29 September 2014. In anticipation of the 2014 NATO withdrawal and a subsequent expected push to regain power by the Taliban, the anti-Taliban United Front (Northern Alliance) groups have started to regroup under the umbrella of the National Coalition of Afghanistan (political arm) and the National Front of Afghanistan (military arm).

Geography

A landlocked mountainous country with plains in the north and southwest, Afghanistan is variously described as being located within Central Asia or South Asia. It is part of the US coined Greater Middle East Muslim world, which lies between latitudes 29° N and 39° N, and longitudes 60° E and 75° E. The country's highest point is Noshaq, at 7,492 m (24,580 ft) above sea level. It has a continental climate with harsh winters in the central highlands, the glaciated northeast (around Nuristan), and the Wakhan Corridor, where the average temperature in January is below "15 °C (5 °F), and hot summers in the low-lying areas of the Sistan Basin of the southwest, the Jalalabad basin in the east, and the Turkistan plains along the Amu River in the north, where temperatures average over 35 °C (95 °F) in July. Despite having numerous rivers and reservoirs, large parts of the country are dry. The endorheic Sistan Basin is one of the driest regions in the world. Aside from the usual rainfall, Afghanistan receives snow during the winter in the Hindu Kush and Pamir Mountains, and the melting snow in the spring season enters the rivers, lakes, and streams. However, two-thirds of the country's water flows into the neighbouring countries of Iran, Pakistan, and Turkmenistan. The state needs more than US$2 billion to rehabilitate its irrigation systems so that the water is properly managed.

The northeastern Hindu Kush mountain range, in and around the Badakhshan Province of Afghanistan, is in a geologically active area where earthquakes may occur almost every year. They can be deadly and destructive sometimes, causing landslides in some parts or avalanches during the winter. The last strong earthquakes were in 1998, which killed about 6,000 people in Badakhshan near Tajikistan. This was followed by the 2002 Hindu Kush earthquakes in which over 150 people were killed and over 1,000 injured. A 2010 earthquake left 11 Afghans dead, over 70 injured, and more than 2,000 houses destroyed.

The country's natural resources include: coal, copper, iron ore, lithium, uranium, rare earth elements, chromite, gold, zinc, talc, barites, sulfur, lead, marble, precious and semi-precious stones, natural gas, and petroleum, among other things. In 2010, US and Afghan government officials estimated that untapped mineral deposits located in 2007 by the US Geological Survey are worth between $900 bn and $3 trillion.

At 652,230 km^2 (251,830 sq mi), Afghanistan is the world's 41st largest country, slightly bigger than France and smaller than Burma, about the size of Texas in the United States. It borders Pakistan in the south and east; Iran in the west; Turkmenistan, Uzbekistan, and Tajikistan in the north; and China in the far east.

Demographics

As of 2012, the population of Afghanistan is around 31,108,077, which includes the roughly 2.7 million Afghan refugees still living in Pakistan and Iran. In 1979, the population was reported to be about 15.5 million. The only city with over a million residents is its capital, Kabul. Other large cities in the country are, in order of population size, Kandahar, Herat, Mazar-i-Sharif, Jalalabad, Lashkar Gah, Taloqan, Khost, Sheberghan, and Ghazni. Urban areas are experiencing rapid population growth following the return of over 5 million expats. According to the Population Reference Bureau, the Afghan population is estimated to increase to 82 million by 2050.

Ethnic Groups

Afghanistan is a multiethnic society, and its historical status as a crossroads has contributed significantly to its diverse ethnic makeup. The population of the country is divided into a wide variety of ethnolinguistic groups. Because a systematic census has not been held in the nation in decades, exact figures about the size and composition of the various ethnic groups are unavailable.

The 2004–present estimates in the above chart are supported by recent national opinion polls that measured how a group of about 804 to 7,760 local residents in Afghanistan felt about the current war, political situation, as well as the economic and social issues affecting their daily lives. Seven of the surveys were conducted between 2004 to 2012 by the Asia Foundation and one between 2004 to 2009 by a combined effort of the broadcasting companies NBC News, BBC, and ARD.

Languages

Pashto and Dari (Persian) are the official languages of Afghanistan; bilingualism is very common. Both are Indo-European languages from the Iranian languages sub-family. Dari has always been the prestige language and a lingua franca for inter-ethnic communication. It is the native tongue of the Tajiks, Hazaras, Aimaks, and Kizilbash. Pashto is the native tongue of the Pashtuns, although many Pashtuns often use Dari and some non-Pashtuns are fluent in Pashto.

Other languages, including Uzbek, Arabic, Turkmen, Balochi, Pashayi, and Nuristani languages (Ashkunu, Kamkata-viri, Vasi-vari, Tregami, and Kalasha-ala), are the native tongues of minority groups across the country and have official status in the regions where they are widely spoken. Minor languages also include Pamiri (Shughni, Munji, Ishkashimi, and Wakhi), Brahui, Hindko, and Kyrgyz. A small percentage of Afghans are also fluent in Urdu, English, and other languages.

Religions

Over 99% of the Afghan population is Muslim; approximately 80–85% are from the Sunni branch, 15–19% are Shi'a, and roughly 3% are non-denominational Muslims. Until the 1890s, the region around Nuristan was known as Kafiristan (land of the kafirs (unbelievers)) because of its non-Muslim inhabitants, the Nuristanis, an ethnically distinct people whose religious practices included animism, polytheism, and shamanism. There are small minorities of Christians, Buddhists, Zoroastrianists, Sikhs, and Hindus. There was a small Jewish community in Afghanistan who had emigrated to Israel and the United States by the end of the twentieth century; only one Jew, Zablon Simintov, remained by 2005.

Governance

Afghanistan is an Islamic republic consisting of three branches, the executive, legislative, and judicial. The nation was led by Hamid Karzai as the President and leader since late 2001 till 2014. Currently the new president is Ashraf Ghani with Abdul Rashid Dostum and Sarwar Danish as vise presidents. Abdullah Abdullah serves as the chief executive officer (CEO). The National Assembly is the legislature, a bicameral body having two chambers, the House of the People and the House of Elders. The Supreme Court is led by Chief Justice Abdul Salam Azimi, a former university professor who had been a legal advisor to the president. The current court is seen as more moderate and led by more technocrats than the previous one, which was dominated by fundamentalist religious figures such as Chief Justice Faisal Ahmad Shinwari, who issued several controversial rulings, including seeking to place a limit on the rights of women.

According to Transparency International's 2010 corruption perceptions index results, Afghanistan was ranked as the third most corrupt country in the world. A January 2010 report published by the United Nations Office on Drugs and Crime revealed that bribery consumed an amount equal to 23% of the GDP of the nation. A number of government ministries are believed to be rife with corruption, and while President Karzai vowed to tackle the problem in late 2009 by stating that "individuals who are involved in corruption will have no place in the government", top government officials were stealing and misusing hundreds of millions of dollars through the Kabul Bank. Although the nation's institutions are newly formed and steps have been taken to arrest some, the United States warned that aid to Afghanistan would be greatly reduced if the corruption is not stopped.

Foreign Relations and Military

The Afghan Ministry of Foreign Affairs is in charge of maintaining the foreign relations of Afghanistan. The state has been a member of the United Nations since 1946. It enjoys strong economic relations with a number of NATO and allied states, particularly the United States, United Kingdom, Germany and Turkey. In 2012, the United States designated Afghanistan as a major non-NATO ally and created the U.S.–Afghanistan Strategic Partnership Agreement. Afghanistan also has friendly diplomatic relations with neighbouring Pakistan, Iran, Turkmenistan, Uzbekistan, Tajikistan, and China, and with regional states such as India, Bangladesh, Kazakhstan, Russia, the UAE, Saudi Arabia, Iraq, Egypt, Japan, and South Korea. It continues to develop diplomatic relations with other countries around the world.

The United Nations Assistance Mission in Afghanistan (UNAMA) was established in 2002 under United Nations Security Council Resolution 1401 in order to help the country recover from decades of war. Today, a number of NATO member states deploy about 38,000 troops in Afghanistan as part of the International Security Assistance Force (ISAF). Its main purpose is to train the Afghan National Security Forces (ANSF). The Afghan Armed Forces are under the Ministry of Defence, which includes the Afghan National Army (ANA) and the Afghan Air Force (AAF). The ANA is divided into 7 major Corps, with the 201st Selab ("Flood") in Kabul followed by the 203rd in Gardez, 205th Atul ("Hero") in Kandahar, 207th in Herat, 209th in Mazar-i-Sharif, and the 215th in Lashkar Gah. The ANA also has a commando brigade, which was established in 2007. The Afghan Defence University (ADU) houses various educational establishments for the Afghan Armed Forces, including the National Military Academy of Afghanistan.

Sharia Law

The National Directorate of Security (NDS) is the nation's domestic intelligence agency, which operates similar to that of the United States Department of Homeland Security (DHS) and has between 15,000 to 30,000 employees. The nation also has about 126,000 national police officers, with plans to recruit more so that the total number can reach 160,000. The Afghan National Police (ANP) is under the Ministry of the Interior and serves as a single law enforcement agency all across the country. The Afghan National Civil Order Police is the main branch of the ANP, which is divided into five Brigades, each commanded by a Brigadier General. These brigades are stationed in Kabul, Gardez, Kandahar, Herat, and Mazar-i-Sharif. Every province has an appointed provincial Chief of Police who is responsible for law enforcement throughout the province.

The police receive most of their training from Western forces under the NATO Training Mission-Afghanistan. According to a 2009 news report, a large proportion of police officers were illiterate and accused of demanding bribes. Jack Kem, deputy to the commander of NATO Training Mission Afghanistan and Combined Security Transition Command Afghanistan, stated that the literacy rate in the ANP would rise to over 50% by January 2012. What began as a voluntary literacy program became mandatory for basic police training in early 2011. Approximately 17% of them tested positive for illegal drug use. In 2009, President Karzai created two anti-corruption units within the Interior Ministry. Former Interior Minister Hanif Atmar said that security officials from the US (FBI), Britain (Scotland Yard), and the European Union will train prosecutors in the unit.

The southern and eastern parts of Afghanistan are the most dangerous due to militant activities and the flourishing drug trade. These particular areas are sometimes patrolled by Taliban insurgents, who often plant improvised explosive devices (IEDs) on roads and carry out suicide bombings. Kidnapping and robberies are also reported. Every year many Afghan police officers are killed in the line of duty in these areas. The Afghan Border Police (ABP) are responsible for protecting the nation's airports and borders, especially the disputed Durand Line border, which is often used by members of criminal organisations and terrorists for their illegal activities. A report in 2011 suggested that up to 3 million people were involved in the illegal drug business in Afghanistan. Many of the attacks on government employees may be ordered by powerful mafia groups. Drugs from Afghanistan are exported to neighbouring countries and worldwide. The Afghan Ministry of Counter Narcotics is tasked to deal with these issues by bringing to justice major drug traffickers.

Economy

Afghanistan is an impoverished and least developed country, one of the world's poorest because of decades of war and lack of foreign investment. As of 2013, the nation's GDP stands at about $45.3 billion with an exchange rate of $20.65 billion, and the GDP per capita is $1,100. The country's exports totaled $2.6 billion in 2010. Its unemployment rate is about 35% and roughly the same percentage of its citizens live below the poverty line. According to a 2009 report, about 42% of the population lives on less than $1 a day. The nation has less than $1.5 billion in external debt and is recovering with the assistance of the world community.

The Afghan economy has been growing at about 10% per year in the last decade, which is due to the infusion of over $50 billion in international aid and remittances from Afghan expats. It is also due to improvements made to the transportation system and agricultural production, which is the backbone of the nation's economy. The country is known for producing some of the finest pomegranates, grapes, apricots, melons, and several other fresh and dry fruits, including nuts. Many sources indicate that as much as 11% or more of Afghanistan's economy is derived from the cultivation and sale of opium, and Afghanistan is widely considered the world's largest producer of opium despite Afghan government and international efforts to eradicate the crop.

While the nation's current account deficit is largely financed with donor money, only a small portion is provided directly to the government budget. The rest is provided to non-budgetary expenditure and donor-designated projects through the United Nations system and non-governmental organisations. The Afghan Ministry of Finance is focusing on improved revenue collection and public sector expenditure discipline. For example, government revenues increased 31% to $1.7 billion from March 2010 to March 2011.

Da Afghanistan Bank serves as the central bank of the nation and the "Afghani" (AFN) is the national currency, with an exchange rate of about 47 Afghanis to 1 US dollar. Since 2003, over 16 new banks have opened in the country, including Afghanistan International Bank, Kabul Bank, Azizi Bank, Pashtany Bank, Standard Chartered Bank, and First Micro Finance Bank.

One of the main drivers for the current economic recovery is the return of over 5 million expatriates, who brought with them fresh energy, entrepreneurship and wealth-creating skills as well as much needed funds to start up businesses. For the first time since the 1970s, Afghans have involved themselves in construction, one of the largest industries in the country. Some of the major national construction projects include the $35 billion *New Kabul City* next to the capital, the *Ghazi Amanullah Khan City* near Jalalabad, and the *Aino Mena* in Kandahar. Similar development projects have also begun in Herat, Mazar-e-Sharif, and other cities. In addition, a number of companies and small factories began operating in different parts of the country, which not only provide revenues to the government but also create new jobs. Improvements to the business environment have resulted in more than $1.5 billion in telecom investment and created more than 100,000 jobs since 2003. Afghan rugs are becoming popular again, allowing many carpet dealers around the country to hire more workers.

Afghanistan is a member of SAARC, ECO, and OIC. It is hoping to join SCO soon to develop closer economic ties with neighbouring and regional countries in the so-called *New Silk Road* trade project. Foreign Minister Zalmai Rassoul told the media in 2011 that his nation's "goal is to achieve an Afghan economy whose growth is based on trade, private enterprise and investment". Experts believe that this will revolutionize the economy of the region. Opium production in Afghanistan soared to a record in 2007 with about 3 million people reported to be involved in the business, but then declined significantly in the years following. The government started programs to help reduce poppy cultivation, and by 2010 it was reported that 24 out of the 34 provinces were free from poppy growing.

In June 2012, India advocated for private investments in the resource rich country and the creation of a suitable environment therefore.

Transportation and Infrastructure

Air

Air transport in Afghanistan is provided by the national carrier, Ariana Afghan Airlines (AAA), and by private companies such as Afghan Jet International, East Horizon Airlines, Kam Air, Pamir Airways, and Safi Airways. Airlines from a number of countries also provide flights in and out of the country. These include Air India, Emirates, Gulf Air, Iran Aseman Airlines, Pakistan International Airlines, and Turkish Airlines.

The country has four international airports: Herat International Airport, Hamid Karzai International Airport (formerly Kabul International Airport), Kandahar International Airport, and Mazar-e Sharif International Airport. There are also around a dozen domestic airports with flights to Kabul and/or Herat.

Rail

As of 2014, the country has only two rail links, one a 75 km line from Kheyrabad to the Uzbekistan border and the other a 10 km long line from Toraghundi to the Turkmenistan border. Both lines are used for freight only and there is no passenger service as of yet. There are various proposals for the construction of additional rail lines in the country. In 2013, the presidents of Afghanistan, Turkmenistan, and Uzbekistan attended the groundbreaking ceremony for a 225 km line between Turkmenistan-Andkhvoy-Mazar-i-Sharif-Kheyrabad. The line will link at Kheyrabad with the existing line to the Uzbekistan border. Plans exist for a rail line from Kabul to the eastern border town of

Torkham, where it will connect with Pakistan Railways. There are also plans to finish a rail line between Khaf, Iran and Herat, Afghanistan.

Roads

Travelling by bus in Afghanistan remains dangerous due to careless and intoxicated bus drivers as well as militant activities. The buses are usually older model Mercedes-Benz and owned by private companies. Serious traffic accidents are common on Afghan roads and highways, particularly on the Kabul–Kandahar and the Kabul–Jalalabad Road.

Newer automobiles have recently become more widely available after the rebuilding of roads and highways. They are imported from the United Arab Emirates through Pakistan and Iran. As of 2012, vehicles more than 10 years old are banned from being imported into the country. The development of the nation's road network is a major boost for the economy due to trade with neighbouring countries. Postal services in Afghanistan are provided by the publicly owned Afghan Post and private companies such as FedEx, DHL, and others.

Communication

Telecommunication services in the country are provided by Afghan Wireless, Etisalat, Roshan, MTN Group, and Afghan Telecom. In 2006, the Afghan Ministry of Communications signed a $64.5 million agreement with ZTE for the establishment of a countrywide optical fibre cable network. As of 2011, Afghanistan had around 17 million GSM phone subscribers and over 1 million internet users, but only had about 75,000 fixed telephone lines and a little over 190,000 CDMA subscribers. 3G services are provided by Etisalat and MTN Group. In 2014, Afghanistan leased a space satellite from Eutelsat, called AFGHANSAT 1.

Health

According to the Human Development Index, Afghanistan is the 15th least developed country in the world. The average life expectancy is estimated to be around 60 years for both sexes. The country has the ninth highest total fertility rate in the world, at 5.64 children born/woman (according to 2012 estimates). It has one of the highest maternal mortality rate in the world, estimated in 2010 at 460 deaths/100,000 live births, and the highest infant mortality rate in the world (deaths of babies under one year), estimated in 2012 to be 119.41 deaths/1,000 live births. Data from 2010 suggest that one in ten children die before they are five years old. The Ministry of Public Health plans to cut the infant mortality rate to 400 for every 100,000 live births before 2020. The country currently has more than 3,000 midwives, with an additional 300 to 400 being trained each year.

A number of hospitals and clinics have been built over the last decade, with the most advanced treatments being available in Kabul. The French Medical Institute for Children and Indira Gandhi Childrens Hospital in Kabul are the leading children's hospitals in the country. Some of the other main hospitals in Kabul include the 350-bed Jamhuriat Hospital and the Jinnah Hospital, which is still under construction. There are also a number of well-equipped military-controlled hospitals in different regions of the country.

It was reported in 2006 that nearly 60% of the population lives within a two hour walk of the nearest health facility, up from 9% in 2002. The latest surveys show that 57% of Afghans say they have good or very good access to clinics or hospitals. The nation has one of the highest incidences of people with disabilities, with around a million people affected. About 80,000 people are missing limbs; most of these were injured by landmines. Non-governmental charities such as Save the Children and Mahboba's Promise assist orphans in association with governmental structures. Demographic and Health Surveys is working with the Indian Institute of Health Management Research and others to conduct a survey in Afghanistan focusing on maternal death, among other things.

Education and Culture

Education in the country includes K–12 and higher education, which is supervised by the Ministry of Education and the Ministry of Higher Education. The nation's education system was destroyed due to the decades of war, but it began reviving after the Karzai administration came to power in late 2001. More than 5,000 schools were built or renovated in the last decade, with more than 100,000 teachers being trained and recruited. More than seven million male and female students are enrolled in schools, with about 100,000 being enrolled in different universities around the country; at least 35% of these students are female. As of 2013, there are 16,000 schools across Afghanistan. Education Minister Ghulam Farooq Wardak stated that another 8,000 schools are required to be constructed for the remaining 3 million children who are deprived of education.

Kabul University reopened in 2002 to both male and female students. In 2006, the American University of Afghanistan was established in Kabul, with the aim of providing a world-class, English-language, co-educational learning environment in Afghanistan. The capital of Kabul serves as the learning centre of Afghanistan, with many of the best educational institutions being based there. Major universities outside of Kabul include Kandahar University in the south, Herat University in the northwest, Balkh University in the north, Nangarhar University and Khost University in the east. The National Military Academy of Afghanistan, modelled after the United States Military Academy at West Point, is a four-year military development institution dedicated to graduating officers for the Afghan Armed Forces. The $200 million Afghan Defence University is under construction near Qargha in Kabul. The United States is building six faculties of education and five provincial teacher training colleges around the country, two large secondary schools in Kabul, and one school in Jalalabad.

The literacy rate of the entire population has been very low but is now rising because more students go to schools. In 2010, the United States began establishing a number of Lincoln learning centres in Afghanistan. They are set up to serve as programming platforms offering English language classes, library facilities, programming venues, Internet connectivity, and educational and other counselling services. A goal of the program is to reach at least 4,000 Afghan citizens per month per location. The Afghan National Security Forces are provided with mandatory literacy courses. In addition to this, Baghch-e-Simsim (based on the American Sesame Street) was launched in late 2011 to help young Afghan children learn.

In 2009 and 2010, a 5,000 OLPC - One Laptop Per Child schools deployment took place in Kandahar with funding from an anonymous foundation. The OLPC team seeks local support to undertake larger deployment.

Culture

The Afghan culture has been around for over two millennia, tracing back to at least the time of the Achaemenid Empire in 500 BCE. It is mostly a nomadic and tribal society, with different regions of the country having their own traditions, reflecting the multi-cultural and multi-lingual character of the nation. In the southern and eastern region the people live according to the Pashtun culture by following Pashtunwali, which is an ancient way of life that is still preserved. The remainder of the country is culturally Persian and Turkic. Some non-Pashtuns who live in proximity with Pashtuns have adopted Pashtunwali in a process called Pashtunization (or *Afghanization*), while some Pashtuns have been Persianized. Millions of Afghans who have been living in Pakistan and Iran over the last 30 years have been influenced by the cultures of those neighbouring nations.

Afghans display pride in their culture, nation, ancestry, and above all, their religion and independence. Like other highlanders, they are regarded with mingled apprehension and condescension, for their high regard for personal honour, for their tribe loyalty and for their readiness to use force to settle disputes. As tribal warfare and internecine feuding has been one of their chief occupations since time immemorial, this individualistic trait has made it difficult for foreigners to conquer them. Tony Heathcote considers the tribal system to be the best way of organising large groups of people in a country that is geographically difficult, and in a society that, from a materialistic point of view, has an uncomplicated lifestyle. There are an estimated 60 major Pashtun tribes, and the Afghan nomads are estimated at about 2–3 million.

The nation has a complex history that has survived either in its current cultures or in the form of various languages and monuments. However, many of its historic monuments have been damaged in recent wars. The two famous Buddhas of Bamiyan were destroyed by the Taliban, who regarded them as idolatrous. Despite that, archaeologists are still finding Buddhist relics in different parts of the country, some of them dating back to the 2nd century. This indicates that Buddhism was widespread in Afghanistan.

Other historical places include the cities of Herat, Kandahar, Ghazni, Mazar-i-Sharif, and Zarang. The Minaret of Jam in the Hari River valley is a UNESCO World Heritage site. A cloak reputedly worn by Islam's Prophet Muhammad is kept inside the Shrine of the Cloak in Kandahar, a city founded by Alexander and the first capital of Afghanistan. The citadel of Alexander in the western city of Herat has been renovated in recent years and is a popular attraction for tourists. In the north of the country is the Shrine of Hazrat Ali, believed by many to be the location where Ali was buried. The Afghan Ministry of Information and Culture is renovating 42 historic sites in Ghazni until 2013, when the province will be declared as the capital of Islamic civilization. The National Museum of Afghanistan is located in Kabul.

Although literacy is low, classic Persian and Pashto poetry plays an important role in the Afghan culture. Poetry has always been one of the major educational pillars in the region, to the level that it has integrated itself into culture. Some notable poets include Rumi, Rabi'a Balkhi, Sanai, Jami, Khushal Khan Khattak, Rahman Baba, Khalilullah Khalili, and Parween Pazhwak.

Bangladesh

Bangladesh, officially the People's Republic of Bangladesh, is a country in South Asia. It is bordered by India to its west, north and east; Burma to its southeast and separated from Nepal and Bhutan by the Chicken's Neck corridor. To its south, it faces the Bay of Bengal. Bangladesh is the world's eighth-most populous country, with over 160 million people, and among the most densely populated countries. It forms part of the ethno-linguistic region of Bengal, along with the neighbouring Indian states of West Bengal and Tripura.

The present-day borders of Bangladesh took shape during the Partition of Bengal and British India in 1947, when the region used to be known as East Pakistan, as a part of the newly formed state of Pakistan. It was separated from West Pakistan by 1,400 km of Indian territory. Due to political exclusion, ethnic and linguistic discrimination and economic neglect by the politically dominant western wing, nationalism, popular agitation and civil disobedience led to the Bangladesh Liberation War and independence in 1971. After independence, the new state endured poverty, famine, political turmoil and military coups. The restoration of democracy in 1991 has been followed by relative calm and economic progress. In 2014, the Bangladeshi general election was boycotted by major opposition parties, resulting in a parliament and government dominated by the Awami League and its smaller coalition partners.

Bangladesh is a unitary parliamentary republic with an elected parliament called the Jatiyo Sangshad. The native Bengalis form the country's largest ethnic group, along with indigenous peoples in northern and southeastern districts. Geographically, the country is dominated by the fertile Bengal delta, the world's largest delta. This also gives Bangladesh a unique name tag "The land of rivers".

Bangladesh is a Next Eleven emerging economy. It has achieved significant strides in human and social development since independence, including in progress in gender equity, universal primary education, food production, health and population control. However, Bangladesh continues to face numerous political, economic, social and environmental challenges, including political instability, corruption, poverty, overpopulation and climate change. Bangladesh is a founding member of SAARC, the Developing 8 Countries and BIMSTEC. It contributes one of the largest peacekeeping forces to the United Nations. It is a member of the Commonwealth of Nations, the Organisation of Islamic Cooperation and the Non-Aligned Movement.

History of Bangladesh

Antiquity

Remnants of civilization in the greater Bengal region date back four thousand years to when the region was settled by ancient Dravidian, Indo-Aryan, Tibeto-Burman and Austroasiatic peoples.

The exact origin of the word "Bangla" or "Bengal" is unclear, though it is believed to be derived from *Bang/Vanga*, the Dravidian-speaking tribe that settled in the area around the year 1000 BCE. Under Islamic rule, the region came to be known to the Muslim world in Persian as *Bangalah*.

The region was known to the ancient Greek and Roman world as *Gangaridai* or *nation of Ganges*. Though still largely unclear, the early history of Bengal featured a succession of city states, maritime kingdoms and pan-Indian empires, as well as a tussle between Hinduism and Buddhism for dominance. The ancient political units of the region consisted of Vanga, Samatata, Harikela and Pundravardhana.

The Mauryan Empire led by Ashoka the Great conquered Bengal in the second century BCE. After the collapse of the Gupta Empire, a local ruler named Shashanka rose to power and founded the Gauda kingdom. After a period of anarchy, the Bengali Buddhist Pala dynasty ruled the region for four hundred years, followed by the Hindu Sena Dynasty and Candra Dynasty.

Islamic Bengal

Islam was introduced to the Bengal region during the 7th century by Arab Muslim traders and Sufi missionaries, and the subsequent Muslim conquest of Bengal in the 12th century lead to the rooting of Islam across the region. Bakhtiar Khilji, a Turkic general, defeated Lakshman Sen of the Sena dynasty and conquered large parts of Bengal in the year 1204.

The region was ruled by the Sultanate of Bengal and the Baro-Bhuiyan confederacy for the next few hundred years. By the 16th century, the Mughal Empire controlled Bengal, and Dhaka became an important provincial centre of Mughal administration.

Bengal was probably the wealthiest part of the subcontinent until the 16th century. From 1517 onwards, Portuguese traders from Goa were traversing the sea route to Bengal. Only in 1537 were they allowed to settle and open customs houses at Chittagong. In 1577, the Mughal emperor Akbar permitted the Portuguese to build permanent settlements and churches in Bengal.

Colonialism

The influence of European traders grew until the British East India Company gained control of Bengal following the Battle of Plassey in 1757. The bloody rebellion of 1857—known as the Sepoy Mutiny—resulted in a transfer of authority to the crown with a British viceroy running the administration. During colonial rule, famine racked South Asia many times, including the war-induced Great Bengal famine of 1943, which claimed 3 million lives.

After the foundation of the British Indian Empire, Bengal was still under the heavy influence of British culture including architecture and art. The Indian Independence Movement was still underway in effort to overthrow the British Empire, and many Bengali people contributed to that effort. At the same time as the Islamic and Hindu conflicts occurred, Bengal would be split into two states. Between 1905 and 1911, an abortive attempt was made to divide the province of Bengal into two zones.

East Pakistan

Following the exit of the British Empire in 1947, Bengal was partitioned along religious lines, with the western part going to newly created India and the eastern part (Muslim majority) joining Pakistan as a province called East Bengal (later renamed East Pakistan), with Dhaka as its capital.

In 1950, land reform was accomplished in East Bengal with the abolishment of the feudal zamindari system. Despite the economic and demographic weight of the east, Pakistan's government and military were largely dominated by the upper classes from the west. The Bengali Language Movement of 1952 was the first sign of friction between the two wings of Pakistan. Dissatisfaction with the central government over economic and cultural issues continued to rise through the next decade, during which the Awami League emerged as the political voice of the Bengali-speaking population.

It agitated for autonomy in the 1960s, and in 1966, its president, Sheikh Mujibur Rahman (Mujib), was jailed; he was released in 1969 after an unprecedented popular uprising. In 1970, a massive cyclone devastated the coast of East Pakistan, killing up to half a million people, and the central government's response was seen as poor. The anger of the Bengali population was compounded when Sheikh Mujibur Rahman, whose Awami League had won a majority in Parliament in the 1970 elections, was blocked from taking office.

After staging compromise talks with Mujibur Rahman, President Yahya Khan and military officials launched Operation Searchlight, a sustained military assault on East Pakistan, and arrested Mujibur Rahman in the early hours of 26 March 1971. Yahya's methods were extremely bloody, and the violence of the war resulted in many civilian deaths. Yahya's chief targets included intellectuals and Hindus, and about one million refugees fled to neighbouring India. Estimates of those massacred throughout the war range from thirty thousand to three million. Mujibur Rahman was ultimately released on 8 January 1972 as a result of direct US intervention.

Awami League leaders set up a government-in-exile in Calcutta, India. The exile government formally took oath at Meherpur, in the Kustia district of East Pakistan, on 17 April 1971, with Tajuddin Ahmad as the first Prime Minister and Syed Nazrul Islam as the Acting President. The Bangladesh Liberation War lasted for nine months. A resistance force known as the Mukti Bahini was formed from the Bangladesh Forces (consisting of Bengali regular forces) in alliance with civilian fighters such as the Kader Bahini and the Hemayet Bahini. Led by General M. A. G. Osmani, the Bangladesh Forces were organised into eleven sectors and, as part of Mukti Bahini, conducted a massive guerrilla war against the Pakistan Forces. The war witnessed the 1971 Bangladesh genocide, in which the Pakistan Army and its allied religious militias carried out a wide-scale elimination of Bengali civilians, intellectuals, youth, students, politicians, activists and religious minorities. By winter, Bangladesh-India Allied Forces defeated the Pakistan Army, culminating in its surrender and the Liberation of Dhaka on 16 December 1971.

Modern Bangladesh

After independence, the Constitution of Bangladesh established a unitary secular multiparty parliamentary democratic system. The Awami League won the first general elections in 1973 with a massive mandate, gaining an absolute parliamentary majority. A nationwide famine occurred during 1973 and 1974, and in early 1975, Mujib initiated a one-party socialist rule with his newly formed BAKSAL. On 15 August 1975, Mujib and most of his family members were assassinated by mid-level military officers. Vice President Khandaker Mushtaq Ahmed was sworn in as President with most of Mujib's cabinet intact. Two Army uprisings on 3 November and 7 November 1975 led to a reorganised structure of power. A state of emergency was declared to restore order and calm. Mushtaq resigned, and the country was placed under temporary martial law, with three service chiefs serving as deputies to the new president, Justice Abu Sayem, who also became the Chief Martial Law Administrator. Lieutenant General Ziaur Rahman took over the presidency in 1977 when Justice Sayem resigned. President Zia reinstated multi-party politics, introduced free markets, and founded the Bangladesh Nationalist Party (BNP). Zia's rule ended when he was assassinated by elements of the military in 1981. Bangladesh's next major ruler was Lieutenant General Hossain Mohammad Ershad, who gained power in a coup on 24 March 1982, and ruled until 6 December 1990, when he was forced to resign after a revolt of all major political parties and the public, along with pressure from Western donors (which was a major shift in international policy after the fall of the Soviet Union).

Figure: *Founding leader Sheikh Mujibur Rahman signs the Constitution of Bangladesh into law on 16 December 1972*

Since then, Bangladesh has reverted to a parliamentary democracy. Zia's widow, Khaleda Zia, led the Bangladesh Nationalist Party to parliamentary victory at the general election in 1991 and became the first female Prime Minister in Bangladeshi history. However, the Awami League, headed by Sheikh Hasina, one of Mujib's surviving daughters, won the next election in 1996. The Awami League lost again to the Bangladesh Nationalist Party in 2001. Widespread political unrest followed the resignation of the BNP in late October 2006, but the caretaker government worked to bring the parties to election within the required ninety days. At the last minute in early January, the Awami League withdrew from the election scheduled for later that month. On 11 January 2007, the military intervened to support both a state of emergency and a continuing but neutral caretaker government under a newly appointed Chief Advisor, who was not a politician. The country had suffered for decades from extensive corruption, disorder, and political violence. The caretaker government worked to root out corruption from all levels of government. It arrested on corruption charges more than 160 people, including politicians, civil servants, and businessmen, among whom were both major party leaders, some of their senior staff, and two sons of Khaleda Zia.

After working to clean up the system, the caretaker government held what was described by observers as a largely free and fair election on 29 December 2008. The Awami League's Sheikh Hasina won with a two-thirds landslide in the elections; she took the oath of Prime Minister on 6 January 2009.

Politics and Law

Government

Bangladesh is a unitary state and parliamentary democracy. Direct elections in which all citizens, aged 18 or over, can vote are held every five years for the unicameral parliament known as the Jatiyo Sangshad. Currently it has 350 members (including 50 reserved seats for women) elected from single-member constituencies. The Prime Minister, as the head of government, forms the cabinet and runs the day-to-day affairs of state. The Prime Minister is formally appointed by the President but must also be a member of parliament who commands the confidence of the majority.

The President is the head of state, albeit mainly ceremonially in his/her elected post; however, the President's powers are substantially expanded during the tenure of a caretaker government, which is responsible for the conduct of elections and transfer of power. The officers of the caretaker government must be non-partisan and are given three months to complete their task. This transitional arrangement was pioneered by Bangladesh in its 1991 election and then institutionalised in 1996 through its 13th constitutional amendment.

Major parties in Bangladesh include the Awami League, the Bangladesh Nationalist Party (BNP), the Jatiya Party and the Jamaat-e-Islami. Sheikh Hasina's Awami League aligns with more leftist parties, whereas Khaleda Zia's BNP has politically been allied with

Islamist parties like the Jamaat but practices secular politics. The former two have been bitter, dominant political rivals for over 15 years; each is related to one of the leaders of the independence movement. The Awami League-BNP rivalry has been punctuated by protests, violence and murder. Student politics are particularly strong in Bangladesh, a legacy from the liberation movement era, as almost all parties have highly active student wings, and student leaders have been elected to the Jatiyo Sangshad.

On 11 January 2007, following widespread political unrest, emergency law was declared and a caretaker government was appointed to administer the next general election. The 22 January 2007 election was postponed indefinitely as the Army-backed caretaker government of Fakhruddin Ahmed aimed to prepare a new voter list and crack down on corruption. They also assisted the interim government of Bangladesh in a drive against corruption, which resulted in Bangladesh's position in Transparency International's Corruption Perceptions Index changed from the very bottom, where they had been for 3 years in a row, to 147th in just 1 year. A large alliance led by the Bangladesh Awami League won in a 29 December 2008 landslide victory, gaining 230 seats among 300 seats in the parliament.

Law & Judiciary

Bangladeshi law is primarily in accordance with the English legal system, although since 1947 the legal scenario of Bangladesh has significantly drifted from the West owing to differences in socio-cultural values and religious guidelines. Laws are loosely based on English common law, but family laws such as marriage and inheritance are based on religious scriptures, and therefore differ between religious communities. The Constitution of Bangladesh was drafted in 1972 and has undergone 15 amendments.

The highest judicial body is the Supreme Court, with justices appointed by the President. The judicial and law enforcement institutions are comparatively weak. On 1 November 2007, Bangladesh successfully separated the Judiciary Branch from the Executive, but several black laws, including the Special Powers Act, still influence the rulers. It is expected that this separation will make the judiciary stronger and more impartial.

Foreign Relations and Military

Bangladesh pursues a moderate foreign policy which places heavy reliance on multinational diplomacy, especially at the United Nations. In 1974, Bangladesh joined both the Commonwealth of Nations and the United Nations and has since been elected to serve two terms on the Security Council – in 1978–1979 and 2000–2001. In the 1980s, Bangladesh pioneered the creation of the South Asian Association for Regional Cooperation (SAARC), the first regional intergovernmental body in South Asia. It is also a founding member of the Bay of Bengal Initiative and the Developing 8 Countries.

Bangladesh's most important and complex foreign relationship is with neighbouring India. The relationship is borne out of historical and cultural affinities, as well as India's alliance with Bangladeshi nationalists during the liberation of Bangladesh in 1971. However, bilateral ties have gone through several hiccups in the last forty years. A major source of tension is water-sharing on 56 common rivers, as well as border security and India's barriers to trade and investments. Both countries have also at times accused each other of harbouring insurgent groups. Recognising the importance of good relations, regional security and South Asian economic integration, the two countries have sought to revive relations in recent years, and have formed strategic partnerships to develop regional connectivity, infrastructure, greater trade, mutual access to markets, energy, environmental protection and cultural projects. India's eastern states, as well as Nepal and Bhutan, are keen to gain access to Bangladesh's Chittagong and Mongla ports.

Bangladesh enjoys very warm ties with the People's Republic of China, and particularly in the last decade there has been increased economic cooperation between them. Between 2006 and 2007, trade between the two nations rose by 28.5% and there have been agreements to grant various Bangladeshi commodities tariff-free access to the Chinese market. Cooperation between the Military of Bangladesh and the People's Liberation Army is also increasing, with joint military agreements signed and Bangladesh purchasing Chinese arms which range from small arms to large naval surface combat ships such as the Chinese Type 053H1 Missile Frigate.

Bangladesh is a major South Asian ally of the United States. The two countries have long-standing partnerships in development, defence, energy, business, trade, education, health and the environment. As of 2011, American aid to Bangladesh totalled over US$6 billion. American companies are the largest foreign investors in country, and the US is also the largest market for Bangladeshi exports. In the 1991 Gulf War, Bangladesh participated in the US-led multinational coalition to liberate Kuwait. It supports the US-led reconstruction of Afghanistan, where Bangladeshi non-governmental agencies, such as BRAC, are extensively involved in Afghan reconstruction efforts. The US Military and the Bangladesh Armed Forces have long-standing strategic relations and host frequent joint military exercises, particularly in counter-terrorism and maritime security.

The US has also assisted Bangladesh with massive relief operations in the aftermath of several natural disasters, such as the 1991 Bangladesh cyclone and Cyclone Sidr. In 2010, President Barack Obama announced a $1 billion aid package for Bangladesh, to be utilised from 2010 to 2015, in addressing challenges of food security, health and climate change. In 2011, Secretary of State Hillary Clinton and Foreign Minister Dipu Moni launched annual strategic dialogues between the two countries.

As of 2012, the current strength of the army is around 300,000 including reservists, the air force 22,000, and navy 24,000. In addition to traditional defence roles, the military has been called on to provide support to civil authorities for disaster relief and internal security during periods of political unrest. Bangladesh is not currently active in any ongoing war, but it contributed 2,300 troops during Operation Desert Storm in 1991, and is the world's largest contributor (10,736) to UN peacekeeping forces. In May 2007, Bangladesh had major deployments in Democratic Republic of Congo, Liberia, Sudan, Timor-Leste and Côte d'Ivoire.

Divisions

Divisions are subdivided into districts (*zila*). There are 64 districts in Bangladesh, each further subdivided into *upazila* (subdistricts) or *thana*. The area within each police station, except for those in metropolitan areas, is divided into several *unions*, with each union consisting of multiple villages. In the metropolitan areas, police stations are divided into wards, which are further divided into *mahallas*. There are no elected officials at the divisional or district levels, and the administration is composed only of government officials. Direct elections are held for each union (or ward), electing a chairperson and a number of members. In 1997, a parliamentary act was passed to reserve three seats (out of 12) in every union for female candidates.

Dhaka is the capital and largest city of Bangladesh. The cities with a city corporation, having mayoral elections, include Dhaka South, Dhaka North, Chittagong, Khulna, Sylhet, Rajshahi, Barisal, Rangpur, Comilla and Gazipur. Other major cities, these and other municipalities electing a chairperson, include Mymensingh, Gopalganj, Jessore, Bogra, Dinajpur, Saidapur, Narayanganj and Rangamati. Both the municipal heads are elected for a span of five years.

Economy

Bangladesh is a developing nation and a rapidly growing market-based economy. It is one of the world's leading exporters of textiles and garments, as well as fish, seafood and jute, and has globally competitive emerging industries in shipbuilding, life sciences and technology. The country also has a strong social enterprise sector and is the birthplace of microfinance.Bangladesh has substantially decreased its dependency on foreign grants and loans from 85% (In 1988) to 2% (In 2010) for its annual development budget. Its per capita income as of 2013 is US$1,044 compared to the world average of $8,985. In December 2005, the Central Bank of Bangladesh projected GDP growth around 6.5%.

Bangladesh has seen a dramatic increase in foreign direct investment. In order to enhance economic growth, the government set up several export processing zones to attract foreign investment. These are managed by the Bangladesh Export Processing Zone Authority.

Goldman Sachs recognised the Bangladeshi economy as one of the Next Eleven. Citigroup identified Bangladesh as a 3G country with significant potential to generate global growth. The insufficient power supply constitutes an obstacle to growth. According to the World Bank, "among Bangladesh's most significant obstacles to growth are poor governance and weak public institutions." In April 2010, Standard & Poor's awarded Bangladesh a BB- for a long term in credit rating which is below India and well over Pakistan and Sri Lanka.

One significant contributor to the development of the economy has been the widespread propagation of microcredit by Muhammad Yunus (awarded the Nobel Peace Prize in 2006) through the Grameen Bank. By the late 1990s, Grameen Bank had 2.3 million members, along with 2.5 million members of other similar organisations.

Bangladesh government is planning for construction of the largest deep sea port in South Asia at Sonadia Island. The 500 billion taka project will be completed in multiple phases and enable Bangladesh to service the whole region as a maritime transport and logistics hub. India, China, Bhutan, Nepal and other neighbouring countries will be able to take full advantage of the strategic location and the privileges given to Bangladesh because of its Least developed country status, for exporting goods that are manufactured in Bangladesh.

Religion

Islam is the state religion even though Bangladesh is secular. Islam is the largest religion of Bangladesh, making up 86.6% of population.

Hinduism makes up 12.1% of the population, Buddhism 1% and others of 0.3% of the population. The majority of Muslims are Sunni, roughly 4% are non-denominational Muslims and a small number are Shia, and about 100,000 Ahmadi Muslims. Bangladesh has the fourth largest Muslim population after Indonesia, Pakistan and India. Hindus are the second biggest religious group in Bangladesh, and the third largest in the world after India and Nepal.

After Bangladesh gained independence from Pakistan, Secularism was included in the original Constitution of Bangladesh in 1972 as one of the Four State Principles, the others being Democracy, Nationalism and Socialism. In 2010, the High Court upheld the secular principles of the 1972 constitution but allowed to keep Islam as the state religion. Bangladesh follows secular government system in democratic state. However, Bangladesh also follows combined system of state laws and individual religious laws applicable to people of respective religious group.

Some people in Bangladesh practice Sufism, as historically Islam was brought to the region by Sufi saints. Sufi influences in the region go back many centuries. The largest gathering of Muslims in the country is the Bishwa Ijtema, held annually by the Tablighi Jamaat. The Ijtema is the second largest Muslim congregation in the world after the Hajj.

Education

Bangladesh has a low literacy rate, estimated at 61.3% for males and 52.2% for females in 2010. The educational system in Bangladesh is three-tiered and highly subsidized. The government of Bangladesh operates many schools in the primary, secondary, and higher secondary levels. It also subsidises parts of the funding for many private schools. In the tertiary education sector, the government also funds more than 15 state universities through the University Grants Commission.

The education system is divided into 5 levels: Primary (from grades 1 to 5), Junior Secondary (from grades 6 to 8), Secondary (from grades 9 to 10), Higher Secondary (from grades 11 to 12) and tertiary. The five years of lower secondary education concludes with a Secondary School Certificate (SSC) Examination, but since 2009 it concludes with a Primary Education Closing (PEC) Examination. Also earlier Students who pass this examination proceed to four years Secondary or matriculation training, which culminate in a Secondary School Certificate (SSC) Examination, but since 2010 the Primary Education Closing (PEC) passed examinees proceed to three years Junior Secondary, which culminate in a Junior School Certificate (JSC)

Examination. Then students who pass this examination proceed to two years Secondary or matriculation training, which culminate in a Secondary School Certificate (SSC) Examination. Students who pass this examination proceed to two years of Higher Secondary or intermediate training, which culminate in a Higher Secondary School Certificate (HSC) Examination.

Education is mainly offered in Bengali, but English is also commonly taught and used. A large number of Muslim families send their children to attend part-time courses or even to pursue full-time religious education, which is imparted in Bengali and Arabic in madrasahs.

Bangladesh conforms fully to the Education For All (EFA) objectives, the Millennium Development Goals (MDG) and international declarations. Article 17 of the Bangladesh Constitution provides that all children between the ages of six and ten years receive a basic education free of charge.

Universities in Bangladesh are mainly categorized into three different types: public university (government owned and subsidized), private university (private sector owned universities) and international university (operated and funded by international organisations). Bangladesh has some thirty-four public, sixty-four private and two international universities. National University has the largest enrollment among them and University of Dhaka (established 1921) is the oldest university of the country. Islamic University of Technology, commonly known as IUT is a subsidiary organ of the Organisation of the Islamic Cooperation (OIC), representing fifty seven member countries from Asia, Africa, Europe and South America. BUET and SUST are also two top universities of the country. Bangladeshi universities are accredited by and affiliated with the University Grants Commission (UGC), a commission created according to the Presidential Order (P.O. No 10 of 1973) of the Government of the People's Republic of Bangladesh.

Health

Health and education levels remain relatively low, although they have improved recently as poverty (26% at 2012) levels have decreased. In the rural areas, village doctors with little or no formal training constitute 62% of the healthcare providers practicing modern medicine and the formally trained providers are occupying a mere 4% of the total health workforce. A survey conducted by Future Health Systems revealed significant deficiencies in treatment practices of village doctors, with a wide prevalence of harmful and inappropriate drug prescriptions. There are market incentives for accessing health care through informal providers and it is important to understand these markets in order to facilitate collaboration across actors and institutions in order to provide incentives for better performance.

A 2007 study of 1000 households in rural Bangladesh found that direct costs (payment to formal and informal health care providers) and indirect costs (loss of earnings associated with workdays lost because of illness) associated with illness were important deterrents to accessing health care from qualified healthcare providers. A community survey with 6183 individuals in rural Bangladesh found a clear gender difference in treatment-seeking behaviour, with women less likely to seek treatment compared to men. The use of skilled birth attendants, however, has risen between 2005 and 2007 by women in all wealth quintiles except the highest quintile. A pilot community empowerment tool, called a health watch, was successfully developed and implemented in south-eastern Bangladesh in order to improve uptake and monitoring of public health services.

The poor health conditions in Bangladesh is attributed by the lack of healthcare and services provision by the government. The total expenditure on healthcare as a percentage of their GDP was only 3.35% in 2009, according to a World Bank report published in 2010. The number of hospital beds per 10,000 population is 4. The General government expenditure on healthcare as a percentage of total government expenditure was only 7.9% as of 2009 and the citizens pay most of their health care bills as the out-of-pocket expenditure as a percentage of private expenditure on health is 96.5%.

Malnutrition has been a persistent problem for the poverty-stricken country. The World Bank estimates that Bangladesh is ranked 1st in the world of the number of children suffering from malnutrition. In Bangladesh, 26% of the population are undernourished and 46% of the children suffers from moderate to severe underweight problem. 43% of children under 5 years old are stunted. One in five preschool age children are vitamin A deficient and one in two are anemic. Child malnutrition in Bangladesh is amongst the highest in the world. Two-thirds of the children, under the age of five, are under-nourished and about 60% of them, who are under six, are stunted. More than 45 percent of rural families and 76 percent of urban families were below the acceptable caloric intake level.

Pakistan

Pakistan, officially the Islamic Republic of Pakistan, is a sovereign country in South Asia. With a population exceeding 180 million people, it is the sixth most populous country and with an area covering 796,095 km^2 (307,374 sq mi), it is the 36th largest country in the world in terms of area. Pakistan has a 1,046-kilometre (650 mi) coastline along the Arabian Sea and the Gulf of Oman in the south and is bordered by India to the east, Afghanistan to the west, Iran to the southwest and China in the far northeast. It is separated from Tajikistan by Afghanistan's narrow Wakhan Corridor in the north, and also shares a marine border with Oman.

The territory that now constitutes Pakistan was previously home to several ancient cultures, including the Mehrgarh of the Neolithic and the Bronze Age Indus Valley Civilisation, and was later home to kingdoms ruled by people of different faiths and cultures, including Hindus, Indo-Greeks, Muslims, Turco-Mongols, Afghans and Sikhs. The area has been ruled by numerous empires and dynasties, including the Indian Mauryan Empire, the Persian Achaemenid Empire, Alexander of Macedonia, the Arab Umayyad Caliphate, the Mongol Empire, the Mughal Empire, the Durrani Empire, the Sikh Empire and the British Empire. As a result of the Pakistan Movement led by Muhammad Ali Jinnah and the subcontinent's struggle for independence, Pakistan was created in 1947 as an independent nation for Muslims from the regions in the east and west of Subcontinent where there was a Muslim majority. Initially a dominion, Pakistan adopted a new constitution in 1956, becoming an Islamic republic. A civil war in 1971 resulted in the secession of East Pakistan as the new country of Bangladesh.

Pakistan is a federal parliamentary republic consisting of four provinces and four federal territories. It is an ethnically and linguistically diverse country, with a similar variation in its geography and wildlife. A regional and middle power, Pakistan has the seventh largest standing armed forces in the world and is also a nuclear power as well as a declared nuclear-weapons state, being the only nation in the Muslim world, and the second in South Asia, to have that status. It has a semi-industrialised economy with a well-integrated agriculture sector, its economy is the 26th largest in the world in terms of purchasing power and 45th largest in terms of nominal GDP and is also characterized among the emerging and growth-leading economies of the world.

The post-independence history of Pakistan has been characterised by periods of military rule, political instability and conflicts with neighbouring India. The country continues to face challenging problems, including overpopulation, terrorism, poverty, illiteracy, and corruption. It ranked 16th on the 2012 Happy Planet Index. It is a member of the United Nations, the Commonwealth of Nations, the Next Eleven

Economies, ECO, UfC, D8, Cairns Group, Kyoto Protocol, ICCPR, RCD, UNCHR, Group of Eleven, CPFTA, Group of 24, the G20 developing nations, ECOSOC, founding member of the Organisation of Islamic Cooperation, SAARC and CERN.

Independence and Modern Pakistan

After independence, the President of the Muslim League, Mohammed Ali Jinnah, became the new nation's first Governor-General, and the Secretary General of the Muslim League, Nawabzada Liaquat Ali Khan became the first Prime Minister. From 1947 to 1956, Pakistan was a dominion in the Commonwealth of Nations under two monarchs. In 1947, George VI relinquished the title of Emperor of India and became King of Pakistan. He retained that title until his death on 6 February 1952, after which Queen Elizabeth II became Queen of Pakistan. She retained that title until Pakistan became an Islamic and Parliamentary republic in 1956, but civilian rule was stalled by a military coup led by the Army Commander-in-Chief, General Ayub Khan. The country experienced exceptional growth until a second war with India took place in 1965 and led to economic downfall and internal instability. Ayub Khan's successor, General Yahya Khan (President from 1969 to 1971), had to deal with a devastating cyclone which caused 500,000 deaths in East Pakistan.

Figure: *Zulfikar Ali Bhutto along with Field Marshal Ayub Khan signing the Tashkent Declaration which brought an end to the Indo-Pakistani War of 1965.*

In 1970, Pakistan held its first democratic elections since independence, that were meant to mark a transition from military rule to democracy, but after the East Pakistani Awami League won, Yahya Khan and the ruling elite in West Pakistan refused to hand over power. There was civil unrest in the East, and the Pakistan Army launched a military operation on 25 March 1971, aiming to regain control of the province. The genocide carried out during this operation led to a declaration of independence and to the waging of a war of liberation by the Bengali Mukti Bahini forces in East Pakistan, with support from India. However, in West Pakistan the conflict was described as a civil war as opposed to War of Liberation.

Independent estimates of civilian deaths during this period range from 300,000 to 3 million. Attacks on Indian military bases by the Pakistan Air Force in December 1971 sparked the Indo-Pakistani War of 1971, which ended with the formal secession of East Pakistan as the independent state of Bangladesh.

Figure: *Pakistan's first Prime Minister Liaquat Ali Khan with President Harry S. Truman of United States.*

With Pakistan's defeat in the war, Yahya Khan was replaced by Zulfikar Ali Bhutto as Chief Martial Law Administrator. Civilian rule resumed from 1972 to 1977. During this period Pakistan began to build nuclear weapons; the country's first atomic power plant was inaugurated in 1972. Civilian rule ended with a military coup in 1977, and in 1979 General Zia-ul-Haq became the third military president. Military government lasted until 1988, during which Pakistan became one of the fastest-growing economies in South Asia. Zia consolidated nuclear development and increased Islamization of the state. During this period, Pakistan helped to subsidise and distribute US resources to factions of the Mujahideen movement against the 1979 Soviet invasion of Afghanistan.

Zia died in a plane crash in 1988, and Benazir Bhutto, daughter of Zulfikar Ali Bhutto, was elected as the first female Prime Minister of Pakistan. She was followed by Nawaz Sharif, and over the next decade the two leaders fought for power, alternating in office while the country's situation worsened; economic indicators fell sharply, in contrast to the 1980s. This period is marked by political instability, misgovernance and corruption. In May 1998, while Sharif was Prime Minister, India tested five nuclear weapons and tension with India heightened to an extreme: Pakistan detonated six nuclear weapons of its own in the *Chagai-I* and *Chagai-II* tests later in the same month. Military tension between the two countries in the Kargil district led to the Kargil War of 1999, after which General Pervez Musharraf took over through a bloodless coup d'état and assumed vast executive powers.

***Figure:** U.S President George W. Bush with his Pakistani counterpart in Islamabad. Pakistan is a leading member of U.S led War on Terror.*

Musharraf ruled Pakistan as head of state from 1999 to 2001 and as President from 2001 to 2008, a period of extensive economic reform and Pakistan's involvement in the US-led war on terrorism. On 15 November 2007, Pakistan's National Assembly became the first to complete its full five-year term, and new elections were called. After the assassination of Benazir Bhutto in December 2007, her Pakistan Peoples Party (PPP) won the largest number of seats in the 2008 elections, and party member Yousaf Raza Gillani was sworn in as Prime Minister. Musharraf resigned from the presidency on 18 August 2008 when threatened with impeachment, and was succeeded by Asif Ali Zardari. Gillani was disqualified from membership of parliament and as prime minister by the Supreme Court of Pakistan in June 2012. By its own estimates, Pakistan's involvement in the war on terrorism has cost up to $67.93 billion, thousands of casualties and nearly 3 million displaced civilians. The Pakistani general election of 2013 saw the Pakistan Muslim League (N) achieve a majority, following which Nawaz Sharif became elected as the Prime Minister of Pakistan, returning to the post for the third time after fourteen years, in a democratic transition. However claims of electoral fraud, together with allegations of nepotism and corruption dogged his third term, resulting in widespread protests, and resignations by opposition members. He nonetheless resisted calls to step down, while shoring up support in the parliament.

Politics

Pakistan is a democratic parliamentary federal republic with Islam as the state religion. The first Constitution of Pakistan was adopted in 1956 but suspended by Ayub Khan in 1958. The Constitution of 1973—suspended by Zia-ul-Haq in 1977 but reinstated in 1985—is the country's most important document, laying the foundations of the current government. The Pakistani military establishment has played an influential role in mainstream politics throughout Pakistan's political history. Presidents brought in by military coups ruled in 1958–1971, 1977–1988 and 1999–2008. Pakistan today is a multiparty system parliamentry state with clear division of power and responsibilities between branches of government. The first successful demonstrative transaction was held in May 2013. As of 2013 elections, the three main political parties in the country are Pakistan Muslim League led by Nawaz Sharif, Pakistan Peoples Party led by Bilawal Bhutto Zardari and Pakistan Movement for Justice led by Imran Khan.

- Head of State: The president who is elected by an electoral college is the ceremonial head of the state and is the civilian commander-in-chief of the Pakistan Armed Forces (with Chairman Joint Chiefs of Staff Committee as its principal military adviser), but military appointments and key confirmations in the armed forces are made by the prime minister after reviewing the reports on their merit and performances. Almost all appointed officers in the judicial branches, military chiefs, chairman and branches, and legislatures require the executive confirmation from the prime minister, whom the President must consult, by law. However, the powers to pardon and grant clemency vest with the President of Pakistan.
- Legislative: The bicameral legislature comprises a 100-member Senate and a 342-member National Assembly. Members of the National Assembly are elected through the first-past-the-post system under universal adult suffrage, representing electoral districts known as National Assembly constituencies. According to the constitution, the 70 seats reserved for women and religious minorities are allocated to the political parties

according to their proportional representation. Senate members are elected by provincial legislators, with all of provinces have equal representation.

- Executive: The prime minister is usually the leader of the largest party or a coalition in the National Assembly. He serves as the head of government and is designated to exercise as the country's chief executive. The premier is responsible for appointing a cabinet consisting of ministers and advisors as well as running the government operations, taking and authorizing executive decisions, appointments and recommendations that require executive confirmation of the Prime Minister.
- Provincial governments: Each of the four province has a similar system of government, with a directly elected Provincial Assembly in which the leader of the largest party or coalition is elected Chief Minister. Chief Ministers oversees the provincial government and head the provincial cabinet, it is common in Pakistan to have different ruling parties or coalitions in the provinces. The provincial assemblies have power to make laws and approve provincial budget which is commonly presented by the provincial finance minister every fiscal year. Provincial governors who play role as the ceremonial head of province are appointed by the President.
- Judiciary: The judiciary of Pakistan is a hierarchical system with two classes of courts: the superior (or higher) judiciary and the subordinate (or lower) judiciary. The superior judiciary is composed of the Supreme Court of Pakistan, the Federal Shariat Court and five High Courts, with the Supreme Court at the apex. The Constitution of Pakistan entrusts the superior judiciary with the obligation to preserve, protect and defend the constitution. Neither the Supreme Court nor a High Court may exercise jurisdiction in relation to Tribal Areas, except otherwise provided for. The disputed regions of Azad Kashmir and Gilgit–Baltistan have separate court systems

Foreign Relations of Pakistan

Pakistan is the second most populous Muslim country (after Indonesia), and its status as a declared nuclear power, being the only Islamic nation to have that status, plays a part in its international role. Pakistan claims to maintain an independent foreign policy, especially when it comes to issues such as development of nuclear weapons, construction of nuclear reactors, foreign military purchases and other issues that are vital to its national interests. Pakistan has a strategic geopolitical location at the corridor of world major maritime oil supply lines, and has proximity to the resource and oil rich central Asian countries. Pakistan is a founding member of the Organisation of Islamic Cooperation (OIC), is ranked by the US as a major non-NATO ally in the war against terrorism, and has the world's eighth-largest standing military force in terms of number of active personnel.

Pakistan's foreign policy focuses on security against threats to national identity and territorial integrity, and on the cultivation of close relations with Muslim countries. A 2004 briefing on foreign policy for Pakistani Parliamentarians says, "Pakistan highlights sovereign equality of states, bilateralism, mutuality of interests, and non-interference in each other's domestic affairs as the cardinal features of its foreign policy." The country is an active member of the United Nations. It is a founding member of the Organisation of Islamic Cooperation (OIC), in which it has promoted Musharraf's concept of "Enlightened Moderation". Pakistan is also a member of Commonwealth of Nations, the South Asian Association for Regional Cooperation (SAARC), the Economic Cooperation Organisation (ECO) and the G20 developing nations. India's nuclear tests were seen as a threat to Pakistan and led it to establish itself as a nuclear power. Pakistan now maintains a policy of "credible minimum deterrence".

Pakistan maintains good relations with all Arab and most other Muslim countries. Since the Sino-Indian War of 1962, Pakistan's closest strategic, military and economic ally has been China. The relationship has survived changes of governments and variations in the regional and global situation. Chinese cooperation with Pakistan has reached economic high points, with substantial Chinese investment in Pakistan's infrastructural expansion including the Pakistani deep-water port at Gwadar. Both countries have an ongoing free trade agreement. Pakistan has served as China's main bridge between Muslim countries. Pakistan also played an important role in bridging the communication gap between China and the West by facilitating the 1972 Nixon visit to China.

Pakistan and India continue to be rivals. The Kashmir conflict remains the major point of rift; three of their four wars were over this territory. Pakistan has had mixed relations with the United States. As an anti-Soviet power in the 1950s and during Soviet-Afghan War in the 1980s, Pakistan was one of the closest allies of the US, but relations soured in the 1990s when the US imposed sanctions because of Pakistan's possession and testing of nuclear weapons. The US war on terrorism led initially to an improvement in the relationship, but it was strained by a divergence of interests and resulting mistrust during the war in Afghanistan and by issues related to terrorism. Since 1948, there has been an ongoing, and at times fluctuating, violent conflict in the southwestern province of Balochistan between various Baloch separatist groups, who seek greater political autonomy, and the central government of Pakistan.

Administrative Divisions

Pakistan is a federation of four provinces: Punjab, Sindh, Khyber Pakhtunkhwa and Balochistan, as well as the Islamabad Capital Territory and the Federally Administered Tribal Areas in the northwest, which include the Frontier Regions. The government of Pakistan exercises *de facto* jurisdiction over the western parts of the disputed Kashmir region, organised into the separate political entities Azad Kashmir and Gilgit–Baltistan (formerly Northern Areas). The *Gilgit–Baltistan Empowerment and Self-Governance Order* of 2009 assigned a province-like status to the latter, giving it self-government.

Local government follows a three-tier system of districts, tehsils and union councils, with an elected body at each tier. There are about 130 districts altogether, of which Azad Kashmir has ten and Gilgit–Baltistan seven. The Tribal Areas comprise seven tribal agencies and six small frontier regions detached from neighbouring districts.

Law enforcement in Pakistan is carried out by federal and provincial police agencies. The four provinces and the Islamabad Capital Territory each have a civilian police force with jurisdiction limited to the relevant province or territory. At the federal level, there are a number of civilian agencies with nationwide jurisdictions; including the Federal Investigation Agency, the National Highways and Motorway Police, and several paramilitary forces such as the Pakistan Rangers and the Frontier Corps.

The court system of Pakistan is organised as a hierarchy, with the Supreme Court at the apex, below which are High Courts, Federal Shariat Courts (one in each province and one in the federal capital), District Courts (one in each district), Judicial Magistrate Courts (in every town and city), Executive Magistrate Courts and Civil Courts. Pakistan's penal code has limited jurisdiction in the Tribal Areas, where law is largely derived from tribal customs.

Military

The armed forces of Pakistan are the eighth largest in the world in terms of numbers in full-time service, with about 617,000 personnel on active duty and 513,000 reservists in 2010. They came into existence after independence in 1947, and the military establishment has frequently been involved in the politics of Pakistan ever since. The Chairman joint chiefs is the highest principle officer in the armed forces, and the chief military adviser to the government though the chairman has no authority over the three branches of armed forces. The three main branches are the Army, the Navy, and the Air Force, and they are supported by a number of paramilitary forces.

The National Command Authority is responsible for employment, for control of the development of all strategic nuclear organisations and for Pakistan's nuclear doctrine under the nuclear defence theory. Pakistan's defence forces maintain close military relations with China and the United States and import military equipment mainly from them. The defence forces of China and Pakistan occasionally carry out joint military exercises. Conscription may be introduced in times of emergency, but it has never been imposed.

Since independence, Pakistan has been involved in four wars with neighbouring India, beginning in 1947 with the First Kashmir War, when Pakistan gained control of present-day Azad Kashmir and Gilgit–Baltistan. The two countries were at war again in 1965 and in 1971, and most recently in the Kargil War of 1999. The Army has also been engaged in several skirmishes with Afghanistan on the western Durand Line border. In 1961, it repelled an Afghan incursion in the Bajaur Agency near the Durand Line border. During the Soviet war in Afghanistan, Pakistan's military provided support to the mujahideen rebels through its ISI agency. Pakistani forces also shot down several intruding Soviet/Afghan aircraft during the 1980s, one of which belonged to Alexander Rutskoy.

Apart from its own conflicts, Pakistan has been an active participant in United Nations peacekeeping missions. It played a major role in rescuing trapped American soldiers from Mogadishu, Somalia, in 1993 in Operation Gothic Serpent. Pakistani armed forces are the largest troop contributors to UN peacekeeping missions.

Pakistan maintained significant numbers of troops in some Arab countries in defence, training and advisory roles. During the Six-Day War in 1967 and the Yom Kippur War in October 1973, PAF pilots volunteered to go to the Middle East to support Egypt and Syria, which were in a state of war with Israel; they shot down ten Israeli planes in the Six-Day War. In 1979, at the request of the Saudi government, commandos of the Pakistani Special Service Group were rushed to assist Saudi forces in Mecca to lead the operation of the Grand Mosque

Seizure. In 1991 Pakistan got involved with the Gulf War and sent 5,000 troops as part of a US-led coalition, specifically for the defence of Saudi Arabia.

Pakistani armed forces have been engaged in a war in North-West Pakistan since 2001, mainly against the Tehrik-i-Taliban Pakistan. Major operations undertaken by the Army include Operation Black Thunderstorm and Operation Rah-e-Nijat.

Kashmir Conflict

The Kashmir conflict is a territorial dispute between India and Pakistan over the Kashmir region, the most northwesterly region of South Asia. The two countries have fought at least three wars over Kashmir—the Indo-Pakistani War of 1947, 1965, 1971 and 1999—and several skirmishes over the Siachen Glacier. India claims the entire state of Jammu and Kashmir and administers approximately 45.1% of the region, including most of Jammu, the Kashmir Valley, Ladakh, and the Siachen Glacier. India's claim is contested by Pakistan, which controls approximately 38.2% of Kashmir, consisting of Azad Kashmir and the northern areas of Gilgit and Baltistan.

The conflict of Kashmir has its origin in 1947, when British India was separated into the two states of Pakistan and India. As part of the partition process, both countries had agreed that the rulers of princely states would be allowed to opt for membership of either Pakistan or India, or in special cases to remain independent. India claims Kashmir on the basis of the Instrument of Accession, a legal agreement with Kashmir's leaders executed by Maharaja Hari Singh, then ruler of Kashmir, agreeing to accede the area to India. Pakistan claims Kashmir on the basis of a Muslim majority and of geography, the same principles that were applied for the creation of the two independent states. India referred the dispute to the United Nations on 1 January 1948. In a resolution in 1948, the UN asked Pakistan to remove most of its troops. A plebiscite would then be held. However, Pakistan failed to vacate the region. A ceasefire was reached in 1949 and a Line of Control was established, dividing Kashmir between the two countries.

Pakistan claims that its position is for the right of the people of Jammu and Kashmir to determine their future through impartial elections as mandated by the United Nations, while India has stated that Kashmir is an integral part of India, referring to the 1972 Simla Agreement and to the fact that elections take place regularly. Certain Kashmiri independence groups believe that Kashmir should be independent of both India and Pakistan.

Law Enforcement

Law enforcement in Pakistan is carried out by several federal and provincial police agencies. The four provinces and the Islamabad Capital Territory each have a civilian police force with jurisdiction extending only to the relevant province or territory. At the federal level, there are a number of civilian agencies with nationwide jurisdictions including the Federal Investigation Agency and the National Highways and Motorway Police, as well as several paramilitary forces including the Pakistan Rangers and the Frontier Corps.

The most senior officers of all the civilian police forces also form part of the Police Service of Pakistan, which is a component of the civil service of Pakistan. The five regional policies are namely Balochistan Police, Capital Territory Police, Frontier Police, Punjab Police and Sindh Police. Pakistan also has a National Highways & Motorway Police which is responsible for enforcement of traffic and safety laws, security and recovery on Pakistan's National Highways and Motorway network. Regional police departments also maintain respective Elite Police which is specialised in counter-terrorist operations and VIP security duties. Pakistan Rangers are an internal security force with the prime objective to provide and maintain security in war zones and areas of conflict as well as maintaining law and order which includes providing assistance to the police.

Geography and Climate

Pakistan covers an area of 796,095 km^2 (307,374 sq mi), approximately equal to the combined land areas of France and the United Kingdom. It is the 36th largest nation by total area, although this ranking varies depending on how the disputed territory of Kashmir is counted. Pakistan has a 1,046 km (650 mi) coastline along the Arabian Sea and the Gulf of Oman in the south and land borders of 6,774 km (4,209 mi) in total: 2,430 km (1,510 mi) with Afghanistan, 523 km (325 mi) with China, 2,912 km (1,809 mi) with India and 909 km (565 mi) with Iran. It shares a marine border with Oman, and is separated from Tajikistan by the cold, narrow Wakhan Corridor. Pakistan occupies a geopolitically important location at the crossroads of South Asia, the Middle East and Central Asia.

Geologically, Pakistan overlaps the Indian tectonic plate in its Sindh and Punjab provinces; Balochistan and most of Khyber Pakhtunkhwa are within the Eurasian plate, mainly on the Iranian plateau. Gilgit–Baltistan and Azad Kashmir lie along the edge of the Indian plate and hence are prone to violent earthquakes. Ranging from the coastal areas of the south to the glaciated mountains of the north, Pakistan's landscapes vary from plains to deserts, forests, hills and plateaus .

Pakistan is divided into three major geographic areas: the northern highlands, the Indus River plain and the Balochistan Plateau. The northern highlands contain the Karakoram, Hindu Kush and Pamir mountain ranges, which contain some of the world's highest peaks, including five of the fourteen eight-thousanders (mountain peaks over 8,000 metres or 26,250 feet), which attract adventurers and mountaineers from all over the world, notably K2 (8,611 m or 28,251 ft) and Nanga Parbat (8,126 m or 26,660 ft). The Balochistan Plateau lies in the west and the Thar Desert in the east. The 1,609 km (1,000 mi) Indus River and its tributaries flow through the country from the Kashmir region to the Arabian Sea. There is an expanse of alluvial plains along it in Punjab and Sindh.

The climate varies from tropical to temperate, with arid conditions in the coastal south. There is a monsoon season with frequent flooding due to heavy rainfall, and a dry season with significantly less rainfall or none at all. There are four distinct seasons: a cool, dry winter from December through February; a hot, dry spring from March through May; the summer rainy season, or southwest monsoon period, from June through September; and the retreating monsoon period of October and November. Rainfall varies greatly from year to year, and patterns of alternate flooding and drought are common.

Infrastructure

Economy: Pakistan is a rapidly developing country and is one of the Next Eleven, the eleven countries that, along with the BRICs, have a high potential to become the world's largest economies in the 21st century. However, after decades of war and social instability, as of 2013, serious deficiencies in basic services such as railway transportation and electric power generation had developed. The economy is semi-industrialized, with centres of growth along the Indus River. The diversified economies of Karachi and Punjab's urban centres coexist with less developed areas in other parts of the country. Pakistan's estimated nominal GDP as of 2011 is US$202 billion. The GDP by PPP is US$488.6 billion. The estimated nominal per capita GDP is US$1,197, GDP (PPP) per capita is US$2,851 (international dollars), and debt-to-GDP ratio is 55.5%. A 2010 report by RAD-AID positioned Pakistan's economy at 27th largest in the world by purchasing power and 45th largest in absolute dollars. It is South Asia's second largest economy, representing about 15 percent of regional GDP.

Goldman Sachs economist expects that by 2050, Pakistan would become the 18th largest economy in the world with a GDP of US$3.33 trillion. Pakistan's economic growth since its inception has been varied. It has been slow during periods of civilian rule, but excellent during the three periods of military rule, although the foundation for sustainable and equitable growth was not formed. The early to middle 2000s was a period of rapid reform; the government raised development spending, which reduced poverty levels by 10% and increased GDP by 3%. The economy cooled again from 2007. Inflation reached 25% in 2008 and Pakistan had to depend on a fiscal policy backed by the International Monetary Fund to avoid possible bankruptcy. A year later, the Asian Development Bank reported that Pakistan's economic crisis was easing. The inflation rate for the fiscal year 2010–11 was 14.1%. On January 2014, a survey conducted by the *Japan External Trade Organisation* placed Pakistan just behind Taiwan in terms of business generated by Japanese companies. Pakistan's data was generated from 27 Japanese firms doing business here. The results found that 74.1% of the Japanese companies estimated operating profit in 2013.

Pakistan is one of the largest producers of natural commodities, and its labour market is the 10th largest in the world. The 7 million strong Pakistani diaspora, contributed US$11.2 billion to the economy in FY2011. The major source countries of remittances to Pakistan include UAE, USA, Saudi Arabia, GCC countries (including Bahrain, Kuwait, Qatar and Oman), Australia, Canada, Japan, UK and EU countries like Norway, Switzerland, etc. . According to the World Trade Organisation Pakistan's share of overall world exports is declining; it contributed only 0.128% in 2007. The trade deficit in the fiscal year 2010–11 was US$11.217 billion.

The structure of the Pakistani economy has changed from a mainly agricultural to a strong service base. Agriculture now accounts for only 21.2% of the GDP. Even so, according to the United Nations Food and Agriculture Organisation, Pakistan produced 21,591,400 metric tons of wheat in 2005, more than all of Africa (20,304,585 metric tons) and nearly as much as all of South America (24,557,784 metric tons). Between 2002 and 2007 there was substantial foreign investment in Pakistan's banking and energy sectors. Other important industries include clothing and textiles (accounting for nearly 60% of exports), food processing, chemicals manufacture, iron and steel. There is great potential for tourism in Pakistan, but it is severely affected by the country's instability. Pakistan's cement is also fast growing mainly because of demand from Afghanistan and countries boosting real estate sector, In 2013 Pakistan exported 7,708,557 metric tons of cement. Pakistan has an installed capacity of 44,768,250 metric tons of cement and 42,636,428 metric tons of clinker. In the 2012–2013 cement industry in Pakistan became the most profitable sector of economy.

Foreign direct investment (FDI) in Pakistan soared by 180.6 per cent year-on-year to US$2.22 billion and portfolio investment by 276 per cent to $407.4 million during the first nine months of fiscal year 2006, the State Bank of Pakistan (SBP) reported on 24 April.

During July–March 2005–06, FDI year-on-year increased to $2.224 billion from only $792.6 million and portfolio investment to $407.4 million, whereas it was $108.1 million in the corresponding period last year, according to the latest statistics released by the State Bank. Pakistan has achieved FDI of almost $8.4 billion in the financial year 06/07, surpassing the government target of $4 billion. Foreign investment had significantly declined by 2010, dropping by 54.6% due to Pakistan's political instability and weak law and order, according to the Bank of Pakistan.

The textile sector enjoys a pivotal position in the exports of Pakistan. Pakistan is the 8th largest exporter of textile products in Asia. This sector contributes 9.5% to the GDP and provides employment to about 15 million people or roughly 30% of the 49 million workforce of the country. Pakistan is the 4th largest producer of cotton with the third largest spinning capacity in Asia after China and India, and contributes 5% to the global spinning capacity. China is the second largest buyer of Pakistani textiles, importing $1.527 billion of textiles last fiscal. Unlike US where mostly value added textiles are imported, China buys only cotton yarn and cotton fabric from Pakistan. In 2012, Pakistani textile products accounted for 3.3% or $1.07b of total UK's textile imports, 12.4% or $4.61b of total Chinese textile imports, 2.98% or $2.98b of total US's textile imports, 1.6% or $0.88b of total German textile imports and 0.7% or $0.888b of total Indian textile imports.

The Pakistani competitive yet profitable banking sector is continuously improving with a diversified pattern of ownership due to an active participation of foreign and local stakeholders. It has resulted into an increased competition among banks to attract a greater number of customers by the provision of quality services for long-term benefits. Now there are 6 full-fledged Islamic banks and 13 conventional banks offering products and services. Islamic banking and finance in Pakistan has experienced phenomenal growth. Islamic deposits – held by full-fledged Islamic banks and Islamic windows of conventional banks at present stand at 9.7% of total bank deposits in the country.

Transport

The transport sector accounts for 10.5% of Pakistan's GDP. Its road infrastructure is better than those of India, Bangladesh and Indonesia, but the rail system lags behind those of India and China, and aviation infrastructure also needs improvement. There is scarcely any inland water transportation system, and coastal shipping only meets minor local requirements.

Roads form the backbone of Pakistan's transport system; a total road length of 259,618 km accounts for 91% of passenger and 96% of freight traffic. Road transport services are largely in the hands of the private sector, which handles around 95% of freight traffic. The National Highway Authority is responsible for the maintenance of national highways and motorways. The highway and motorway system depends mainly on north–south links, connecting the southern ports to the populous provinces of Punjab and NWFP. Although this network only accounts for 4.2% of total road length, it carries 85 percent of the country's traffic. Pakistan Railways, under the Ministry of Railways, operates the railroad system. Rail was the primary means of transport till 1970. In the two decades from around 1990, there was a marked shift in traffic from rail to highways. Now the railway's share of inland traffic is only 10% for passengers and 4% for freight traffic. The total rail track decreased from 8,775 km in 1990–91 to 7,791 km in 2011. Pakistan expects to use the rail service to boost foreign trade with China, Iran and Turkey.

Pakistan had 35 airports in 2007–08. The state-run Pakistan International Airlines is the major airline; it carries about 73% of domestic passengers and all domestic freight. Karachi's Jinnah International Airport is the principal international gateway to Pakistan, although Islamabad and Lahore also handle significant amounts of traffic. Pakistan's major seaports are Karachi, Muhammad bin Qasim and Gwadar, which is still under construction.

Science and Technology

Pakistan is active in physics and mathematics research. Every year, scientists from around the world are invited by the Pakistan Academy of Sciences and the Pakistan Government to participate in the International Nathiagali Summer College on Physics. Pakistan hosted an international seminar on *Physics in Developing Countries* for International Year of Physics 2005. Pakistani theoretical physicist Abdus Salam won a Nobel Prize in Physics for his work on the electroweak interaction.

In medicine, Salimuzzaman Siddiqui was the first Pakistani scientist to bring the therapeutic constituents of the Neem tree to the attention of natural products chemists. Pakistani neurosurgeon Ayub Ommaya invented the Ommaya reservoir, a system for treatment of brain tumours and other brain conditions.

Pakistan has an active space program led by its space research agency, SUPARCO. Polish-Pakistani aerospace engineer W. J. M. Turowicz developed and supervised the launch of the Rehbar-I rocket from Pakistani soil, making Pakistan the first South Asian country to launch a rocket into space. Pakistan launched its first satellite, Badr-I, from China in 1990, becoming the first Muslim country and second South Asian country to put a satellite into space. In 1998, Pakistan became the seventh country in the world to successfully develop its own nuclear weapons.

Pakistan is one of a small number of countries that have an active research presence in Antarctica. The Pakistan Antarctic Programme was established in 1991. Pakistan has two summer research stations on the continent and plans to open another base, which will operate all year round. Electricity in Pakistan is generated and distributed by two vertically integrated public sector utilities: the Karachi Electric Supply Corporation (KESC) for Karachi and the Water and Power Development Authority (WAPDA) for the rest of Pakistan. Nuclear power in Pakistan is provided by three licensed commercial nuclear power plants under Pakistan Atomic Energy Commission (PAEC). Pakistan is the first Muslim country in the world to embark on a nuclear power program. Commercial nuclear power plants generate roughly 3% of Pakistan's electricity, compared with about 64% from thermal and 33% from hydroelectric power.

Religion

Pakistan is the second most populous Muslim-majority country and has the second largest Shia population in the world. About 97% of Pakistanis are Muslim. The majority are Sunni, with an estimated 5–20% Shia. A further 2.3% are Ahmadis, who are officially considered non-Muslims by virtue of a 1974 constitutional amendment. There are also several Quraniyoon communities. Sectarian violence among Muslim denominations has increased in recent times with over 400 targeted deaths of Shias in the year 2012 alone. After the Quetta blast in 2013, there were country-wide protests by Shia Muslims supported by fellow Sunni Muslims calling an end to sectarian violence in the country and urging for Shia-Sunni unity in the country. Ahmadis are particularly persecuted, especially since 1974 when they were banned from calling themselves Muslims. In 1984 Ahmadiyya places of worship were banned from being called "mosques". As of 2012, 12% of Pakistani Muslims self-identify as non-denominational Muslims.

Islam to some extent syncretized with pre-Islamic influences, resulting in a religion with some traditions distinct from those of the Arab world. Two Sufis whose shrines receive much national attention are Ali Hajweri in Lahore (ca. 12th century) and Shahbaz Qalander in Sehwan, Sindh (ca. 12th century). Sufism, a mystical Islamic tradition, has a long history and a large popular following in Pakistan. Popular Sufi culture is centred on Thursday night gatherings at shrines and annual festivals which feature Sufi music and dance. Contemporary Islamic fundamentalists criticize its popular character, which in their view, does not accurately reflect the teachings and practice of the Prophet and his companions.

After Islam, Hinduism and Christianity are the largest religions in Pakistan, with 2,800,000 (1.6%) adherents each in 2005. They are followed by the Bahá'í Faith, which has a following of 30,000, then Sikhism, Buddhism and Zoroastrianism, each claiming 20,000 adherents, and a very small community of Jains. There is a Roman Catholic community in Karachi which was established by Goan and Tamil migrants when Karachi's infrastructure was being developed by the British during colonial administration between World War I and II.

Culture and Society

Pakistani society is largely hierarchical, emphasising local cultural etiquettes and traditional Islamic values that govern personal and political life. The basic family unit is the extended family, although there has been a growing trend towards nuclear families for socio-economic reasons. The traditional dress for both men and women is the Shalwar Kameez; trousers and shirts are also popular among men. The middle class has increased to around 35 million and the upper and upper-middle classes to around 17 million in recent decades, and power is shifting from rural landowners to the urbanised elites. Pakistani festivals like Eid ul-Fitr, Eid al-Adha and Ramadan are mostly religious in origin. Increasing globalisation has resulted in Pakistan ranking 56th on the A.T. Kearney/FP Globalization Index.

Chapter 2

Islamic Countries in Africa

Algeria

Algeria, officially People's Democratic Republic of Algeria, is a country in the Maghreb region of North Africa on the Mediterranean coast. Its capital and most populous city is Algiers. With a total area of 2,381,741 square kilometres (919,595 sq mi), 90% of which is desert, Algeria is the tenth-largest country in the world, and the largest in Africa and in the Mediterranean. The country is bordered in the northeast by Tunisia, in the east by Libya, in the west by Morocco, in the southwest by Western Sahara, Mauritania, and Mali, in the southeast by Niger, and in the north by the Mediterranean Sea.

Flag Emblem

The territory of today's Algeria was the home of many prehistoric cultures, including Aterian and Capsian and the "Proto-Imazicen" cultures. Its area has known many empires and dynasties, including ancient Amazic Numidians, Phoenecians, Lybio-Punic Carthaginians, Romans, Vandals, Byzantines, Arab Umayyads, Arab Abbasids, Multi-Ethnic Fatimids, Amazic Hammadids, Amazic Almoravids, Amazic Almohads, Turkish Ottomans and the French colonial empire. In recent decades Algeria and other nations of the "Desert Belt" have experienced an identity crisis; in response Algeria and Morocco have nationalized Tamazict, the language of their 13,000 year old people. Algeria is a semi-presidential republic consisting of 48 provinces and 1541 communes. With a population of 37.9 million, it is the 35th most populated country on Earth. Abdelaziz Bouteflika has been the President of Algeria since 1999 and has won four consecutive elections. However, according to the Democracy Index, Algeria is an authoritarian regime.

Algeria's economy is largely based on hydrocarbons, due to which manufacturing has suffered from Dutch disease. The country supplies large amounts of natural gas to Europe, and energy exports are the backbone of the economy. According to OPEC Algeria has the 17th largest reserves of oil in the world, and the second largest in Africa, while it has the 9th largest reserves of natural gas. Sonatrach, the national oil company, is the largest company in Africa.

Algeria has the second largest military in North Africa with the largest defence budget in Africa. Algeria has had a peaceful nuclear program since the 1990s. Algeria is a member of the African Union, the Arab League, OPEC, and the United Nations, and is a founding member of the Arab Maghreb Union.

The French Colonisation of Algeria

On the pretext of a slight to their consul, the French invaded and captured Algiers in 1830. The conquest of Algeria by the French took some time and resulted in considerable bloodshed. A combination of violence and disease epidemics caused the indigenous Algerian population to decline by nearly one-third from 1830 to 1872. The population of Algeria, which stood at about 1.5 million in 1830, reached nearly 11 million in 1960. French policy was predicated on "civilizing" the country. Algeria's social fabric suffered during the occupation: literacy plummeted. During this period, a small but influential French-speaking indigenous elite was formed, made up of Berbers mostly from Kabyles. As a consequence, French government favoured the Kabyles. About 80% of Indigenous Schools were constructed for Kabyles.

Figure: *Emir Abdelkaderin 1865*

From 1848 until independence, France administered the whole Mediterranean region of Algeria as an integral part and dèpartement of the nation. One of France's longest-held overseas territories, Algeria became a destination for hundreds of thousands of European immigrants, who became known as *colons* and later, as *Pied-Noirs.* Between 1825 and 1847, 50,000 French people emigrated to Algeria. These settlers benefited from the French government's confiscation of communal land from tribal peoples, and the application of modern agricultural techniques that increased the amount of arable land.

Gradually, dissatisfaction among the Muslim population, which lacked political and economic status in the colonial system, gave rise to demands for greater political autonomy, and eventually independence, from France. Tensions between the two population groups came to a head in 1954, when the first violent events of what was later called the Algerian War began. Historians have estimated that between 30,000 and 150,000 Harkis and their dependents were killed by the Front de Libération Nationale (FLN) or by lynch mobs in Algeria. The FLN used terrorist attacks in Algeria and France as part of its war, and the French conducted severe reprisals and repression led to the death of 1.5 million Algerian and hundreds of thousand injuries, orphans and widows. The war concluded in 1962, when Algeria gained complete independence following the March 1962 Evian agreements and the July 1962 self-determination referendum.

Independence

***Figure:** Houari Boumediene*

Algeria's first president was the FLN leader Ahmed Ben Bella. Morocco's claim to portions of western Algeria led to the Sand War in 1963. Ben Bella was overthrown in 1965 by Houari Boumediene, his former ally and defence minister. Under Ben Bella, the government had become increasingly socialist and authoritarian; Boumédienne continued this trend. But, he relied much more on the army for his support, and reduced the sole legal party to a symbolic role. He collectivised agriculture and launched a massive industrialization drive. Oil extraction facilities were nationalized. This was especially beneficial to the leadership after the international 1973 oil crisis.

In the 1960s and 1970s under President Houari Boumediene, Algeria pursued a programme of industrialisation within a state-controlled socialist economy. Boumediene's successor, Chadli Bendjedid, introduced some liberal economic reforms. He promoted a policy of Arabisation in Algerian society and public life. Teachers of Arabic, brought in from other Muslim countries, spread radical Islamic thought in schools and sowed the seeds of political Islamism. The Algerian economy became increasingly dependent on oil, leading to hardship when the price collapsed during the 1980s oil glut. Economic recession caused by the crash in world oil prices resulted in Algerian social unrest during the 1980s; by the end of the decade, Bendjedid introduced a multiparty system. Political parties developed, such as the Islamic Salvation Front (FIS), a broad coalition of Islamist groups.

Civil War and Aftermath

In December 1991 the Islamic Salvation Front dominated the first of two rounds of legislative elections. Fearing the election of an Islamist government, the authorities intervened on 11 January 1992, cancelling the elections. Bendjedid resigned and a High Council of State was installed to act as Presidency. It banned the FIS, triggering a civil insurgency between the Front's armed wing, the Armed Islamic Group, and the national armed forces, in which more than 100,000 people are thought to have died. The Islamist militants conducted a violent campaign of civilian massacres. At several points in the conflict, the situation in Algeria became a point of international concern, most notably during the crisis surrounding Air France Flight 8969, a hijacking perpetrated by the Armed Islamic Group. The Armed Islamic Group declared a ceasefire in October 1997.

Algeria held elections in 1999, considered biased by international observers and most opposition groups which were won by President Abdelaziz Bouteflika. He worked to restore political stability to the country and announced a 'Civil Concord' initiative, approved in a referendum, under which many political prisoners were pardoned, and several thousand members of armed groups were granted exemption from prosecution under a limited amnesty, in force until 13 January 2000. The AIS disbanded and levels of insurgent violence fell rapidly. The Groupe Salafiste pour la Prédication et le Combat (GSPC), a splinter group of the Group Islamic Armée, continued a terrorist campaign against the Government.

Bouteflika was re-elected in the April 2004 presidential election after campaigning on a programme of national reconciliation. The programme comprised economic, institutional, political and social reform to modernise the country, raise living standards, and tackle the causes of alienation. It also included a second amnesty initiative, the Charter for Peace and National Reconciliation, which was approved in a referendum in September 2005. It offered amnesty to most guerrillas and Government security forces.

In November 2008, the Algerian Constitution was amended following a vote in Parliament, removing the two-term limit on Presidential incumbents. This change enabled Bouteflika to stand for re-election in the 2009 presidential elections, and he was re-elected in April 2009. During his election campaign and following his re-election, Bouteflika promised to extend the programme of national reconciliation and a $150-billion spending programme to create three million new jobs, the construction of one million new housing units, and to continue public sector and infrastructure modernisation programmes.

A continuing series of protests throughout the country started on 28 December 2010, inspired by similar protests across the Middle East and North Africa. On 24 February 2011, the government lifted Algeria's 19-year-old state of emergency. The government enacted legislation dealing with political parties, the electoral code, and the representation of women in elected bodies. In April 2011, Bouteflika promised further constitutional and political reform. However, elections are routinely criticized by opposition groups as unfair and international human rights groups say that media censorship and harassment of political opponents continue.

Politics

Algeria is an authoritarian regime, according to the Democracy Index 2010. The Freedom of the Press 2009 report gives it rating "Not Free".

Elected politicians are considered to have relatively little sway over Algeria. Instead, a group of unelected civilian and military "décideurs", known as "le pouvoir" ("the power"), actually rule the country, even deciding who should be president. The most powerful man may be Mohamed Mediène, head of the military intelligence. In recent years, many of these generals have died or retired. After the death of General Larbi Belkheir, Bouteflika put loyalists in key posts, notably at Sonatrach, and secured constitutional amendments that make him re-electable indefinitely.

The head of state is the president of Algeria, who is elected for a five-year term. The president was formerly limited to two five-year terms, but a constitutional amendment passed by the Parliament on 11 November 2008 removed this limitation. Algeria has universal suffrage at 18 years of age. The President is the head of the army, the Council of Ministers and the High Security Council. He appoints the Prime Minister who is also the head of government.

The Algerian parliament is bicameral; the lower house, the People's National Assembly, has 462 members who are directly elected for five-year terms, while the upper house, the Council of the Nation, has 144 members serving six-year terms, of which 96 members are chosen by local assemblies and 48 are appointed by the president. According to the constitution, no political association may be formed if it is "based on differences in religion, language, race, gender, profession or region". In addition, political campaigns must be exempt from the aforementioned subjects.

Parliamentary elections were last held in May 2012, and were judged to be largely free by international monitors, though local groups alleged fraud and irregularities. In the elections, the FLN won 221 seats, the military-backed National Rally for Democracy won 70, and the Islamist Green Algeria Alliance won 47.

Foreign Relations

In October 2009, Algeria cancelled a weapons deal with France over the possibility of inclusion of Israeli parts in them. Tensions between Algeria and Morocco in relation to the Western Sahara have been an obstacle to tightening the Arab Maghreb Union, nominally established in 1989, but which has carried little practical weight.

Algeria is included in the European Union's European Neighbourhood Policy (ENP) which aims at bringing the EU and its neighbours closer. Giving incentives and rewarding best performers, as well as offering funds in a faster and more flexible manner, are the two main principles underlying the European Neighbourhood Instrument (ENI) that came into force in 2014. It has a budget of €15.4 billion and provides the bulk of funding through a number of programmes.

Military

The military of Algeria consists of the People's National Army (ANP), the Algerian National Navy (MRA), and the Algerian Air Force (QJJ), plus the Territorial Air Defence Force. It is the direct successor of the Armée de Libération Nationale (ALN), the armed wing of the nationalist National Liberation Front which fought French colonial occupation during the Algerian War of Independence (1954–62).

Total military personnel include 147,000 active, 150,000 reserve, and 187,000 paramilitary staff (2008 estimate). Service in the military is compulsory for men aged 19–30, for a total of 12 months. The military expenditure was 4.3% of the gross domestic product (GDP) in 2012. Algeria has the second largest military in North Africa with the largest defence budget in Africa ($10.3 billion).

In 2007, the Algerian Air Force signed a deal with Russia to purchase 49 MiG-29SMT and 6 MiG-29UBT at an estimated cost of $1.9 billion. It also agreed to return old aircraft purchased from the former USSR. Russia is also building two 636-type diesel submarines for Algeria.

Economy

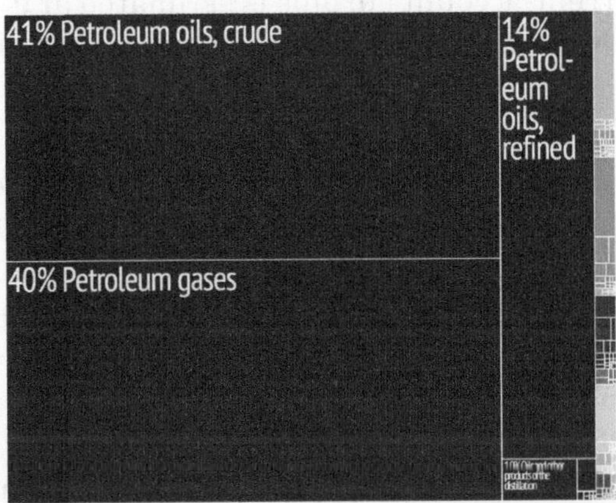

Figure: *Graphical depiction of the country's exports in 28 colour-coded categories.*

Algeria is classified as an upper middle income country by the World Bank. Algeria's currency is the dinar (DZD). The economy remains dominated by the state, a legacy of the country's socialist post-independence development model. In recent years, the Algerian government has halted the privatization of state-owned industries and imposed restrictions on imports and foreign involvement in its economy.

Algeria has struggled to develop industries outside hydrocarbons in part because of high costs and an inert state bureaucracy. The government's efforts to diversify the economy by attracting foreign and domestic investment outside the energy sector have done little to reduce high youth unemployment rates or to address housing shortages. The country is facing a number of short-term and medium-term problems, including the need to diversify the economy, strengthen political, economic and financial reforms, improve the business climate and reduce inequalities amongst regions.

A wave of economic protests in February and March 2011 prompted the Algerian government to offer more than $23 billion in public grants and retroactive salary and benefit increases. Public spending has increased by 27% annually during the past 5 years. The 2010–14 public-investment programme will cost US$286 billion, 40% of which will go to human development.

The Algerian economy grew by 2.6% in 2011, driven by public spending, in particular in the construction and public-works sector, and by growing internal demand. If hydrocarbons are excluded, growth has been estimated at 4.8%. Growth of 3% is expected in 2012, rising to 4.2% in 2013. The rate of inflation was 4% and the budget deficit 3% of GDP. The current-account surplus is estimated at 9.3% of GDP and at the end of December 2011, official reserves were put at US$182 billion. Inflation, the lowest in the region, has remained stable at 4% on average between 2003 and 2007.

In 2011 Algeria announced a budgetary surplus of $26.9 billion, 62% increase in comparison to 2010 surplus. In general, the country exported $73 billion worth of commodities while it imported $46 billion.

Thanks to strong hydrocarbon revenues, Algeria has a cushion of $173 billion in foreign currency reserves and a large hydrocarbon stabilization fund. In addition, Algeria's external debt is extremely low at about 2% of GDP. The economy remains very dependent on hydrocarbon wealth, and, despite high foreign exchange reserves (US$178 billion, equivalent to three years of imports), current expenditure growth makes Algeria's budget more vulnerable to the risk of prolonged lower hydrocarbon revenues.

In 2011, the agricultural sector and services recorded growth of 10% and 5.3%, respectively. About 14% of the labour force are employed in the agricultural sector. Fiscal policy in 2011 remained expansionist and made it possible to maintain the pace of public investment and to contain the strong demand for jobs and housing. Algeria has not joined the WTO, despite several years of negotiations.

In March 2006, Russia agreed to erase $4.74 billion of Algeria's Soviet-era debt during a visit by Russian President Vladimir Putin to the country, the first by a Russian leader in half a century. In return, Algerian President Abdelaziz Bouteflika agreed to buy $7.5 billion worth of combat planes, air-defence systems and other arms from Russia, according to the head of Russia's state arms exporter Rosoboronexport.

Hydrocarbons

Algeria, whose economy is reliant on petroleum, has been an OPEC member since 1969. Its crude oil production stands at around 1.1 million barrels/day, but it is also a major gas producer and exporter, with important links to Europe. Hydrocarbons have long been the backbone of the economy, accounting for roughly 60% of budget revenues, 30% of GDP, and over 95% of export earnings. Algeria has the 10th-largest reserves of natural gas in the world and is the sixth-largest gas exporter. The U.S. Energy Information Administration reported that in 2005, Algeria had 160 trillion cubic feet ($4.5^3 \times 10$ m^3) of proven natural-gas reserves. It also ranks 16th in oil reserves.

Non-hydrocarbon growth for 2011 was projected at 5%. To cope with social demands, the authorities raised expenditure, especially on basic food support, employment creation, support for SMEs, and higher salaries. High hydrocarbon prices have improved the current account and the already large international reserves position.

Income from oil and gas rose in 2011 as a result of continuing high oil prices, though the trend in production volume is downwards. Production from the oil and gas sector in terms of volume, continues to decline, dropping from 43.2 million tonnes to 32 million tonnes between 2007 and 2011. Nevertheless, the sector accounted for 98% of the total volume of exports in 2011, against 48% in 1962, and 70% of budgetary receipts, or USD 71.4 billion.

The Algerian national oil company is Sonatrach, which plays a key role in all aspects of the oil and natural gas sectors in Algeria. All foreign operators must work in partnership with Sonatrach, which usually has majority ownership in production-sharing agreements.

Labour Market

Despite a decline in total unemployment, youth and women unemployment is high. Unemployment particularly affects the young, with a jobless rate of 21.5% among the 15–24 age group.

The overall rate of unemployment was 10% in 2011, but remained higher among young people, with a rate of 21.5% for those aged between 15 and 24. The government strengthened in 2011 the job programmes introduced in 1988, in particular in the framework of the programme to aid those seeking work (Dispositif d'Aide à l'Insertion Professionnelle).

Nigeria

Nigeria, officially the Federal Republic of Nigeria, is a federal constitutional republic comprising 36 states and its Federal Capital Territory, Abuja. Nigeria is located in West Africa and shares land borders with the Republic of Benin in the west, Chad and Cameroon in the east, and Niger in the north. Its coast in the south lies on the Gulf of Guinea in the Atlantic Ocean.

The site of many former kingdoms and empires, the modern political state of Nigeria has its origins in the British colonization of the region during the late nineteenth to early twentieth centuries; it emerged from the combination of two neighbouring British protectorates: the Southern Nigeria Protectorate and Northern Nigeria Protectorate. During the colonial period, the British set up administrative and legal structures whilst retaining traditional chiefdoms. Nigeria achieved independence in 1960, but plunged into civil war several years later. It has since alternated between democratically-elected civilian governments and military dictatorships, with its 2011 presidential elections being viewed as the first to be conducted reasonably freely and fairly.

Nigeria is often referred to as the "Giant of Africa", due to its large population and economy. With approximately 174 million inhabitants, Nigeria is the most populous country in Africa and the seventh most populous country in the world. Nigeria has one of the largest populations of youth in the world. The country is inhabited by over 500 ethnic groups, of which the three largest are the Hausa, Igbo and Yoruba. Regarding religion, Nigeria is roughly divided in half between Christians, who live mostly in the southern and central parts of the country, and Muslims, concentrated mostly in the northern and southwestern regions. A minority of the population practice religions indigenous to Nigeria, such as those native to Igbo and Yoruba peoples.

In 2014, Nigeria's economy (GDP) became the largest in Africa, worth more than $500 billion, and overtook South Africa to become the world's 21st largest economy. Furthermore, the debt-to-GDP ratio is only 11 percent (8 percent below the 2012 ratio). By 2050, Nigeria is expected to become one of the world's top 20 economies. The country's oil reserves have played a major role in its growing wealth and influence. Nigeria is considered to be an emerging market by the World Bank and has been identified as a regional power in Africa. It is also a member of the MINT group of countries, which are widely seen as the globe's next "BRIC-like" economies. It is also listed among the "Next Eleven" economies set to become among the biggest in the world. Nigeria is a member of the Commonwealth of Nations, the African Union, OPEC, and the United Nations among other international organisations.

History

The Nok people of Northern Nigeria produced the earliest terracotta sculptures found in the country. The Nok civilization flourished between 500 B.C. and 200 A.D. In the northern part of the country, Kano and Katsina have a recorded history dating to around 999 AD. Hausa kingdoms and the Kanem-Bornu Empire prospered as trade posts between North and West Africa.

At the beginning of the 19th century, Usman dan Fodio directed a successful *jihad* and created and led the centralised Fulani Empire (also known as the Sokoto Caliphate). The territory controlled by the resultant state included much of modern-day northern and central Nigeria; it lasted until the 1903 break-up of the Empire into various European colonies.

The Yoruba kingdoms of Ife and Oyo in southwestern Nigeria became prominent in the 12th and 14th centuries, respectively. Yoruba mythology states that Ile-If[1] is the source of the human race and pre-dates any other civilisation. The oldest signs of human settlement at If[1]'s current site date back to the 9th century, and its material culture includes terracotta and bronze figures.

Oyo, at its territorial zenith in the late 17th to early 18th centuries, extended its influence from western Nigeria to modern-day Togo. The Edo Kingdom of Benin is located in southwestern Nigeria. Benin's power lasted between the 15th and 19th centuries. Their dominance reached as far as the city of Eko (an Edo name later changed to Lagos by the Portuguese) and further.

The Kingdom of Nri of the Igbo people, one of the oldest kingdoms in Nigeria, consolidated in the 10th century and continued until it lost its sovereignty to the British in 1911. Nri was ruled by the Eze Nri, and the city of Nri is considered to be the foundation of Igbo culture. Nri and Aguleri, where the Igbo creation myth originates, are in the territory of the Umeuri clan. Members of the clan trace their lineages back to the patriarchal king-figure Eri. In West Africa, the oldest bronzes made using the lost-wax process were from Igbo Ukwu, a city under Nri influence.

Middle Ages (1500-1800)

For centuries, various peoples in modern-day Nigeria traded overland with traders from North Africa. Cities in the area became regional centres in a broad network of trade routes that spanned western, central and northern Africa. In the 16th century, Spanish and Portuguese explorers were the first Europeans to begin significant, direct trade with peoples of modern-day Nigeria, at the port they named Lagos and in Calabar. Europeans traded goods with peoples at the coast; coastal trade with Europeans also marked the beginnings of the Atlantic slave trade.

Traditionally, peoples captured in war were made slaves by the conquerors. Usually, the captives were taken back to the conquerors' territory as forced labour; after time, they were sometimes acculturated and absorbed into the conquerors' society. Slavery also existed in the territories comprising modern-day Nigeria;. its scope was broadest towards the end of the 19th century. According to the *Encyclopedia of African History*, "It is estimated that by the 1890s the largest slave population of the world, about 2 million people, was concentrated in the territories of the Sokoto Caliphate. The use of slave labour was extensive, especially in agriculture."

A changing legal imperative (transatlantic slave trade outlawed by Britain in 1807) and economic imperative (a desire for political and social stability) led most European powers to support widespread cultivation of agricultural products, such as the palm, for use in European industry.

British Nigeria (1800-1960)

The slave trade was engaged in by European state and non-state actors such as Great Britain, the Netherlands, Portugal and private companies, as well as various African states and non-state actors. With rising anti-slavery sentiment at home and changing economic realities, Great Britain outlawed the international slave trade in 1807. Following the Napoleonic Wars, Great Britain established the West Africa Squadron in an attempt to halt the international traffic in slaves. It stopped ships of other nations that were leaving the African coast with slaves; the seized slaves were taken to Freetown, a colony in West Africa originally established for the resettlement of freed slaves from Britain.

In 1885, British claims to a West African sphere of influence received recognition from other European nations. The following year, it chartered the Royal Niger Company under the leadership of Sir George Taubman Goldie. In 1900 the company's territory came under the control of the British government, which moved to consolidate its hold over the area of modern Nigeria. On 1 January 1901, Nigeria became a British protectorate, and part of the British Empire, the foremost world power at the time. In the late 19th and early 20th centuries the independent kingdoms of what would become Nigeria fought a number of conflicts against the British Empire's efforts to expand its territory. By war, the British conquered Benin in 1897, and, in the Anglo-Aro War (1901–1902), defeated other opponents. The restraint or conquest of these states opened up the Niger area to British rule.

In 1914, the British formally united the Niger area as the *Colony and Protectorate of Nigeria.* Administratively, Nigeria remain divided into the northern and southern Protectorates and Lagos Colony. Inhabitants of the southern region sustained more interaction, economic and cultural, with the British and other Europeans due to the coastal economy.

Christian missions established Western educational institutions in the Protectorates. Under Britain's policy of indirect rule and validation of Islamic tradition, the Crown did not encourage the operation of Christian missions in the northern, Islamic part of the country. Some children of the southern elite went to Great Britain to pursue higher education. By independence in 1960, regional differences in "modern" educational access were marked. The legacy, though less pronounced, continues to the present-day. Imbalances between North and South were expressed in Nigeria's political life as well. For instance, northern Nigeria did not outlaw slavery until 1936 whilst in other parts of Nigeria slavery was abolished soon after colonialism.

Following World War II, in response to the growth of Nigerian nationalism and demands for independence, successive constitutions legislated by the British government moved Nigeria toward self-government on a representative and increasingly federal basis. By the middle of the 20th century, a great wave for independence was sweeping across Africa. Nigeria achieved independence in 1960.

Independence (1960)

On 1 October 1960, Nigeria gained its independence from the United Kingdom. Nigeria's government was a coalition of conservative parties: the Nigerian People's Congress (NPC), a party dominated by Northerners and those of the Islamic faith, and the Igbo and Christian-dominated National Council of Nigeria and the Cameroons (NCNC) led by Nnamdi Azikiwe. Azikiwe became Nigeria's maiden Governor-General in 1960. The opposition comprised the comparatively liberal Action Group (AG), which was largely dominated by the Yoruba and led by Obafemi Awolowo. The cultural and political differences between Nigeria's dominant ethnic groups - the Hausa ('Northerners'), Igbo ('Easterners') and Yoruba ('Westerners') - were sharp.

An imbalance was created in the polity by the result of the 1961 plebiscite. Southern Cameroon opted to join the Republic of Cameroon while Northern Cameroons chose to remain in Nigeria. The northern part of the country was now far larger than the southern part. In 1963, the nation established a Federal Republic, with Azikiwe as its first president. When elections were held in 1965, the Nigerian National Democratic Party came to power in Nigeria's Western Region.

Civil War (1967-1970)

The disquilibrium and perceived corruption of the electoral and political process led, in 1966, to several back-to-back military coups. The first coup was in January 1966 and led by Igbo soldiers under Majors Emmanuel Ifeajuna and Chukwuma Kaduna Nzeogwu. It was partially successful; the coup plotters murdered Prime Minister Abubakar Tafawa Balewa, Premier Ahmadu Bello of the Northern Region and Premier Ladoke Akintola of the Western Region. But, the coup plotters struggled to form a central government. President Nwafor Orizu handed over government control to the Army, then under the command of another Igbo officer, General JTU Aguiyi-Ironsi.

Later, the counter-coup of 1966, supported primarily by Northern military officers, facilitated the rise of Lt. Colonel Yakubu Gowon to head of state. This sequence of events led to an increase in ethnic tension and violence.

In May 1967, the Eastern Region declared independence as a state called the Republic of Biafra, under the leadership of Lt Colonel Emeka Ojukwu. The Nigerian Civil War began as the official Nigerian government side (predominated by soldiers from the North and West) attacked Biafra (Southeastern) on 6 July 1967 at Garkem. The 30 month war, with a long siege of Biafra and its isolation from trade and supplies, ended in January 1970. Estimates of the number of dead in the former Eastern Region are between 1 and 3 million people, from warfare, disease, and starvation, during the 30-month civil war .

France, Egypt, the Soviet Union, Britain and others were deeply involved in the civil war behind the scenes. Britain and the Soviet Union were the main military backers of the Nigerian government while France and others aided the Biafrans. Nigeria used Egyptian pilots for their air force.

Military Juntas (1970-1999)

During the oil boom of the 1970s, Nigeria joined OPEC and the huge revenue generated made the economy richer. Despite huge revenues from oil production and sale, the military administration did little to improve the standard of living of the population, help small and medium businesses, or invest in infrastructure. As oil revenues fuelled the rise of federal subventions to states, the federal government became the centre of political struggle and the threshold of power in the country. As oil production and revenue rose, the Nigerian government became increasingly dependent on oil revenues and the international commodity markets for budgetary and economic concerns. It did not develop other sources of the economy for economic stability. That spelled doom to federalism in Nigeria.

Beginning in 1979, Nigerians participated in a brief return to democracy when Olusegun Obasanjo transferred power to the civilian regime of Shehu Shagari. The Shagari government became viewed as corrupt and incompetent by virtually all sectors of Nigerian society. The military coup of Muhammadu Buhari shortly after the regime's fraudulent re-election in 1984 was generally viewed as a positive development. Buhari promised major reforms, but his government fared little better than its predecessor. His regime was overthrown by another military coup in 1985.

The new head of state, Ibrahim Babangida, declared himself president and commander in chief of the armed forces and the ruling Supreme Military Council. He set 1990 as the official deadline for a return to democratic governance. Babangida's tenure was marked by a flurry of political activity: he instituted the International Monetary Fund's Structural Adjustment Program (SAP) to aid in the repayment of the country's crushing international debt, which most federal revenue was dedicated to servicing. He enrolled Nigeria in the Organisation of the Islamic Conference, which aggravated religious tensions in the country.

After Babangida survived an abortive coup, he pushed back the promised return to democracy to 1992. Free and fair elections were finally held on 12 June 1993, with a presidential victory for Moshood Kashimawo Olawale Abiola. Babangida annulled the elections, leading to mass civilian violent protests which effectively shut down the country for weeks. Babangida finally kept his promise to relinquish office to a civilian-run government, but not before appointing Ernest Shonekan as head of the interim government. Babangida's regime has been considered the most corrupt, and responsible for creating a culture of corruption in Nigeria.

Shonekan's caretaker regime was overwhelmed in late 1993 by the military coup of General Sani Abacha. Abacha used violence on a wide scale to suppress the continuing civilian unrest. He shifted money to offshore accounts in various western European banks and voided coup plots by bribing army generals. Several hundred million dollars in accounts traced to him were discovered in 1999. The regime came to an end in 1998 when the dictator was found dead amid questionable circumstances. His successor, General Abdulsalami Abubakar, adopted a new constitution on 5 May 1999, which provided for multiparty elections. On 29 May 1999 Abubakar transferred power to the winner of the elections, Obasanjo, who had since retired from the military.

Democratization (1999)

Nigeria regained democracy in 1999 when it elected Olusegun Obasanjo, the former military head of state, as the new President of Nigeria. This ended almost 33 years of military rule (from 1966 until 1999), excluding the short-lived second republic (between 1979 and 1983) by military dictators who seized power in coups d'état and counter-coups during the Nigerian military juntas of 1966–1979 and 1983–1998. Although the elections which brought Obasanjo to power in 1999 and again in 2003 were condemned as unfree and unfair, Nigeria has shown marked improvements in attempts to tackle government corruption and to hasten development.

Ethnic violence for control over the oil-producing Niger Delta region and inadequate infrastructures are some of the issues in the country. Umaru Yar'Adua of the People's Democratic Party (PDP) came into power in the general election of 2007. The international community has been observing Nigerian elections to encourage a free and fair process, and condemned this one as being severely flawed.

Yar'Adua died on 5 May 2010. Dr. Goodluck Jonathan was sworn in as Yar'Adua's replacement on 6 May 2010, becoming Nigeria's 14th Head of State, while his vice-president, Namadi Sambo, an architect and former Kaduna State governor, was chosen on 18 May 2010, by the National Assembly. His confirmation followed President Jonathan's nomination of Sambo to that position.

Goodluck Jonathan served as Nigeria's president till 16 April 2011, when a new presidential election in Nigeria was conducted. Jonathan of the PDP was declared the winner on 19 April 2011, having won the election with a total of 22,495,187 of the 39,469,484 votes cast, to stand ahead of Muhammadu Buhari from the main opposition party, the Congress for Progressive Change (CPC), which won 12,214,853 of the total votes cast. The international media reported the elections as having run smoothly with relatively little violence or voter fraud, in contrast to previous elections.

Government and Politics

Nigeria is a Federal Republic modelled after the United States, with executive power exercised by the president. It is influenced by the Westminster System model in the composition and management of the upper and lower houses of the bicameral legislature. The president presides as both Head of State and head of the national executive; the leader is elected by popular vote to a maximum of two 4-year terms.

The president's power is checked by a Senate and a House of Representatives, which are combined in a bicameral body called the National Assembly. The Senate is a 109-seat body with three members from each state and one from the capital region of Abuja; members are elected by popular vote to four-year terms. The House contains 360 seats, with the number of seats per state is determined by population.

Ethnocentrism, tribalism, religious persecution, and prebendalism have affected Nigerian politics both prior and subsequent to independence in 1960. Kin-selective altruism has made its way into Nigerian politics, resulting in tribalist efforts to concentrate Federal power to a particular region of their interests. Nationalism has also led to active secessionist movements such as MASSOB, Nationalist movements such as Oodua Peoples Congress, Movement for the Emancipation of the Niger Delta and a civil war. Nigeria's three largest ethnic groups (Hausa, Igbo and Yoruba) have maintained historical preeminence in Nigerian politics; competition amongst these three groups has fuelled corruption and graft.

Because of the above issues, Nigeria's political parties are pan-national and secular in character (though this does not preclude the continuing preeminence of the dominant ethnicities). The major political parties at present include the ruling People's Democratic Party of Nigeria, which maintains 223 seats in the House and 76 in the Senate (61.9% and 69.7% respectively); the opposition All Nigeria People's Party has 96 House seats and 27 in the Senate (26.6% and 24.7%). About twenty minor opposition parties are registered.

The immediate past president, Olusegun Obasanjo, acknowledged fraud and other electoral "lapses" but said the result reflected opinion polls. In a national television address in 2007, he added that if Nigerians did not like the victory of his handpicked successor, they would have an opportunity to vote again in four years.

As in many other African societies, prebendalism and high rates of corruption continue to constitute major challenges to Nigeria. All major parties have practised vote rigging and other means of coercion in order to remain competitive. In 1983, the policy institute at Kuru concluded that only the 1959 and 1979 elections to that time were conducted with minimal vote rigging.

Law

There are three distinct systems of law in Nigeria:

- Common law, derived from its British colonial past, and a development of its own after independence;
- Customary law, derived from indigenous traditional norms and practice, including the dispute resolution meetings of pre-colonial Yorubaland secret societies and the ¸kp[1] and ÌkÍñkÍ of Igboland and Ibibioland;
- Sharia law, used only in the predominantly Muslim northern states of the country. It is an Islamic legal system that had been used long before the colonial administration. In late 1999, Zamfara emphasized its use, with eleven other northern states following suit. These states are Kano, Katsina, Niger, Bauchi, Borno, Kaduna, Gombe, Sokoto, Jigawa, Yobe, and Kebbi.

The country has a judicial branch, the highest court of which is the Supreme Court of Nigeria.

Foreign Relations

Upon gaining independence in 1960, Nigeria made African unity the centrepiece of its foreign policy and played a leading role in the fight against the apartheid government in South Africa. One notable exception to the African focus was Nigeria's close relationship developed with Israel throughout the 1960s. The latter nation sponsored and oversaw the construction of Nigeria's parliament buildings.

Nigeria's foreign policy was tested in the 1970s after the country emerged united from its own civil war. It supported movements against white minority governments in the Southern Africa sub-region. Nigeria backed the African National Congress (ANC) by taking a committed tough line with regard to the South African government and their military actions in southern Africa. Nigeria was also a founding member of the Organisation for African Unity (now the African Union), and has tremendous influence in West Africa and Africa on the whole. Nigeria has additionally founded regional cooperative efforts in West Africa, functioning as standard-bearer for the Economic Community of West African States (ECOWAS) and ECOMOG, economic and military organisations, respectively.

With this African-centred stance, Nigeria readily sent troops to the Congo at the behest of the United Nations shortly after independence (and has maintained membership since that time). Nigeria also supported several Pan African and pro-self government causes in the 1970s, including garnering support for Angola's MPLA, SWAPO in Namibia, and aiding opposition to the minority governments of Portuguese Mozambique, and Rhodesia.

Nigeria retains membership in the Non-Aligned Movement. In late November 2006, it organised an Africa-South America Summit in Abuja to promote what some attendees termed "South-South" linkages on a variety of fronts. Nigeria is also a member of the International Criminal Court, and the Commonwealth of Nations. It was temporarily expelled from the latter in 1995 when ruled by the Abacha regime.

Nigeria has remained a key player in the international oil industry since the 1970s, and maintains membership in Organisation of the Petroleum Exporting Countries (OPEC), which it joined in July 1971. Its status as a major petroleum producer figures prominently in its sometimes volatile international relations with both developed countries, notably the United States, and the developing countries of China, Jamaica, and Ghana and Kenya in Africa.

Millions of Nigerians have emigrated at times of economic hardship, primarily to Europe, North America and Australia. It is estimated that over a million Nigerians have emigrated to the United States and constitute the Nigerian American populace. Individuals in many such Diasporic communities have joined the "Egbe Omo Yoruba" society, a national association of Yoruba descendants in North America.

Military

The Nigerian Military are charged with protecting The Federal Republic of Nigeria, promoting Nigeria's global security interests, and supporting peacekeeping efforts especially in West Africa. This is in support of the doctrine sometimes called Pax Nigeriana.

The Nigerian Military consist of an army, a navy, and an air force. The military in Nigeria have played a major role in the country's history since independence. Various juntas have seized control of the country and ruled it through most of its history. Its last period of rule ended in 1999 following the sudden death of former dictator Sani Abacha in 1998. His successor, Abdulsalam Abubakar, handed over power to the democratically elected government of Olusegun Obasanjo in 1999.

As Africa's most populated country, Nigeria has repositioned its military as a peacekeeping force on the continent. Since 1995, the

Nigerian military, through ECOMOG mandates, have been deployed as peacekeepers in Liberia (1997), Ivory Coast (1997–1999), Sierra Leone 1997–1999. Under an African Union mandate, it has stationed forces in Sudan's Darfur region to try to establish peace.

Economy

Nigeria is classified as a mixed economy emerging market, and has already reached lower middle income status according to the World Bank, with its abundant supply of natural resources, well-developed financial, legal, communications, transport sectors and stock exchange (the Nigerian Stock Exchange), which is the second largest in Africa.

Nigeria was ranked 30th in the world in terms of GDP (PPP) in 2012. Nigeria is the United States' largest trading partner in sub-Saharan Africa and supplies a fifth of its oil (11% of oil imports). It has the seventh-largest trade surplus with the US of any country worldwide. Nigeria is the 50th-largest export market for US goods and the 14th-largest exporter of goods to the US. The United States is the country's largest foreign investor. The International Monetary Fund (IMF) projected economic growth of 9% in 2008 and 8.3% in 2009. The IMF further projects an 8% growth in the Nigerian economy in 2011.

February 2011: According to Citigroup, Nigeria will get the highest average GDP growth in the world between 2010–2050. Nigeria is one of two countries from Africa among 11 Global Growth Generators countries. Previously, economic development had been hindered by years of military rule, corruption, and mismanagement. The restoration of democracy and subsequent economic reforms have successfully put Nigeria back on track towards achieving its full economic potential. As of 2014 it is the largest economy in Africa, having overtaken South Africa.

During the oil boom of the 1970s, Nigeria accumulated a significant foreign debt to finance major infrastructural investments. With the fall of oil prices during the 1980s oil glut Nigeria struggled to keep up with its loan payments and eventually defaulted on its principal debt repayments, limiting repayment to the interest portion of the loans. Arrears and penalty interest accumulated on the unpaid principal which increased the size of the debt. After negotiations by the Nigeria authorities, in October 2005 Nigeria and its Paris Club creditors reached an agreement in which Nigeria repurchased its debt at a discount of approximately 60%. Nigeria used part of its oil profits to pay the residual 40%, freeing up at least $1.15 billion annually for poverty reduction programmes. Nigeria made history in April 2006 by becoming the first African Country to completely pay off its debt (estimated $30 billion) owed to the Paris Club.

Oil

Nigeria is the 12th largest producer of petroleum in the world and the 8th largest exporter, and has the 10th largest proven reserves. (The country joined OPEC in 1971). Petroleum plays a large role in the Nigerian economy, accounting for 40% of GDP and 80% of Government earnings. However, agitation for better resource control in the Niger Delta, its main oil producing region, has led to disruptions in oil production and prevents the country from exporting at 100% capacity.

The Niger Delta Nembe Creek Oil field was discovered in 1973 and produces from middle Miocene deltaic sandstone-shale in an anticline structural trap at a depth of 2–4 km. In June 2013, the company announced a strategic review of its operations in Nigeria, hinting that assets could be divested. While many international oil companies have operated there for decades, by 2014 most were making moves to divest their interests, citing a range of issues including oil theft. In August 2014, Shell Oil Company said it was finalizing its interests in four Nigerian oil fields.

Overseas Remittances

Next to petrodollars, the second biggest source of foreign exchange earnings for Nigeria are remittances sent home by Nigerians living abroad. In 2014, 17.5 million Nigerians reside in foreign countries, with the UK and the USA having more than 2 million Nigerians each.

According to the International Organisation for Migration, Nigeria witnessed a dramatic increase in remittances sent home from overseas Nigerians, going from USD 2.3 billion in 2004 to 17.9 billion in 2007, representing 6.7% of GDP. The United States accounts for the largest portion of official remittances, followed by the United Kingdom, Italy, Canada, Spain and France. On the African continent, Egypt, Equatorial Guinea, Chad, Libya and South Africa are important source countries of remittance flows to Nigeria, while China is the biggest remittance-sending country in Asia.

Services

Nigeria has one of the fastest growing telecommunications markets in the world, major emerging market operators (like MTN, Etisalat, Zain and Globacom) basing their largest and most profitable centres in the country. The government has recently begun expanding this infrastructure to space based communications. Nigeria has a space satellite which is monitored at the Nigerian National Space Research and Development Agency Headquarters in Abuja.

Nigeria has a highly developed financial services sector, with a mix of local and international banks, asset management companies, brokerage houses, insurance companies and brokers, private equity funds and investment banks.

Mining

Nigeria also has a wide array of underexploited mineral resources which include natural gas, coal, bauxite, tantalite, gold, tin, iron ore, limestone, niobium, lead and zinc. Despite huge deposits of these natural resources, the mining industry in Nigeria is still in its infancy.

Manufacturing

Nigeria has a manufacturing industry which includes leather and textiles (centred Kano, Abeokuta, Onitsha, and Lagos), Nigeria currently has an indigenous auto manufacturing company; Innoson Motors located in Nnewi. It produces Buses and SUVs.car manufacturing (for the French car manufacturer Peugeot as well as for the English truck manufacturer Bedford, now a subsidiary of General Motors), t-shirts, plastics and processed food.

Nigeria in recent years has been embracing industrialization, It currently has an indigenous vehicle manufacturing company, *Innoson Motors (IVM)* which manufactures Rapid Transit Buses, Trucks and SUVs with an upcoming introduction of Cars. Nigeria also has few Electronic manufacturers like Zinox, the first Branded Nigerian Computer and Electronic gadgets (like tablet PCs) manufacturers. In 2013, Nigeria introduced a policy regarding import duty on vehicles to encourage local manufacturing companies in the country. In this regard, some foreign vehicle manufacturing companies like *Nissan* have made known their plans to have manufacturing plants in Nigeria. Ogun is considered to be the current Nigeria's industrial hub, as most factories are located in Ogun and more companies are moving there, followed by Lagos.

Government Satellites

The Nigerian government has commissioned the overseas production and launch of four satellites. The Nigeriasat-1 was the first satellite to be built under the Nigerian government sponsorship. The satellite was launched from Russia on 27 September 2003. Nigeriasat-1 was part of the world-wide Disaster Monitoring Constellation System. The primary objectives of the Nigeriasat-1 were: to give early warning signals of environmental disaster; to help detect and control desertification in the northern part of Nigeria; to assist in demographic planning; to establish the relationship between malaria vectors and the environment that breeds malaria and to give early warning signals on future outbreaks of meningitis using remote sensing technology; to provide the technology needed to bring education to all parts of the country through distant learning; and to aid in conflict resolution and border disputes by mapping out state and International borders.

NigeriaSat-2, Nigeria's second satellite, was built as a high-resolution earth satellite by Surrey Space Technology Limited, a United Kingdom-based satellite technology company. It has 2.5-metre resolution panchromatic (very high resolution), 5-metre multispectral (high resolution, NIR red, green and red bands), and 32-metre multispectral (medium resolution, NIR red, green and red bands) antennas, with a ground receiving station in Abuja. The NigeriaSat-2 spacecraft alone was built at a cost of over £35 million. This satellite was launched into orbit from a military base in China.

NigComSat-1, a Nigerian satellite built in 2004, was Nigeria's third satellite and Africa's first communication satellite. It was launched on 13 May 2007, aboard a Chinese Long March 3B carrier rocket, from the Xichang Satellite Launch Centre in China. The spacecraft was operated by NigComSat and the Nigerian Space Agency, NASRDA. On 11 November 2008, NigComSat-1 failed in orbit after running out of power due to an anomaly in its solar array. It was based on the Chinese DFH-4 satellite bus, and carries a variety of transponders: 4 C-band; 14 Ku-band; 8 Ka-band; and 2 L-band. It was designed to provide coverage to many parts of Africa, and the Ka-band transponders would also cover Italy.

On 10 November 2008 (0900 GMT), the satellite was reportedly switched off for analysis and to avoid a possible collision with other satellites. According to Nigerian Communications Satellite Limited, it was put into "emergency mode operation in order to effect mitigation and repairs". The satellite eventually failed after losing power on 11 November 2008.

On 24 March 2009, the Nigerian Federal Ministry of Science and Technology, NigComSat Ltd. and CGWIC signed another contract for the in-orbit delivery of the NigComSat-1R satellite. NigComSat-1R was also a DFH-4 satellite, and the replacement for the failed NigComSat-1 was successfully launched into orbit by China in Xichang on December 19, 2011. The satellite according to Nigerian President Goodluck Jonathan which was paid for by the insurance policy on NigComSat-1 which de-orbited in 2009, would have a positive impact on national development in various sectors such as communications, internet services, health, agriculture, environmental protection and national security.

Ethnic Groups

Nigeria has more than 250 ethnic groups, with varying languages and customs, creating a country of rich ethnic diversity. The largest ethnic groups are the Hausa, Yoruba, Igbo and Fulani, accounting for more than 70% of the population, while the Edo, Ijaw, Kanuri, Ibibio, Ebira, Nupe, Gwari, Itsekiri, Jukun, Urhobo, Igala, Idoma and Tiv comprise between 25 and 30%; other minorities make up the remaining 5%.

The middle belt of Nigeria is known for its diversity of ethnic groups, including the Pyem, Goemai, and Kofyar. The official population count of each of Nigeria's ethnicities has always remained controversial and disputed as members of different ethnic groups believe the census is rigged to give a particular group (usually believed to be northern groups) numerical superiority.

There are small minorities of British, American, East Indian, Chinese (est. 50,000), white Zimbabwean, Japanese, Greek, Syrian and Lebanese immigrants in Nigeria. Immigrants also include those from other West African or East African nations. These minorities mostly reside in major cities such as Lagos and Abuja, or in the Niger Delta as employees for the major oil companies. A number of Cubans settled in Nigeria as political refugees following the Cuban Revolution.

In the middle of the 19th century, a number of ex-slaves of Afro-Cuban and Afro-Brazilian descent and emigrants from Sierra Leone established communities in Lagos and other regions of Nigeria. Many ex-slaves came to Nigeria following the emancipation of slaves in the Americas. Many of the immigrants, sometimes called Saros (immigrants from Sierra Leone) and Amaro (ex-slaves from Brazil) later became prominent merchants and missionaries in these cities.

Languages

In some areas of Nigeria, ethnic groups speak more than one language. The official language of Nigeria, English, was chosen to facilitate the cultural and linguistic unity of the country, due to the influence of British colonisation that ended in 1960.

Many French speakers from surrounding countries influence the English spoken in border regions of Nigeria and some Nigerian citizens have become fluent enough in French to work in the surrounding countries. The French spoken in Nigeria may be mixed with some native languages but is mostly spoken like the French spoken in Benin. French may also be mixed with English as it is in Cameroon. Most of the population speak English and their native language.

The major languages spoken in Nigeria represent three major families of African languages: the majority are Niger–Congo languages, such as Igbo, Yoruba and Fulfulde; Hausa is Afro-Asiatic; and Kanuri, spoken in the northeast, primarily in Borno and Yobe State, is part of the Nilo-Saharan family.

Even though most ethnic groups prefer to communicate in their own languages, English as the official language is widely used for education, business transactions and for official purposes. English as a first language is used only by a small minority of the country's urban elite, and it is not spoken at all in some rural areas. Hausa is the most widely spoken of the 3 main languages spoken in Nigeria itself (Igbo, Hausa and Yoruba) but unlike the Yorubas and Igbos, the Hausas tend not to travel far outside Nigeria itself.

With the majority of Nigeria's populace in the rural areas, the major languages of communication in the country remain indigenous languages. Some of the largest of these, notably Yoruba and Igbo, have derived standardised languages from a number of different dialects and are widely spoken by those ethnic groups. Nigerian Pidgin English, often known simply as 'Pidgin' or 'Broken' (Broken English), is also a popular lingua franca, though with varying regional influences on dialect and slang. The pidgin English or Nigerian English is widely spoken within the Niger Delta Regions, predominately in Warri, Sapele, Port Harcourt, Agenebode, Ewu, and Benin City.

Religion

Figure: *The Abuja National Mosque.*

Nigeria is religiously diverse society with Islam and Christianity being the most widely professed religions. According to recent estimates,

50% of Nigeria's population adheres to Islam (mainly Sunni). Christianity is practiced by 48% of the population (74% Protestant, 25% Catholic, 1% other Christian). Adherents of Animism and other religions collectively represent 1.4% of the population.

All religions represented in Nigeria were practiced in every major city in 1990. Islam dominated the north and had a number of supporters in the South Western, Yoruba part of the country. Nigeria has the largest Muslim population in sub-Saharan Africa. Protestantism and local syncretic Christianity are also in evidence in Yoruba areas, while Catholicism dominates the Igbo and closely related areas. Both Protestantism and Catholicism dominated in the Ibibio, Annang, and the Efik kiosa lands.

The 1963 census indicated that 47% of Nigerians were Muslim, 35% Christian, and 18% members of local indigenous congregations; the results of this census were disputed however. If accurate, this indicated a sharp increase since 1953 in the number of Christians (up 13%); a slight decline among those professing indigenous beliefs, compared with 20%; and only a modest (4%) increase of Muslims.

The vast majority of Muslims in Nigeria are Sunni belonging to Maliki school of jurisprudence; however, a sizeable minority also belongs to Shafi madhhab. A large number of Sunni Muslims are members of Sufi brotherhoods. Most Sufis follow the Qadiriyya, Tijaniyyah and/or the Mouride movements. A significant Shia minority exists. Some northern states have incorporated Sharia law into their previously secular legal systems, which has brought about some controversy. Kano State has sought to incorporate Sharia law into its constitution. The majority of Quranists follow the Kalo Kato or Quraniyyun movement. There are also Ahmadiyya and Mahdiyya minorities.

According to a 2001 report of The World Factbook by CIA, about 50% of Nigeria's population was Muslim, 40% were Christians and 10% adhered to local religions. Other sources give higher estimates for the country's Christian population. A 2012 report on religion and public life by the Pew Research Centre stated that in 2010, 49.3 percent of Nigeria's population was Christian, 48.8 percent was Muslim, and 1.9 percent were followers of indigenous and other religions, or unaffiliated.

The 2010 census of Association of Religion Data Archives has also reported that 46.5 percent of the total population was Christian, slightly larger than the Muslim population (45.5 percent), while 7.7 percent were members of other religious groups. However, these estimates should be taken with caution because sample data is mostly collected from major urban areas in the south, which are predominantly Christian.

Among Christians, the Pew Research survey found that 74% were Protestant, 25% were Catholic, and 1% belonged to other Christian denominations, including a small Orthodox Christian community. In terms of Nigeria's major ethnic groups, the Hausa ethnic group (predominant in the north) was found to be 95% Muslim and 5% Christian, the Yoruba tribe (predominant in the west) was 55% Muslim, 35% Christian and 10% adherents of other religions, while the Igbos (predominant in the east) and the Ijaw (south) were 98% Christian, with 2% practicing traditional religions. The middle belt of Nigeria contains the largest number of minority ethnic groups in Nigeria, who were found to be mostly Christians and members of traditional religions, with a small proportion of Muslims.

Leading Protestant churches in the country include the Church of Nigeria of the Anglican Communion, the Assemblies of God Church, the Nigerian Baptist Convention and The Synagogue, Church Of All Nations Since the 1990s, there has been significant growth in many other churches, particularly those of Evangelical theology. These include the Redeemed Christian Church of God, Winners' Chapel, Christ Apostolic Church (the first Aladura Movement in Nigeria), Deeper Christian Life Ministry, Evangelical Church of West Africa, Mountain of Fire and Miracles, Christ Embassy, The Synagogue Church Of All Nations. In addition, The Church of Jesus Christ of Latter-day Saints, the Aladura Church, the Seventh-day Adventist and various indigenous churches have also experienced growth. Other leading Protestant churches in the country are the Church of Nigeria of the Anglican Communion, the Assemblies of God Church, the Nigerian Baptist Convention and The Synagogue, Church Of All Nations.

The Yoruba area contains a large Anglican population, while Igboland is predominantly Catholic and the Edo area is composed predominantly of members of the Assemblies of God, which was introduced into Nigeria by Augustus Ehurie Wogu and his associates at Old Umuahia. Further, Nigeria has become an African hub for the Grail Movement and the Hare Krishnas, and the largest temple of the Eckankar religion is in Port Harcourt, Rivers State, with a total capacity of 10,000.

Crime

Nigeria is home to a substantial network of organised crime, active especially in drug trafficking. Nigerian criminal groups are heavily involved in drug trafficking, shipping heroin from Asian countries to Europe and America; and cocaine from South America to Europe and South Africa. . The various Nigerian Confraternities or "campus cults" are active in both organised crime and in political violence as well as providing a network of corruption within Nigeria. As confraternities have extensive connections with political and military figures, they offer excellent alumni networking opportunities. The Supreme Vikings Confraternity, for example, boasts that twelve members of the Rivers State House of Assembly are cult members. On lower levels of society, there are the "area boys", organised gangs mostly active in Lagos who specialise in mugging and small-scale drug dealing. According to official statistics, gang violence in Lagos resulted in 273 civilians and 84 policemen killed in the period of August 2000 to May 2001.

Internationally, Nigeria is infamous for a form of bank fraud dubbed *419*, a type of advance fee fraud (named after Section 419 of the Nigerian Penal Code) along with the "Nigerian scam", a form of confidence trick practiced by individuals and criminal syndicates. These scams involve a complicit Nigerian bank (the laws being set up loosely to allow it) and a scammer who claims to have money he needs to obtain from that bank. The victim is talked into exchanging bank account information on the premise that the money will be transferred to him, and then he'll get to keep a cut. In reality, money is taken out instead, and/or large fees (which seem small in comparison with the imaginary wealth he awaits) are deducted.

In 2003, the Nigerian Economic and Financial Crimes Commission (or EFCC) was created, ostensibly to combat this and other forms of organised financial crime. There is also some major piracy in Nigeria, with attacks directed at all types of vessels. Consistent with the rise of Nigeria as an increasingly dangerous hot spot, 28 of the 30 seafarers kidnapped as of January–June 2013 were in Nigeria, not in Somalia (the remaining two were in Togo). Additionally, the single death to date in 2013 occurred in Nigeria.

Nigeria is also pervaded by political corruption. It is ranked 143 out of 182 countries in Transparency International's 2011 Corruption Perceptions Index. More than $400 billion was stolen from the treasury by Nigeria's leaders between 1960 and 1999.

Egypt Arab Republic

Egypt is an Afro-Asiatic transcontinental country spanning the northeast corner of Africa and southwest corner of Asia, via a land bridge formed by the Sinai Peninsula. Most of Egypt's territory of

1,010,000 square kilometres (390,000 sq mi) lies within the Nile Valley of North Africa, but it is also considered a Mediterranean country as it is bordered by the Mediterranean Sea to the north. It is also bordered by the Gaza Strip and Israel to the northeast, the Gulf of Aqaba to the east, the Red Sea to the east and south, Sudan to the south and Libya to the west.

With over 87 million inhabitants, Egypt is the largest country in North Africa and the Arab World, the third-largest in Africa, and the fifteenth-most populous in the world. The great majority of its people live near the banks of the Nile River, an area of about 40,000 square kilometres (15,000 sq mi), where the only arable land is found. The large regions of the Sahara Desert, which constitute most of Egypt's territory, are sparsely inhabited. About half of Egypt's residents live in urban areas, with most spread across the densely populated centres of greater Cairo, Alexandria and other major cities in the Nile Delta.

Egypt has one of the longest histories of any modern country, arising in the tenth millennium BCE as one of the world's first nation states. Considered a cradle of civilization, Ancient Egypt experienced some of the earliest developments of writing, agriculture, urbanisation, organised religion and central government in history. Iconic monuments such as the Giza Necropolis and its Great Sphinx, as well the ruins of Memphis, Thebes, Karnak, and the Valley of the Kings, reflect this legacy and remain a significant focus of archaeological study and popular interest worldwide. Egypt's rich cultural heritage is an integral part of its national identity, having endured and at times assimilated various foreign influences, including Greek, Persian, Roman, Arab, Ottoman, and European.

Modern Egypt is considered to be a regional and middle power, with significant cultural, political, and military influence in North Africa, the Middle East and the Muslim world. Its economy is one of the largest and most diversified in the Middle East, with sectors such as tourism, agriculture, industry and services at almost equal production levels. In 2011, long term President Hosni Mubarak stepped down amid mass protests. Later elections saw the rise of the Muslim Brotherhood, which was ousted by the army a year later amid mass protests.

History of Egypt

Prehistory and Ancient Egypt

There is evidence of rock carvings along the Nile terraces and in desert oases. In the 10th millennium BC, a culture of hunter-gatherers and fishers was replaced by a grain-grinding culture. Climate changes or overgrazing around 8000 BC began to desiccate the pastoral lands of Egypt, forming the Sahara. Early tribal peoples migrated to the Nile River where they developed a settled agricultural economy and more centralised society.

By about 6000 BC, a Neolithic culture rooted in the Nile Valley. During the Neolithic era, several predynastic cultures developed independently in Upper and Lower Egypt. The Badarian culture and the successor Naqada series are generally regarded as precursors to dynastic Egypt. The earliest known Lower Egyptian site, Merimda, predates the Badarian by about seven hundred years. Contemporaneous Lower Egyptian communities coexisted with their southern counterparts for more than two thousand years, remaining culturally distinct, but maintaining frequent contact through trade. The earliest known evidence of Egyptian hieroglyphic inscriptions appeared during the predynastic period on Naqada III pottery vessels, dated to about 3200 BC.

Figure: *The Giza Necropolis is the oldest of the ancient Wonders and the only one still in existence*

A unified kingdom was founded c. 3150 BC by King Menes, leading to a series of dynasties that ruled Egypt for the next three millennia. Egyptian culture flourished during this long period and remained distinctively Egyptian in its religion, arts, language and customs. The first two ruling dynasties of a unified Egypt set the stage for the Old Kingdom period, *c.* 2700–2200 BC., which constructed many pyramids, most notably the Third Dynasty pyramid of Djoser and the Fourth Dynasty Giza pyramids.

The First Intermediate Period ushered in a time of political upheaval for about 150 years. Stronger Nile floods and stabilisation of government, however, brought back renewed prosperity for the country in the Middle Kingdom *c.* 2040 BC, reaching a peak during the reign of Pharaoh Amenemhat III. A second period of disunity heralded the arrival of the first foreign ruling dynasty in Egypt, that of the Semitic

Hyksos. The Hyksos invaders took over much of Lower Egypt around 1650 BC and founded a new capital at Avaris. They were driven out by an Upper Egyptian force led by Ahmose I, who founded the Eighteenth Dynasty and relocated the capital from Memphis to Thebes.

The New Kingdom *c.* 1550–1070 BC began with the Eighteenth Dynasty, marking the rise of Egypt as an international power that expanded during its greatest extension to an empire as far south as Tombos in Nubia, and included parts of the Levant in the east. This period is noted for some of the most well known Pharaohs, including Hatshepsut, Thutmose III, and his wife Nefertiti, Tutankhamun and Ramesses II. The first historically attested expression of monotheism came during this period as Atenism. Frequent contacts with other nations brought new ideas to the New Kingdom. The country was later invaded and conquered by Libyans, Nubians and Assyrians, but native Egyptians eventually drove them out and regained control of their country.

The Thirtieth Dynasty was the last native ruling dynasty during the Pharaonic epoch. It fell to the Persians in 343 BC after the last native Pharaoh, King Nectanebo II, was defeated in battle.

Ptolemaic and Roman Egypt

The Ptolemaic Kingdom was a powerful Hellenistic state, extending from southern Syria in the east, to Cyrene to the west, and south to the frontier with Nubia. Alexandria became the capital city and a centre of Greek culture and trade. To gain recognition by the native Egyptian populace, they named themselves as the successors to the Pharaohs. The later Ptolemies took on Egyptian traditions, had themselves portrayed on public monuments in Egyptian style and dress, and participated in Egyptian religious life.

The last ruler from the Ptolemaic line was Cleopatra VII, who committed suicide following the burial of her lover Mark Antony who had died in her arms (from a self-inflicted stab wound), after Octavian had captured Alexandria and her mercenary forces had fled. The Ptolemies faced rebellions of native Egyptians often caused by an unwanted regime and were involved in foreign and civil wars that led to the decline of the kingdom and its annexation by Rome. Nevertheless Hellenistic culture continued to thrive in Egypt well after the Muslim conquest.

Christianity was brought to Egypt by Saint Mark the Evangelist in the 1st century. Diocletian's reign marked the transition from the Roman to the Byzantine era in Egypt, when a great number of Egyptian

Christians were persecuted. The New Testament had by then been translated into Egyptian. After the Council of Chalcedon in AD 451, a distinct Egyptian Coptic Church was firmly established.

Middle Ages

The Byzantines were able to regain control of the country after a brief Persian invasion early in the 7th century, until 639–42, when Egypt was invaded and conquered by the Islamic Empire by the Muslim Arabs. When they defeated the Byzantine Armies in Egypt, the Arabs brought Sunni Islam to the country. Early in this period, Egyptians began to blend their new faith with indigenous beliefs and practices, leading to various Sufi orders that have flourished to this day. These earlier rites had survived the period of Coptic Christianity.

During Muhammad's Era

The Islamic Prophet Muhammad's first interaction with the people of Egypt was during the Expedition of Zaid ibn Haritha (Hisma). He sent Hatib bin Abi Baltaeh with a letter to the king of Egypt called Muqawqis In the letter Muhammad said: "I invite you to accept Islam, Allah the sublime, shall reward you doubly. But if you refuse to do so, you will bear the burden of the transgression of all the Copts". During this expedition one of Muhammad's envoys Dihyah bin Khalifa Kalbi was attacked, Muhammad sent Zayd ibn Haritha to help him. Dihya approached the Banu Dubayb (a tribe which converted to Islam and had good relations with Muslims) for help. When the news reached Muhammad, he immediately dispatched Zayd ibn Haritha with 500 men to punish them. The Muslim army fought with Banu Judham, killed several of them (inflicting heavy casualties), including their chief, Al-Hunayd ibn Arid and his son, and captured 1000 camels, 5000 of their cattle and a 100 women and boys. The new chief of the Banu Judham who had embraced Islam appealed to Muhammad to release his fellow tribesmean, and Muhammad released them.

Islamic Era

Muslim rulers nominated by the Islamic Caliphate remained in control of Egypt for the next six centuries, with Cairo as the seat of the Caliphate under the Fatimids. With the end of the Kurdish Ayyubid dynasty, the Mamluks, a Turco-Circassian military caste, took control about AD 1250. By the late 13th century, Egypt linked the Red Sea, India, Malaya, and East Indies. The mid-14th-century Black Death killed about 40% of the country's population. Hatib bin Abi Baltaeh to the king of Egypt called Muqawqis to invite him to Islam.

Egypt Eyalet

Egypt was conquered by the Ottoman Turks in 1517, after which it became a province of the Ottoman Empire. The defencive militarisation damaged its civil society and economic institutions. The weakening of the economic system combined with the effects of plague left Egypt vulnerable to foreign invasion. Portuguese traders took over their trade. Between 1687 and 1731, Egypt experienced six famines. The 1784 famine cost it roughly one-sixth of its population.

Egypt was always a difficult province for the Ottoman Sultans to control, due in part to the continuing power and influence of the Mamluks, the Egyptian military caste who had ruled the country for centuries. As such, Egypt remained semi-autonomous under the Mamluks until it was invaded by the French forces of Napoleon I in 1798. After the French were expelled, power was seized in 1805 by Muhammad Ali Pasha, an Albanian military commander of the Ottoman army in Egypt.

Egypt under the Muhammad Ali dynasty remained nominally an Ottoman province. It was granted the status of an autonomous vassal state or *Khedivate* in 1867. Isma'il and Tewfik Pasha governed Egypt as a quasi-independent state under Ottoman suzerainty until the British occupation of 1882. Nevertheless, the Khedivate of Egypt (1867–1914) remained a de jure Ottoman province until 5 November 1914, when it was declared a British protectorate in reaction to the decision of the Young Turks of the Ottoman Empire to join the First World War on the side of the Central Powers.

Muhammad Ali Dynasty

After the French were defeated by the British, a power vacuum was created in Egypt, and a three-way power struggle ensued between the Ottoman Turks, Egyptian Mamluks who had ruled Egypt for centuries, and Albanian mercenaries in the service of the Ottomans. It ended in victory for the Albanians led by Muhammad Ali.

While he carried the title of viceroy of Egypt, his subordination to the Ottoman porte was merely nominal. Muhammad Ali established a dynasty that was to rule Egypt until the revolution of 1952. In later years, the dynasty became a British puppet.

The introduction in 1820 of long-staple cotton transformed its agriculture into a cash-crop monoculture before the end of the century, concentrating land ownership and shifting production towards international markets.

Muhammad Ali annexed Northern Sudan (1820–1824), Syria (1833), and parts of Arabia and Anatolia; but in 1841 the European powers, fearful lest he topple the Ottoman Empire itself, forced him to return most of his conquests to the Ottomans. His military ambition required him to modernise the country: he built industries, a system of canals for irrigation and transport, and reformed the civil service.

Muhammad Ali Pasha evolved the military from one that convened under the tradition of the corvée to a great modernised army. He introduced conscription of the male peasantry in 19th century Egypt, and took a novel approach to create his great army, strengthening it with numbers and in skill. Education and training of the new soldiers was not an option; the new concepts were furthermore enforced by isolation. The men were held in barracks to avoid distraction of their growth as a military unit to be reckoned with. The resentment for the military way of life eventually faded from the men and a new ideology took hold, one of nationalism and pride. It was with the help of this newly reborn martial unit that Muhammad Ali imposed his rule over Egypt.

Muhammad Ali was succeeded briefly by his son Ibrahim (in September 1848), then by a grandson Abbas I (in November 1848), then by Said (in 1854), and Isma'il (in 1863).

The Suez Canal, built in partnership with the French, was completed in 1869. Its construction led to enormous debt to European banks, and caused popular discontent because of the onerous taxation it required. In 1875 Ismail was forced to sell Egypt's share in the canal to the British Government. Within three years this led to the imposition of British and French controllers who sat in the Egyptian cabinet, and, "with the financial power of the bondholders behind them, were the real power in the Government."

Local dissatisfaction with Ismail and with European intrusion led to the formation of the first nationalist groupings in 1879, with Ahmad Urabi a prominent figure. Fearing a reduction of their control, the UK and France intervened militarily, bombarding Alexandria and crushing the Egyptian army at the battle of Tel el-Kebir. They reinstalled Ismail's son Tewfik as figurehead of a *de facto* British protectorate. In 1906, the Dinshaway Incident prompted many neutral Egyptians to join the nationalist movement.

In 1914, the Protectorate was made official, and the title of the head of state was changed to *sultan*, to repudiate the vestigial suzerainty of the Ottoman sultan, who was backing the Central powers in World War I. Abbas II was deposed as khedive and replaced by his uncle, Hussein Kamel, as sultan.

After the First World War, Saad Zaghlul and the Wafd Party led the Egyptian nationalist movement to a majority at the local Legislative Assembly. When the British exiled Zaghlul and his associates to Malta on 8 March 1919, the country arose in its first modern revolution. The revolt led the UK government to issue a unilateral declaration of Egypt's independence on 22 February 1922.

The new government drafted and implemented a constitution in 1923 based on a parliamentary system. Saad Zaghlul was popularly elected as Prime Minister of Egypt in 1924. In 1936, the Anglo-Egyptian Treaty was concluded. Continued instability due to remaining British influence and increasing political involvement by the king led to the dissolution of the parliament in a military *coup d'état* known as the 1952 Revolution. The Free Officers Movement forced King Farouk to abdicate in support of his son Fuad. British military presence in Egypt lasted until 1954.

Republic

Following the 1952 Revolution by the Free Officers Movement, the rule of Egypt passed to military hands. On 18 June 1953, the Egyptian Republic was declared, with General Muhammad Naguib as the first President of the Republic.

Reign of President Nasser

Naguib was forced to resign in 1954 by Gamal Abdel Nasser – the real architect of the 1952 movement – and was later put under house arrest. Nasser assumed power as President in June 1956. British forces completed their withdrawal from the occupied Suez Canal Zone on 13 June 1956. He nationalised the Suez Canal on 26 July 1956, prompting the 1956 Suez Crisis.

In 1958, Egypt and Syria formed a sovereign union known as the United Arab Republic. The union was short-lived, ending in 1961 when Syria seceded, thus ending the union. During most of its existence, the United Arab Republic was also in a loose confederation with North Yemen (formerly the Mutawakkilite Kingdom of Yemen), known as the United Arab States. In 1959, the All-Palestine Government of the Gaza Strip, an Egyptian client state, was absorbed into United Arab Republic under the pretext of Arab union, and was never restored.

In early 1960s, Egypt became fully involved in the North Yemen Civil War. The Egyptian President, Gamal Abdel Nasser, supported the Yemeni republicans with as many as 70,000 Egyptian troops and chemical weapons. Despite several military moves and peace conferences, the war sank into a stalemate. Egyptian commitment in Yemen was greatly undermined later.

In mid May 1967, the Soviet Union issued warnings to Nasser of an impending Israeli attack on Syria. Although the chief of staff Mohamed Fawzi verified them as "baseless", Nasser took 3 successive steps that made the war virtually inevitable: On 14 May he deployed his troops in Sinai near the border with Israel, On 19 May expelled the UN peacekeepers stationed in the Sinai Peninsula border with Israel, and on 23 May closed Straits of Tiran to Israeli shipping. On 26 May Nasser declared, "*The battle will be a general one and our basic objective will be to destroy Israel*". Israel re-iterated that the Straits of Tiran closure was a Casus belli. In the 1967 Six Day War, Israel attacked Egypt, and occupied Sinai Peninsula and the Gaza Strip, which Egypt had occupied since the 1948 Arab–Israeli War. During the 1967 war, an Emergency Law was enacted, and remained in effect until 2012, with the exception of an 18-month break in 1980/81. Under this law, police powers were extended, constitutional rights suspended and censorship is legalised.

At the time of the fall of the Egyptian monarchy in the early 1950s, less than half a million Egyptians were considered upper class and rich, four million middle class and 17 million lower class and poor. Fewer than half of all primary-school-age children attended school, and most of them being boys. Nasser's policies changed this. Land reform and distribution, the dramatic growth in university education, and government support to national industries greatly improved social mobility and flattened the social curve. From academic year 1953-54 through 1965-66, overall public school enrolments more than doubled. Millions of previously poor Egyptians, through education and jobs in the public sector, joined the middle class. Doctors, engineers, teachers, lawyers, journalists, constituted the bulk of the swelling middle class in Egypt under Nasser. During the 60's, the Egyptian economy went from sluggishness to the verge of collapse, the society became less free, and Nasser's appeal waned considerably.

Reign of President Sadat

In 1970, President Nasser died and was succeeded by Anwar Sadat. Sadat switched Egypt's Cold War allegiance from the Soviet Union to the United States, expelling Soviet advisors in 1972. He launched the Infitah economic reform policy, while clamping down on religious and secular opposition. In 1973, Egypt, along with Syria, launched the October War, a surprise attack to regain part of the Sinai territory Israel had captured 6 years earlier. It presented Sadat with a victory that allowed him to regain the Sinai later in return for peace with Israel.

In 1975, Sadat shifted Nasser's economic policies and sought to use his popularity to reduce government regulations and encourage foreign investment through his program of Infitah. Through this policy, incentives such as reduced taxes and import tariffs attracted some investors, but investments however were mainly directed at low risk and profitable ventures like tourism and construction, abandoning Egypt's infant industries. Even though Sadat's policy was intended to modernise Egypt and assist the middle class, it mainly benefited the higher class, and, because of the elimination of subsidies on basic foodstuffs, led to the 1977 Egyptian Bread Riots.

Sadat made a historic visit to Israel in 1977, which led to the 1979 peace treaty in exchange for Israeli withdrawal from Sinai. Sadat's initiative sparked enormous controversy in the Arab world and led to Egypt's expulsion from the Arab League, but it was supported by most Egyptians. However, Sadat was assassinated by an Islamic extremist.

Reign of President Mubarak

Hosni Mubarak came to power after the assassination of Sadat in a referendum in which he was the only candidate.

Hosni Mubarak reaffirmed Egypt's relationship with Israel yet eased the tensions with Egypt's Arab neighbours as well. Domestically, Mubarak faced many serious problems. Even though farm and industry output expanded, the economy could not keep pace with the population boom. Mass poverty and unemployment led rural families to stream into cities like Cairo where they ended up in crowded slums, barely managing to survive.

In the 1980s, 1990s, and 2000s, terrorist attacks in Egypt became numerous and severe, and began to target Christian Copts and foreign tourists as well as government officials. In the 1990s an Islamist group, Al-Gama'a al-Islamiyya, engaged in an extended campaign of violence, from the murders and attempted murders of prominent writers and intellectuals, to the repeated targeting of tourists and foreigners. Serious damage was done to the largest sector of Egypt's economy—tourism—and in turn to the government, but it also devastated the livelihoods of many of the people on whom the group depended for support.

During Mubarak's reign, the political scene was dominated by the National Democratic Party, which was created by Sadat in 1978. It passed 1993 Syndicates Law, 1995 Press Law, and 1999 Nongovernmental Associations Law which hampered freedoms of association and expression by imposing new regulations and draconian penalties on violations. As a result, by the late 1990s parliamentary politics had become virtually irrelevant and alternative avenues for political expression were curtailed as well. On 17 November 1997, 62 people, mostly tourists, were massacred near Luxor. In late February 2005, Mubarak announced a reform of the presidential election law, paving the way for multi-candidate polls for the first time since the 1952 movement. However, the new law placed restrictions on the candidates, and led to Mubarak's easy re-election victory. Voter turnout was less than 25%. Election observers also alleged government interference in the election process. After the election, Mubarak imprisoned Ayman Nour, the runner-up.

Human Rights Watch's 2006 report on Egypt detailed serious human rights violations, including routine torture, arbitrary detentions and trials before military and state security courts. In 2007, Amnesty International released a report alleging that Egypt had become an international centre for torture, where other nations send suspects for interrogation, often as part of the War on Terror. Egypt's foreign ministry quickly issued a rebuttal to this report.

Constitutional changes voted on 19 March 2007 prohibited parties from using religion as a basis for political activity, allowed the drafting of a new anti-terrorism law, authorised broad police powers of arrest and surveillance, and gave the president power to dissolve parliament and end judicial election monitoring. In 2009, Dr. Ali El Deen Hilal Dessouki, Media Secretary of the National Democratic Party (NDP), described Egypt as a "pharaonic" political system, and democracy as a "long term goal". Dessouki also stated that "the real centre of power in Egypt is the military".

Revolution

On 25 January 2011, widespread protests began against Mubarak's government. On 11 February 2011, Mubarak resigned and fled Cairo. Jubilant celebrations broke out in Cairo's Tahrir Square at the news. The Egyptian military then assumed the power to govern. Mohamed Hussein Tantawi, chairman of the Supreme Council of the Armed Forces, became the *de facto* interim head of state. On 13 February 2011, the military dissolved the parliament and suspended the constitution.

A constitutional referendum was held on 19 March 2011. On 28 November 2011, Egypt held its first parliamentary election since the previous regime had been in power. Turnout was high and there were no reports of major irregularities or violence. Mohamed Morsi was elected president on 24 June 2012. On 2 August 2012, Egypt's Prime Minister Hisham Qandil announced his 35 member cabinet comprising 28 newcomers including four from the Muslim Brotherhood.

Liberal and secular groups walked out of the constituent assembly because they believed that it would impose strict Islamic practices, while Muslim Brotherhood backers threw their support behind Morsi. On 22 November 2012, President Morsi issued a declaration immunising his decrees from challenge and seeking to protect the work of the constituent assembly.

The move led to massive protests and violent action throughout Egypt. On 5 December 2012, tens of thousands of supporters and opponents of president Morsi clashed, in what was described as the largest violent battle between Islamists and their foes since the country's revolution. Mohamed Morsi offered a "national dialogue" with opposition leaders but refused to cancel the December 2012 constitutional referendum. On 30 June 2013, massive protests were organised across Egypt against Morsi's rule, leading to the ousting of Morsi by the military on 3 July 2013, where the military removed Morsi from power in a coup d'état and installed an interim government.

On 4 July 2013, 68-year old Egyptian judge Adly Mansour was sworn in as acting president over the new government following the removal of Morsi. The military-backed Egyptian authorities cracked down on the Muslim Brotherhood and its supporters, jailing thousands and killing hundreds of street protesters. Many of the Muslim Brotherhood leaders and activists have either been sentenced to death or life imprisonment in a series of mass trials.

On 18 January 2014, the interim government instituted a new constitution following a referendum in which 98.1% of voters were supportive. Participation was low with only 38.6% of registered voters participating although this was higher than the 33% who voted in a referendum during Morsi's tenure. On 26 March 2014 Abdel Fattah el-Sisi the head of the Egyptian Armed Forces, who at this time was in control of the country, resigned from the military, announcing he would stand as a candidate in the 2014 presidential election. The poll, held between 26 and 28 May 2014, resulted in a landslide victory for el-Sisi. Sisi sworn into office as President of Egypt on 8 June 2014. The Muslim Brotherhood and some liberal and secular activist groups boycotted the vote. Even though the military-backed authorities extended voting to a third day, the 46% turnout was lower than the 52% turnout in the 2012 election.

Politics

The House of Representatives, whose members are elected to serve five-year terms, is Specialised in the Legislature power. Elections were last held between November 2011 and January 2012 which was later dissolved. The next parliamentary election will be held within 6 months of the constitution's ratification on 18 January 2014. Originally, the parliament was to be formed before the president was elected, but interim president Adly Mansour pushed the date. The Egyptian presidential election, 2014 took place on 26–28 May 2014. Official figures showed a turnout of 25,578,233 or 47.5%, with Abdel Fattah el-Sisi winning with 23.78 million votes, or 96.91% compared to 757,511 (3.09%) for Hamdeen Sabahi.

On 3 July 2013 following millions of protesters demonstrated across Egypt against Morsi reported as one of the biggest protests in world history. then-General Abdul Fatah Al-Sisi announced the removal of President Morsi from office and suspending the constitution for modification. 50-member constitution committee was formed for modifying the constitution which was later published for public voting and was adopted in 18 January 2014.

In 2013, the Freedom House rated political rights in Egypt at "5" (with 1 representing the most free and 7 the least), civil liberties as "5" which gave it the freedom rating of "Partly Free." Egyptian nationalism predates its Arab counterpart by many decades, having roots in the 19th century and becoming the dominant mode of expression of Egyptian anti-colonial activists and intellectuals until the early 20th century. The ideology espoused by Islamists such as the Muslim Brotherhood is mostly supported by the lower-middle strata of Egyptian society.

Egypt has the oldest continuous parliamentary tradition in the Arab world. The first popular assembly was established in 1866. It was disbanded as a result of the British occupation of 1882, and the British allowed only a consultative body to sit. In 1923, however, after the country's independence was declared, a new constitution provided for a parliamentary monarchy.

Law

The legal system is based on Islamic and civil law (particularly Napoleonic codes); and judicial review by a Supreme Court, which accepts compulsory International Court of Justice jurisdiction only with reservations.

Islamic jurisprudence is the principal source of legislation. Sharia courts and qadis are run and licensed by the Ministry of Justice. The personal status law that regulates matters such as marriage, divorce and child custody is governed by Sharia. In a family court, a woman's testimony is worth half of a man's testimony.

***Figure:** Supreme Constitutional Court of Egypt.*

On 26 December 2012, the Muslim Brotherhood attempted to institutionalise a controversial new constitution. It was approved by the public in a referendum held 15–22 December 2012 with 64% support, but with only 33% electorate participation. It replaced the 2011 Provisional Constitution of Egypt, adopted following the revolution.

The Penal code was unique as it contains a "Blasphemy Law." The present court system allows a death penalty including against an absent individual tried *in absentia*. Several Americans and Canadians were sentenced to death in 2012.

On 18 January 2014, the interim government successfully institutionalised a more secular constitution sets up a president and parliament. The president is elected to a four year term and may serve 2 terms. The parliament may impeach the president. Under the constitution, there is a guarantee of gender equality and absolute freedom of thought. The military retains the ability to appoint the national Minister of Defence for the next 8 years. Under the constitution, political parties may not be based on "religion, race, gender or geography".

Military

The Egyptian Armed forces have a combined troop strength of around 468,500 active personnel in addition 1,000,000 reservists for a total of 1,468,500 strong.

According to the former chair of Israel's Knesset Foreign Affairs and Defence Committee, Yuval Steinitz, the Egyptian Air Force has roughly the same number of modern warplanes as the Israeli Air Force and far more Western tanks, artillery, anti-aircraft batteries and warships than the IDF. Egypt is speculated by Israel to be the second country in the region with a spy satellite, EgyptSat 1 in addition to EgyptSat 2 launched on 16 April 2014.

Figure: *Egyptian Air Force F-16 refuelling during Operation Bright Star*

The Egyptian military has dozens of factories manufacturing weapons as well as consumer goods. The Armed Forces' inventory includes equipment from different countries around the world. Equipment from the former Soviet Union is being progressively replaced by more modern US, French, and British equipment, a significant portion of which is built under license in Egypt, such as the M1 Abrams tank.

The Egyptian Navy is the largest navy in Africa and Middle East and the Arab World, and is the seventh largest in the world measured by the number of vessels.

The United States of America provides Egypt with annual military assistance, which in 2009 amounted to US$1.3 billion (inflation adjusted US$ 1.43 billion in 2014).

The military has a lot of influence in the political life of Egypt as well as the economy and it exempts itself from laws that apply to other sectors. It also enjoys considerable power, prestige and independence within the state and has been widely considered part of the Egyptian "deep state".

Human Rights

The Egyptian Organisation for Human Rights is one of the longest-standing bodies for the defence of human rights in Egypt. In 2003, the government established the National Council for Human Rights. The council came under heavy criticism by local activists, who contend it was a propaganda tool for the government to excuse its own violations and to give legitimacy to repressive laws such as the Emergency Law.

Protesters from the Third Square movement: "Neither Morsi nor the military", 31 July 2013

The Pew Forum on Religion & Public Life ranks Egypt as the fifth worst country in the world for religious freedom. The United States Commission on International Religious Freedom, a bipartisan independent agency of the US government, has placed Egypt on its watch list of countries that require close monitoring due to the nature and extent of violations of religious freedom engaged in or tolerated by the government. According to a 2010 Pew Global Attitudes survey, 84% of Egyptians polled supported the death penalty for those who leave Islam; 77% supported whippings and cutting off of hands for theft and robbery; and 82% support stoning a person who commits adultery.

Coptic Christians face discrimination at multiple levels of the government, ranging from disproportionate representation in government ministries to laws that limit their ability to build or repair churches. Intolerance of Baháʼís and non-orthodox Muslim sects, such as Sufis, Shi'a and Ahmadis, also remains a problem. When the government moved to computerise identification cards, members of religious minorities, such as Baháʼís, could not obtain identification documents. An Egyptian court ruled in early 2008 that members of other faiths may obtain identity cards without listing their faiths, and without becoming officially recognised.

Clashes continue between police and supporters of former President Mohamed Morsi, at least 595 civilians were killed in Cairo on 14 August 2013, the worst mass killing in Egypt's modern history.

Egypt actively practises capital punishment. Egypt's authorities do not release figures on death sentences and executions, despite repeated requests over the years by human rights organisations. The United Nations human rights office and various NGOs expressed "deep alarm" after an Egyptian Minya Criminal Court sentenced 529 people to death in a single hearing on 25 March 2014. Sentenced supporters of former President Mohamed Morsi will be executed for their alleged role in violence following his ousting in July 2013. The judgment was condemned as a violation of international law. By May 2014, approximately 16,000 people (and as high as more than 40,000 by one independent count), mostly Brotherhood members or supporters, have been imprisoned after the coup after the Muslim Brotherhood was labeled as terrorist organisation by the post-coup interim Egyptian government.

Foreign Relations

The permanent headquarters of the Arab League are located in Cairo and the body's secretary general has traditionally been Egyptian. This position is currently held by former foreign minister Nabil el-Araby. The Arab League briefly moved from Egypt to Tunis in 1978 to protest the Egypt-Israel Peace Treaty, but it later returned to Cairo in 1989. Saudi Arabia, the United Arab Emirates and Kuwait, have pledged more than $20bn to help Egypt overcome its economic difficulties since the Egyptian military overthrew Islamist president Mohamed Morsi in July 2013.

Following the 1973 war and the subsequent peace treaty, Egypt became the first Arab nation to establish diplomatic relations with Israel. Despite that, Israel is still widely considered as a hostile state by the majority of Egyptians. Egypt has played a historical role as a mediator in resolving various disputes in the Middle East, most notably its handling of the Israeli-Palestinian conflict and the peace process. Egypt's ceasefire and truce brokering efforts in Gaza have been hardly challenged following Israel's evacuation of its settlements from the strip in 2005, despite increasing animosity towards the Hamas government in Gaza after the ouster of Mohamed Morsi, and despite recent attempts by countries like Turkey and Qatar to take over this role.

Ties between Egypt and other non-Arab Middle Eastern nations, including Iran and Turkey, have often been tense: Iran, partly due to its rivalry with Saudi Arabia, the United Arab Emirates and other Gulf monarchies who have traditionally maintained strong ties with Egypt; and Turkey due to its government's support for the now-banned Muslim Brotherhood in Egypt.

In 1989, Egypt was designated as a major non-NATO ally of the United States. In 2011, the U.S. provided a military assistance of US$1.3 billion, and an economic assistance of US$250 million. Nevertheless, ties between the two countries have temporarily soured since the July 2013 military coup that deposed Islamist president Mohamed Morsi. The Obama administration condemned Egypt's violent crackdown on the Muslim Brotherhood and its supporters, cancelling future military exercises and halting the delivery of F-16 fighters to the Egyptian Armed Forces. However, both countries have started to normalize relations in mid-2014, calling for each other's support in the fight against regional and international terrorism. In a 2014 news story, BBC reported: "The US has revealed it has released $575m (£338m) in military aid to Egypt that had been frozen since the ousting of President Mohammed Morsi last year."

Simultaneously, relations with Russia have improved significantly following Mohamed Morsi's removal and both countries have worked since then to strengthen military and trade ties among other aspects of bilateral cooperation.

Egypt is a founding member of the Non-Aligned Movement and the United Nations. Former Egyptian Deputy Prime Minister Boutros Boutros-Ghali served as Secretary-General of the United Nations from 1991 to 1996.

In the 21st century, Egypt has had a major problem with immigration, as millions of persons from other African nations flee poverty and war. Border control methods can be "harsh, sometimes lethal."

Economy

Egypt's economy depends mainly on agriculture, media, petroleum imports, natural gas, and tourism; there are also more than three million Egyptians working abroad, mainly in Saudi Arabia, the Persian Gulf and Europe. The completion of the Aswan High Dam in 1970 and the resultant Lake Nasser have altered the time-honoured place of the Nile River in the agriculture and ecology of Egypt. A rapidly growing population, limited arable land, and dependence on the Nile all continue to overtax resources and stress the economy.

The government has invested in communications and physical infrastructure. Egypt has received United States foreign aid since 1979 (an average of $2.2 billion per year) and is the third-largest recipient of such funds from the United States following the Iraq war. Egypt's economy mainly relies on these sources of income: tourism, remittances from Egyptians working abroad and revenues from the Suez Canal.

Egypt has a developed energy market based on coal, oil, natural gas, and hydro power. Substantial coal deposits in the northeast Sinai are mined at the rate of about 600,000 tonnes (590,000 long tons; 660,000 short tons) per year. Oil and gas are produced in the western desert regions, the Gulf of Suez, and the Nile Delta. Egypt has huge reserves of gas, estimated at 1,940 cubic kilometres (470 cu mi), and LNG up to 2012 exported to many countries. In 2013, the Egyptian General Petroleum Co (EGPC) said the country will cut exports of natural gas and tell major industries to slow output this summer to avoid an energy crisis and stave off political unrest, Reuters has reported. Egypt is counting on top liquid natural gas (LNG) exporter Qatar to obtain additional gas volumes in summer, while encouraging factories to plan their annual maintenance for those months of peak demand, said EGPC chairman, Tarek El Barkatawy. Egypt produces its own energy, but has been a net oil importer since 2008 and is rapidly becoming a net importer of natural gas.

Economic conditions have started to improve considerably, after a period of stagnation, due to the adoption of more liberal economic policies by the government as well as increased revenues from tourism and a booming stock market. In its annual report, the International Monetary Fund (IMF) has rated Egypt as one of the top countries in the world undertaking economic reforms. Some major economic reforms undertaken by the government since 2003 include a dramatic slashing of customs and tariffs. A new taxation law implemented in 2005 decreased corporate taxes from 40% to the current 20%, resulting in a stated 100% increase in tax revenue by the year 2006.

Foreign direct investment (FDI) in Egypt increased considerably before the removal of Hosni Mubarak, exceeding $6 billion in 2006, due to economic liberalisation and privatization measures taken by minister of investment Mahmoud Mohieddin. Since the fall of Hosni Mubarak in 2011, Egypt has experienced a drastic fall in both foreign investment and tourism revenues, followed by a 60% drop in foreign exchange reserves, a 3% drop in growth, and a rapid devaluation of the Egyptian pound.

Although one of the main obstacles still facing the Egyptian economy is the limited trickle down of wealth to the average population, many Egyptians criticise their government for higher prices of basic goods while their standards of living or purchasing power remains relatively stagnant. Corruption is often cited by Egyptians as the main impediment to further economic growth. The government promised major reconstruction of the country's infrastructure, using money paid for the newly acquired third mobile license ($3 billion) by Etisalat in 2006. In the Corruption Perceptions Index 2013, Egypt was ranked 114 out of 177.

Figure: *Suez Canal*

Egypt's most prominent multinational companies are the Orascom Group and Raya Contact Centre. The information technology (IT) sector has expanded rapidly in the past few years, with many start-ups selling outsourcing services to North America and Europe, operating with companies such as Microsoft, Oracle and other major corporations, as well as many small and medium size enterprises. Some of these companies are the Xceed Contact Centre, Raya, E Group Connections and C3. The IT sector has been stimulated by new Egyptian entrepreneurs with government encouragement.

An estimated 2.7 million Egyptians abroad contribute actively to the development of their country through remittances (US$7.8 billion in 2009), as well as circulation of human and social capital and investment. Remittances, money earned by Egyptians living abroad and sent home, reached a record US$21 billion in 2012, according to the World Bank.

Egyptian society is moderately unequal in terms of income distribution, with an estimated 35 - 40% of Egypt's population earning less than the equivalent of $2 a day, while only around 2–3% may be considered wealthy.

Demographics

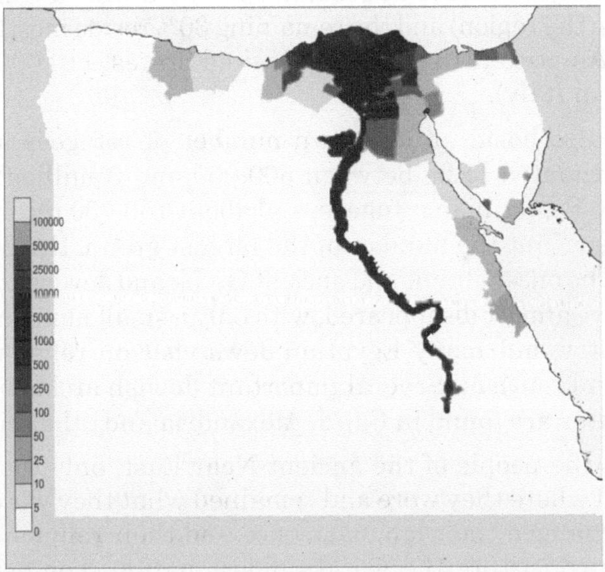

Figure: *Egypt population density (people per km²)*

Egypt is the most populated country in the Middle East, and the third most populous on the African continent, with about 84 million inhabitants as of 2013. Its population grew rapidly from 1970 to 2010 due to medical advances and increases in agricultural productivity enabled by the Green Revolution. Egypt's population was estimated at only 3 million when Napoleon invaded the country in 1798.

Egypt's people are highly urbanised, being concentrated along the Nile (notably Cairo and Alexandria), in the Delta and near the Suez Canal. Egyptians are divided demographically into those who live in the major urban centres and the fellahin, or farmers, that reside in rural villages.

Ethnic Egyptians are by far the largest ethnic group in the country, constituting 91% of the total population. Ethnic minorities include the Abazas, Turks, Greeks, Bedouin Arab tribes living in the eastern deserts and the Sinai Peninsula, the Berber-speaking Siwis (Amazigh) of the Siwa Oasis, and the Nubian communities clustered along the Nile. There are also tribal Beja communities concentrated in the south-eastern-most corner of the country, and a number of Dom clans mostly in the Nile Delta and Faiyum who are progressively becoming assimilated as urbanisation increases.

According to the International Organisation for Migration, an estimated 2.7 million Egyptians live abroad. Approximately 70% of Egyptian migrants live in Arab countries (923,600 in Saudi Arabia, 332,600 in Libya, 226,850 in Jordan, 190,550 in Kuwait with the rest elsewhere in the region) and the remaining 30% reside mostly in Europe and North America (318,000 in the United States, 110,000 in Canada and 90,000 in Italy).

Egypt also hosts an unknown number of refugees and asylum seekers, estimated to be between 500,000 and 3 million. There are some 70,000 Palestinian refugees, and about 150,000 recently arrived Iraqi refugees, but the number of the largest group, the Sudanese, is contested. The once-vibrant and ancient Greek and Jewish communities in Egypt have almost disappeared, with only a small number remaining in the country, but many Egyptian Jews visit on religious or other occasions and tourism. Several important Jewish archaeological and historical sites are found in Cairo, Alexandria and other cities.

Among the people of the ancient Near East, only the Egyptians have stayed where they were and remained what they were, although they have changed their language once and their religion twice. In a sense, they constitute the world's oldest nation. For most of their history, Egypt has been a state, but only in recent years has it been truly a nation-state, with a government claiming the allegiance of its subjects on the basis of a common identity.

Languages

The official language of the Republic is Modern Standard Arabic. The spoken languages are: Egyptian Arabic (68%), Sa'idi Arabic (29%),

Eastern Egyptian Bedawi Arabic (1.6%), Sudanese Arabic (0.6%), Domari (0.3%), Nobiin (0.3%), Beja (0.1%), Siwi and others. Additionally, Greek, Armenian and Italian are the main languages of immigrants. In Alexandria in the 19th century there was a large community of Italian Egyptians and Italian was the "lingua franca" of the city.

The main foreign languages taught in schools, by order of popularity, are English, French, German and Italian.

Historical Egyptian languages, also known as Copto-Egyptian, consist of ancient Egyptian and Coptic, and form a separate branch among the family of Afro-Asiatic languages. The "Koiné" dialect of the Greek language, though not native to Egypt, was important in Hellenistic Alexandria. It was used extensively in the philosophy and science of that culture. Later translations from Greek to Arabic became the subject of study by Arab scholars.

Religion

Egypt is a predominantly Sunni Muslim country with Islam as its state religion. The percentage of adherents of various religions is a controversial topic in Egypt. An estimated 90% are identified as Muslim, 9% as Coptic Christians, and 1% as other Christian denominations. Non-denominational Muslims form roughly 12% of the population.

After Islam arrived in the 7th century, Egypt emerged as a centre of politics and culture in the Muslim world. Under Anwar Sadat, Islam became the official state religion and Sharia the main source of law. It is estimated that 15 million Egyptians follow Native Sufi orders, with the Sufi leadership asserting that the numbers are much greater as many Egyptian Sufis are not officially registered with a Sufi order. There is also a minority of Shi'a. The Jerusalem Centre for Public Affairs estimates the Shia population at 1 to 2.2 million and could measure as much as 3 million. The Ahmadiyya population is estimated at less than 50 thousand, whereas the Salafi (ultra-conservative) population is estimated at five to six million. Cairo is famous for its numerous mosque minarets and has been dubbed *"The City of 1,000 Minarets"*.

Of the Christian minority in Egypt over 90% belong to the native Coptic Orthodox Church of Alexandria, an Oriental Orthodox Christian Church. Other native Egyptian Christians are adherents of the Coptic Catholic Church, the Evangelical Church of Egypt and various other Protestant denominations. Non-native Christian communities are largely found in the urban regions of Cairo and Alexandria, the largest formerly being the Christians of Syro-Lebanese, or "Levantine", descent who belong to Greek Catholic, Greek Orthodox, and Maronite Catholic denominations. Syro-Lebanese Christians formerly had a much larger community in Egypt before the Nasser regime and the adoption of laws of nationalisation. Ethnic Greeks also made up a large Greek Orthodox population in the past. Likewise Armenians made up the then larger Armenian Orthodox and Catholic communities, with Italian Egyptians largely making up the Roman Catholic community.

Egypt hosts two major religious institutions, the Coptic Orthodox Church of Alexandria, established in the middle of the 1st century CE by Saint Mark the Evangelist, and Al-Azhar University, founded in 970 CE by the Fatimids as the first Islamic School and University in the world.

Egypt recognises only three religions: Islam, Christianity, and Judaism. Other faiths and minority Muslim sects practised by Egyptians, such as the small Bahá'í and Ahmadi community, are not recognised by the state, and face persecution. Individuals, particularly Baha'is and atheists, wishing to include such religions on their mandatory state issued identification cards are denied this ability, and are put in the position of either not obtaining required identification or lying about their faith. A 2008 court ruling allowed members of unrecognised faiths to obtain identification and leave the religion field blank.

Libya Peoples Socialist Arab Republic

Libya, officially the State of Libya, is a country in the Maghreb region of North Africa bordered by the Mediterranean Sea to the north, Egypt to the east, Sudan to the southeast, Chad and Niger to the south, and Algeria and Tunisia to the west. The three traditional parts of the country are Tripolitania, Fezzan and Cyrenaica. With an area of almost 1.8 million square kilometres (700,000 sq mi), Libya is the fourth largest country in Africa, and is the 17th largest country in the world.

The largest city and capital, Tripoli, is home to over one million of Libya's six million people. Libya has the 10th-largest proven oil reserves of any country in the world.

Libya has been inhabited by Berbers since the Late Bronze Age. The Phoenicians established trading posts in western Libya, and Ancient Greek colonists established city-states in eastern Libya. Libya was variously ruled by Persians, Egyptians and Greek-Egyptians before becoming a part of the Roman Empire. Libya was an early centre of Christianity. During the 7th Century, invasions brought Islam and Arab colonization. In the sixteenth century the Spanish Empire and the Knights of St John occupied Tripoli, until Ottoman rule began in 1551. Libya was involved in the Barbary Wars of the 18th and 19th centuries. Ottoman rule continued until the twentieth century Italian occupation of Libya and large-scale Italian immigration. Italian rule ended during the Second World War, during which Libya was an important area of warfare. Libya became an independent kingdom in 1951. In 1969 Muammar Gaddafi seized power, beginning a period of improved living standards and brutal suppression of dissent.

The Libyan Civil War, also referred to as the Libyan Revolution, was a 2011 armed conflict in the North African country of Libya, fought between forces loyal to Colonel Muammar Gaddafi and those seeking to oust his government. The war was preceded by protests in Zawiya, 8 August 2009 and finally ignited by protests in Benghazi beginning on Tuesday, 15 February 2011, which led to clashes with security forces that fired on the crowd. The protests escalated into a rebellion that spread across the country, with the forces opposing Gaddafi establishing an interim governing body, the National Transitional Council.

The United Nations Security Council passed an initial resolution on 26 February, freezing the assets of Gaddafi and his inner circle and restricting their travel, and referred the matter to the International Criminal Court for investigation. In early March, Gaddafi's forces rallied, pushed eastwards and re-took several coastal cities before reaching Benghazi. A further U.N. resolution authorised member states to establish and enforce a no-fly zone over Libya, and to use "all necessary measures" to prevent attacks on civilians. The Gaddafi government then announced a ceasefire, but failed to uphold it, though it then accused rebels of violating the ceasefire when they continued to fight as well. Throughout the conflict, rebels rejected government offers of a ceasefire and efforts by the African Union to end the fighting because the plans set forth did not include the removal of Gaddafi, Since then, Libya has experienced instability and political violence. Instability has severely affected both commerce and oil production.

Libya is theoretically governed by a parliament known as the House of Representatives elected in the June 2014 elections. However the parliament's control of the country is severely limited by the internal conflict against Islamist militias, which control Tripoli. Officially, the House of Representatives took over from the General National Congress, which was elected in July 2012 to serve until January 2014. However, a minority of the General National Congress, having lost the elections, reconvened in August 2014. This New General National Congress meets in Tripoli, while the elected House of Representatives meets in Tobruk. At a meeting of the European Parliament Committee on Foreign Affairs on 2 December 2014, UN Special Representative Bernadino Leon described Libya as a non-state.

Islamic Libya

Under the command of 'Amr ibn al-'As, the Rashidun army conquered Cyrenaica. In 647 an army led by Abdullah ibn Saad took Tripoli from the Byzantines definitively. The Fezzan was conquered by Uqba ibn Nafi in 663. The Berber tribes of the hinterland accepted Islam, however they resisted Arab political rule.

For the next several decades, Libya was under the purview of the Umayyad Caliph of Damascus until the Abbasids overthrew the Umayyads in 750, and Libya came under the rule of Baghdad. When Caliph Harun al-Rashid appointed Ibrahim ibn al-Aghlab as his governor of Ifriqiya in 800, Libya enjoyed considerable local autonomy under the Aghlabid dynasty. By the end of the 9th century, the Shiite Fatimids controlled Western Libya, and ruled the entire region in 972 and appointed Bologhine ibn Ziri as governor. Ibn Ziri's Berber Zirid dynasty ultimately broke away from the Shiite Fatimids, and recognised the Sunni Abbasids of Baghdad as rightful Caliphs. In retaliation, the Fatimids brought about the migration of thousands from two troublesome Arab Bedouin tribes, the Banu Sulaym and Banu Hilal to North Africa. This act drastically altered the fabric of the Libyan countryside, and cemented the cultural and linguistic Arabisation of the region.

Zirid rule in Tripolitania was short-lived though, and already in 1001 the Berbers of the Banu Khazrun broke away. Tripolitania remained under their control until 1146, when the region was overtaken by the Normans of Sicily. It was not until 1159 that the Moroccan Almohad leader Abd al-Mu'min reconquered Tripoli from European rule. For the next 50 years, Tripolitania was the scene of numerous battles between the Almohad rulers and insurgents of the Banu Ghaniya. Later, a general of the Almohads, Muhammad ibn Abu Hafs, ruled Libya from 1207 to 1221 before the later establishment of a Tunisian Hafsid dynasty independent from the Almohads. The Hafsids ruled Tripolitania for nearly 300 years. By the 16th century however, the Hafsids became increasingly caught up in the power struggle between Spain and the Ottoman Empire.

Ottoman Tripolitania

After a successful invasion of Tripoli by Habsburg Spain in 1510, and its handover to the Knights of St. John, the Ottoman admiral Sinan Pasha finally took control of Libya in 1551. His successor Turgut Reis was named the Bey of Tripoli and later Pasha of Tripoli in 1556. By 1565, administrative authority as regent in Tripoli was vested in a *pasha* appointed directly by the *sultan* in Constantinople/Istanbul. In the 1580s, the rulers of Fezzan gave their allegiance to the sultan, and although Ottoman authority was absent in Cyrenaica, a *bey* was stationed in Benghazi late in the next century to act as agent of the government in Tripoli. European slaves and large numbers of enslaved blacks transported from Sudan were also a feature of everyday life in Tripoli. In 1551, Turgut Reis enslaved almost the entire population of the Maltese island of Gozo, some 6,300 people, sending them to Libya.

In time, real power came to rest with the pasha's corps of janissaries. In 1611 the *deys* staged a coup against the pasha, and Dey Sulayman was appointed as head of government. For the next hundred years, a series of *deys* effectively ruled Tripolitania. The two most important Deys were Mehmed Saqizli (r. 1631–49) and Osman Saqizli (r. 1649–72), both also Pasha, who ruled effectively the region. The latter conquered also Cyrenaica.

Lacking direction from the Ottoman government, Tripoli lapsed into a period of military anarchy during which coup followed coup and few deys survived in office more than a year. One such coup was led by Turkish officer Ahmed Karamanli. The Karamanlis ruled from 1711 until 1835 mainly in Tripolitania, but had influence in Cyrenaica and Fezzan as well by the mid-18th century. Ahmad's successors proved to be less capable than himself, however, the region's delicate balance of power allowed the Karamanli. The 1793–95 Tripolitanian civil war occurred in those years. In 1793, Turkish officer Ali Benghul deposed Hamet Karamanli and briefly restored Tripolitania to Ottoman rule. However, Hamet's brother Yusuf (r. 1795–1832) reestablished Tripolitania's independence.

In the early 19th century war broke out between the United States and Tripolitania, and a series of battles ensued in what came to be known as the First Barbary War and the Second Barbary War. By 1819, the various treaties of the Napoleonic Wars had forced the Barbary states to give up piracy almost entirely, and Tripolitania's economy began to crumble. As Yusuf weakened, factions sprung up around his three sons; civil war soon resulted. Ottoman Sultan Mahmud II sent in troops ostensibly to restore order, marking the end of both the Karamanli dynasty and an independent Tripolitania. Order was not recovered easily, and the revolt of the Libyan under Abd-El-Gelil and Gûma ben Khalifa lasted until the death of the latter in 1858. The second period of direct Ottoman rule saw administrative changes, and what seemed as greater order in the governance of the three provinces of Libya.

Italian Libya

After the Italo-Turkish War (1911–1912), Italy simultaneously turned the three regions into colonies. From 1912 to 1927, the territory of Libya was known as Italian North Africa. From 1927 to 1934, the territory was split into two colonies, Italian Cyrenaica and Italian Tripolitania, run by Italian governors. Some 150,000 Italians settled in Libya, constituting roughly 20% of the total population.

In 1934, Italy adopted the name "Libya" (used by the Ancient Greeks for all of North Africa, except Egypt) as the official name of the colony (made up of the three provinces of Cyrenaica, Tripolitania and Fezzan). Omar Mukhtar was the resistance leader against the Italian colonization and became a national hero despite his capture and execution on 16 September 1931. His face is currently printed on the Libyan ten dinar note in memory and recognition of his patriotism. Idris al-Mahdi as-Senussi (later King Idris I), Emir of Cyrenaica, led the Libyan resistance to Italian occupation between the two world wars. Ilan Pappé estimates that between 1928 and 1932 the Italian military "killed half the Bedouin population (directly or through disease and starvation in camps)." Italian historian Emilio Gentile estimates 50,000 deaths resulting from the suppression of resistance.

In June 1940, Italy entered World War II. Libya became the setting for the hard-fought North African Campaign that ultimately ended in defeat for Italy and its German ally in 1943.

From 1943 to 1951, Libya was under Allied occupation. The British military administered the two former Italian Libyan provinces of Tripolitana and Cyrenaïca, while the French administered the province of Fezzan. In 1944, Idris returned from exile in Cairo but declined to resume permanent residence in Cyrenaica until the removal of some aspects of foreign control in 1947. Under the terms of the 1947 peace treaty with the Allies, Italy relinquished all claims to Libya.

Independence, Kingdom of Libya and Libya under Gaddafi

On 24 December 1951, Libya declared its independence as the United Kingdom of Libya, a constitutional and hereditary monarchy under King Idris, Libya's only monarch. The discovery of significant oil reserves in 1959 and the subsequent income from petroleum sales enabled one of the world's poorest nations to establish an extremely wealthy state. Although oil drastically improved the Libyan government's finances, resentment among some factions began to build over the increased concentration of the nation's wealth in the hands of King Idris.

***Figure:** King Idris I led the country into independence in 1951 and became its first head of state*

On 1 September 1969, a small group of military officers led by 27-year-old army officer Muammar Gaddafi staged a coup d'état against King Idris, launching the Al Fateh Revolution. Gaddafi was referred to as the "Brother Leader and Guide of the Revolution" in government statements and the official Libyan press.

On 2 March 1977, Libya officially became the "Great Socialist People's Libyan Arab Jamahiriya". Gaddafi officially passed power to the General People's Committees and henceforth claimed to be no more than a symbolic figurehead. Dissidence against the new system was not tolerated. At around the same time the Jamahiriya was established, Gaddafi authorized the execution of twenty-two officers who had participated in a 1975 attempted military coup, in addition to the execution of several civilians. The new "*jamahiriya*" governance structure he established was officially referred to as "direct democracy", though the government refused to publish election results.

Libya's system of governance during the *Jamahiriya* era was based on Gaddafi's theories outlined in his *The Green Book*, published in 1975. Under the *Jamahiriya* system, political issues for debate were raised at local level around the country, convened by any one of about 2,000 local "people's committees". The committees would then pass their votes to a central general committee formed by elected members, where votes at the local congresses would finally influence the outcomes of national decisions.

In February 1977, Libya started delivering military supplies to Goukouni Oueddei and the People's Armed Forces in Chad. The Chadian–Libyan conflict began in earnest when Libya's support of rebel forces in northern Chad escalated into an invasion. Later that same year, Libya and Egypt fought a four-day border war that came to be known as the Libyan-Egyptian War, both nations agreed to a ceasefire under the mediation of the Algerian president Houari Boumediène. Hundreds of Libyans lost their lives in the war against Tanzania, when Gaddafi tried to save his friend Idi Amin. Gaddafi financed various other groups from anti-nuclear movements to Australian trade unions.

From 1977 onward, per capita income in the country rose to more than US $11,000, the fifth-highest in Africa, while the Human Development Index became the highest in Africa and greater than that of Saudi Arabia. This was achieved without borrowing any foreign loans, keeping Libya debt-free. The Great Manmade River was also built to allow free access to fresh water across large parts of the country. In addition, financial support was provided for university scholarships and employment programs.

Much of the country's income from oil, which soared in the 1970s, was spent on arms purchases and on sponsoring dozens of paramilitaries and terrorist groups around the world. An American airstrike failed to kill Gaddafi in 1986. Libya was finally put under United Nations sanctions after the bombing of a commercial flight killed hundreds of travellers.

A gathering of more than 200 African kings and traditional rulers, meeting on 27 August 2008 in the Libyan town of Benghazi, conferred on Colonel Gaddafi the title "King of Kings of Africa". Sheikh Abdilmajid of Tanzania said traditional rulers were more influential in Africa than their respective governments.

2011 Revolution

After the Arab Spring movements overturned the rulers of Tunisia and Egypt, Libya experienced a full-scale revolt beginning on 17 February 2011. By 20 February, the unrest had spread to Tripoli. On 27 February 2011, the National Transitional Council was established to administer the areas of Libya under rebel control. On 10 March 2011, France became the first state to officially recognise the council as the legitimate representative of the Libyan people.

Pro-Gaddafi forces were able to respond militarily to rebel pushes in Western Libya and launched a counterattack along the coast toward Benghazi, the *de facto* centre of the uprising. The town of Zawiya, 48 kilometres (30 mi) from Tripoli, was bombarded by air force planes and army tanks and seized by Jamahiriya troops, "exercising a level of brutality not yet seen in the conflict."

Organs of the United Nations, including United Nations Secretary General Ban Ki-moon and the United Nations Human Rights Council, condemned the crackdown as violating international law, with the latter body expelling Libya outright in an unprecedented action urged by Libya's own delegation to the UN.

On 17 March 2011 the UN Security Council passed Resolution 1973 with a 10–0 vote and five abstentions including Russia and China. The resolution sanctioned the establishment of a no-fly zone and the use of "all means necessary" to protect civilians within Libya. On 19 March, the first act of NATO allies to secure the no-fly zone by destroying Libyan air defences began when French military jets entered Libyan airspace on a reconnaissance mission heralding attacks on enemy targets. In the weeks that followed, American forces were in the forefront of NATO operations against Libya. More than 8,000 American personnel in warships and aircraft were deployed in the area. At least 3,000 targets were struck in 14,202 strike sorties, 716 of them in Tripoli and 492 in Brega. The American air offencive included flights of B-2 Stealth bombers, each bomber armed with sixteen 2000-pound bombs, flying out of and returning to their base in Missouri on the continental United States. Clearly the support provided by the NATO airforces was pivotal in the ultimate success of the revolution.

By 22 August 2011, rebel fighters had entered Tripoli and occupied Green Square, which they renamed Martyrs' Square in honour of those killed since 17 February 2011. On 20 October 2011 the last heavy fighting of the uprising came to an end in the city of Sirte, where Gadhafi was captured and killed. The defeat of loyalist forces was celebrated on 23 October 2011, three days after the fall of Sirte. At least 30,000 Libyans died in the civil war.

Post-Gaddafi Era

Since the defeat of loyalist forces, Libya has been torn among numerous, rival, armed militias affiliated to regions, cities and tribes, while the central government has been weak and unable to bring its authority over the country. Competing militias have lined up against each other in a political struggle between Islamist politicians and their opponents. On 7 July 2012, Libyans had voted in their first parliamentary elections since the end of the former regime. On 8 August 2012, the National Transitional Council officially handed power to the wholly elected General National Congress, which was tasked with the formation of an interim government and the drafting of a new Libyan Constitution to be approved in a general referendum.

On 25 August 2012, in what Reuters reported to be apparently "the most blatant sectarian attack" since the end of the civil war, unnamed organised assailants bulldozed a Sufi mosque with graves, in broad daylight in the centre of the Libyan capital Tripoli. It was the second such razing of a Sufi site in two days.

On 11 September 2012, the 2012 Benghazi attack occurred, in which Islamic militants were able to successfully attack the American consulate in Benghazi and to kill the American ambassador to Libya, J. Christopher Stevens.

On 7 October 2012, Libya's Prime Minister-elect Mustafa A.G. Abushagur stepped down after failing a second time to win parliamentary approval for a new cabinet. On 14 October 2012, the General National Congress elected former GNC member and human rights lawyer Ali Zeidan as prime minister-designate. Zeidan was sworn in after his cabinet was approved by the GNC. On March 11, after having been ousted by the GNC for his inability to halt a rogue oil shipment, Prime Minister Zeiden stepped down, and was replaced by Prime Minister Abdullah al-Thani. On 25 March 2014, in the face of mounting instability, al-Thani's government briefly explored the possibility of the restoration of the Libyan monarchy.

Operation Dignity: On 16 May 2014 retired Libyan general Khalifa Haftar launched an aerial and ground attack in Benghazi, targeting Islamic militant groups entrenched within the city. This attack was made without any authorization from the central government. Haftar dubbed his anti-Islamist military operation as Operation Dignity. As a part of this operation, on 18 May 2014 in Tripoli, the parliament building was stormed by troops loyal to Haftar, in what some members of the Libyan government described as an attempted coup. Haftar claims to be cleansing Libya of a certain radical militant Islamic terrorist element which he describes as having "infected the country", many allegedly from foreign sources. He has proclaimed the General National Council to be dissolved, and claims to aim for the establishment of a duly elected government without any ties to Islamist militias. *Operation Dignity* has been greeted by various marches and demonstrations of support, attended by thousands of Libyan citizens in Tripoli, Benghazi and in other Libyan cities.

Briefly from May 25 through June 5, Prime Minister Abdullah al-Thani resigned and was nominally replaced by Ahmed Maiteeq. This temporary resignation by al-Thani came shortly after al-Thani's family had been threatened and attacked by gunmen. In hopes of quelling the violence and defusing the widening power struggle and stand-off with

General Haftar, parliamentary elections were held on 25 June 2014. Less than half the eligible voters turned out to vote, reflecting ongoing uncertainties regarding the Libyan political system. Still, many observers were surprised that the elections appeared to have been smoother, less violent, and more transparent than expected. Initial election returns indicated strong gains by secularist and federalist forces. Finalized official elections results are not due for release until mid July. On 26 June 2014, shortly after the elections, Salwa Bughaighis, a human rights lawyer in Benghazi, who was a critic of both Muammar Gaddafi and several of the Islamist militias which overthrew him, was assassinated in her home.

On June 26, the outgoing GNC announced that the new incoming *House of Representatives* would be headquartered in Benghazi. Additionally the *Constitutional Assembly Group*, the group of lawmakers tasked in January to draft a new constitution, is already housed in the eastern Libyan city of Beida, east of Bengazi. The House of Representatives was scheduled to open on 1 August 2014. The move from Tripoli to Benghazi was intended to assure citizens in the East that they were members of the Libyan state of equal importance to those in the West. Obvious security concerns for both legislative groups remain.

On 2 July 2014 Prime Minister Abdullah al-Thani completed negotiations for a settlement agreement with factions still holding oil ports which then remained shuttered due to factional infighting. Al-Thani's brokered agreement reopened the two remaining blockaded major oil ports in the country, thus ending the country's oil crisis. The government however remained weak with rival militias vying for power in many parts of the country. The interim government was contemplating requesting international support to help stabilize the country, which the foreign minister told the UN Security Council was becoming a "failed state." As the security situation deteriorated further, western nations began closing their diplomatic missions and evacuating their citizens. The United States and French embassies closed in late July 2014, while the UK embassy closed in early August 2014. On 12 August 2014 masked gunmen assassinated the Tripoli police chief Colonel Mohammed Sweissi.

Geography

Libya extends over 1,759,540 square kilometres (679,362 sq mi), making it the 17th largest nation in the world by size. Libya is somewhat smaller than Indonesia in land area, and roughly the size of the U.S. state of Alaska. It is bound to the north by the Mediterranean Sea, the west by Tunisia and Algeria, the southwest by Niger, the south by

Chad and Sudan and to the east by Egypt. Libya lies between latitudes 19° and 34°N, and longitudes 9° and 26°E.

At 1,770 kilometres (1,100 mi), Libya's coastline is the longest of any African country bordering the Mediterranean. The portion of the Mediterranean Sea north of Libya is often called the Libyan Sea. The climate is mostly extremely dry and desertlike in nature. However, the northern regions enjoy a milder Mediterranean climate.

Natural hazards come in the form of hot, dry, dust-laden sirocco (known in Libya as the *gibli*). This is a southern wind blowing from one to four days in spring and autumn. There are also dust storms and sandstorms. Oases can also be found scattered throughout Libya, the most important of which are Ghadames and Kufra.. Libya is one of the sunniest and driest countries in the world due to prevailing presence of desert environment.

Libyan Desert

The Libyan Desert, which covers much of Libya, is one of the most arid and sun-baked places on earth. In places, decades may pass without seeing any rainfall at all, and even in the highlands rainfall seldom happens, once every 5–10 years. At Uweinat, as of 2006 the last recorded rainfall was in September 1998. There is a large depression, the Qattara Depression, just south of the northernmost scarp, with Siwa Oasis at its western extremity. The depression continues in a shallower form west, to the oases of Jaghbub and Jalu. Likewise, the temperature in the Libyan Desert can be extreme; on 13 September 1922 the town of 'Aziziya, which is located southwest of Tripoli, recorded an air temperature of 57.8 °C (136.0 °F), considered to be a world record. In September 2012, however, the world record figure of 57.8 °C was overturned by the World Meteorological Organisation.

There are a few scattered uninhabited small oases, usually linked to the major depressions, where water can be found by digging to a few feet in depth. In the west there is a widely dispersed group of oases in unconnected shallow depressions, the Kufra group, consisting of Tazerbo, Rebianae and Kufra. Aside from the scarps, the general flatness is only interrupted by a series of plateaus and massifs near the centre of the Libyan Desert, around the convergence of the Egyptian-Sudanese-Libyan borders.

Slightly further to the south are the massifs of Arkenu, Uweinat and Kissu. These granite mountains are ancient, having formed long before the sandstones surrounding them. Arkenu and Western Uweinat are ring complexes very similar to those in the Aïr Mountains. Eastern

Uweinat (the highest point in the Libyan Desert) is a raised sandstone plateau adjacent to the granite part further west. The plain to the north of Uweinat is dotted with eroded volcanic features. With the discovery of oil in the 1950s also came the discovery of a massive aquifer underneath much of the country. The water in this aquifer pre-dates the last ice ages and the Sahara Desert itself. This area also contains the Arkenu structures, which were once though to be two impact craters.

Government and Politics

The legislature of Libya is the unicameral Council of Deputies in Tobruk.

The former legislature was the General National Congress, which had 200 seats.

On 7 July 2012, Libyans voted in parliamentary elections, the first free elections in almost 40 years. Around thirty women were elected to become members of parliament. Early results of the vote showed the National Forces Alliance, led by former interim Prime Minister Mahmoud Jibril, as front runner. The Justice and Construction Party, affiliated to the Muslim Brotherhood, has done less well than similar parties in Egypt and Tunisia. It won 17 out of 80 seats that were contested by parties, but about 60 independents have since joined its caucus.

As of January 2013, there was mounting public pressure on the National Congress to set up a drafting body to create a new constitution. Congress had not yet decided whether the members of the body would be elected or appointed.

On 30 March 2014 General National Congress voted to replace itself with new Council of Deputies. The new legislature allocates 30 seats for women, will have 200 seats overall (with individuals able to run as members of political parties) and allows Libyans of foreign nationalities to run for office.

Following the 2012 elections, Freedom House improved Libya's rating from Not Free to Partly Free, and now considers the country to be an electoral democracy.

Gaddafi merged civil and sharia courts in 1973. Civil courts now employ sharia judges who sit in regular courts of appeal and specialise in sharia appellate cases. Laws regarding personal status are derived from Islamic law.

Military

The Libyan National Army comprises a ground army, an air force and a navy. It is currently being re-established by the Libyan government, as Libya's previous national army was defeated in the Libyan Civil War and disbanded. As of May 2012, an estimated 35,000 personnel have joined its ranks.

As of November 2012, it was deemed to be still in the embryonic stage of development. President Mohammed el-Megarif promised that empowering the army and police force is the government's biggest priority. President el-Megarif also ordered that all of the country's militias must come under government authority or disband.

Militias have so far refused to be integrated into a central security force. Many of these militias are disciplined, but the most powerful of them answer only to the executive councils of various Libyan cities. These militias make up the so-called Libyan Shield, a parallel national force, which operates at the request, rather than at the order, of the defence ministry.

Foreign Relations

Libya's foreign policies have fluctuated since 1951. As a Kingdom, Libya maintained a definitively pro-Western stance, and was recognised as belonging to the conservative traditionalist bloc in the League of Arab States (the present-day Arab League), of which it became a member in 1953. The government was also friendly towards Western countries such as the United Kingdom, United States, France, Italy, Greece, and established full diplomatic relations with the Soviet Union in 1955. Although the government supported Arab causes, including the Moroccan and Algerian independence movements, it took little active part in the Arab-Israeli dispute or the tumultuous inter-Arab politics of the 1950s and early 1960s. The Kingdom was noted for its close association with the West, while it steered a conservative course at home.

After the 1969 coup, Muammar Gaddafi closed American and British bases and partly nationalized foreign oil and commercial interests in Libya. Gaddafi was known for backing a number of leaders viewed as anathema to Westernization and political liberalism, including Ugandan President Idi Amin, Central African Emperor Jean-Bédel Bokassa, Ethiopian strongman Haile Mariam Mengistu, Liberian President Charles Taylor, and Yugoslav President Slobodan Miloševiæ.

Relations with the West were strained by a series of incidents for most of Gaddafi's rule, including the killing of London policewoman Yvonne Fletcher, the bombing of a West Berlin nightclub frequented by U.S. servicemen, and the bombing of Pan Am Flight 103, which led to UN sanctions in the 1990s, though by the late 2000s, the United States and other Western powers had normalised relations with Libya.

Gaddafi's decision to abandon the pursuit of weapons of mass destruction after the Iraq War saw Iraqi dictator Saddam Hussein overthrown and put on trial led to Libya being hailed as a success for Western soft power initiatives in the War on Terror. In October 2010, Gaddafi apologized to African leaders on behalf of Arab nations for their involvement in the African slave trade.

Libya is included in the European Union's European Neighbourhood Policy (ENP) which aims at bringing the EU and its neighbours closer.

Administrative Divisions

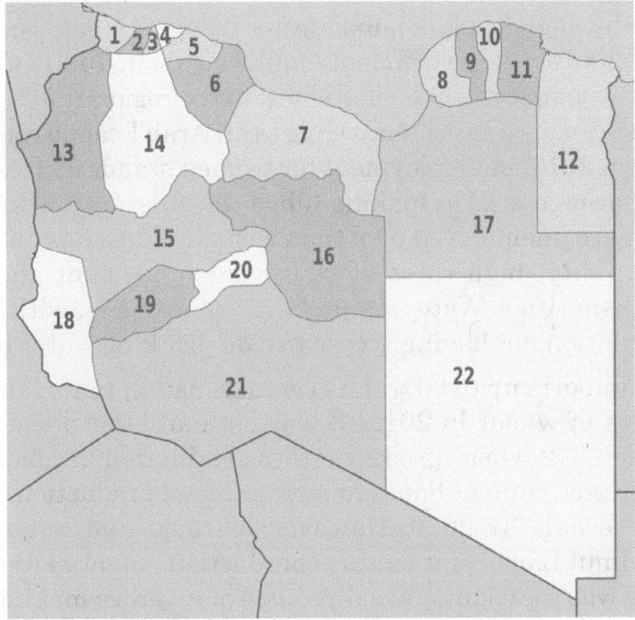

Figure: *Districts of Libya since 2007*

Historically the area of Libya was considered three provinces (or states), Tripolitania in the northwest, Barka (Cyrenaica) in the east, and Fezzan in the southwest. It was the conquest by Italy in the Italo-Turkish War that united them in a single political unit.

Economy

The Libyan economy depends primarily upon revenues from the oil sector, which accounts for 80% of GDP and 97% of exports. Libya holds the largest proven oil reserves in Africa and is an important contributor to the global supply of light, sweet crude. Apart from petroleum, the other natural resources are natural gas and gypsum. The International Monetary Fund estimated Libya's real GDP growth at 122% in 2012 and 16.7% in 2013, after a 60% plunge in 2011.

The World Bank defines Libya as an 'Upper Middle Income Economy', along with only seven other African countries. Substantial revenues from the energy sector, coupled with a small population, give Libya one of the highest per capita GDPs in Africa. This allowed the Libyan Arab Jamahiriya state to provide an extensive level of social security, particularly in the fields of housing and education.

Libya faces many structural problems including a lack of institutions, weak governance, and chronic structural unemployment. The economy displays a lack of economic diversification and significant reliance on immigrant labour. Libya has traditionally relied on unsustainably high levels of public sector hiring to create employment. In the mid-2000s, the government employed about 70% of all national employees. Unemployment is the highest in the region at 21%, according to the latest census figures. According to an Arab League report, based on data from 2010, unemployment for women stands at 18% while for the figure for men is 21%, making Libya the only Arab country where there are more unemployed men than women. Libya has high levels of social inequality, high rates of youth unemployment and regional economic disparities. Water supply is also a problem, with some 28% of the population not having access to safe drinking water in 2000.

Libya imports up to 90% of its cereal consumption requirements, and imports of wheat in 2012/13 was estimated at about 1 million tonnes. The 2012 wheat production was estimated at about 200,000 tonnes. The government hopes to increase food production to 800,000 tonnes of cereals by 2020. However, natural and environmental conditions limit Libya's agricultural production potential. Before 1958, agriculture was the country's main source of revenue, making up about 30% of GDP. With the discovery of oil in 1958, the size of the agriculture sector declined rapidly, comprising less than 5% GDP by 2005.

The country joined OPEC in 1962. Libya is not a WTO member, but negotiations for its accession started in 2004.

In the early 1980s, Libya was one of the wealthiest countries in the world; its GDP per capita was higher than some developed countries.

In the early 2000s officials of the Jamahiriya era carried out economic reforms to reintegrate Libya into the global economy. UN sanctions were lifted in September 2003, and Libya announced in December 2003 that it would abandon programs to build weapons of mass destruction. Other steps have included applying for membership of the World Trade Organisation, reducing subsidies, and announcing plans for privatization. Authorities privatized more than 100 government owned companies after

2003 in industries including oil refining, tourism and real estate, of which 29 were 100% foreign owned. Many international oil companies returned to the country, including oil giants Shell and ExxonMobil. After sanctions were lifted there was a gradual increase of air traffic, and by 2005 there were 1.5 million yearly air travellers. Libya had long been a notoriously difficult country for Western tourists to visit due to stringent visa requirements.

In 2007 Saif al-Islam Gaddafi, the second-eldest son of Muammar Gaddafi, was involved in a green development project called the Green Mountain Sustainable Development Area, which sought to bring tourism to Cyrene and to preserve Greek ruins in the area.

In August 2011 it was estimated that it would take at least 10 years to rebuild Libya's infrastructure. Even before the 2011 war, Libya's infrastructure was in a poor state due to "utter neglect" by Gaddafi's administration, according to the NTC. By October 2012, the economy had recovered from the 2011 conflict, with oil production returning to near normal levels. Oil production was more than 1.6 million barrels per day before the war. By October 2012, the average oil production has surpassed 1.4 million bpd. The resumption of production was made possible due to the quick return of major Western companies, like Total, Eni, Repsol, Wintershall and Occidental.

Demographics

Libya is a large country with a relatively small population, but the population is concentrated very narrowly along the coast. Population density is about 50 persons per km² (130/sq. mi.) in the two northern regions of Tripolitania and Cyrenaica, but falls to less than one person per km² (2.6/sq. mi.) elsewhere. Ninety percent of the people live in less than 10% of the area, primarily along the coast. About 88% of the population is urban, mostly concentrated in the three largest cities, Tripoli, Benghazi and Misrata. Libya has a population of about 6.5 million, 27.7% of whom are under the age of 15. In 1984 the population was 3.6 million, an increase from the 1.54 million reported in 1964.

There are about 140 tribes and clans in Libya. Family life is important for Libyan families, the majority of which live in apartment blocks and other independent housing units, with precise modes of housing depending on their income and wealth. Although the Libyan Arabs traditionally lived nomadic lifestyles in tents, they have now settled in various towns and cities. Because of this, their old ways of life are gradually fading out. An unknown small number of Libyans still live in the desert as their families have done for centuries. Most of the population has occupations in industry and services, and a small percentage is in agriculture.

According to the *World Refugee Survey 2008*, published by the U.S. Committee for Refugees and Immigrants, Libya hosted a population of refugees and asylum seekers numbering approximately 16,000 in 2007. Of this group, approximately 9,000 persons were from Palestine, 3,200 from Sudan, 2,500 from Somalia and 1,100 from Iraq. Libya reportedly deported thousands of illegal entrants in 2007 without giving them the opportunity to apply for asylum. Refugees faced discrimination from Libyan officials when moving in the country and seeking employment.

Ethnic Groups

The original inhabitants of Libya belonged predominantly to various Berber ethnic groups; however, the long series of foreign invasions – particularly by Arabs and Turks – have had a profound and lasting influence on Libya's demographics. Today, Libyans are primarily Arabs, and some are a mixture of Arab and Berber ethnicities, or a mixture of Arab and Turkish ethnicities. The Turkish minority are often called "Kouloughlis" and are concentrated in and around villages and towns. Other ethnic minorities include Libyan blacks, the Tuaregs, and the Tebou.

Among foreign residents, the largest groups are citizens of other African nations – including North Africans (primarily Egyptians) – and Sub-Saharan Africans. In 2011, there were also an estimated 60,000 Bangladeshis, 30,000 Chinese and 30,000 Filipinos in Libya. Libya is home to a large illegal population which numbers more than one million, mostly Egyptians and Sub-Saharan Africans. Libya has a small Italian minority. Previously, there was a visible presence of Italian settlers, but many left after independence in 1947 and many more left in 1970 after the accession of Muammar Gaddafi.

Languages

The main language spoken in Libya is Arabic (the Libyan dialect), and Modern Standard Arabic is also the official language. Italian and English are sometimes spoken in the big cities, although Italian speakers are mainly among the older generation.

Religion

About 97% of the population in Libya are Muslims, most of whom belong to the Sunni branch. Small numbers of Ibadi Muslims, Sufis and Ahmadis also live in the country.

Before the 1930s, the Senussi Movement was the primary Islamic movement in Libya. This was a religious revival adapted to desert life. Its *zawaaya* (lodges) were found in Tripolitania and Fezzan, but Senussi influence was strongest in Cyrenaica. Rescuing the region from unrest and anarchy, the Senussi movement gave the Cyrenaican tribal people a religious attachment and feelings of unity and purpose. This Islamic movement, which was eventually destroyed by both Italian invasion and later the Gaddafi government, was very conservative and somewhat different from the Islam that exists in Libya today. Gaddafi asserted that he was a devout Muslim, and his government was taking a role in supporting Islamic institutions and in worldwide proselytising on behalf of Islam.

There are small foreign communities of Christians. Coptic Orthodox Christianity, which is the Christian Church of Egypt, is the largest and most historical Christian denomination in Libya. There are about 60,000 Egyptian Copts in Libya. Most Copts in Libya are Egyptian with a small minority of them native Libyans who remained Christian after Islam came to Libya from Egypt. There are three Coptic Churches in Libya, one in Tripoli, one in Benghazi, and one in Misurata. The Coptic Church has grown in recent years in Libya as a small number of Libyans have converted to Christianity and the growing immigration of Egyptian Copts to Libya. There are an estimated 40,000 Roman Catholics in Libya who are served by two Bishops, one in Tripoli (serving the Italian community) and one in Benghazi (serving the Maltese community). There is also a small Anglican community, made up mostly of African immigrant workers in Tripoli; it is part of the Anglican Diocese of Egypt. People have been arrested on suspicion of being Christian missionaries, as proselytising is illegal.

Libya was once the home of one of the oldest Jewish communities in the world, dating back to at least 300 BC. In 1942, the Italian Fascist authorities set up forced labour camps south of Tripoli for the Jews, including Giado (about 3,000 Jews) and Gharyan, Jeren, and Tigrinna. In Giado some 500 Jews died of weakness, hunger, and disease. In 1942, Jews who were not in the concentration camps were heavily restricted in their economic activity and all men between 18 and 45 years were drafted for forced labour. In August 1942, Jews from Tripolitania were interned in a concentration camp at Sidi Azaz. In the three years after November 1945, more than 140 Jews were murdered, and hundreds more wounded, in a series of pogroms. By 1948, about 38,000 Jews remained in the country. Upon Libya's independence in 1951, most of the Jewish community emigrated.

Chapter 3

Islamic Countries in South-East

Indonesia

Indonesia, officially the Republic of Indonesia, is a sovereign state in Southeast Asia and Oceania. Indonesia is an archipelago comprising thousands of islands. It encompasses 33 provinces and 1 Special Administrative Region (for being governed by a pre-colonial monarchy) with an estimated population of over 252 million people, making it the world's fourth most populous country. Indonesia's republican form of government comprises an elected legislature and president. The nation's capital city is Jakarta. The country shares land borders with Papua New Guinea, East Timor, and Malaysia. Other neighbouring countries include Singapore, the Philippines, Australia, Palau, and the Indian territory of the Andaman and Nicobar Islands. Indonesia is a founding member of ASEAN and a member of the G-20 major economies. The Indonesian economy is the world's 17th largest by nominal GDP.

The Indonesian archipelago has been an important trade region since at least the 7th century, when Srivijaya and then later Majapahit traded with China and India. Local rulers gradually absorbed foreign cultural, religious and political models from the early centuries CE, and Hindu and Buddhist kingdoms flourished. Indonesian history has been influenced by foreign powers drawn to its natural resources. Muslim traders brought the now-dominant Islam, while European powers brought Christianity and fought one another to monopolize trade in the Spice Islands of Maluku during the Age of Discovery. Following three and a half centuries of Dutch colonialism, Indonesia secured its independence after World War II. Indonesia's history has since been turbulent, with challenges posed by natural disasters, mass slaughter, corruption, separatism, a democratization process, and periods of rapid economic change.

Indonesia consists of hundreds of distinct native ethnic and linguistic groups. The largest – and politically dominant – ethnic group are the Javanese. A shared identity has developed, defined by a national language, ethnic diversity, religious pluralism within a majority Muslim population, and a history of colonialism and rebellion against it. Indonesia's national motto, *"Bhinneka Tunggal Ika"* ("Unity in Diversity" *literally,* "many, yet one"), articulates the diversity that shapes the country. Despite its large population and densely populated regions, Indonesia has vast areas of wilderness that support the world's second highest level of biodiversity. The country has abundant natural resources, yet poverty remains widespread.

History

Fossils and the remains of tools show that the Indonesian archipelago was inhabited by *Homo erectus*, popularly known as "Java Man", between 1.5 million years ago and as recently as 35,000 years ago. *Homo sapiens* reached the region by around 45,000 years ago. In 2011 evidence was uncovered in neighbouring East Timor showing that 42,000 years ago these early settlers were catching and consuming large numbers of big deep sea fish such as tuna, and that they had the technology needed to make ocean crossings to reach Australia and other islands.

Austronesian peoples, who form the majority of the modern population, migrated to South East Asia from Taiwan. They arrived in Indonesia around 2000 BCE, and as they spread through the archipelago, pushed the indigenous Melanesian peoples to the far eastern regions. Ideal agricultural conditions, and the mastering of wet-field rice cultivation as early as the 8th century BCE, allowed villages, towns, and small kingdoms to flourish by the 1st century CE. Indonesia's strategic sea-lane position fostered inter-island and international trade, including links with Indian kingdoms and China, which were established several centuries BCE. Trade has since fundamentally shaped Indonesian history.

Hinduism and Mahayana Buddhism arrived in Indonesia in the 4th and 5th century, as trade with India intensified under the south Indian Pallava dynasty.

From the 7th century, the powerful Srivijaya naval kingdom flourished as a result of trade and the influences of Hinduism and Buddhism that were imported with it. Between the 8th and 10th centuries, the agricultural Buddhist Sailendra and Hindu Mataram dynasties thrived and declined in inland Java, leaving grand religious monuments such as Sailendra's Borobudur and Mataram's Prambanan. The Hindu Majapahit kingdom was founded in eastern Java in the late 13th century, and under Gajah Mada, its influence stretched over much of Indonesia.

Although Muslim traders first travelled through Southeast Asia early in the Islamic era, the earliest evidence of Islamized populations in Indonesia dates to the 13th century in northern Sumatra. Other Indonesian areas gradually adopted Islam, and it was the dominant religion in Java and Sumatra by the end of the 16th century. For the most part, Islam overlaid and mixed with existing cultural and religious influences, which shaped the predominant form of Islam in Indonesia, particularly in Java. The first regular contact between Europeans and the peoples of Indonesia began in 1512, when Portuguese traders, led by Francisco Serrão, sought to monopolize the sources of nutmeg, cloves, and cubeb pepper in Maluku. Dutch and British traders followed. In 1602 the Dutch established the Dutch East India Company (VOC) and became the dominant European power. Following bankruptcy, the VOC was formally dissolved in 1800, and the government of the Netherlands established the Dutch East Indies as a nationalized colony.

For most of the colonial period, Dutch control over the archipelago was tenuous outside of coastal strongholds; only in the early 20th century did Dutch dominance extend to what was to become Indonesia's present boundaries. Japanese occupation during the Second World War ended Dutch rule and encouraged the previously suppressed Indonesian independence movement. A later UN report stated that four million people died in Indonesia as a result of the Japanese occupation. Two days after the surrender of Japan in August 1945, Sukarno, an influential nationalist leader, declared independence and was appointed President. The Netherlands tried to reestablish their rule, and the resulting conflict ended in December 1949, when in the face of international pressure, the Dutch formally recognised Indonesian independence with the exception of the Dutch territory of West New Guinea, which was incorporated into Indonesia following the 1962 New York Agreement, and the UN-mandated Act of Free Choice of 1969 which was questionable and has resulted in a longtime independence movement.

Sukarno moved Indonesia from democracy towards authoritarianism, and maintained his power base by balancing the opposing forces of the military and the Communist Party of Indonesia (PKI). An attempted coup on 30 September 1965 was countered by the army, who led a violent anti-communist purge, during which the PKI was blamed for the coup and effectively destroyed. Around 500,000 people are estimated to have been killed. The head of the military, General Suharto, outmaneuvered the politically weakened Sukarno and was formally appointed president in March 1968. His New Order administration was supported by the US government, and encouraged foreign direct investment in Indonesia, which was a major factor in the subsequent three decades of substantial economic growth. However, the authoritarian "New Order" was widely accused of corruption and suppression of political opposition.

Figure: *Sukarno, Indonesia's founding President.*

Indonesia was the country hardest hit by the late 1990s Asian financial crisis. This led to popular protest against the New Order which led to Suharto's resignation in May 1998. In 1999, East Timor voted to secede from Indonesia, after a twenty-five-year military occupation that was marked by international condemnation of repression of the East Timorese. Since Suharto's resignation, a strengthening of democratic processes has included a regional autonomy program, and the first direct presidential election in 2004. Political and economic instability, social unrest, corruption, and terrorism slowed progress; however, in the last five years the economy has performed strongly. Although relations among different religious and ethnic groups are largely harmonious, sectarian discontent and violence have persisted. A political settlement to an armed separatist conflict in Aceh was achieved in 2005.

Government and Politics

Indonesia is a republic with a presidential system. As a unitary state, power is concentrated in the central government. Following the resignation of President Suharto in 1998, Indonesian political and governmental structures have undergone major reforms. Four amendments to the 1945 Constitution of Indonesia have revamped the executive, judicial, and legislative branches. The president of Indonesia is the head of state and head of government, commander-in-chief of the Indonesian National Armed Forces, and the director of domestic governance, policy-making, and foreign affairs. The president appoints a council of ministers, who are not required to be elected members of the legislature. The 2004 presidential election was the first in which the people directly elected the president and vice president. The president may serve a maximum of two consecutive five-year terms.

The highest representative body at national level is the People's Consultative Assembly (MPR). Its main functions are supporting and amending the constitution, inaugurating the president, and formalizing broad outlines of state policy. It has the power to impeach the president. The MPR comprises two houses; the People's Representative Council (DPR), with 560 members, and the Regional Representative Council (DPD), with 132 members. The DPR passes legislation and monitors the executive branch; party-aligned members are elected for five-year terms by proportional representation. Reforms since 1998 have markedly increased the DPR's role in national governance. The DPD is a new chamber for matters of regional management.

Most civil disputes appear before a State Court (Pengadilan Negeri); appeals are heard before the High Court (Pengadilan Tinggi). The Supreme Court (Mahkamah Agung) is the country's highest court, and hears final cessation appeals and conducts case reviews. Other courts include the Commercial Court, which handles bankruptcy and insolvency; a State Administrative Court (Pengadilan Tata Negara) to hear administrative law cases against the government; a Constitutional Court (Mahkamah Konstitusi) to hear disputes concerning legality of law, general elections, dissolution of political parties, and the scope of authority of state institutions; and a Religious Court (Pengadilan Agama) to deal with codified Sharia Law cases.

Foreign Relations and Military

In contrast to Sukarno's anti-imperialistic antipathy to western powers and tensions with Malaysia, Indonesia's foreign relations since the Suharto "New Order" have been based on economic and political cooperation with Western nations. Indonesia maintains close relationships with its neighbours in Asia, and is a founding member of ASEAN and the East Asia Summit. The nation restored relations with the People's Republic of China in 1990 following a freeze in place since anti-communist purges early in the Suharto era. Indonesia has been a member of the United Nations since 1950, and was a founder of the Non-Aligned Movement (NAM) and the Organisation of the Islamic Conference (OIC, now the Organisation of Islamic Cooperation). Indonesia is signatory to the ASEAN Free Trade Area agreement, the Cairns Group, and the WTO, and has historically been a member of OPEC, although it withdrew in 2008 as it was no longer a net exporter of oil. Indonesia has received humanitarian and development aid since 1966, in particular from the United States, western Europe, Australia, and Japan.

The Indonesian Government has worked with other countries to apprehend and prosecute perpetrators of major bombings linked to militant Islamism and Al-Qaeda. The deadliest bombing killed 202 people (including 164 international tourists) in the Bali resort town of Kuta in 2002. The attacks, and subsequent travel warnings issued by other countries, severely damaged Indonesia's tourism industry and foreign investment prospects.

Indonesia's armed forces (TNI) include the Army (TNI–AD), Navy (TNI–AL, which includes marines), and Air Force (TNI–AU). The army has about 400,000 active-duty personnel. Defence spending in the national budget was 4% of GDP in 2006, and is controversially supplemented by revenue from military commercial interests and foundations. One of the reforms following the 1998 resignation of Suharto was the removal of formal TNI representation in parliament; nevertheless, its political influence remains extensive.

Separatist movements in the provinces of Aceh and Papua have led to armed conflict, and subsequent allegations of human rights abuses and brutality from all sides. Following a sporadic thirty-year guerrilla war between the Free Aceh Movement (GAM) and the Indonesian military, a ceasefire agreement was reached in 2005. In Papua, there has been a significant, albeit imperfect, implementation of regional autonomy laws, and a reported decline in the levels of violence and human rights abuses, since the presidency of Susilo Bambang Yudhoyono.

Administrative Divisions

Administratively, Indonesia consists of 34 provinces, five of which have special status. Each province has its own legislature and governor.

The provinces are subdivided into regencies (*kabupaten*) and cities (*kota*), which are further subdivided into districts (*kecamatan* or *distrik* in Papua and West Papua), and again into administrative villages (either *desa, kelurahan, kampung, nagari* in West Sumatra, or *gampong* in Aceh). Village is the lowest level of government administration in Indonesia. Furthermore, a village is divided into several community groups (Rukun-Warga (RW)) which are further divided into neighbourhood groups (Rukun-Tetangga (RT)). In Java the *desa* (village) is divided further into smaller units called *dusun* or *dukuh* (hamlets), these units are the same as Rukun-Warga. Following the implementation of regional autonomy measures in 2001, the regencies and cities have become the key administrative units, responsible for providing most government services. The village administration level is the most influential on a citizen's daily life and handles matters of a village or neighbourhood through an elected *lurah* or *kepala desa* (village chief).

The provinces of Aceh, Jakarta, Yogyakarta, Papua, and West Papua have greater legislative privileges and a higher degree of autonomy from the central government than the other provinces. The Acehnese government, for example, has the right to create certain elements of an independent legal system; in 2003, it instituted a form of *Sharia Law* (Islamic law). Yogyakarta was granted the status of Special Region in recognition of its pivotal role in supporting Indonesian Republicans during the Indonesian Revolution and its willingness to join Indonesia as a republic. Papua, formerly known as Irian Jaya, was granted special autonomy status in 2001 and was split into Papua and West Papua in February 2003. Jakarta is the country's special capital region.

Economy

Indonesia has a mixed economy in which both the private sector and government play significant roles. The country is the largest economy in Southeast Asia and a member of the G-20 major economies. Indonesia's estimated gross domestic product (nominal), as of 2012 was US$928.274 billion with estimated nominal per capita GDP was US$3,797, and per capita GDP PPP was US$4,943 (international dollars). The gross domestic product (GDP) is about $1 trillion and the debt ratio to the GDP is 26%. According to World Bank affiliated report based on 2011 data, the Indonesian economy was the world's 10th largest by nominal GDP (PPP based), with the country contributing 2.3 percent of global economic output. The industry sector is the economy's largest and accounts for 46.4% of GDP (2012), this is followed by services (38.6%) and agriculture (14.4%). However, since 2012, the service sector has employed more people than other sectors, accounting for 48.9% of the total labour force, this has been followed by agriculture (38.6%) and industry (22.2%). Agriculture, however, had been the country's largest employer for centuries.

According to World Trade Organisation data, Indonesia was the 27th biggest exporting country in the world in 2010, moving up three places from a year before. Indonesia's main export markets (2009) are Japan (17.28%), Singapore (11.29%), the United States (10.81%), and China (7.62%). The major suppliers of imports to Indonesia are Singapore (24.96%), China (12.52%), and Japan (8.92%). In 2005, Indonesia ran a trade surplus with export revenues of US$83.64 billion and import expenditure of US$62.02 billion. The country has extensive natural resources, including crude oil, natural gas, tin, copper, and gold. Indonesia's major imports include machinery and equipment, chemicals, fuels, and foodstuffs. And the country's major export commodities include oil and gas, electrical appliances, plywood, rubber, and textiles.

The tourism sector contributes to around US$9 billion of foreign exchange in 2012, and ranked as the 4th largest among goods and services export sectors. Singapore, Malaysia, Australia, China and Japan are the top five source of visitors to Indonesia.

In the 1960s the economy deteriorated drastically as a result of political instability, a young and inexperienced government, and economic nationalism, which resulted in severe poverty and hunger. By the time of Sukarno's downfall in the mid-1960s, the economy was in chaos with 1,000% annual inflation, shrinking export revenues, crumbling infrastructure, factories operating at minimal capacity, and negligible investment. Following President Sukarno's downfall in the mid-1960s, the New Order administration brought a degree of discipline to economic policy that quickly brought inflation down, stabilized the currency, rescheduled foreign debt, and attracted foreign aid and investment. Indonesia was until recently Southeast Asia's only member of OPEC, and the 1970s oil price raises provided an export revenue windfall that contributed to sustained high economic growth rates, averaging over 7% from 1968 to 1981. Following further reforms in the late 1980s, foreign investment flowed into Indonesia, particularly into the rapidly developing export-oriented manufacturing sector, and from 1989 to 1997, the Indonesian economy grew by an average of over 7%.

Indonesia was the country hardest hit by the Asian financial crisis of 1997–98. During the crisis there were sudden and large capital outflows leading the rupiah to go into free fall. Against the US dollar the rupiah dropped from about Rp 2,600 in late 1997 to a low point of around Rp 17,000 some months later and the economy shrank by a remarkable 13.7%. These developments led to widespread economic distress across the economy and contributed to the political crisis of 1998 which saw Suharto resign as president. The rupiah later stabilised in the Rp. 8,000 range and economic growth returned to 4% per year by 2000. However, the currency still fluctuates, dropping below Rp 11,000 per dollar in September 2013. In addition, corruption has been a persistent problem. Transparency International, for example, has since ranked Indonesia below 100 in its Corruption Perceptions Index. Since 2007, however, with the improvement in banking sector and domestic consumption, national economic growth has accelerated to over 6% annually and this helped the country weather the 2008–2009 global recession. The Indonesian economy performed strongly during the Global Financial Crisis and in 2012 its GDP grew by over 6%. The country regained its investment grade rating in late 2011 after losing it in the 1997. However, as of 2012, an estimated 11.7% of the population lived below the poverty line and the official open unemployment rate was 6.1%.

Demographics

According to the 2010 national census, the population of Indonesia is 237.6 million, with high population growth at 1.9%. 58% of the population lives in Java, the world's most populous island. In 1961 the first post-colonial census gave a total population of 97 million. Population is expected to grow to around 269 million by 2020 and 321 million by 2050.

There are around 300 distinct native ethnic groups in Indonesia, and 742 different languages and dialects. Most Indonesians are descended from Austronesian-speaking peoples whose languages can be traced to Proto-Austronesian (PAn), which possibly originated in Taiwan. Another major grouping are Melanesians, who inhabit eastern Indonesia. The largest ethnic group is the Javanese, who comprise 42% of the population, and are politically and culturally dominant. The Sundanese, ethnic Malays, and Madurese are the largest non-Javanese groups. A sense of Indonesian nationhood exists alongside strong regional identities. Social, religious and ethnic tensions have triggered horrendous violence. Chinese Indonesians are an influential ethnic minority comprising 3–4% of the population. Much of the country's privately owned commerce and wealth is Chinese-Indonesian-controlled. Chinese businesses in Indonesia are part of the larger bamboo network, a network of overseas Chinese businesses operating in the markets of Southeast Asia that share common family and cultural ties. This has contributed to considerable resentment, and even anti-Chinese violence.

The official national language is Indonesian, a form of Malay. It is based on the prestige dialect of Malay, that of the Johor-Riau Sultanate, which for centuries had been the lingua franca of the archipelago, standards of which are the official languages in Singapore, Malaysia and Brunei. Indonesian is universally taught in schools, consequently it is spoken by nearly every Indonesian. It is the language of business, politics, national media, education, and academia. It was promoted by Indonesian nationalists in the 1920s, and declared the official language under the name *Bahasa Indonesia* on the proclamation of independence in 1945. Most Indonesians speak at least one of the several hundred local languages and dialects, often as their first language. Of these, Javanese is the most widely spoken as the language of the largest ethnic group. On the other hand, Papua has over 270 indigenous Papuan and Austronesian languages, in a region of about 2.7 million people.

While religious freedom is stipulated in the Indonesian constitution, the government officially recognises only six religions: Islam, Protestantism, Roman Catholicism, Hinduism, Buddhism, and Confucianism. Indonesia is the world's most populous Muslim-majority nation, at 87.2% in 2010, with the majority being Sunni (99%). The Shias and Ahmadis respectively constitute 0.5% and 0.2% of the Muslim population. On 21 May 2011 the Indonesian Sunni-Shia Council (MUHSIN) was established. The council aims to hold gatherings, dialogues and social activities. It was an answer to violence committed in the name of religion. Seven percent of the population was Christian, 1.7% Hindu, and 0.9% Buddhist or other. Most Indonesian Hindus are Balinese, and most Buddhists in modern-day Indonesia are ethnic Chinese. Though now minority religions, Hinduism and Buddhism remain defining influences in Indonesian culture. Islam was first adopted by Indonesians in northern Sumatra in the 13th century, through the influence of traders, and became the country's dominant religion by the 16th century. Roman Catholicism was brought to Indonesia by early Portuguese colonialists and missionaries, and the Protestant denominations are largely a result of Dutch Calvinist and Lutheran missionary efforts during the country's colonial period. A large proportion of Indonesians—such as the Javanese *abangan*, Balinese Hindus, and Dayak Christians—practice a less orthodox, syncretic form of their religion, which draws on local customs and beliefs.

Education in Indonesia is compulsory for twelve years. Parents can choose between state-run, non sectarian public schools supervised by the Department of National Education (Depdiknas) or private or semi-private religious (usually Islamic) schools supervised and financed by the Department of Religious Affairs. The enrolment rate is 94% for primary education (2011), 75% for secondary education, and 27% for tertiary education. The literacy rate is 93% (2011).

Malaysia

Malaysia is a federal constitutional monarchy located in Southeast Asia. It consists of thirteen states and three federal territories and has a total landmass of 329,847 square kilometres (127,350 sq mi) separated by the South China Sea into two similarly sized regions, Peninsular Malaysia and East Malaysia (Malaysian Borneo). Peninsular Malaysia shares a land and maritime border with Thailand and maritime borders with Singapore, Vietnam, and Indonesia. East Malaysia shares land and maritime borders with Brunei and Indonesia and a maritime border with the Philippines. The capital city is Kuala Lumpur, while Putrajaya is the seat of the federal government. In 2010 the population was 28.33 million, with 22.6 million living in Peninsular Malaysia. The southernmost point of continental Eurasia, Tanjung Piai, is in Malaysia, located in the tropics. It is one of 17 megadiverse countries on earth, with large numbers of endemic species.

Malaysia has its origins in the Malay Kingdoms present in the area which, from the 18th century, became subject to the British Empire. The first British territories were known as the Straits Settlements, whose establishment was followed by the Malay kingdoms becoming British protectorates. The territories on Peninsular Malaysia were first unified as the Malayan Union in 1946. Malaya was restructured as the Federation of Malaya in 1948, and achieved independence on 31 August 1957. Malaya united with North Borneo, Sarawak, and Singapore on 16 September 1963, with *si* being added to give the new country the name Malaysia. Less than two years later in 1965, Singapore was expelled from the federation.

The country is multi-ethnic and multi-cultural, which plays a large role in politics. The constitution declares Islam the state religion while protecting freedom of religion. The government system is closely modelled on the Westminster parliamentary system and the legal system is based on common law. The head of state is the king, known as the Yang di-Pertuan Agong. He is an elected monarch chosen from the hereditary rulers of the nine Malay states every five years. The head of government is the Prime Minister.

Since independence, Malaysia has had one of the best economic records in Asia, with GDP growing at an average 6.5% per annum for almost 50 years. The economy has traditionally been fuelled by its natural resources, but is expanding in the sectors of science, tourism, commerce and medical tourism. Today, Malaysia has a newly industrialised market economy, ranked third largest in Southeast Asia and 29th largest in the world. It is a founding member of the Association of Southeast Asian Nations, the East Asia Summit and the Organisation of Islamic Cooperation, and a member of Asia-Pacific Economic Cooperation, the Commonwealth of Nations, and the Non-Aligned Movement.

History

Evidence of modern human habitation in Malaysia dates back 40,000 years. In the Malay Peninsular, the first inhabitants are thought to be Negritos. Traders and settlers from India and China arrived as early as the 1st century AD, establishing trading ports and coastal towns in the 2nd and 3rd centuries. Their presence resulted in strong Indian and Chinese influence on the local cultures, and the people of the Malay Peninsula adopted the religions of Hinduism and Buddhism. Sanskrit inscriptions appear as early as the 4th or 5th century. The Kingdom of Langkasuka arose around the 2nd century in the northern area of the Malay Peninsula, lasting until about the 15th century. Between the 7th and 13th centuries, much of the southern Malay Peninsula was part of the maritime Srivijaya empire. After the fall of Srivijaya, the Majapahit empire had influence over most of Peninsular Malaysia and the Malay Archipelago. Islam began to spread among Malays in the 14th century. In the early 15th century, Parameswara, a prince of the former Srivijayan empire, founded the Malacca Sultanate, commonly considered the first independent state in the peninsula area. Malacca was an important commercial centre during this time, attracting trade from around the region.

In 1511, Malacca was conquered by Portugal, after which it was taken by the Dutch in 1641. In 1786, the British Empire established a presence in Malaya, when the Sultan of Kedah leased Penang to the British East India Company. The British obtained the town of Singapore in 1819, and in 1824 took control of Malacca following the Anglo-Dutch Treaty. By 1826, the British directly controlled Penang, Malacca, Singapore, and the island of Labuan, which they established as the crown colony of the Straits Settlements. By the 20th century, the states of Pahang, Selangor, Perak, and Negeri Sembilan, known together as the Federated Malay States, had British Residents appointed to advise the Malay rulers, to whom the rulers were bound to defer by treaty.

The remaining five states in the peninsula, known as the Unfederated Malay States, while not directly under British rule, also accepted British advisers around the turn of the 20th century. Development on the Peninsula and Borneo were generally separate until the 19th century. Under British rule the immigration of Chinese and Indians to serve as labourers was encouraged. The area that is now Sabah came under British control as North Borneo when both the Sultan of Brunei and the Sultan of Sulu transferred their respective territorial rights of ownership, between 1877 and 1878. In 1842, Sarawak was ceded by the Sultan of Brunei to James Brooke, whose successors ruled as the White Rajahs over an independent kingdom until 1946, when it became a Crown colony.

In the Second World War the Japanese army invaded and occupied Malaya, North Borneo, Sarawak, and Singapore for over three years. During this time, ethnic tensions were raised and nationalism grew. Popular support for independence increased after Malaya was reconquered by Allied Forces. Post-war British plans to unite the administration of Malaya under a single crown colony called the Malayan Union met with strong opposition from the Malays, who opposed the weakening of the Malay rulers and the granting of citizenship to the ethnic Chinese. The Malayan Union, established in 1946 and consisting of all the British possessions in the Malay Peninsula with the exception of Singapore, was quickly dissolved and replaced by the Federation of Malaya, which restored the autonomy of the rulers of the Malay states under British protection. During this time, mostly Chinese rebels under the leadership of the Malayan Communist Party launched guerrilla operations designed to force the British out of Malaya. The Malayan Emergency lasted from 1948 to 1960, and involved a long anti-insurgency campaign by Commonwealth troops in Malaya. After this a plan was put in place to federate Malaya with the crown colonies of North Borneo (which joined as Sabah), Sarawak, and Singapore. The proposed date of federation was 31 August 1963, however, the date was delayed until 16 September 1963 due to opposition from Indonesia's Sukarno and the Sarawak United Peoples' Party.

Federation brought heightened tensions including a conflict with Indonesia, Singapore's eventual exit in 1965, and racial strife. This strife culminated in the 13 May race riots in 1969. After the riots, the controversial New Economic Policy was launched by Prime Minister Tun Abdul Razak, trying to increase the share of the economy held by the *bumiputera*. Under Prime Minister Mahathir Mohamad there was a period of rapid economic growth and urbanisation beginning in the

1980s. The economy shifted from being agriculturally based to one based on manufacturing and industry. Numerous mega-projects were completed, such as the Petronas Towers, the North-South Expressway, the Multimedia Super Corridor, and the new federal administrative capital of Putrajaya. However, in the late 1990s the Asian financial crisis almost caused the collapse of the currency and the stock and property markets.

Government and Politics

Malaysia is a federal constitutional elective monarchy. The system of government is closely modelled on that of the Westminster parliamentary system, a legacy of British colonial rule. The head of state is the Yang di-Pertuan Agong, commonly referred to as the King. The King is elected to a five-year term by and from among the nine hereditary rulers of the Malay states; the other four states, which have titular Governors, do not participate in the selection. By informal agreement the position is systematically rotated among the nine, and has been held by Abdul Halim of Kedah since December 2011. The King's role has been largely ceremonial since changes to the constitution in 1994, picking ministers and members of the upper house.

Legislative power is divided between federal and state legislatures. The bicameral federal parliament consists of the lower house, the House of Representatives and the upper house, the Senate. The 222-member House of Representatives is elected for a maximum term of five years from single-member constituencies. All 70 senators sit for three-year terms; 26 are elected by the 13 state assemblies, and the remaining 44 are appointed by the King upon the Prime Minister's recommendation. The parliament follows a multi-party system and the government is elected through a first-past-the-post system. Since independence Malaysia has been governed by a multi-party coalition known as the Barisan Nasional.

Each state has a unicameral State Legislative Assembly whose members are elected from single-member constituencies. State governments are led by Chief Ministers, who are state assembly members from the majority party in the assembly. In each of the states with a hereditary ruler, the Chief Minister is normally required to be a Malay, appointed by the ruler upon the recommendation of the Prime Minister. Parliamentary elections are held at least once every five years, the most recent of which took place in May 2013. Registered voters of age 21 and above may vote for the members of the House of Representatives and, in most of the states, for the state legislative chamber. Voting is not mandatory. Except for state elections in Sarawak, by convention state elections are held concurrently with the federal election.

Executive power is vested in the Cabinet, led by the Prime Minister. The prime minister must be a member of the house of representatives, who in the opinion of the King, commands a majority in parliament. The cabinet is chosen from members of both houses of Parliament. The Prime Minister is both the head of cabinet and the head of government. The incumbent, Najib Razak, appointed in 2009, is the sixth prime minister.

Malaysia's legal system is based on English Common Law. Although the judiciary is theoretically independent, its independence has been called into question and the appointment of judges lacks accountability and transparency. The highest court in the judicial system is the Federal Court, followed by the Court of Appeal and two high courts, one for Peninsular Malaysia and one for East Malaysia. Malaysia also has a special court to hear cases brought by or against royalty. The death penalty is in use for crimes such as murder, terrorism and drug trafficking. Separate from and running parallel to the civil courts are the Syariah Courts, which apply Shariah law to Muslims in the areas of family law and religious observances.

Race is a significant force in politics, and many political parties are ethnically based. Affirmative actions such as the New Economic Policy and the National Development Policy which superseded it, were implemented to advance the standing of the *bumiputera*, consisting of Malays and the indigenous tribes who are considered the original inhabitants of Malaysia, over non-*bumiputera* such as Malaysian Chinese and Malaysian Indians. These policies provide preferential treatment to *bumiputera* in employment, education, scholarships, business, and access to cheaper housing and assisted savings. However, it has generated greater interethnic resentment. There is ongoing debate over whether the laws and society of Malaysia should reflect secular or Islamic principles. Islamic criminal laws passed by the Pan-Malaysian Islamic Party in state legislative assembly of Kelantan have been blocked by the federal government on the basis that criminal laws are the responsibility of the federal government.

Foreign Relations and Military

A founding member of the Association of Southeast Asian Nations (ASEAN) and the Organisation of Islamic Cooperation (OIC), the country participates in many international organisations such as the

United Nations, the Asia-Pacific Economic Cooperation, the Developing 8 Countries, and the Non-Aligned Movement (NAM). It has chaired ASEAN, the OIC, and the NAM in the past. A former British colony, it is also a member of the Commonwealth of Nations. Kuala Lumpur was the site of the first East Asia Summit in 2005.

Malaysia's foreign policy is officially based on the principle of neutrality and maintaining peaceful relations with all countries, regardless of their political system. The government attaches a high priority to the security and stability of Southeast Asia, and seeks to further develop relations with other countries in the region. Historically the government has tried to portray Malaysia as a progressive Islamic nation while strengthening relations with other Islamic states. A strong tenet of Malaysia's policy is national sovereignty and the right of a country to control its domestic affairs.

The policy towards territorial disputes by the government is one of pragmatism, with the government solving disputes in a number of ways, such as bringing the case to the International Court of Justice. The Spratly Islands are disputed by many states in the area, and the entirety of the South China Sea is claimed by China. Nevertheless, unlike its neighbours of Vietnam and the Philippines, Malaysia has avoided any conflicts with China. Brunei and Malaysia in 2009 announced an end to claims of each other's land, and to resolve issues related to their maritime borders. The Philippines has a dormant claim to the eastern part of Sabah. Singapore's land reclamation has caused tensions, and maritime border disputes exist with Indonesia.

Malaysia has never recognised Israel and has no diplomatic ties with it. It has remained a strong supporter of the State of Palestine, and has called for Israel to be taken to the International Criminal Court over the Gaza flotilla raid. Malaysian peacekeeping forces are present in Lebanon and have contributed to many other UN peacekeeping missions.

The Malaysian Armed Forces have three branches, the Royal Malaysian Navy, the Malaysian Army, and the Royal Malaysian Air Force. There is no conscription, and the required age for voluntary military service is 18. The military uses 1.5% of the country's GDP, and employs 1.23% of Malaysia's manpower. Currently, Malaysia is undergoing major program to expand and modernise all three branches of its armed forces.

The Five Power Defence Arrangements is a regional security initiative which has been in place for almost 40 years. It involves joint military exercises held among Malaysia, Singapore, Australia, New Zealand, and the United Kingdom. Joint exercises and war games also been held with Brunei, Indonesia and the United States. Malaysia, Philippines and Thailand have agreed to host joint security force exercises to secure their maritime border and tackle issues such as illegal immigration and smuggling. There are fears that unrest in the Muslim areas of the Mindanao, Philippines and southern Thailand could spill over into Malaysia.

Economy

Malaysia is a relatively open state-oriented and newly industrialised market economy. The state plays a significant but declining role in guiding economic activity through macroeconomic plans. Malaysia has had one of the best economic records in Asia, with GDP growing an average 6.5 per cent annually from 1957 to 2005. In 2014, the GDP (PPP) was about $746.821 billion, the third largest economy in ASEAN and the 28th largest in the world. In 1991, former Prime Minister of Malaysia, Mahathir bin Mohamad outlined his ideal in Vision 2020, in which Malaysia would become a self-sufficient industrialised nation by 2020. Najib Razak has said Malaysia could attain developed country status much earlier from the actual target in 2020, adding the country has two program concept such as Government Transformation Programme and the Economic Transformation Programme. According to a report of HSBC, Malaysia will become the world's 21st largest economy by 2050, with a GDP of $1.2 trillion (Year 2000 dollars) and a GDP per capita of $29,247 (Year 2000 dollars). The report also says "The electronic equipment, petroleum, and liquefied natural gas producer will see a substantial increase in income per capita. Malaysian life expectancy, relatively high level of schooling, and above average fertility rate will help in its rapid expansion". Viktor Shvets, the managing director of Credit Suisse, has said "Malaysia has all the right ingredients to become a developed nation".

In the 1970s, the predominantly mining and agricultural-based economy began a transition towards a more multi-sector economy. Since the 1980s, the industrial sector, with a high level of investment, has led the country's growth. The economy recovered from the 1997 Asian financial crisis earlier than neighbouring countries did, and has since recovered to the levels of the pre-crisis era with a GDP per capita of $14,800. Economic inequalities exist between different ethnic groups. The Chinese make up about one-third of the population, but accounts for 70 per cent of the country's market capitalisation. Chinese businesses in Malaysia are part of the larger bamboo network, a network of overseas Chinese businesses in the Southeast Asian market sharing common family and cultural ties.

Figure: *The Petronas Towers house the headquarters of the national oil company Petronas and are the tallest twin-towers in the world.*

International trade, facilitated by the shipping route in adjacent Strait of Malacca, and manufacturing are the key sectors. Malaysia is an exporter of natural and agricultural resources, and petroleum is a major export. Malaysia has once been the largest producer of tin, rubber and palm oil in the world. Manufacturing has a large influence in the country's economy, although Malaysia's economic structure has been moving away from it. Malaysia remains one of the world's largest producers of palm oil.

In an effort to diversify the economy and make it less dependent on export goods, the government has pushed to increase tourism to Malaysia. As a result, tourism has become Malaysia's third largest source of foreign exchange, although it is threatened by the negative effects of the growing industrial economy, with large amounts of air and water pollution along with deforestation affecting tourism. The tourism sector came under some pressure in 2014 when the national carrier Malaysia Airlines had one of its planes disappear in March, while another was brought down by a missile over Ukraine in July, resulting in the loss of a total 537 passengers and crew. The state of the airline, which had been unprofitable for 3 years, prompted the government in August 2014 to nationalise the airline by buying up the 30 per cent it did not already own. Between 2013 and 2014, Malaysia has been listed as one of the best places to retire in the world too, with the country in third position on the Global Retirement Index. This in part was the result of the Malaysia My Second Home programme to allow foreigners to live in the country on a long-stay visa for up to 10 years.

The country has developed into a centre of Islamic banking, and is the country with the highest numbers of female workers in that industry. Knowledge-based services are also expanding. To create a self-reliant defencive ability and support national development, Malaysia privatised some of its military facilities in the 1970s. The privatisation has created defence industry, which in 1999 was brought under the Malaysia Defence Industry Council. The government continues to promote this sector and its competitiveness, actively marketing the defence industry.

Science policies in Malaysia are regulated by the Ministry of Science, Technology, and Innovation. The country is one of the world's largest exporters of semiconductor devices, electrical devices, and IT and communication products. Malaysia began developing its own space programme in 2002, and in 2006, Russia agreed to transport one Malaysian to the International Space Station as part of a multi-billion dollar purchase of 18 Russian Sukhoi Su-30MKM fighter jets by the Royal Malaysian Air Force. The government has invested in building satellites in through the RazakSAT programme.

Infrastructure

The infrastructure of Malaysia is one of the most developed in Asia. Its telecommunications network is second only to Singapore's in Southeast Asia, with 4.7 million fixed-line subscribers and more than 30 million cellular subscribers. The country has seven international ports, the major one being the Port Klang. There are 200 industrial parks along with specialised parks such as Technology Park Malaysia and Kulim Hi-Tech Park. Fresh water is available to over 95 per cent of the population. During the colonial period, development was mainly concentrated in economically powerful cities and in areas forming security concerns. Although rural areas have been the focus of great development, they still lag behind areas such as the West Coast of Peninsular Malaysia. The telecommunication network, although strong in urban areas, is less available to the rural population.

Malaysia's road network covers 144,403 kilometres (89,728 mi) and includes 1,821 kilometres (1,132 mi) of expressways. The longest highway of the country, the North-South Expressway, extends over 800 kilometres (497 mi) between the Thai border and Singapore. In Budget 2015, the government announced a RM27 billion (US$8.23 billion) budget for the implementation of the Pan Borneo Highway project, which aims to upgrade all trunk roads to dual carriage expressways, bringing the standard of East Malaysian highways to the same level of quality of West Malaysian highways Malaysia has 118 airports, of which 38 are paved. The country's official airline is Malaysia Airlines, providing international and domestic air service alongside two other carriers. The railway system is state-run, and covers a total of 1,849 kilometres (1,149 mi). Relatively inexpensive elevated Light Rail Transit systems are used in some cities, such as Kuala Lumpur. The Asean Rail Express is a railway service that connects Kuala Lumpur to Bangkok, and is intended to eventually stretch from Singapore to China.

Traditionally, energy production in Malaysia has been based on oil and natural gas. The country has 13 GW of electrical generation capacity. However, the country only has 33 years of natural gas reserves, and 19 years of oil reserves, while the demand for energy is increasing. In response, the government is expanding into renewable energy sources. Sixteen per cent of electricity generation is hydroelectric, the remaining 84 per cent being thermal. The oil and gas industry is dominated by state owned Petronas, and the energy sector as a whole is regulated by the Energy Commission of Malaysia, a statutory commission that governs the energy in the peninsula and Sabah, under the terms of the Electricity Commission Act of 2001.

Demographics

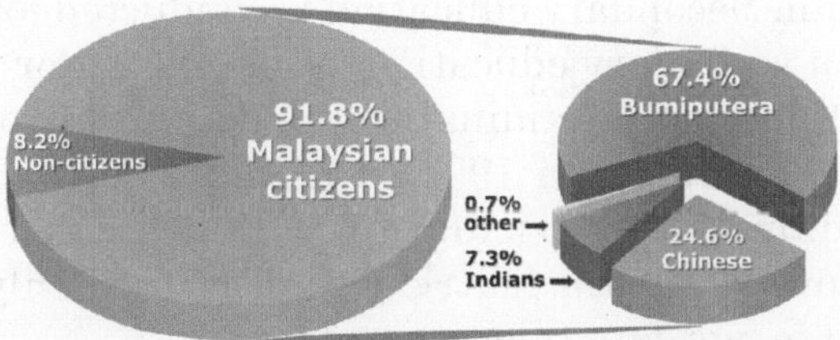

Figure: *The percentage distribution of Malaysian population by ethnic group based on 2010 census.*

As of the 2010 census, the population of Malaysia was 28,334,135, making it the 42nd most populated country. The population of Malaysia consists of many ethnic groups. In 2010, Malaysian citizens, of which *bumiputera* were 67.4%, made up 91.8% of the population. According to constitutional definition, Malays are Muslims who practice Malay customs and culture. They play a dominant role politically. *Bumiputera* status is also accorded to certain non-Malay indigenous peoples, including ethnic Thais, Khmers, Chams and the natives of Sabah and Sarawak. Non-Malay *bumiputera* make up more than half of Sarawak's population and over two thirds of Sabah's population. There also exist aboriginal groups in much smaller numbers on the peninsula, where they are collectively known as the Orang Asli. Laws over who gets *bumiputera* status vary between states.

Other minorities who lack *bumiputera* status make up a large amount of the population. 24.6 per cent of the population are of Chinese descent, while those of Indian descent comprise 7.3 per cent of the population. The Chinese have historically been dominant in the business and commerce community, and form a plurality of the population of Penang. Immigrants from India, the majority of them Tamils, began arriving in Malaysia early in the 19th century. Malaysian citizenship is not automatically granted to those born in Malaysia, but is granted to a child born of two Malaysian parents outside Malaysia. Dual citizenship is not permitted. Citizenship in the states of Sabah and Sarawak in Malaysian Borneo are distinct from citizenship in Peninsular Malaysia for immigration purposes. Every citizen is issued a biometric smart chip identity card known as *MyKad* at the age of 12, and must carry the card at all times.

The education system features a non-compulsory kindergarten education followed by six years of compulsory primary education, and five years of optional secondary education. Schools in the primary education system are divided into two categories: national primary schools, which teach in Malay, and vernacular schools, which teach in Chinese or Tamil. Secondary education is conducted for five years. In the final year of secondary education, students sit for the Malaysian Certificate of Education examination. Since the introduction of the matriculation programme in 1999, students who completed the 12-month programme in matriculation colleges can enroll in local universities. However, in the matriculation system, only 10 per cent of places are open to non-*bumiputera* students.

The infant mortality rate in 2009 was 6 deaths per 1000 births, and life expectancy at birth in 2009 was 75 years. With the aim of developing Malaysia into a medical tourism destination, 5 per cent of the government social sector development budget is spent on health care. The population in concentrated on Peninsular Malaysia where

20 million of approximately 28 million Malaysians live. 70 per cent of the population is urban. Kuala Lumpur is the capital and the largest city in Malaysia, as well as its main commercial and financial centre. Putrajaya, a purpose-built city constructed from 1999, is the seat of government, as many executive and judicial branches of the federal government were moved there to ease growing congestion within Kuala Lumpur.

Due to the rise in labour-intensive industries, the country is estimated to have over 3 million migrant workers; about 10 per cent of the population. Sabah-based NGOs estimate that out of the 3 million that make up the population of Sabah, 2 million are illegal immigrants. Malaysia hosts a population of refugees and asylum seekers numbering approximately 171,500.

Of this population, approximately 79,000 are from Burma, 72,400 from the Philippines, and 17,700 from Indonesia. Malaysian officials are reported to have turned deportees directly over to human smugglers in 2007, and Malaysia employs RELA, a volunteer militia with a history of controversies, to enforce its immigration law.

Chapter 4

Islamic States in Middle-East

Bahrain

Bahrain, officially the Kingdom of Bahrain, is a small island country situated near the western shores of the Persian Gulf. It is an archipelago with Bahrain Island, the largest land mass, at 55 km (34 mi) long by 18 km (11 mi) wide. Saudi Arabia lies to the west and is connected to Bahrain by the King Fahd Causeway while Iran lies 200 km (124 mi) to the north across the Persian Gulf. The peninsula of Qatar is to the southeast across the Gulf of Bahrain. The population in 2010 stood at 1,234,571, including 666,172 non-nationals.

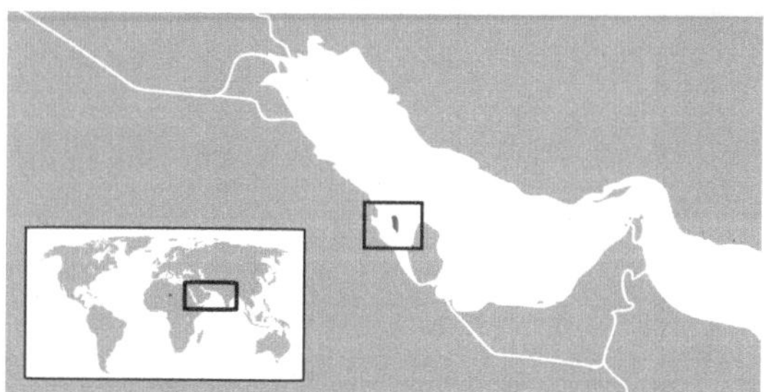

Figure: *Location of Bahrain (green)*

Bahrain is the site of the ancient land of the Dilmun civilisation. Bahrain was one of the earliest areas to convert to Islam in 628 AD. Following a period of Arab rule, Bahrain was occupied by the Portuguese in 1521, who in turn were expelled in 1602 by Shah Abbas I of the Safavid empire. In 1783, the Bani Utbah clan captured Bahrain from the Qajars and has since been ruled by the Al Khalifa royal family, with Ahmed al Fateh as Bahrain's first hakim. In the late 1800s, following successive treaties with the British, Bahrain became a protectorate of the United Kingdom. In 1971, Bahrain declared independence. Formerly a state, Bahrain was declared a Kingdom in 2002. Since early 2011, the country has experienced sustained protests and unrest inspired by the regional Arab Spring, particularly by the majority Shia population.

Bahrain has the first post-oil economy in the Persian Gulf because the Bahraini economy does not rely on oil. Since the late 20th century, Bahrain has heavily invested in the banking and tourism sectors. The country's capital, Manama, is home to many large financial structures. Bahrain has a high Human Development Index (ranked 48th in the world) and was recognised by the World Bank as a high income economy. The United States designated Bahrain a major non-NATO ally in 2001. As of October 2014, Bahrain is ruled by an "authoritarian regime" and is rated as "Not Free" by the U.S.-based non-governmental Freedom House.

History of Bahrain

Pre-Islamic Era

Bahrain was home to the Dilmun civilization, an important Bronze Age trade centre linking Mesopotamia and the Indus Valley. Bahrain was later ruled by the Assyrians and Babylonians.

Bahrain's pre-Islamic population consisted of Christian Arabs (mostly Abd al-Qays), Persians (Zoroastrians), Jews and Aramaic-speaking agriculturalists. According to Robert Bertram Serjeant, the Baharna may be the Arabized "descendants of converts from the original population of Christians (Aramaeans), Jews and Persians inhabiting the island and cultivated coastal provinces of Eastern Arabia at the time of the Muslim conquest". The sedentary people of pre-Islamic Bahrain were Aramaic speakers and to some degree Persian speakers, while Syriac functioned as a liturgical language.

From the 6th to 3rd century BC, Bahrain was added to the Persian Empire by the Achaemenian dynasty. By about 250 BC, the Parthians brought the Persian Gulf under its control and extended its influence as far as Oman. In order to control trade routes, the Parthians established garrisons along the southern coast of the Persian Gulf.

During the classical era, Bahrain was referred to by the ancient Greeks as *Tylos*, the centre of pearl trading, when Nearchus came to discover Bahrain serving under Alexander the Great. The Greek admiral Nearchus is believed to have been the first of Alexander's commanders to visit Bahrain, and he found a verdant land that was part of a wide trading network; he recorded: "That in the island of Tylos, situated in the Persian Gulf, are large plantations of cotton tree, from which are manufactured clothes called *sindones*, a very different degrees of value, some being costly, others less expensive. The use of these is not confined to India, but extends to Arabia." The Greek historian, Theophrastus, states that much of Bahrain were covered in these cotton trees and that Bahrain was famous for exporting walking canes engraved with emblems that were customarily carried in Babylon.

Alexander had planned to settle in Bahrain with Greek colonists, and although it is not clear that this happened on the scale he envisaged, Bahrain was very much part of the Hellenised world: the language of the upper classes was Greek (although Aramaic was in everyday use), while Zeus was worshipped in the form of the Arabian sun-god Shams. Bahrain even became the site of Greek athletic contests.

The Greek historian Strabo believed the Phoenicians originate from Bahrain. Herodotus also believed that the homeland of the Phoenicians was Bahrain. This theory was accepted by the 19th-century German classicist Arnold Heeren who said that: "In the Greek geographers, for instance, we read of two islands, named Tyrus or Tylos, and Arad, Bahrain, which boasted that they were the mother country of the Phoenicians, and exhibited relics of Phoenician temples." The people of Tyre in particular have long maintained Persian Gulf origins, and the similarity in the words "Tylos" and "Tyre" has been commented upon. However, there is little evidence of occupation at all in Bahrain during the time when such migration had supposedly taken place.

The name Tylos is thought to be a Hellenisation of the Semitic, Tilmun (from Dilmun). The term Tylos was commonly used for the islands until Ptolemy's *Geographia* when the inhabitants are referred to as 'Thilouanoi'. Some place names in Bahrain go back to the Tylos era, for instance, the residential suburb of Arad in Muharraq, is believed to originate from "Arados", the ancient Greek name for Muharraq.

In the 3rd century AD, Ardashir I, the first ruler of the Sassanid dynasty, marched on Oman and Bahrain, where he defeated Sanatruq the ruler of Bahrain. At this time, Bahrain was known as Mishmahig (which in Middle-Persian/Pahlavi means "ewe-fish").

Bahrain was also the site of worship of a shark deity called Awal. Worshipers built a large statue to Awal in Muharraq, although it has now been lost. For many centuries after *Tylos*, Bahrian was known as *Awal*. By the 5th century, Bahrain became the centre for Nestorian Christianity, with the village Samahij as the seat of bishops. In 410, according to the Oriental Syriac Church synodal records, a bishop named Batai was excommunicated from the church in Bahrain. As a sect, the Nestorians were often persecuted as heretics by the Byzantine

Empire, but Bahrain was outside the Empire's control offering some safety. The names of several Muharraq villages today reflect Bahrain's Christian legacy, with Al Dair meaning "the monastery".

Muhammad's Era

Muhammad's first interaction with the people of Bahrain was the Al Kudr Invasion. Muhammad ordered a surprise attack on the Banu Salim tribe for allegedly plotting to attack Medina. He had gotten news that some tribes were amassing an army on march from Bahrain. But the tribesmen retreated when they learnt Muhammad was leading an army to face them.

Traditional Islamic Accounts State that Al-Alâ Al-Harami was sent as an envoy during the Expedition of Zaid ibn Haritha (Hisma) to the Bahrain region by the prophet Muhammad in 628 AD and that Munzir ibn-Sawa al-Tamimi, the local ruler, responded to his mission and converted the entire area.

Islamic Era

In 899 AD, the Qarmatians, a millenarian Ismaili Muslim sect seized Bahrain, seeking to create a utopian society based on reason and redistribution of property among initiates. Thereafter, the Qarmatians demanded tribute from the caliph in Baghdad, and in 930 AD sacked Mecca and Medina, bringing the sacred Black Stone back to their base in Ahsa, in medieval Bahrain, for ransom. According to historian Al-Juwayni, the stone was returned 22 years later in 951 under mysterious circumstances. Wrapped in a sack, it was thrown into the Great Mosque of Kufa in Iraq, accompanied by a note saying "By command we took it, and by command we have brought it back." The theft and removal of the Black Stone caused it to break into seven pieces.

Following a 976 AD defeat by the Abbasids, the Qarmations were overthrown by the Arab Uyunid dynasty of al-Hasa, who took over the entire Bahrain region in 1076. The Uyunids controlled Bahrain until 1235, when the archipelago was briefly occupied by the Persian ruler of Fars. In 1253, the Bedouin Usfurids brought down the Uyunid dynasty, thereby gaining control over eastern Arabia, including the islands of Bahrain. In 1330, the archipelago became a tributary state of the rulers of Hormuz, though locally the islands were controlled by the Shi'ite Jarwanid dynasty of Qatif. In the mid-15th century, the archipelago came under the rule of the Jabrids, a Bedouin dynasty also based in Al-Ahsa that ruled most of eastern Arabia.

Portuguese Control

In 1521, the Portuguese allied with Hormuz and seized Bahrain from the Jabrid ruler Migrin ibn Zamil, who was killed during the takeover. Portuguese rule lasted for around 80 years, during which time they depended mainly on Sunni Persian governors. The Portuguese were expelled from the islands in 1602 by Abbas I of the Safavid dynasty of Persia, which gave impetus to Shia Islam. For the next two centuries, Persian rulers retained control of the archipelago, interrupted by the 1717 and 1738 invasions of the Ibadhis of Oman. During most of this period, they resorted to governing Bahrain indirectly, either through the city of Bushehr or through immigrant Sunni Arab clans. The latter were tribes returning to the Arabian side of the Persian Gulf from Persian territories in the north who were known as *Huwala* (literally: those that have changed or moved). In 1753, the Huwala clan of Nasr Al-Madhkur invaded Bahrain on behalf of the Iranian Zand leader Karim Khan Zand and restored direct Iranian rule.

1782-1783 Unrest in Bahrain

In 1783, Nasr Al-Madhkur, ruler of Bahrain and Bushire, lost the islands of Bahrain following his defeat by the Bani Utbah tribe at the 1782 Battle of Zubarah. Bahrain was not new territory to the Bani Utbah; they had been a presence there since the 17th century. During that time, they started purchasing date palm gardens in Bahrain; a document shows that 81 years before arrival of the Al-Khalifa, one of the shaikhs of the Al Bin Ali tribe (an offshoot of the Bani Utbah) had bought a palm garden from Mariam bint Ahmed Al Sindi in Sitra island.

The Al Bin Ali were the dominant group controlling the town of Zubarah on the Qatar peninsula, originally the centre of power of the Bani Utbah. After the Bani Utbah gained control of Bahrain, the Al Bin Ali had a practically independent status there as a self-governing tribe. They used a flag with four red and three white stripes, called the Al-Sulami flag in Bahrain, Qatar, Kuwait, and the Eastern province of the Kingdom of Saudi Arabia. Later, different Arab family clans and tribes from Qatar moved to Bahrain to settle after the fall of Nasr Al-Madhkur of Bushehr. These families included the Al Khalifa, Al-Ma'awdah, Al-Fadhil, Al-Mannai, Al-Noaimi, Al-Sulaiti, Al-Sadah, Al-Thawadi and other families and tribes.

The Al Khalifa family moved to Bahrain in 1797. Originally, they lived in Umm Qasr where they preyed on the caravans of Basra and pirated ships in the Shatt al-Arab waterway until Turks expelled them to Kuwait where they remained until 1766. In the early 19th century,

Bahrain was invaded by both the Omanis and the Al Sauds. In 1802 it was governed by a twelve-year-old child, when the Omani ruler Sayyid Sultan installed his son, Salim, as Governor in the Arad Fort. In 1820, the Al Khalifa tribe were recognised by Great Britain as the rulers ("Al-Hakim" in Arabic) of Bahrain after signing a treaty relationship. However, ten years later they were forced to pay yearly tributes to Egypt despite seeking Persian and British protection.

In 1860, the Al Khalifas used the same tactic when the British tried to overpower Bahrain. Writing letters to the Persians and Ottomans, Al Khalifas agreed to place Bahrain under the latter's protection in March due to offering better conditions. Eventually the Government of British India overpowered Bahrain when the Persians refused to protect it. Colonel Pelly signed a new treaty with Al Khalifas placing Bahrain under British rule and protection. Following the Qatari–Bahraini War in 1868, British representatives signed another agreement with the Al Khalifas. It specified that the ruler could not dispose of any of his territory except to the United Kingdom and could not enter into relationships with any foreign government without British consent. In return the British promised to protect Bahrain from all aggression by sea and to lend support in case of land attack. More importantly the British promised to support the rule of the Al Khalifa in Bahrain, securing its unstable position as rulers of the country. Other agreements in 1880 and 1892 sealed the protectorate status of Bahrain to the British.

Unrest amongst the people of Bahrain began when Britain officially established complete dominance over the territory in 1892. The first revolt and widespread uprising took place in March 1895 against Sheikh Issa bin Ali, then ruler of Bahrain. Sheikh Issa was the first of the Al Khalifa to rule without Persian relations. Sir Arnold Wilson, Britain's representative in the Persian Gulf and author of *The Persian Gulf*, arrived in Bahrain from Muscat at this time. The uprising developed further with some protesters killed by British forces.

Economic Prosperity - 19th Century

Peace and trade brought a new prosperity. Bahrain was no longer dependent upon pearling, and by the mid-19th century, it became the pre-eminent trading centre in the Persian Gulf, overtaking rivals Basra, Kuwait and finally in the 1870s, Muscat. At the same time, Bahrain's socio-economic development began to diverge from the rest of the Persian Gulf: it transformed itself from a trading centre into a modern state. This process was spurred by the attraction of large numbers of Persian, Huwala, and Indian merchant families who set up businesses on the island, making it the nexus of a vast web of trade routes across the Persian Gulf, Persia and the Indian sub-continent. A contemporary account of Manama in 1862 found:

"Mixed with the indigenous population [of Manamah] are numerous strangers and settlers, some of whom have been established here for many generations back, attracted from other lands by the profits of either commerce or the pearl fishery, and still retaining more or less the physiognomy and garb of their native countries. Thus the gay-coloured dress of the southern Persian, the saffron-stained vest of Oman, the white robe of Nejed, and the striped gown of Bagdad, are often to be seen mingling with the light garments of Bahreyn, its blue and red turban, its white silk-fringed cloth worn Banian fashion round the waist, and its frock-like overall; while a small but unmistakable colony of Indians, merchants by profession, and mainly from Gujarat, Cutch, and their vicinity, keep up here all their peculiarities of costume and manner, and live among the motley crowd, 'among them, but not of them'.

WG Palgrave, *Narrative of a Year's Journey through Central and Eastern Arabia (1862–3)* "

Palgrave's description of Manama's coffee houses in the mid-19th century portrays them as cosmopolitan venues in contrast to what he describes as the 'closely knit and bigoted universe of central Arabia'. Palgrave describes a people with an open – even urbane – outlook: "Of religious controversy I have never heard one word. In short, instead of Zelators and fanatics, camel-drivers and Bedouins, we have at Bahrain [Manama] something like 'men of the world, who know the world like men' a great relief to the mind; certainly it was so to mine."

The great trading families that emerged during this period have been compared to the Borgias and Medicis and their great wealth gave them extensive power, and among the most prominent were the Persian Al Safar family, who held the position of Native Agents of Britain in 19th Century. The Al Safar enjoyed an 'exceptionally close' relationship with the Al Khalifa clan from 1869, although the al-Khalifa never intermarried with them – it has been speculated that this could be related to political reasons (to limit the Safars' influence with the ruling family) and possibly for religious reasons (because the Safars were Shia).

As a result of Bahrain's trade with India, the cultural influence of the subcontinent grew dramatically, with styles of dress, cuisine, and education showing a marked Indian influence. According to Exeter University's James Onley "In these and countless other ways, Eastern Arabia's ports and people were as much a part of the Indian Ocean world as they were a part of the Arab world."

Early 20th Century

In 1911, a group of Bahraini merchants demanded restrictions on the British influence in the country. The group's leaders were subsequently arrested and exiled to India. In 1923, the British introduced administrative reforms and replaced Sheikh Issa bin Ali with his son. Some clerical opponents and families such as al Dossari left or were exiled to Saudi Arabia and Iran. Three years later the British placed the country under the *de facto* rule of Charles Belgrave who operated as an adviser to the ruler until 1957. Belgrave brought a number of reforms such as establishment of the country's first modern school in 1919, the Persian Gulf's first girls school in 1928 and the abolition of slavery in 1937. At the same time, the pearl diving industry developed at a rapid pace.

In 1927, Rezâ Shâh, then Shah of Iran, demanded sovereignty over Bahrain in a letter to the League of Nations. A move that prompted Belgrave to undertake harsh measures including encouraging conflicts between Shia and Sunni Muslims in order to bring down the uprisings and limit the Iranian influence. Belgrave even went further by suggesting to rename the Persian Gulf to the "Arabian Gulf"; however, the proposal was refused by the British government. Britain's interest in Bahrain's development was motivated by concerns over Saudi and Iranian ambitions in the region.

The Bahrain Petroleum Company (Bapco), a subsidiary of the Standard Oil Company of California (Socal), discovered oil in 1931 and production began the following year. This was to bring rapid modernisation to Bahrain. Relations with the United Kingdom became closer, as evidenced by the British Royal Navy moving its entire Middle Eastern command from Bushehr in Iran to Bahrain in 1935.

Bahrain participated in the Second World War on the Allied side, joining on 10 September 1939. On 19 October 1940, four Italian SM.82s bombers bombed Bahrain alongside Dhahran oilfields in Saudi Arabia, targeting Allied-operated oil refineries. Although minimal damage was caused in both locations, the attack forced the Allies to upgrade Bahrain's defences, an action which further stretched Allied military resources.

After World War II, increasing anti-British sentiment spread throughout the Arab World and led to riots in Bahrain. The riots focused on the Jewish community. In 1948, following rising hostilities and looting, most members of Bahrain's Jewish community abandoned their properties and evacuated to Bombay, later settling in Israel (Pardes Hanna-Karkur) and the United Kingdom. As of 2008, 37 Jews remained in the country. In the 1950s, the National Union Committee, formed by reformists following sectarian clashes, demanded an elected popular assembly, removal of Belgrave and carried out a number of protests and general strikes. In 1965 a month-long uprising broke out after hundreds of workers at the Bahrain Petroleum Company were laid off.

Independence

On 15 August 1971, Bahrain declared independence and signed a new treaty of friendship with the United Kingdom. Bahrain joined the United Nations and the Arab League later in the year. The oil boom of the 1970s benefited Bahrain greatly, although the subsequent downturn hurt the economy. The country had already begun diversification of its economy and benefited further from Lebanese Civil War in the 1970s and 1980s, when Bahrain replaced Beirut as the Middle East's financial hub after Lebanon's large banking sector was driven out of the country by the war.

Following the 1979 Islamic revolution in Iran, in 1981 Bahraini Shî'a fundamentalists orchestrated a failed coup attempt under the auspices of a front organisation, the Islamic Front for the Liberation of Bahrain. The coup would have installed a Shî'a cleric exiled in Iran, Hujjatu l-Islâm Hâdî al-Mudarrisî, as supreme leader heading a theocratic government. In December 1994, a group of youths threw stones at female runners during an international marathon for running bare-legged. The resulting clash with police soon grew into civil unrest.

A popular uprising occurred between 1994 and 2000 in which leftists, liberals and Islamists joined forces. The event resulted in approximately forty deaths and ended after Hamad ibn Isa Al Khalifa became the Emir of Bahrain in 1999. A referendum on 14–15 February 2001 massively supported the National Action Charter. He instituted elections for parliament, gave women the right to vote, and released all political prisoners. As part of the adoption of the National Action Charter on 14 February 2002, Bahrain changed its formal name from the State (*dawla*) of Bahrain to the Kingdom of Bahrain.

The country participated in military action against the Taliban in October 2001 by deploying a frigate in the Arabian Sea for rescue and humanitarian operations. As a result, in November of that year, US president George W. Bush's administration designated Bahrain as a "major non-NATO ally". Bahrain opposed the invasion of Iraq and had offered Saddam Hussein asylum in the days prior to the invasion. Relations improved with neighbouring Qatar after the border dispute over the Hawar Islands was resolved by the International Court of Justice in The Hague in 2001. Following the political liberalisation of the country, Bahrain negotiated a free trade agreement with the United States in 2004.

Bahraini Uprising

Inspired by the regional Arab Spring, Bahrain's Shia majority started large protests against its Sunni rulers in early 2011. The government initially allowed protests following a pre-dawn raid on protesters camped in Pearl Roundabout. A month later it requested security assistance from Saudi Arabia and other GCC countries and declared a three-month state of emergency. The government then launched a crackdown on opposition that included conducting thousands of arrests. Almost daily clashes between protesters and security forces led to dozens of deaths. Protests, sometimes staged by opposition parties, are ongoing. More than 80 civilians and 13 policemen were killed as of March 2014. The lack of coverage by Arab media in the Persian Gulf as compared to other Arab Spring uprisings has sparked several controversies.

Politics of Bahrain

Figure: *Isa Bin Salman,1968.*

Bahrain under the Al-Khalifa regime claims to be a constitutional monarchy headed by the King, Shaikh Hamad bin Isa Al Khalifa; however, given its dictatorial oppression, lack of parliamentary power and lack of an independent judiciary, most observers assert that Bahrain is an absolute monarchy. King Hamad enjoys wide executive authorities which include appointing the Prime Minister and his ministers, commanding the army, chairing the Higher Judicial Council, appointing the parliament's upper half and dissolving its elected lower half. The head of government is the unelected Prime Minister, Shaikh Khalîfa bin Salman Al Khalifa, the uncle of the current king who has served in this position since 1971, making him the longest serving prime minister in the world. In 2010, about half of the government was composed of Al Khalifa family.

Bahrain has a bicameral National Assembly (*al-Jam'iyyah al-Watani*) consisting of the Shura Council (*Majlis Al-Shura*) with 40 seats and the Council of Representatives (*Majlis Al-Nuwab*) with 40 seats. The 40 members of the Shura are appointed by the king. In the Council of Representatives, 40 members are elected by absolute majority vote in single-member constituencies to serve 4-year terms. The appointed council "exercises a *de facto* veto" over the elected, because draft acts must be approved by it in order they pass into law. After that the king may ratify and issue the act or return it within six months to the National Assembly where it may only pass into law if approved by two thirds of both councils.

In 1973, the country held its first parliamentary elections; however, two years later, the late emir dissolved the parliament and suspended the constitution after it rejected the State Security Law. The period between 2002 and 2010 saw three parliamentary elections. The first, held in 2002 was boycotted by the opposition, Al Wefaq, which won a majority in the second in 2006 and third in 2010. The 2011 by-election was held to replace 18 members of Al Wefaq who resigned in protest against government crackdown.

The opening up of politics saw big gains for both Shîa and Sunnî Islamists in elections, which gave them a parliamentary platform to pursue their policies. It gave a new prominence to clerics within the political system, with the most senior Shia religious leader, Sheikh Isa Qassim, playing a vital role. This was especially evident when in 2005 the government called off the Shia branch of the "Family law" after over 100,000 Shia took to the streets. Islamists opposed the law because "neither elected MPs nor the government has the authority to change the law because these institutions could misinterpret the word of God". The law was supported by women activists who said they were "suffering in silence". They managed to organise a rally attended by 500 participants. Ghada Jamsheer, a leading woman activist said the government was using the law as a "bargaining tool with opposition Islamic groups".

Analysts of democratisation in the Middle East cite the Islamists' references to respect for human rights in their justification for these programmes as evidence that these groups can serve as a progressive force in the region. Some Islamist parties have been particularly critical of the government's readiness to sign international treaties such as the United Nations' International Convention on Civil and Political Rights. At a parliamentary session in June 2006 to discuss ratification of the Convention, Sheikh Adel Mouwda, the former leader of salafist party, Asalah, explained the party's objections: "The convention has been tailored by our enemies, God kill them all, to serve their needs and protect their interests rather than ours. This why we have eyes from the American Embassy watching us during our sessions, to ensure things are swinging their way".

Human Rights

The period between 1975 and 1999 known as the "State Security Law Era", saw wide range of human rights violations including arbitrary arrests, detention without trial, torture and forced exile. After the Emir Hamad Al Khalifa (now king) succeeded his father Isa Al Khalifa in 1999, he introduced wide reforms and human rights improved significantly. These moves were described by Amnesty International as representing a "historic period of human rights".

Human rights conditions started to decline by 2007 when torture began to be employed again. In 2011, Human Rights Watch described the country's human rights situation as "dismal". Due to this, Bahrain lost some of the high International rankings it had gained before.

In 2011, Bahrain was criticised for its crackdown on the Arab spring uprising. In September, a government appointed commission confirmed reports of grave human rights violations including systematic torture. The government promised to introduce reforms and avoid repeating the "painful events". However, reports by human rights organisations Amnesty International and Human Rights Watch issued in April 2012 said the same violations were still happening.

The documentary TV film "Bahrain: Shouting in the Dark" which was produced by the Qatari channel "Al Jazeera", talks about the Bahraini protests during 2011. This TV film showed all the violations that have been taken against the rights of Bahraini citizens during the uprising. It also caused some problems between the Bahraini and the Qatari governments. Relations between Bahrain and Qatar improved following a meeting of the Gulf Cooperation Council in November 2014 in which it was announced Bahrain diplomats would return to Qatar.

Women's Rights

Women's political rights in Bahrain saw an important step forward when women were granted the right to vote and stand in national elections for the first time in the 2002 election. However, no women were elected to office in that year's polls. Instead, Shî'a and Sunnî Islamists dominated the election, collectively winning a majority of seats. In response to the failure of women candidates, six were appointed to the Shura Council, which also includes representatives of the Kingdom's indigenous Jewish and Christian communities. Dr. Nada Haffadh became the country's first female cabinet minister on her appointment as Minister of Health in 2004. The quasi-governmental women's group, the Supreme Council for Women, trained female candidates to take part in the 2006 general election. When Bahrain was elected to head the United Nations General Assembly in 2006 it appointed lawyer and women's rights activist Haya bint Rashid Al Khalifa President of the United Nations General Assembly, only the third woman in history to head the world body. Female activist Ghada Jamsheer said "The government used women's rights as a decorative tool on the international level." She referred to the reforms as "artificial and marginal" and accused the government of "hinder[ing] non-governmental women societies".

In 2006, Lateefa Al Gaood became the first female MP after winning by default. The number rose to four after the 2011 by-elections. In 2008, Houda Nonoo was appointed ambassador to the United States making her the first Jewish ambassador of any Arab country. In 2011, Alice Samaan, a Christian woman was appointed ambassador to the UK.

Media

Bahraini journalists risk prosecution for offences which include "undermining" the government and religion. Self-censorship is widespread. Journalists were targeted by officials during anti-government protests in 2011. Three editors from opposition daily Al-Wasat (Bahraini newspaper) were sacked and later fined for publishing "false" news. Several foreign correspondents were expelled.

Most domestic broadcasters are state-run. An independent commission, set up to look into the unrest, found that state media coverage was at times inflammatory. It said opposition groups suffered from lack of access to mainstream media, and recommended that the government "consider relaxing censorship". Bahrain will host the Saudi-financed Alarab News Channel, expected to launch in December 2012. It will be based at a planned "Media City". An opposition satellite station, Lualua TV, operates from London but has found its signals blocked.

By June 2012, Bahrain had 961,000 internet users. The platform "provides a welcome free space for journalists, although one that is increasingly monitored", according to Reporters Without Borders. Rigorous filtering targets political, human rights, religious material and content deemed obscene. Bloggers and other netizens were among those detained during protests in 2011.

Military

The kingdom has a small but well equipped military called the Bahrain Defence Force (BDF), numbering around 13,000 personnel. The supreme commander of the Bahraini military is King Hamad bin Isa Al Khalifa and the deputy supreme commander is the Crown Prince, Salman bin Hamad bin Isa Al Khalifa.

The BDF is primarily equipped with United States equipment, such as the F16 Fighting Falcon, F5 Freedom Fighter, UH60 Blackhawk, M60A3 tanks, and the ex-USS *Jack Williams*, an Oliver Hazard Perry class frigate renamed the RBNS *Sabha*. The Government of Bahrain has close relations with the United States, having signed a cooperative agreement with the United States Military and has provided the United States a base in Juffair since the early 1990s, although a US naval presence existed since 1948. This is the home of the headquarters for Commander, *United States Naval Forces Central Command* (COMUSNAVCENT) / *United States Fifth Fleet* (COMFIFTHFLT), and around 6,000 United States military personnel.

Foreign Relations

Bahrain established bilateral relations with 190 countries worldwide. As of 2012, Bahrain maintains a network of 25 embassies, 3 consulates and 4 permanent missions to the Arab League, United Nations and European Union respectively. Bahrain also hosts 36 embassies. Bahrain plays a modest, moderating role in regional politics and adheres to the views of the Arab League on Middle East peace and Palestinian rights by supporting the two state solution. Bahrain is also one of the founding members of the Gulf Cooperation Council. Relations with Iran tend to be tense as a result of a failed coup in 1981 which Bahrain blames Iran for and occasional claims of Iranian sovereignty over Bahrain by ultra-conservative elements in the Iranian public.

Governorates

The first municipality in Bahrain was the 8-member Manama municipality which was established in July 1919. Members of the municipality were elected annually; the municipality was said to have been the first municipality to be established in the Arab world. The municipality was in charge of cleaning roads and renting buildings to tenants and shops. By 1929, it undertook road expansions as well as opening markets and slaughterhouses. In 1958, the municipality started water purification projects. In 1960, Bahrain comprised four municipalities including *Manama*, *Hidd*, *Al Muharraq*, and *Riffa*. Over the next 30 years, the 4 municipalities were divided into 12 municipalities as settlements such as Hamad Town and Isa Town grew. These municipalities were administered from Manama under a central municipal council whose members are appointed by the king.

Economy

According to a January 2006 report by the United Nations Economic and Social Commission for Western Asia, Bahrain has the fastest growing economy in the Arab world. Bahrain also has the freest economy in the Middle East and is twelfth freest overall in the world based on the 2011 Index of Economic Freedom published by the Heritage Foundation/*Wall Street Journal.*

In 2008, Bahrain was named the world's fastest growing financial centre by the City of London's Global Financial Centres Index. Bahrain's banking and financial services sector, particularly Islamic banking, have benefited from the regional boom driven by demand for oil. Petroleum production and processing account is Bahrain's most exported product, accounting for 60% of export receipts, 70% of government revenues, and 11% of GDP. Aluminium production is the second most exported product, followed by finance and construction materials.

Economic conditions have fluctuated with the changing price of oil since 1985, for example during and following the Persian Gulf crisis of 1990–91. With its highly developed communication and transport facilities, Bahrain is home to a number of multinational firms and construction proceeds on several major industrial projects. A large share of exports consist of petroleum products made from imported crude oil, which accounted for 51% of the country's imports in 2007. Bahrain depends heavily on food imports to feed its growing population; it relies heavily on meat imports from Australia and also imports 75% of its total fruit consumption needs. Since only 2.9% of the country's land is arable, agriculture contributes to 0.5% of Bahrain's GDP. In 2004, Bahrain signed the US-Bahrain Free Trade Agreement, which will reduce certain trade barriers between the two nations. Due to the combination of the global financial crisis and the recent unrest, the growth rate decreased to 2.2% which is the lowest growth rate since 1994.

Unemployment, especially among the young, and the depletion of both oil and underground water resources are major long-term economic problems. In 2008, the jobless figure was at 4%, with women over represented at 85% of the total. In 2007 Bahrain became the first Arab country to institute unemployment benefits as part of a series of labour reforms instigated under Minister of Labour, Dr. Majeed Al Alawi.

Infrastructure

Bahrain has one main international airport, the Bahrain International Airport (BIA) which is located on the island of Muharraq, in the north-east. The airport handled more than 100,000 flights and more than 8 million passengers in 2010. Bahrain's national carrier, Gulf Air operates and bases itself in the BIA.

Bahrain has a well-developed road network, particularly in Manama. The discovery of oil in the early 1930s accelerated the creation of multiple roads and highways in Bahrain, connecting several isolated villages, such as Budaiya, to Manama.

To the east, a bridge connected Manama to Muharraq since 1929, a new causeway was built in 1941 which replaced the old wooden bridge. Currently there are three modern bridges connecting the two locations. Transits between the two islands peaked after the construction of the Bahrain International Airport in 1932. Ring roads and highways were later built to connect Manama to the villages of the Northern Governorate and towards towns in central and southern Bahrain.

The four main islands and all the towns and villages are linked by well-constructed roads. There were 3,164 km (1,966 mi) of roadways in 2002, of which 2,433 km (1,512 mi) were paved. A causeway stretching over 2.8 km (2 mi), connect Manama with Muharraq Island, and another bridge joins Sitra to the main island. The King Fahd Causeway, measuring 24 km (15 mi), links Bahrain with the Saudi Arabian mainland via the island of Umm an-Nasan. It was completed in December 1986, and financed by Saudi Arabia. In 2008, there were 17,743,495 passengers transiting through the causeway.

Bahrain's port of Mina Salman is the main seaport of the country and consists of 15 berths. In 2001, Bahrain had a merchant fleet of eight ships of 1,000 GRT or over, totaling 270,784 GRT. Private vehicles and taxis are the primary means of transportation in the city.

Telecommunications

The telecommunications sector in Bahrain officially started in 1981 with the establishment of Bahrain's first telecommunications company, Batelco and until 2004, it monopolised the sector. In 1981, there were more than 45,000 telephones in use in the country. By 1999, Batelco had more than 100,000 mobile contracts. In 2002, under pressure from international bodies, Bahrain implemented its telecommunications law which included the establishment of an independent *Telecommunications Regulatory Authority* (TRA). In 2004, Zain (a rebranded version of MTC Vodafone) started operations in Bahrain and in 2010 VIVA (owned by STC Group) become the third company to provide mobile services.

Bahrain has been connected to the internet since 1995 with the country's domain suffix is '.bh'. The country's connectivity score (a statistic which measures both Internet access and fixed and mobile telephone lines) is 210.4 percent per person, while the regional average in Arab States of the Persian Gulf is 135.37 percent. The number of

Bahraini internet users has risen from 40,000 in 2000 to 250,000 in 2008, or from 5.95 to 33 percent of the population. As of August 2013, the TRA has licensed 22 Internet Service Providers.

Demographics

In 2010, Bahrain's population grew to 1.2 million, of which 568,399 were Bahraini and 666,172 were non-nationals. It had risen from 1.05 million (517,368 non-nationals) in 2007, the year when Bahrain's population crossed the one million mark. Though a majority of the population is Middle Eastern, a sizeable number of people from South Asia live in the country. In 2008, approximately 290,000 Indian nationals lived in Bahrain, making them the single largest expatriate community in the country. Bahrain is the fourth most densely populated sovereign state in the world with a population density of 1,646 people per km^2 in 2010. The only sovereign states with larger population densities are city states. Much of this population is concentrated in the north of the country with the Southern Governorate being the least densely populated part. The north of the country is so urbanised that it is considered by some to be one large metropolitan area.

Ethnic Groups

Bahraini people are ethnically diverse. There are at least 8–9 different ethnic groups of Bahraini citizens. Shia Bahraini citizens are divided into two main ethnic groups: Bahrani and Ajam. Most Shia Bahrainis are ethnic Baharna. The Baharna are descendants of the original pre-Islamic inhabitants of Bahrain. The pre-Islamic population of Bahrain consisted of Christianized Arabs (mostly Abd al-Qays), Aramean Christians, Persian-speaking Zoroastrians and Jewish agriculturalists. According to Robert Bertram Serjeant, the Baharna may be the Arabized "descendants of converts from the original population of Christians (Aramaeans), Jews and ancient Persians inhabiting the island and cultivated coastal provinces of Eastern Arabia at the time of the Arab conquest". The sedentary people of pre-Islamic Bahrain were mainly Aramaic speakers and to some degree Persian speakers while Syriac functioned as a liturgical language.

The Ajam are ethnic Persian Shias. Unlike the Baharna, Ajam are not ethnic Arabs. Shia Persians form large communities in Manama and Muharraq. Bahraini Persians maintain a distinct culture and language, but have long since assimilated into Bahraini culture; they tend to identify themselves as Persian Bahrainis than Iranians. 22% of Bahraini citizens are ethnic Persian Shias. A tiny minority of Shia Bahraini citizens are ethnic Hasawis from Al-Hasa.

Among Sunni Bahraini citizens, there are also many different ethnic groups. Sunni Bahrainis are mainly divided into two main ethnic groups: urban Arabs (al Arab) and Huwala. The urban Arabs are mostly descendants of Sunni Arabs from central Arabia who were traditionally pearl-divers, merchants, sailors, traders and fishermen in the pre-oil era. The urban Arabs are the most influential ethnic group in Bahrain, they hold most government positions and the Bahraini monarchy are ethnic urban Arabs. Urban Arabs have traditionally lived in areas such as Zallaq, Muharraq, Riffa and Hawar islands. The Huwala are descendants of Sunni Iranians; some of them are ethnic Persians, and a tiny minority of them are ethnic Sunni Arabs who intermingled with the Persians. Many Huwala originally lived in Awadhiya and Hoora. The Huwala form a significant part of Bahrain's elite and merchant class.

In addition to these ethnic groups, there are also Balochs, Afro-Arabs, Indians and ethnic tribal people. The Bahraini Baloch are descendants of the Iranian Baloch. Most Bahrainis of African origin come from east Africa and have traditionally lived on Muharraq Island and in Riffa. A portion of Indian Bahrainis are descendants of wealthy Indian merchants from the pre-oil era, known as the Bania. A smaller group of Sunni Bahraini citizens are descendants of naturalized Palestinian refugees and other Levant Arab immigrants.

Religion

The state religion of Bahrain is Islam and most Bahraini citizens are Muslim. There are no official figures for the proportion of Shia and Sunni among the Muslims of Bahrain, but approximately 65–75% percent of Bahraini Muslims are Shia.

There is a native Christian community in Bahrain. Christian Bahraini citizens number 1,000 people. The majority of Christian Bahraini citizens tend to be Orthodox Christians, with the largest church by membership being the Greek Orthodox Church. They enjoy religious and social freedom, and Bahrain has some Christian members in the Bahraini government. Expatriate Christians make up the majority of Christians in Bahrain, while native Christian Bahrainis (who hold Bahraini citizenship) make up a smaller community. Alees Samaan, the current Bahraini ambassador to the United Kingdom is a native Christian. Bahrain also has a native Jewish community numbering thirty-seven Bahraini citizens. Various sources cite Bahrain's native Jewish community as being from 36 to 50 people, Bahraini Jews are active in politics. A Jewish businessman, Ebrahim Daoud Nonoo, was appointed to the upper house of parliament (Shura Council). In 2008, the Jewish Bahraini politician Houda Nonoo was named Bahrain's ambassador to the United States. Bahrain also has a native Bahá'í community. Baha'is constitute approximately 1% of Bahrain's total population.

Due to an influx of immigrants and guest workers from Southern Asian countries, such as India, Philippines and Sri Lanka, the overall percentage of Muslims in the country has declined in recent years. According to the 2001 census, 81.2% of Bahrain's population was Muslim, 10% were Christian, and 9.8% practised Hinduism or other religions. The 2010 census records that the Muslim proportion had fallen to 70.2% (the 2010 census did not differentiate between the non-Muslim religions). Bahrain government officials rejected reports from Bahraini opposition that the administration was trying to alter the country's demographics by naturalizing Sunni Syrians.

Languages

Arabic is the official language of Bahrain, though English is widely used. Bahrani Arabic is the most widely spoken dialect of the Arabic language, though this differs slightly from standard Arabic. Arabic plays an important role in political life, as, according to article 57 (c) of Bahrain's constitution, an MP must be fluent in Arabic to stand for parliament. Among the Bahraini and non-Bahraini population, many people speak Persian, the official language of Iran, or Urdu, the official language of Pakistan. Malayalam and Nepali are also widely spoken in the Nepalese workers and Gurkha Soldiers community. Hindi is spoken among significant Indian communities. Many commercial institutions and road signs are bilingual, displaying both English and Arabic.

Education

Education is compulsory for children between the ages of 6 and 14. Education is free for Bahraini citizens in public schools, with the Bahraini Ministry of Education providing free textbooks. Coeducation is not used in public schools, with boys and girls segregated into separate schools.

At the beginning of the 20th century, Qur'anic schools (*Kuttab*) were the only form of education in Bahrain. They were traditional schools aimed at teaching children and youth the reading of the Qur'an. After World War I, Bahrain became open to western influences, and a demand for modern educational institutions appeared. 1919 marked the beginning of modern public school system in Bahrain when the Al-Hidaya Al-Khalifia School for boys opened in Muharraq. In 1926, the Education Committee opened the second public school for boys in

Manama, and in 1928 the first public school for girls was opened in Muharraq. As of 2011, there are a total of 126,981 students studying in public schools.

In 2004, King Hamad ibn Isa Al Khalifa introduced the "King Hamad Schools of Future" project that uses Information Communication Technology to support K–12 education in Bahrain. The project's objective is to connect all schools within the kingdom with the Internet. In addition to British intermediate schools, the island is served by the Bahrain School (BS). The BS is a United States Department of Defence school that provides a K-12 curriculum including International Baccalaureate offerings. There are also private schools that offer either the IB Diploma Programme or United Kingdom's A-Levels.

Bahrain also encourages institutions of higher learning, drawing on expatriate talent and the increasing pool of Bahrain nationals returning from abroad with advanced degrees. The University of Bahrain was established for standard undergraduate and graduate study, and the King Abdulaziz University College of Health Sciences, operating under the direction of the Ministry of Health, trains physicians, nurses, pharmacists, and paramedics. The 2001 National Action Charter paved the way for the formation of private universities such as the Ahlia University in Manama and University College of Bahrain in Saar. The Royal University for Women (RUW), established in 2005, was the first private, purpose-built, international University in Bahrain dedicated solely to educating women. The University of London External has appointed MCG (Management Consultancy Group) as the regional representative office in Bahrain for distance learning programmes. MCG is one of the oldest private institutes in the country. Institutes have also opened which educate South Asian students, such as the Pakistan Urdu School, Bahrain and the Indian School, Bahrain. A few prominent institutions are DePaul University, Bentley University, the Ernst & Young Training Institute, NYIT and the Birla Institute of Technology International Centre. In 2004, the Royal College of Surgeons in Ireland (RCSI) set up a constituent medical university in the country. In addition to the Arabian Gulf University, AMA International University and the College of Health Sciences, these are the only medical schools in Bahrain.

Health

Bahrain has a universal health care system, dating back to 1960. Government-provided health care is free to Bahraini citizens and heavily subsidised for non-Bahrainis. Healthcare expenditure accounted for 4.5% of Bahrain's GDP, according to the World Health

Organisation. Bahraini physicians and nurses form a majority of the country's workforce in the health sector, unlike neighbouring Gulf states. The first hospital in Bahrain was the American Mission Hospital, which opened in 1893 as a dispensary. The first public hospital, and also tertiary hospital, to open in Bahrain was the Salmaniya Medical Complex, in the Salmaniya district of Manama, in 1957. Private hospitals are also present throughout the country, such as the International Hospital of Bahrain.

The life expectancy in Bahrain is 73 for males and 76 for females. Compared to many countries in the region, the prevalence of AIDS and HIV is relatively low. Malaria and tuberculosis (TB) do not constitute major problems in Bahrain as neither disease is indigenous to the country. As a result, cases of malaria and TB have declined in recent decades with cases of contractions amongst Bahraini nationals becoming rare. The Ministry of Health sponsors regular vaccination campaigns against TB and other diseases such as hepatitis B.

Bahrain is currently suffering from an obesity epidemic as 28.9% of all males and 38.2% of all females are classified as obese. Bahrain also has one of the highest prevalence of diabetes in the world (5th place), with more than 15% of the Bahraini population suffering from the disease, and accounting for 5% of deaths in the country. Cardiovascular diseases account for 32% of all deaths in Bahrain, being the number one cause of death in the country (the second being cancer). Sickle cell anaemia and thalassaemia are prevalent in the country, with a study concluding that 18% of Bahrainis are carriers of sickle cell anaemia while 24% are carriers of thalassaemia.

Culture

Bahrain is sometimes described as "Middle East lite" due to its combination of modern infrastructure with a Persian Gulf identity. While Islam is the main religion, Bahrainis are known for their tolerance towards the practice of other faiths.

Rules regarding female attire are generally relaxed compared to regional neighbours; the traditional attire of women usually include the hijab or the abaya. Although the traditional male attire is the thobe which also includes traditional headdresses such as the Keffiyeh, Ghutra and Agal, Western clothing is common in the country.

Although Bahrain legalized homosexuality in 1976, including same-sex sodomy, many homosexuals have since been arrested . Another facet of Bahrain's openness is the country's status as the most prolific book publisher in the Arab world, with 132 books published in 2005 for a population of 700,000. In comparison, the 2005 average for the entire Arab world was seven books published per one million people, according to the United Nations Development Programme.

Palestine

The State of Palestine is a *de jure* sovereign state in the Levant. Its independence was declared on 15 November 1988 by the Palestine Liberation Organisation (PLO) in Algiers as a government-in-exile. The State of Palestine claims the West Bank and Gaza Strip, and has designated Jerusalem as its capital, with partial control of those areas assumed in 1994 as the Palestinian Authority. Most of the areas claimed by the State of Palestine have been occupied by Israel since 1967 in the aftermath of the Six-Day War. The State of Palestine applied for full UN Membership in 2011; and in 2012 was recognised as a non-member observer state by the United Nations.

The October 1974 Arab League summit designated the PLO as the "sole legitimate representative of the Palestinian people" and reaffirmed "their right to establish an independent state of urgency." In November 1974, the PLO was recognised as competent on all matters concerning the question of Palestine by the UN General Assembly granting them observer status as a "non-state entity" at the UN. After the 1988 Declaration of Independence, the UN General Assembly officially "acknowledged" the proclamation and decided to use the designation "Palestine" instead of "Palestine Liberation Organisation" in the UN. In spite of this decision, the PLO did not participate at the UN in its capacity of the State of Palestine's government.

In 1993, in the Oslo Accords, Israel acknowledged the PLO negotiating team as "representing the Palestinian people", in return for the PLO recognising Israel's right to exist in peace, acceptance of UN Security Council resolutions 242 and 338, and its rejection of "violence and terrorism". As a result, in 1994 the PLO established the Palestinian National Authority (PNA or PA) territorial administration, that exercises some governmental functions in parts of the West Bank and the Gaza Strip. In 2007, the Hamas takeover of Gaza Strip politically and territorially divided the Palestinians, with Abbas's Fatah left largely ruling the West Bank and recognised internationally as the official Palestinian Authority, while Hamas has secured its control over the Gaza Strip. In April 2011, the Palestinian parties signed an agreement of reconciliation, but its implementation had stalled until a unity government was formed on 2 June 2014.

On 29 November 2012, in a 138-9 vote (with 41 abstentions and 5 absences), the United Nations General Assembly passed resolution 67/

19, upgrading Palestine from an "observer entity" to a "non-member observer state" within the United Nations system, which was described as de facto recognition of the PLO's sovereignty. Palestine's new status is equivalent to that of the Holy See; similarly, Switzerland was a non-member observer state for more than 50 years (until 2002). The UN has permitted Palestine to title its representative office to the UN as "The Permanent Observer Mission of the State of Palestine to the United Nations", and Palestine has instructed its diplomats to officially represent "The State of Palestine"—no longer the Palestinian National Authority. On 17 December 2012, UN Chief of Protocol Yeocheol Yoon declared that "the designation of 'State of Palestine' shall be used by the Secretariat in all official United Nations documents", thus recognising the title 'State of Palestine' as the state's official name for all UN purposes. As of 30 October 2014, 135 (69.9%) of the 193 member states of the United Nations have recognised the State of Palestine. Many of the countries that do not recognise the State of Palestine nevertheless recognise the PLO as the "representative of the Palestinian people". The PLO's Executive Committee is empowered by the Palestinian National Council to perform the functions of government of the State of Palestine. On 25 May 2014 during his visit to the Holy Land, Pope Francis, in a carefully worded statement, made explicit reference to the "State of Palestine".

In 1946, Transjordan gained independence from the British Mandate for Palestine. A year later, the UN adopted a partition plan for a two-state solution in the remaining territory of the mandate. The plan was accepted by the Jewish leadership, but rejected by the Arab leaders and Britain refused to implement the plan. On the eve of final British withdrawal, the Jewish Agency for Israel declared the establishment of the State of Israel according to the proposed UN plan. The Arab Higher Committee did not declare a state of its own and instead, together with Transjordan, Egypt, and the other members of the Arab League of the time, commenced military action resulting in the 1948 Arab–Israeli War. During the war, Israel gained additional territories that were expected to form part of the Arab state under the UN plan. Egypt occupied the Gaza Strip and Transjordan occupied the West Bank. Egypt initially supported the creation of an All-Palestine Government, but disbanded it in 1959. Transjordan never recognised it and instead decided to incorporate the West Bank with its own territory to form Jordan. The annexation was ratified in 1950 but was rejected by the international community. The Six-Day War in 1967, when Egypt, Jordan, and Syria fought against Israel, ended with Israel being in occupation of the West Bank and Gaza Strip, besides other territories.

In 1964, when the West Bank was controlled by Jordan, the Palestine Liberation Organisation was established there with the goal to confront Israel. The Palestinian National Charter of the PLO defines the boundaries of Palestine as the whole remaining territory of the mandate, including Israel. Following the Six-Day War, the PLO moved to Jordan, but later relocated to Lebanon after Black September in 1971. In 1974, the Arab League recognised the PLO as the sole legitimate representative of the Palestinian people, and it gained observer status at the UN General Assembly. After the 1982 Lebanon War, the PLO moved to Tunisia.

In 1979, through the Camp David Accords, Egypt signaled an end to any claim of its own over the Gaza Strip. In July 1988, Jordan ceded its claims to the West Bank—with the exception of guardianship over Haram al-Sharif—to the PLO. In November 1988, the PLO legislature, while in exile, declared the establishment of the "State of Palestine". In the month following, it was quickly recognised by many states, including Egypt and Jordan. In the Palestinian Declaration of Independence, the State of Palestine is described as being established on the "Palestinian territory", without explicitly specifying further. Because of this, some of the countries that recognised the State of Palestine in their statements of recognition refer to the "1967 borders", thus recognising as its territory only the occupied Palestinian territory, and not Israel. The UN membership application submitted by the State of Palestine also specified that it is based on the "1967 borders". During the negotiations of the Oslo Accords, the PLO recognised Israel's right to exist, and Israel recognised the PLO as representative of the Palestinian people. Between 1993 and 1998, the PLO made commitments to change the provisions of its Palestinian National Charter that are inconsistent with the aim for a two-state solution and peaceful coexistence with Israel.

After Israel took control of the West Bank from Jordan and Gaza Strip from Egypt, it began to establish Israeli settlements there. These were organised into Judea and Samaria district (West Bank) and Hof Aza Regional Council (Gaza Strip) in the Southern District. Administration of the Arab population of these territories was performed by the Israeli Civil Administration of the Coordinator of Government Activities in the Territories and by local municipal councils present since before the Israeli takeover. In 1980, Israel decided to freeze elections for these councils and to establish instead Village Leagues, whose officials were under Israeli influence. Later this model became ineffective for both Israel and the Palestinians, and the Village

Leagues began to break up, with the last being the Hebron League, dissolved in February 1988.

As envisioned in the Oslo Accords, Israel allowed the PLO to establish interim administrative institutions in the Palestinian territories, which came in the form of the PNA. It was given civilian control in Area B and civilian and security control in Area A, and remained without involvement in Area C. In 2005, following the implementation of Israel's unilateral disengagement plan, the PNA gained full control of the Gaza Strip with the exception of its borders, airspace, and territorial waters. Following the inter-Palestinian conflict in 2006, Hamas took over control of the Gaza Strip (it already had majority in the PLC), and Fatah took control of the West Bank (and the rest of the PNA institutions). From 2007, the Gaza Strip was governed by Hamas, and the West Bank by Fatah.

McMahon–Hussein Correspondence (1915–1916)

In the early years of World War I, negotiations took place between the British High Commissioner in Egypt Henry McMahon and Sharif of Mecca Husayn bin Ali for an alliance of sorts between the Allies and the Arabs in the Near East against the Ottomans. On 24 October 1915, McMahon sent to Hussein a note which the Arabs came to regard as their "Declaration of Independence". In McMahon's letter, part of the McMahon–Hussein Correspondence, McMahon declared Britain's willingness to recognise the independence of the Arabs, both in the Levant and the Hejaz, subject to certain exemptions. It stated on behalf of the Government of Great Britain that:

The two districts of Mersina and Alexandretta and portions of Syria lying to the west of the districts of Damascus, Homs, Hama and Aleppo cannot be said to be purely Arab, and should be excluded from the limits demanded.

With the above modification, and without prejudice of our existing treaties with Arab chiefs, we accept those limits.

As for those regions lying within those frontiers wherein Great Britain is free to act without detriment to the interest of her ally, France, I am empowered in the name of the Government of Great Britain to give the following assurances and make the following reply to your letter:

Subject to the above modifications, Great Britain is prepared to recognise and support the independence of the Arabs in all the regions within the limits demanded by the Sherif of Mecca.

The exemptions from Arab control of certain areas set out in the McMahon note were to seriously complicate the problems of peace in the Near East. At the time, the Arab portions of the Ottoman Empire were divided into administrative units called *vilayets* and *sanjaks.* Palestine was divided into the *sanjuks* of Acre and Nablus, both of which were a part of the vilayet of Beirut, and an independent *sanjak* of Jerusalem. The areas exempted from Arab control by the McMahon note included "Syria lying to the west of the districts of Damascus, Homs, Hama, and Aleppo." The British understanding was that "Damascus" meant the *vilayet* and not the city of Damascus, and accordingly virtually all of Palestine was excluded from Arab control. The British entered into the secret Sykes–Picot Agreement on 16 May 1916 and the commitment of the Balfour Declaration of 1917, for example, on that understanding.

The Arabs, however, insisted at the 1919 Paris Peace Conference at the end of the war that "Damascus" meant the city of Damascus – which left Palestine in their hands. However, in 1915, these problems of interpretation did not occur to Hussein, who agreed to the British wording. The Arab interpretation of the agreement formed the basis of Arab claims to Palestine at the peace conference.

League of Nations Mandate for Palestine (1920–1948)

Despite Arab objections based in part on the Arab interpretation of the McMahon correspondence noted above, Britain was given the League of Nations Mandate for Palestine. The Mandate was administered as two territories: Palestine and Transjordan, with the Jordan River being the boundary between them. The boundaries under the Mandate also did not follow those sought by the Jewish community, which sought the inclusion of the east bank of the Jordan into the Palestinian territory, to which the objective of the Mandate for a homeland for the Jewish people would apply. It was made clear from before the commencement of the Mandate, and a clause to that effect was inserted in the Mandate, that the objective set out in the Mandate would not apply to Transjordan. Transjordan was destined for early independence. The objective of the Mandate was to apply only to territory west of the Jordan, which was commonly referred to as Palestine by the British administration, and as Eretz Israel by the Jewish community.

The Arab League and the Arab Higher Committee (1945) The framers of the Arab League sought to include the Palestinian Arabs within the framework of the League from its inception. An annex to the League Pact declared:

Even though Palestine was not able to control her own destiny, it was on the basis of the recognition of her independence that the Covenant of the League of Nations determined a system of government for her. Her existence and her independence among the nations can, therefore, no more be questioned *de jure* than the independence of any of the other Arab States... Therefore, the States signatory to the Pact of the Arab League consider that in view of Palestine's special circumstances, the Council of the League should designate an Arab delegate from Palestine to participate in its work until this country enjoys actual independence.

In November 1945, the Arab League reconstituted the Arab Higher Committee comprising twelve members as the supreme executive body of Palestinian Arabs in the territory of the British Mandate of Palestine. The committee was dominated by the Palestine Arab Party and was immediately recognised by Arab League countries. The Mandate government recognised the new Committee two months later. The Constitution of the League of Arab States says the existence and independence of Palestine cannot be questioned *de jure* even though the outward signs of this independence have remained veiled as a result of *force majeure.*

1947-1948 War in Palestine

Partition of Palestine (1948): In 1946, Jewish leaders – including Nahum Goldmann, Rabbi Abba Silver, Moshe Shertok, and David Ben Gurion – proposed a union between Arab Palestine and Transjordan. Also in 1946, leaders of the Zionist movement in the U.S. sought the postponement of a determination of the application by Transjordan for United Nations membership until the status of Mandate Palestine as a whole was determined. However, at its final session the League of Nations recognised the independence of Transjordan, with the agreement of Britain.

The United Nations Special Committee on Palestine (UNSCOP), which was formed to recommend a solution to Britain's dilemma in Palestine, subsequently reported that the proposed Arab state would not be economically viable. The report indicated that the Arab state would be forced to call for financial assistance "from international institutions in the way of loans for expansion of education, public health and other vital social services of a non-self-supporting nature." A technical note from the Secretariat explained that without some redistribution of customs from the Jewish state, Arab Palestine would not be economically viable. The Committee was satisfied that the proposed Jewish State and the City of Jerusalem would be viable.

In 1947, the United Nations proposed the partition of Mandate Palestine into an Arab state, a Jewish state, and a Corpus Separatum for Jerusalem. The United Nations Partition Plan for Palestine was a resolution adopted on 29 November 1947 by the General Assembly of the United Nations. Its title was United Nations General Assembly Resolution 181 (II) Future Government of Palestine. The resolution noted Britain's planned termination of the British Mandate for Palestine and recommended the partition of Palestine into two states, one Arab and one Jewish, with the Jerusalem-Bethlehem area being under special international protection, administered by the United Nations. The resolution included a highly detailed description of the recommended boundaries for each proposed state. The resolution also contained a plan for an economic union between the proposed states, and a plan for the protection of religious and minority rights. The resolution sought to address the conflicting objectives and claims to the Mandate territory of two competing nationalist movements, Zionism (Jewish nationalism) and Arab nationalism, as well as to resolve the plight of Jews displaced as a result of the Holocaust. The resolution called for the withdrawal of British forces and termination of the Mandate by 1 August 1948, and establishment of the new independent states by 1 October 1948.

The Partition Plan was accepted by the Jewish leadership, but rejected by the Arab leaders. The Arab League threatened to take military measures to prevent the partition of Palestine and to ensure the national rights of the Palestinian Arab population. On 14 May 1948, the chairman of the Jewish Agency for Palestine, declared *the establishment of a Jewish state in Eretz-Israel, to be known as the State of Israel.* U.S. President Harry Truman recognised the State of Israel *de facto* the following day. The Arab countries declared war on the newly formed State of Israel heralding the start of the 1948 Arab-Israeli War. On 12 April 1948, the Arab League announced:

The Arab armies shall enter Palestine to rescue it. His Majesty (King Farouk, representing the League) would like to make it clearly understood that such measures should be looked upon as temporary and devoid of any character of the occupation or partition of Palestine, and that after completion of its liberation, that country would be handed over to its owners to rule in the way they like.

Arab–Israeli War (1948)

During the 1948 Arab-Israeli War, Transjordan occupied the area of Cisjordan, now called the West Bank (including East Jerusalem), which it continued to control in accordance with the 1949 Armistice

Agreements and a political union formed in December 1948. Military Proclamation Number 2 of 1948 provided for the application in the West Bank of laws that were applicable in Palestine on the eve of the termination of the Mandate. On 2 November 1948, the military rule was replaced by a civilian administration by virtue of the Law Amending Public Administration Law in Palestine. Military Proclamation Number 17 of 1949, Section 2, vested the King of Jordan with all the powers that were enjoyed by the King of England, his ministers and the High Commissioner of Palestine by the Palestine Order-in-Council, 1922. Section 5 of this law confirmed that all laws, regulations and orders that were applicable in Palestine until the termination of the Mandate would remain in force until repealed or amended.

After the war, which the Israelis call the War of Independence and the Palestinians call the Catastrophe, the 1949 Armistice Agreements established the separation lines between the combatants, leaving Israel in control of some of the areas which had been designated for the Arab state under the Partition Plan, Transjordan in control of the West Bank, Egypt in control of the Gaza Strip and Syria in control of the Himmah Area. The Arab League "supervised" the Egyptian trusteeship of the Palestinian government in Gaza after and secured assurances from Jordan that the 1950 Act of Union was "without prejudice to the final settlement".

The Second Arab-Palestinian Congress was held in Jericho on 1 December 1948 at the end of the war. The delegates proclaimed Abdullah King of Palestine and called for a union of Arab Palestine with the Hashemite Kingdom of Transjordan. Avi Plascov says that Abdullah contacted the Nashashibi opposition, local mayors, mukhars, those opposed to the Husaynis, and opposition members of the AHC. Plascov said that the Palestinian Congresses were conducted in accordance with prevailing Arab custom. He also said that contrary to the widely held belief outside Jordan the representatives did reflect the feelings of a large segment of the population.

The Transjordanian Government agreed to the unification on 7 December 1948, and on 13 December the Transjordanian parliament approved the creation of the Hashemite Kingdom of Jordan. The change of status was reflected by the adoption of this new official name on 21 January 1949. Unification was ratified by a joint Jordanian National Assembly on 24 April 1950 which comprised twenty representatives each from the East and West Bank. The Act of Union contained a protective clause which preserved Arab rights in Palestine "without prejudice to any final settlement".

Many legal scholars say the declaration of the Arab League and the Act of Union implied that Jordan's claim of sovereignty was provisional, because it had always been subject to the emergence of the Palestinian state. A political union was legally established by the series of proclamations, decrees, and parliamentary acts in December 1948. Abdullah thereupon took the title King of Jordan, and he officially changed the country's name to the Hashemite Kingdom of Jordan in April 1949. The 1950 Act of Union confirmed and ratified King Abdullah's actions. Following the annexation of the West Bank, only two countries formally recognised the union: Britain and Pakistan. Thomas Kuttner notes that de facto recognition was granted to the regime, most clearly evidenced by the maintaining of consulates in East Jerusalem by several countries, including the United States. Joseph Weiler agreed, and said that other states had engaged in activities, statements, and resolutions that would be inconsistent with non-recognition. Joseph Massad said that the members of the Arab League granted *de facto* recognition and that the United States had formally recognised the annexation, except for Jerusalem. The policy of the U.S. Department, was stated in a paper on the subject prepared for the Foreign Ministers meetings in London in May was in favour of the incorporation of Central Palestine into Jordan, but desired that it be done gradually and not by sudden proclamation. Once the annexation took place, the Department approved of the action "in the sense that it represents a logical development of the situation which took place as a result of a free expression of the will of the people.... The United States continued to wish to avoid a public expression of approval of the union."

The United States government extended *de jure* recognition to the Government of Transjordan and the Government of Israel on the same day, 31 January 1949. U.S. President Truman told King Abdullah that the policy of the U.S. as regards a final territorial settlement in Palestine had been stated in the General Assembly on 30 November 1948 by the American representative. The U.S. supported Israeli claims to the boundaries set forth in the UN General Assembly resolution of 29 November 1947, but believed that if Israel sought to retain additional territory in Palestine allotted to the Arabs, it should give the Arabs territorial compensation. Clea Bunch said that "President Truman crafted a balanced policy between Israel and its moderate Hashemite neighbours when he simultaneously extended formal recognition to the newly created state of Israel and the Kingdom of Transjordan. These two nations were inevitably linked in the President's mind as twin emergent states: one serving the needs of the refugee Jew, the other absorbing recently displaced Palestinian Arabs. Truman was aware of the private agreements that existed between Jewish Agency leaders and King Abdullah I of Jordan. Thus, it made perfect sense to Truman to favour both states with *de jure* recognition."

Sandra Berliant Kadosh analyzed U.S. policy toward the West Bank in 1948, based largely on the Foreign Relations Documents of the United States. She noted that the U.S. government believed that the most satisfactory solution regarding the disposition of the greater part of Arab Palestine would be incorporation in Transjordan and that the State Department approved the Principle underlying the Jericho resolutions. Kadosh said that the delegates claimed to represent 90 percent of the population, and that they ridiculed the Gaza government. They asserted that it represented only its eighty-odd members.

Egypt supervised an independent government of Palestine in Gaza as a trustee on behalf of the Arab League. An Egyptian Ministerial order dated 1 June 1948 declared that all laws in force during the Mandate would continue to be in force in the Gaza Strip. Another order issued on 8 August 1948 vested an Egyptian Administrator-General with the powers of the High Commissioner. The All-Palestine Government issued a Declaration of the Independent State of Palestine on 1 October 1948. In 1957, the Basic Law of Gaza established a Legislative Council that could pass laws which were given to the High Administrator-General for approval. In March 1962, a Constitution for the Gaza Strip was issued confirming the role of the Legislative Council.

After the War

All-Palestine Government: The All-Palestine Government (Arabic: ÍßæãÉ Úãæã ÝáÓØíä *Hukumat 'umum Filastin*) was established by the Arab League on 22 September 1948, during the 1948 Arab-Israeli War. It was soon recognised by all Arab League members, except Jordan. Though jurisdiction of the Government was declared to cover the whole of the former Mandatory Palestine, its effective jurisdiction was limited to the Gaza Strip. The Prime Minister of the Gaza-seated administration was named Ahmed Hilmi Pasha, and the President was named Haj Amin al-Husseini, former chairman of the Arab Higher Committee.

Shortly thereafter, the Jericho Conference named King Abdullah I of Transjordan, "King of Arab Palestine". The Congress called for the union of Arab Palestine and Transjordan and Abdullah announced his intention to annex the West Bank. The other Arab League member states opposed Abdullah's plan. The U.S. advised the Arab states that the U.S. attitude regarding Israel had been clearly stated in the UN by Dr. Jessup on 20 November 1949. He said that the U.S. supported Israeli claims to the boundaries set forth in the UN General Assembly resolution. However, the U.S. believed that if Israel sought to retain additional territory in Palestine it should give the Arabs other territory as compensation. The Israelis agreed that the boundaries were negotiable, but did not agree to the principle of compensation as a precondition. Israel's Foreign Minister Eban stressed that it was undesirable to undermine what had already been accomplished by the armistice agreements, and maintained that Israel held no territory wrongfully, since her occupation of the areas had been sanctioned by the armistice agreements, as had the occupation of the territory in Palestine held by the Arab states.

In late 1949, under the auspices of the UNCCP, their subsidiary Economic Survey Mission for the Middle East, headed by Gordon R. Clapp, recommended four development projects, involving the Wadi Zerqa basin in Jordan, the Wadi Qelt watershed and stream bed in Arab Palestine, the Litani River in Lebanon, and the Ghab valley in Syria. The World Bank considered the mission's plans positive, and U.S. President Harry Truman subsequently announced that the Foreign Economic Assistance Act of 1950 contained an appropriation of US$27 million for the development projects recommended by the Clapp Mission and to assist Palestinian refugees.

In a diplomatic conversation held on 5 June 1950 between Stuart W. Rockwell of the State Department's Office of African and Near Eastern Affairs and Abdel Monem Rifai, a Counsellor of the Jordan Legation. Rifai asked when the U.S. was going to recognise the union of Arab Palestine and Jordan. Rockwell explained the Department's position, stating that it was not the custom of the U.S. to issue formal statements of recognition every time a foreign country changed its territorial area. The union of Arab Palestine and Jordan had been brought about as a result of the will of the people and the U.S. accepted the fact that Jordanian sovereignty had been extended to the new area. Rifai said he had not realised this and that he was very pleased to learn that the U.S. did in fact recognise the union. The U.S. State Department published this memorandum of conversation in 1978.

The All-Palestine Government was under official Egyptian protection, but on the other hand it had no executive role, but rather mostly political and symbolic. Its importance gradually declined, especially with the government seat relocation from Gaza to Cairo, following the Suez Crisis. In 1959, the All-Palestine entity was officially merged into the United Arab Republic, becoming de facto under

Egyptian military occupation. The All-Palestine Government is regarded by some as the first attempt to establish an independent Palestinian state, whilst most just saw it as an Egyptian puppet, only to be annulled a few years after its creation by no less than President Gamal Abdel Nasser of Egypt.

The Six-Day War (1967)

Between 5 and 10 June 1967, a war – known as the Six-Day War – was fought, in which Israel, defending itself against attacks from many surrounding countries, effectively seized control of the Gaza Strip and the Sinai Peninsula from Egypt, the West Bank, including East Jerusalem from Jordan, and the Golan Heights from Syria.

On 9 June 1967, Israeli Foreign Minister Eban assured the U.S. that it was not seeking territorial aggrandizement and had no "colonial" aspirations. U.S. Secretary of State Dean Rusk stressed to Israel that no settlement with Jordan would be accepted by the global community unless it gave Jordan some special position in the Old City of Jerusalem. The U.S. also assumed Jordan would receive the bulk of the West Bank as that was regarded as Jordanian territory.

On 3 November 1967, U.S. Ambassador Goldberg called on King Hussein of Jordan, saying that the U.S. was committed to the principle of political independence and territorial integrity and was ready to reaffirm it bilaterally and publicly in the Security Council resolution. According to Goldberg, the U.S. believed in territorial integrity, withdrawal, and recognition of secure boundaries. Goldberg said the principle of territorial integrity has two important sub-principles, there must be a withdrawal to recognised and secure frontiers for all countries, not necessarily the old armistice lines, and there must be mutuality in adjustments.

The U.S. President's Special Assistant, Walt Rostow, told Israeli ambassador Harmon that he had already stressed to Foreign Minister Eban that the U.S. expected the thrust of the settlement would be toward security and demilitarisation arrangements rather than toward major changes in the armistice lines. Harmon said the Israeli position was that Jerusalem should be an open city under unified administration, but that the Jordanian interest in Jerusalem could be met through arrangements including "sovereignty". Rostow said the U.S. government assumed (and Harman confirmed) that despite public statements to the contrary, the Government of Israel position on Jerusalem was that which Eban, Harman, and Evron had given several times, that Jerusalem was negotiable.

Rift between Jordan and Palestinian Leadership (1970)

After the events of Black September in Jordan, the rift between the Palestinian leadership and the Kingdom of Jordan continued to widen. The Arab League affirmed the right of the Palestinian people to *self-determination* and called on all the Arab states, including Jordan, to undertake to defend Palestinian national unity and not to interfere in internal Palestinian affairs. The Arab League also 'affirmed the right of the Palestinian people to establish an independent national authority under the command of the Palestine Liberation Organisation, the sole legitimate representative of the Palestinian people in any Palestinian territory that is liberated.' King $ussein dissolved the Jordanian parliament. Half of its members had been West Bank representatives. He renounced Jordanian claims to the West Bank, and allowed the PLO to assume responsibility as the Provisional Government of Palestine. The Kingdom of Jordan, Egypt, and Syria no longer act as the legitimate representatives of the Palestinian people, or their territory.

Rise of the Palestinian Liberation Organisation (1974)

At the Rabat summit conference in 1974, Jordan and the other members of the Arab League declared that the Palestinian Liberation Organisation was the "sole legitimate representative of the [Arab] Palestinian people", thereby relinquishing to that organisation its role as representative of the West Bank.

In a speech delivered on 1 September 1982, U.S. President Ronald Reagan called for a settlement freeze and continued to support full Palestinian autonomy in political union with Jordan. He also said that "It is the United States' position that – in return for peace – the withdrawal provision of Resolution 242 applies to all fronts, including the West Bank and Gaza."

The Amman Agreement of 11 February 1985, declared that the PLO and Jordan would pursue a proposed confederation between the state of Jordan and a Palestinian state. In 1988, King Hussein dissolved the Jordanian parliament and renounced Jordanian claims to the West Bank. The PLO assumed responsibility as the Provisional Government of Palestine and an independent state was declared.

History

Declaration of Independence (1988): Declassified diplomatic documents reveal that in 1974, on the eve of the UN debate that granted the PLO an observer status, some parts of the PLO leadership were considering to proclaim the formation of a Palestinian government in exile at some point. This plan, however, was not carried out.

The Palestinian Declaration of Independence was approved by the Palestinian National Council (PNC) in Algiers on 15 November 1988, by a vote of 253 in favour, 46 against and 10 abstentions. It was read by Yasser Arafat at the closing session of the 19th PNC to a standing ovation. Upon completing the reading of the declaration, Arafat, as Chairman of the Palestine Liberation Organisation assumed the title of "President of Palestine".

Referring to "the historical injustice inflicted on the Palestinian Arab people resulting in their dispersion and depriving them of their right to self-determination," the declaration recalled the Treaty of Lausanne (1923) and UN General Assembly Resolution 181 (1947 Partition Plan) as supporting the rights of Palestinians and Palestine. The declaration then proclaims a "State of Palestine on our Palestinian territory with its capital Jerusalem". The borders of the declared State of Palestine were not specified. The population of the state was referred to by the statement: "The State of Palestine is the state of Palestinians wherever they may be". The state was defined as an Arab country by the statement: "The State of Palestine is an Arab state, an integral and indivisible part of the Arab nation". The declaration was accompanied by a PNC call for multilateral negotiations on the basis of UN Security Council Resolution 242. This call was later termed "the Historic Compromise", as it implied acceptance of the "two-state solution", namely that it no longer questioned the legitimacy of the State of Israel. The PNC's political communiqué accompanying the declaration called only for withdrawal from "Arab Jerusalem" and the other "Arab territories occupied." Arafat's statements in Geneva a month later were accepted by the United States as sufficient to remove the ambiguities it saw in the declaration and to fulfill the longheld conditions for open dialogue with the United States.

As a result of the declaration, the United Nations General Assembly (UNGA) convened, inviting Arafat, Chairman of the PLO to give an address. An UNGA resolution was adopted "acknowledging the proclamation of the State of Palestine by the Palestine National Council on 15 November 1988," and it was further decided that "the designation 'Palestine' should be used in place of the designation 'Palestine Liberation Organisation' in the United Nations system," and it delegate was assigned a seated in the UN General Assembly immediately after non-member states, and before all other observers. One hundred and four states voted for this resolution, forty-four abstained, and two – the United States and Israel – voted against. By mid-December, seventy-five states had recognised Palestine, rising to eighty-nine states by February 1989.

By the 1988 declaration, the PNC empowered its central council to form a government-in-exile when appropriate, and called upon its executive committee to perform the duties of the government-in-exile until its establishment.

Palestinian Authority (1994)

Under the terms of the Oslo Accords signed between Israel and the PLO, the latter assumed control over the Jericho area of the West Bank and the Gaza Strip on 17 May 1994. On 28 September 1995, following the signing of the Israeli-Palestinian Interim Agreement on the West Bank and Gaza Strip, Israeli military forces withdrew from the West Bank towns of Nablus, Ramallah, Jericho, Jenin, Tulkarem, Qalqilya and Bethlehem. In December 1995, the PLO also assumed responsibility for civil administration in 17 areas in Hebron. While the PLO assumed these responsibilities as a result of Oslo, a new temporary interim administrative body was set up as a result of the Accords to carry out these functions on the ground: the Palestinian National Authority (PNA).

An analysis outlining the relationship between the PLO, the PNA (or PA), Palestine and Israel in light of the interim arrangements set out in the Oslo Accords begins by stating that, "Palestine may best be described as a transitional association between the PA and the PLO." It goes on to explain that this transitional association accords the PA responsibility for local government and the PLO responsibility for representation of the Palestinian people in the international arena, while prohibiting it from concluding international agreements that affect the status of the West Bank and Gaza Strip. This situation is said to be accepted by the Palestinian population insofar as it is viewed as a temporary arrangement.

In 2005, following the implementation of Israel's unilateral disengagement plan, PNA gained full control of the Gaza Strip with the exception of its borders, airspace, and territorial waters. This increased the percentage of land in the Gaza strip nominally governed by the PA from 60 percent to 100 percent.

The West Bank and Gaza Strip continued to be considered by the international community to be Occupied Palestinian Territory, notwithstanding the 1988 declaration of Palestinian independence, the limited self-government accorded to the Palestinian Authority as a result of the 1993 Oslo Accords, and Israel's withdrawal from Gaza as part of the Israel's unilateral disengagement plan of 2005, which saw the dismantlement of four Israeli settlements in the West Bank and all settlements in the Gaza Strip.

In March 2008, it was reported that the PA was working to increase the number of countries that recognise Palestine and that a PA representative had signed a bilateral agreement between the State of Palestine and Costa Rica. A recent Al-Haq position paper said the reality is that the PA has entered into various agreements with international organisations and states. These instances of foreign relations undertaken by the PA signify that the Interim Agreement is part of a larger on-going peace process, and that the restrictions on the foreign policy operations of the PA conflict with the inalienable right of the Palestinian people to self-determination, now a norm with a nature of jus cogens, which includes a right to engage in international relations with other peoples.

When the PA is exercising the power that is granted to them by the Oslo Accords, they're acting in the capacity of an agency whose authority is based on an agreement between Israel and the PLO and not as a state.

Split of the Fatah and Hamas

In 2007, after Hamas's legislative victories, the Fatah and Hamas engaged into a violent conflict, taking place mainly in the Gaza Strip, leading to effective collapse of the Palestinian national unity government. After the takeover in Gaza by Hamas on 14 June 2007, Palestinian Authority Chairman Abbas dismissed the Hamas-led government and appointed Salam Fayyad as Prime Minister. Though the new government's authority is claimed to extend to all Palestinian territories, in effect it became limited to the West Bank, as Hamas hasn't recognised the move and continued to rule the Gaza Strip. While PNA budget comes mainly from various aid programs and support of the Arab League, the Hamas Government in Gaza became dependent mainly on Iran until the eruption of the Arab Spring.

2013 Change of Name

Following the successful passage of the 2012 United Nations status resolution which changed Palestine's status at the UN to that of observer state, on 3 January 2013, Abbas signed a presidential decree 1/2013 officially changing the name of the 'Palestinian Authority' to the 'State of Palestine' The decree stated that "Official documents, seals, signs and letterheads of the Palestinian National Authority official and national institutions shall be amended by replacing the name 'Palestinian National Authority' whenever it appears by the name 'State of Palestine' and by adopting the emblem of the State of Palestine." According to international lawyer John V. Whitbeck the decree results in absorbing of the Palestinian Authority into the State of Palestine. On 8 January 2013 the Minister of Communication Safa Naseeruddin, said that because issuing new stamps requires Israeli approval to print them and bring them into the country, it was decided that the new stamps will be printed in Bahrain and the first of these stamps will be used by Palestinian embassies and other diplomatic missions abroad.

On 5 January 2013 Abbas ordered all Palestinian embassies to change any official reference to the Palestinian Authority into State of Palestine. Missions in countries that voted "against" UNGA resolution 67/19 of 2012 are ordered to consult the foreign ministry. Three days later, Omar Awadallah, a foreign ministry official, said that those missions should also use the new name. Some of the countries themselves, such as Norway, Sweden and Spain, stick to the Palestinian Authority term even though they voted "in favour" of the UNGA resolution.

On 6 January 2013, Abbas ordered his cabinet of ministers to prepare regulations to issue new Palestinian passports, official signs and postage stamps in the name of the 'State of Palestine'. Two days later, following negative Israel reaction, it was announced that the change will not apply to documents used at Israel checkpoints in the West Bank and Israeli crossings, unless there is a further decision by Abbas. Saeb Erekat then said the new emblem will be used in correspondence with countries that have recognised a state of Palestine.

For the time being the governments of the renamed Authority established in 1994 and of the State established in 1988 remain distinct. On 5 January 2013 it was announced that it is expected the PLO Central Council would take over the functions of the Palestinian Authority's government and parliament. On the following day, Saeb Erekat, head of the PLO negotiations department, said that the authority should draft a new constitution.

Following the change in name, Turkey became the first state to recognise this change, and on 15 April 2013, the Turkish Consul-General in East Jerusalem ªakir Torunlar presented his credentials as first Turkish Ambassador to the State of Palestine to Palestinian President in Ramallah.

Palestine in the United Nations

2011 United Nations Membership Application: After a two-year impasse in negotiations with Israel, the Palestinian Authority sought to gain recognition as a state according to its 1967 borders with East Jerusalem as its capital from the UN General Assembly in September 2011. A successful application for membership in the UN would require approval from the UN Security Council and a two-thirds majority in the UN General Assembly.

On the prospect of this being successful, U.S. Ambassador to the United Nations Susan Rice alluded to a potential U.S. government withdrawal of UN funding: "This would be exceedingly politically damaging in our domestic context, as you can well imagine. And I cannot frankly think of a greater threat to our ability to maintain financial and political support for the United Nations in Congress than such an outcome." On 28 June, the U.S. Senate passed S.Res. 185 calling on U.S. President Barack Obama to veto the motion and threatening a withdrawal of aid to the West Bank if the Palestinians followed through on their plans. At the likely prospect of a veto, Palestinian leaders signalled they might opt instead for a more limited upgrade to "non-member state" status, which requires only the approval of the UN General Assembly.

Mahmoud Abbas stated he would accept a return to negotiations and abandon the decision if the Israelis agree to the 1967 borders and the right of return for Palestinian refugees. Israel labelled the plan as a unilateral step, to which Foreign Minister Erekat replied,

> *"We are not going [to the UN] for a unilateral declaration of the Palestinian state. We declared our state in 1988 and we have embassies in more than 130 countries and more countries are recognising our state on the 1967 borders. The recognition of the Palestinian state is a sovereignty decision by the countries and it doesn't need to happen through the UN."*

The Arab League formally backed the plan in May, and was officially confirmed by the PLO on 26 June.

On 11 July, the Quartet on the Middle East met to discuss a return to negotiations, but the meeting produced no result. On 13 July, in an interview with *Haaretz*, Palestinian Ambassador to the United Nations Riyad Mansour claimed that 122 states had so far extended formal recognition to the Palestinian state. On the following day, the Arab League released a draft statement which declared a consensus to "go to the United Nations to request the recognition of the State of Palestine with Al Quds as its capital and to move ahead and request a full membership." The league's secretary-general, Nabil al-Arabi, confirmed the statement and said that the application for membership will be submitted by the Arab League. On 18 July, Syria announced that it had formally recognised the State of Palestine, the last Arab state to do so. The decision was welcomed by the league, but met with criticism from some, including former Lebanese prime minister Selim al-Hoss:

"Syria has always been calling for the liberation of Palestine from Israeli occupation and ambitions. The latest stance, however, shows that [Syria] has given up on a national policy that has spanned several decades. ... Why this abandonment of a national principle, and what is the motive behind it? There is no motive except to satisfy international powers that seek to appease Israel".

On 23 September, Abbas delivered to the UN Secretary-General the official application for recognition of a Palestinian state by the UN and a membership in the same organisation. On 11 November a report was approved by the Security Council which concluded that the Council had been unable "to make a unanimous recommendation" on membership for Palestine.

2011 UNESCO Membership

The PLO was accorded observer status at UNESCO in 1974. In 1989, an application for the admission of Palestine as a member state was submitted by a group of seven states during the 131st session of UNESCO's Executive Board. The board postponed a decision until the next session, and the item was included on each session's agenda thereafter, being repeatedly deferred. During the board's 187th session in September 2011, a draft resolution was presented by 24 states requesting that the application be considered and Palestine be granted membership in the organisation. Following consultations between the representatives of the 58-member board, the draft resolution was put for voting on 5 October. The board voted in favour of recommending the application, winning the approval of 40 states. The resolution to admit Palestine as the agency's 195th member state was adopted at the 36th General Conference on 31 October. Of the 185 dues-paying members eligible for voting, 107 were in favour, 14 were against, 52 abstained and 12 were absent. The resolution was submitted by a total of 43 states. Its membership was ratified on 23 November.

2012 United Nations Observer State Status

By September 2012, with their application for full membership stalled, Palestine had decided to pursue an upgrade in status from "observer entity" to "non-member observer state". On 27 November it was announced that the appeal had been officially made, and would be put to a vote in the General Assembly on 29 November, where their status upgrade was expected to be supported by a majority of states. In addition to granting Palestine "non-member observer state status", the draft resolution "expresses the hope that the Security Council will consider favourably the application submitted on 23 September 2011 by the State of Palestine for admission to full membership in the United Nations, endorses the two state solution based on the pre-1967 borders, and stresses the need for an immediate resumption of negotiations between the two parties."

On 29 November 2012, in a 138–9 vote (with 41 abstentions and 5 absences), General Assembly resolution 67/19 passed, upgrading Palestine to "non-member observer state" status in the United Nations. The new status equates Palestine's with that of the Holy See. Switzerland was also a non-member observer state until 2002. The change in status was described by *The Independent* as "*de facto* recognition of the sovereign state of Palestine".

The vote was a historic benchmark for the recognition of the State of Palestine and its people, while a diplomatic setback for Israel and the United States. Status as an observer state in the UN will allow the State of Palestine to participate in general debate at the General Assembly, to co-sponsor resolutions, to join treaties and specialised UN agencies. Even as a non-member state, the Palestinians could join influential international bodies such as the World Trade Organisation, the World Health Organisation, the World Intellectual Property Organisation, the World Bank and the International Criminal Court, where Palestinian Authority tried to have alleged Israeli war crimes in Gaza (2008-2009) investigated. However, in April 2012 prosecutors refused to open the investigation, saying it was not clear if the Palestinians were qualified as a state - as only states can recognise the court's jurisdiction.

The UN nod can also help to affirm the borders of the Palestinian territories that Israel occupied in 1967. Theoretically Palestine could even claim legal rights over its territorial waters and air space as a sovereign state recognised by the UN.

The UN has, after the resolution was passed, permitted Palestine to title its representative office to the UN as "The Permanent Observer Mission of the State of Palestine to the United Nations", seen by many as a reflexion of the UN's *de facto* recognition of the State of Palestine's sovereignty, and Palestine has started to re-title its name accordingly on postal stamps, official documents and passports. The Palestinian authorities have also instructed its diplomats to officially represent "The State of Palestine", as opposed to the "Palestinian National Authority". On 17 December 2012, UN Chief of Protocol Yeocheol Yoon decided that "the designation of 'State of Palestine' shall be used by the Secretariat in all official United Nations documents".

Government

The State of Palestine consists of the following institutions that are associated with the Palestine Liberation Organisation (PLO):

- President of the State of Palestine – appointed by the Palestinian Central Council
- Palestinian National Council – the legislature that established the State of Palestine
- Executive Committee of the Palestine Liberation Organisation – performs the functions of a government in exile, maintaining an extensive foreign-relations network

These should be distinguished from the President of the Palestinian National Authority, Palestinian Legislative Council (PLC) and PNA Cabinet, all of which are instead associated with the Palestinian National Authority. The State of Palestine's founding document is the Palestinian Declaration of Independence, and it should be distinguished from the unrelated PLO Palestinian National Covenant and PNA Palestine Basic Law.

Palestine is divided into sixteen administrative divisions. Five of these divisions, the governorates of Deir al-Balah, Gaza, North Gaza, Khan Yunis and Rafah, are in the Gaza Strip. The combined area of these governorates is 360 square kilometres (360,000 dunams), and their total population in 2007 was 1,416,539. The remaining eleven governorates are in the West Bank, with a population of 2,345,107 in 2007, living in an area of 5,671 square kilometres (5,671,000 dunams).

The governorates in the West Bank are grouped into three areas per the Oslo II Accord. Area A forms 18% of the West Bank by area, and is administered by the Palestinian government. Area B forms 22% of the West Bank, and is under Palestinian civil control, and joint Israeli-Palestinian security control. Area C, except East Jerusalem, forms 60% of the West Bank, and is administered by the Israeli Civil Administration, except that the Palestinian government provides the education and medical services to the 150,000 Palestinians in the area. More than 99% of Area C is off limits to Palestinians. There are about 330,000 Israelis living in settlements in Area C, in the Judea and Samaria Area. Although Area C is under martial law, Israelis living there are judged in Israeli civil courts.

East Jerusalem, the proclaimed capital of Palestine, is administered as part of the Jerusalem District of Israel, but is claimed by Palestine as part of the Jerusalem Governorate. It was annexed by Israel in 1980, but this annexation is not recognised by any other country. Of the 456,000 people in East Jerusalem, rough 60% are Palestinian and 40% are Israeli.

International Recognition and Foreign Relations

Representation of the State of Palestine is performed by the Palestine Liberation Organisation (PLO). In states that recognise the State of Palestine it maintains embassies. The Palestine Liberation Organisation is represented in various international organisations as member, associate or observer. Because of inconclusiveness in sources in some cases it is impossible to distinguish whether the participation is executed by the PLO as representative of the State of Palestine, by the PLO as a non-state entity or by the PNA.

On 15 December 1988, the State of Palestine's declaration of independence of November 1988 was acknowledged in the General Assembly with Resolution 43/177.

As of 30 October 2014, 135 (69.9%) of the 193 member states of the United Nations have recognised the State of Palestine. Many of the countries that do not recognise the State of Palestine nevertheless recognise the PLO as the "representative of the Palestinian people". The PLO's executive committee is empowered by the PNC to perform the functions of government of the State of Palestine.

On 29 November 2012, UN General Assembly resolution 67/19 passed, upgrading Palestine to "non-member observer state" status in the United Nations. The change in status was described as "*de facto* recognition of the sovereign state of Palestine".

On 3 October 2014, new Swedish Prime Minister Stefan Löfven used his inaugural address in parliament to announce that Sweden would recognise the state of Palestine. The official decision to do so was made on 30 October, making Sweden the first long-term member country of the EU to recognise the state of Palestine. Most of the EU's 28 member states have refrained from recognising Palestinian statehood and those that do - such as Hungary, Poland and Slovakia - did so before joining the bloc.

On 13 October 2014, the UK parliament voted by 274 to 12 in favour of recognising Palestine as a state alongside Israel. The House of Commons backed the move "as a contribution to securing a negotiated two-state solution" - although less than half of MPs took part in the vote. However, the UK government is not bound to do anything as a result of the vote: its current policy is that it "reserves the right to recognise a Palestinian state bilaterally at the moment of our choosing and when it can best help bring about peace".

Multilateral Treaties

The State of Palestine is a party to several multilateral treaties, registered with four depositaries: UNESCO, United Nations, the Netherlands and Switzerland. The ratifications of UNESCO conventions took place in 2011/2012 and followed the Palestine becoming a party of UNESCO, while the ratifications of the other conventions were performed in 2014 while negotiations with Israel were in an impasse.

In notifications of 13 May 2014, the United States informed the Secretary General of the United Nations, that it did not consider the "State of Palestine" (parenthesis added by the United States) a sovereign state and would consider itself "not to be in a treaty relationship with the "State of Palestine"". Canada and Israel lodged similar notifications.

European Union Position

In March 1999, the European Union confirmed in the *Berlin Declaration* the Palestinian right to self-determination, including the right to a viable and peaceful sovereign Palestinian State. This right was declared "not subject to any veto".

The EU supports a Palestinian state within the pre-1967 borders, with only minor modifications mutually agreed. Further, the EU advocates Jerusalem as the future capital of both Israel and Palestine.

Legal status

There are a wide variety of views regarding the status of the State of Palestine, both among the states of the international community and among legal scholars. The existence of a state of Palestine, although controversial, is a reality in the opinions of the states that have established bilateral diplomatic relations.

Statehood for the Purposes of the UN Charter

Palestine Liberation Organisation (PLO) had been recognised as "sole legitimate representative of the Palestinian people," competent on all matters concerning the question of Palestine by the UN General Assembly in addition to the right of the Palestinian people in Palestine to national independence and sovereignty, and was granted observer status at the UN General Assembly as a "non-state entity", from 1974. In mid-November 2011, the PLO submitted an official application to become a full member of the UN. A successful application would require approval from the UN Security Council and a two-thirds majority in the UN General Assembly. However, the Security Council's membership committee deadlocked on the issue and had been "unable to make a unanimous recommendation to the Security Council". The report was the result of seven weeks of meetings, detailing myriad disagreements between the council members on whether Palestine fulfills the requirements set forth in the U.N. charter for members countries. With their application for full membership stalled, the PLO sought an upgrade in status, from "observer entity" to "non-member observer state". In November 2012, UN General Assembly accepted the resolution upgrading Palestine to "non-member observer state" within the United Nations system, reasserting PLO as the representative of the Palestinian people.

The UN Charter protects the territorial integrity or political independence of any state from the threat or use of force. Philip Jessup served as a representative of the United States to the United Nations and as a Judge on the International Court of Justice. During the Security Council hearings regarding Israel's application for membership in the UN, he said:

"[W]e already have, among the members of the United Nations, some political entities which do not possess full sovereign power to form their own international policy, which traditionally has been considered characteristic of a State. We know however, that neither at San Francisco nor subsequently has the United Nations considered that complete freedom to frame and manage one's own foreign policy was an essential requisite of United Nations membership.... ...The reason for which I mention the qualification of this aspect of the traditional definition of a State is to underline the point that the term "State", as used and applied in Article 4 of the Charter of the United Nations, may not be wholly identical with the term "State" as it is used and defined in classic textbooks on international law."

In 2009, Riyad al-Maliki, the Palestinian Foreign Minister of the Palestinian National Authority, provided proof that Palestine had been extended legal recognition as a state by 67 other countries, and had bilateral agreements with states in Latin America, Asia, Africa and Europe.

Declaration and Act of State Doctrine

Many states have recognised the State of Palestine since 1988. Under the principles of customary international law, when a government is recognised by another government, recognition is retroactive in effect, and validates all the actions and conduct of the government so recognised from the commencement of its existence.

Stephen Talmon notes that many countries have a formal policy of recognising states, not their governments. In practice, they usually make no formal declarations regarding recognition. He cites several examples including a memorandum on US recognition policy and practice, dated 25 September 1981, which said that recognition would be implied by the US government's dealings with the new government. Many countries have expressed their intention to enter into relations with the State of Palestine. The US formally recognised the West Bank and Gaza Strip as "one area for political, economic, legal and other purposes" in 1997 at the request of the Palestinian Authority. At that time, it asked the public to take notice of that fact through announcements it placed in the *Federal Register*, the official journal of the US government. The USAID West Bank/Gaza, has been tasked with "state-building" projects in the areas of democracy, governance, resources, and infrastructure. Part of the USAID mission is to "provide flexible and discrete support for implementation of the Quartet Road Map", an internationally backed plan which calls for the progressive development of a viable Palestinian State in the West Bank and Gaza. The European Union (EU) has announced similar external relations programs with the Palestinian Authority.

The view of the European states, which did not extend full recognition was expressed by French President François Mitterrand who stated: "Many European countries are not ready to recognise a Palestine state. Others think that between recognition and non-recognition there are significant degrees; I am among these." But, after the PLO recognised the state of Israel, Mitterrand welcomed the PLO leader, Yasser Arafat, in Paris, in May 1989.

Consequences of the Occupation

After 1967, a number of legal arguments were advanced which dismissed the right of Palestinians to self-determination and statehood. They generally proposed that Palestine was a land void of a legitimate sovereign and supported Israeli claims to the remaining territory of the Palestine Mandate. Historian and journalist, Gershom Gorenberg, says that outside of the pro-settlement community in Israel, these positions are considered quirky. He says that, while the Israeli government has used them for PR purposes abroad, it takes entirely different positions when arguing real legal cases before the Israeli Supreme Court. In 2005 Israel decided to dismantle all Israeli settlements in the Gaza Strip and four in the northern West Bank. Gorenberg notes, the government's decision was challenged in the Supreme Court by settlers, and the government won the case by noting the settlements were in territory whose legal status was that of 'belligerent territory'. The government argued that the settlers should have known the settlements were only temporary.

Most UN member states questioned the claim that Israel held better title to the land than the inhabitants, and stressed that statehood was an inalienable right of the Palestinian people. Legal experts, like David John Ball, concluded that "the Palestinians, based on the principles of self-determination and the power of the U.N., appear to hold better title to the territory." The International Court of Justice subsequently reaffirmed the right of the Palestinian people to self-determination and the prohibition under customary and conventional international law against acquisition of territory by war.

The Israeli Supreme Court, sitting as the High Court of Justice, cited a case involving Gaza and said that "The Judea and Samaria areas are held by the State of Israel in belligerent occupation. The legal representative of the state in the area is the military commander. He is not the sovereign in the territory held in belligerent occupation. His power is granted him by public international law regarding belligerent occupation. The legal meaning of this view is twofold: first, Israeli law does not apply in these areas. They have not been "annexed" to Israel. Second, the legal regime which applies in these areas is determined by public international law regarding belligerent occupation."

The court said most Israelis do not have ownership of the land on which they built their houses and businesses in the territory. "They acquired their rights from the military commander, or from persons acting on his behalf. Neither the military commander nor those acting on his behalf are owners of the property, and they cannot transfer rights better than those they have. To the extent that the Israelis built their homes and assets on land which is not private ('state land'), that land is not owned by the military commander. His authority is defined in regulation 55 of The Hague Regulations. . . . The State of Israel acts . . . as the administrator of the state property and as usufructuary of it."

Decisions of International and National Tribunals

The U.S. State Department *Digest of International Law* says that the terms of the Treaty of Lausanne provided for the application of the principles of state succession to the "A" Mandates. The Treaty of Versailles (1920) provisionally recognised the former Ottoman communities as independent nations. It also required Germany to recognise the disposition of the former Ottoman territories and to recognise the new states laid down within their boundaries. The Treaty of Lausanne required the newly created states that acquired the territory to pay annuities on the Ottoman public debt, and to assume responsibility for the administration of concessions that had been granted by the Ottomans. A dispute regarding the status of the territories was settled by an Arbitrator appointed by the Council of the League of Nations. It was decided that Palestine and Transjordan were newly created states according to the terms of the applicable post-war treaties. In its *Judgment No. 5, The Mavrommatis Palestine Concessions*, the Permanent Court of International Justice also decided that Palestine was responsible as the successor state for concessions granted by Ottoman authorities. The Courts of Palestine and Great Britain decided that title to the properties shown on the Ottoman Civil list had been ceded to the government of Palestine as an allied successor state.

State Succession

A legal analysis by the International Court of Justice noted that the Covenant of the League of Nations had provisionally recognised the communities of Palestine as independent nations. The mandate simply marked a transitory period, with the aim and object of leading the mandated territory to become an independent self-governing State. The Court said that specific guarantees regarding freedom of movement and access to the Holy Sites contained in the Treaty of Berlin (1878) had been preserved under the terms of the Palestine Mandate and a chapter of the United Nations Partition Plan for Palestine. In a separate opinion, Judge Higgins argued that since United Nations Security Council Resolution 242 in 1967 to resolution 1515 in 2003, the "key underlying requirements" have been that "Israel is entitled to exist, to be recognised, and to security, and that the Palestinian people are entitled to their territory, to exercise self-determination, and to have their own State", with resolution 1515 endorsing the Road map for peace proposed by the Middle East Quartet, as a means to achieve these obligations through negotiation.

Article 62 (LXII) of the Treaty of Berlin, 13 July 1878 dealt with religious freedom and civil and political rights in all parts of the Ottoman Empire. The guarantees have frequently been referred to as "religious rights" or "minority rights". However, the guarantees included a prohibition against discrimination in civil and political matters. Difference of religion could not be alleged against any person as a ground for exclusion or incapacity in matters relating to the enjoyment of civil or political rights, admission to public employments, functions, and honors, or the exercise of the various professions and industries, "in any locality whatsoever."

The resolution of the San Remo Conference contained a safeguarding clause for all of those rights. The conference accepted the terms of the Mandate with reference to Palestine, on the understanding that there was inserted in the process-verbal a legal undertaking by the Mandatory Power that it would not involve the surrender of the rights hitherto enjoyed by the non-Jewish communities in Palestine. The draft mandates for Mesopotamia and Palestine, and all of the post-war peace treaties contained clauses for the protection of minorities. The mandates invoked the compulsory jurisdiction of the Permanent Court of International Justice in the event of any disputes.

Article 28 of the Mandate required that those rights be safeguarded in perpetuity, under international guarantee. The General Assembly's *Plan for the Future Government of Palestine* placed those rights under UN protection as part of a minority protection plan. It required that they be acknowledged in a Declaration, embodied in the fundamental laws of the states, and in their Constitutions. The partition plan also contained provisions that bound the new states to international agreements and conventions to which Palestine had become a party and held them responsible for its financial obligations. The Declarations of the Independent State of Israel and the Independent State of Palestine acknowledged the protected rights and were accepted as being in line with UN resolution 181(II).

Opinions of Officials and Legal Scholars

Jacob Robinson was a legal advisor to the United Nations delegation of the Jewish Agency for Palestine during the special session of the General Assembly in 1947. He advised the Zionist Executive that the provisional states had come into existence as a result of the resolution of 29 November 1947.

L.C. Green explained that "recognition of statehood is a matter of discretion, it is open to any existing state to accept as a state any entity it wishes, regardless of the existence of territory or an established government."

Alex Takkenberg writes that while "there is no doubt that the entity 'Palestine' should be considered a state *in statu nascendi* and although it is increasingly likely that the ongoing peace process will eventually culminate in the establishment of a Palestinian state, it is premature to conclude that statehood, as defined by international law, is at present (spring 1997) firmly established." Referring to the four criteria of statehood, as outlined in the 1933 Montevideo Convention – that is, a permanent population, a defined territory, government and the capacity to enter into relations with other states – Takkenberg states that the entity known as Palestine does not fully satisfy these criteria.

Conversely John V. Whitbeck, who served as an advisor to the Palestinian negotiation team during negotiations with Israel, writes that "the State of Palestine already exists," and that when, "Judged by these customary criteria [those of the Montevideo Convention], the State of Palestine is on at least as firm a legal footing as the State of Israel." He continues: "The weak link in Palestine's claim to already exist as a state was, until recently, the fourth criterion, "effective control... Yet a Palestinian executive and legislature, democratically elected with the enthusiastic approval of the international community, now exercises 'effective control' over a portion of Palestinian territory in which the great majority of the state's population lives. It can no longer be seriously argued that Palestine's claim to exist falls at the fourth and final hurdle."

For John Quigley, Palestine's existence as a state predates the 1988 declaration. Tracing Palestine's status as an international entity back to the collapse of the Ottoman Empire after World War I, he recalls that the Palestine Mandate (1918–1948), an arrangement made under Article 22 of the Covenant of the League of Nations, held as its "ultimate objective", the "self-determination and independence of the people concerned." He says that in explicitly referring to the Covenant, the 1988 declaration was reaffirming an existing Palestinian statehood. Noting that Palestine under the Mandate entered into bilateral treaties, including one with Great Britain, the Mandatory power, he cites this as an example of its "sovereignty" at that time. He also notes the corollary of the Stimson Doctrine and the customary prohibition on the use of force contained in the Restatement of Foreign Relations Law of the United States, "an entity does not necessarily cease to be a state even if all of its territory has been occupied by a foreign power".

Robert Weston Ash says that Quigley's analysis of the declaration that the Palestinian Authority provided to the International Criminal Court failed to explain a number of key issues. He says the "Palestinian people" to whom sovereignty reverted upon the departure of the British would have included both Jews and Arabs. He suggests that establishes a colourable Jewish —as well as Arab — claim to all of Palestine which tends to refute Professor Quigley's contention that there are no other claimants to that territory. Ash says there are segments of Israeli society that continue to view "Judea and Samaria" as areas promised to the Jews by the Balfour Declaration and says that the Geneva Convention is not applicable to Israel's presence in those territories.

He cites Yehuda Blum's "Missing Reversioner" and Eugene Rostow's related claim that "The right of the Jewish people to settle in Palestine has never been terminated for the West Bank." Quigley has said that the International Court of Justice findings in the "Wall" case regarding the applicability of the Geneva Convention discredited once and for all, as a legal matter, the "missing reversioner" argument. The International Criminal Court has published a summary of arguments which says that some submissions consider that it is clear that the Palestinian National Authority cannot be regarded as a "State", and that some submit that Palestine is recognised as a State by many States and many institutions. The Court says that a conclusive determination on Palestine's declaration will have to be made by the judges at an appropriate moment.

Disputes have arisen as a result of the Conflict of laws between the Palestinian Authority and Israel. Judgments originating in Israeli Courts are not directly enforceable in the Courts of the Palestinian Authority. The District Court of Israel ruled that the Palestinian Authority satisfied the criteria to be legally treated as a sovereign state The ruling was appealed to the Supreme Court of Israel which ruled that the Palestinian Authority cannot be defined as a foreign state, since recognising states is an exclusive authority of the Ministry of Foreign Affairs. The Supreme Court held that the Palestinian Authority can be granted state immunity on an ad hoc basis when it is warranted by the circumstances. The Knesset responded to the willingness of the judges to engage in examination of the notion of 'statehood for the purpose of state immunity' by adopting a measure that makes it possible to grant sovereign immunity to a 'political entity that is not a state' as part of the 2008 Foreign States Immunity Law, Art. 20.

Stefan Talmon notes that "In international law it is true that one generally recognises the Government which exercises effective control over a territory. But this is not an absolute rule without exceptions." James Crawford notes that despite its prevalence, and inclusion in the statehood criteria found in the Montevideo Convention, effectiveness is not the sole or even the critical criterion for statehood. He cites several examples of annexations and governments that have been recognised despite their lack of a territorial foothold. Israeli Prime Minister Netanyahu recently expressed a willingness to recognise the State of Palestine if it will agree to forgo taking effective control of its airspace, military defence, and not enter into alliances with Israel's enemies.

In November 2009, Palestinian officials were reported to be preparing the ground for asking for recognition of a Palestinian State from the Security Council. The state was envisioned to be based on the 1967 Green Line as an international border with Israel and East Jerusalem as its capital. The plan was reported to have support from Arab states, Russia and the UN Secretary General, Ban Ki-moon. The Secretary General said "Today, the State of Israel exists, but the State of Palestine does not." "It is vital that a sovereign State of Palestine is achieved". "This should be on the basis of the 1967 lines with agreed land swaps and a just and agreed solution to the refugee issue." On 29 January 2010, the representative of Palestine deposited a copy of a letter submitted by Prime Minister Fayyad with the UN Secretary-General. The letter reported on the decree issued by Mahmoud Abbas, "President of the State of Palestine", concerning the formation of an independent commission to follow up on the Goldstone report in compliance with General Assembly resolution 64/10 of 5 November 2009.

Paul De Waart says that the Quartet, particularly the United States, as well as western states, do not consider Palestine to be a state as yet. In their view the statehood of Palestine will be the result of bilateral negotiations between Israel and the Palestinian people. He says they have overlooked that under international law it is not anymore a question of creating but of recognising the State of Palestine.

Israeli legal expert Ruth Lapidoth said the Palestinians have already unilaterally declared statehood, and they did not need to do it again. "Recognition of statehood is a political act, and every state has the right to decide for itself whether to recognise another state."

President Abbas said that the State of Palestine was already in existence and that the current battle is to have the state's border recognised.

Jerome Segal wrote about Salam Fayyad's plan for Palestinian statehood. He said lest anyone believe that the 1988 declaration is ancient history, they should read the new Fayyad plan with more care. It cites the 1988 declaration four times, identifying it as having articulated "the foundations of the Palestinian state."

In September 2010, the World Bank released a report which found the Palestinian Authority "well-positioned to establish a state" at any point in the near future. The report highlighted, however, that unless private-sector growth in the Palestinian economy was stimulated, a Palestinian state would remain donor dependent.

In April 2011, the UN's co-ordinator for the Middle East peace process issued a report lauding the Palestinian Authority, describing "aspects of its administration as sufficient for an independent state."

It echoed similar assessments published the week prior by the International Monetary Fund and the World Bank.

Military

The State of Palestine has a paramilitary force called the Palestinian National Security Forces, with the function of maintaining security and protecting Palestinian citizens and the Palestinian State.

Iran

Iran, also known as Persia officially the Islamic Republic of Iran, is a country in Western Asia. It is bordered to the northwest by Armenia and Azerbaijan, with Kazakhstan and Russia across the Caspian Sea; to the northeast by Turkmenistan; to the east by Afghanistan and Pakistan; to the south by the Persian Gulf and the Gulf of Oman; and to the west by Turkey and Iraq. Comprising a land area of 1,648,195 km^2 (636,372 sq mi), it is the second-largest nation in the Middle East and the 18th-largest in the world; with 78.4 million inhabitants, Iran is the world's 17th most populous nation. It is the only country that has both a Caspian Sea and Indian Ocean coastline. Iran has been of geostrategic importance because of its central location in Eurasia and Western Asia and the Strait of Hormuz.

Iran is home to one of the world's oldest civilizations, beginning with the formation of the Proto-Elamite and Elamite kingdom in 3200–2800 BCE. The Iranian Medes unified the country into the first of many empires in 625 BCE, after which it became the dominant cultural and political power in the region. Iran reached the pinnacle of its power during the Achaemenid Empire (First Persian Empire) founded by Cyrus the Great in 550 BCE, which at its greatest extent comprised major portions of the ancient world, stretching from parts of the Balkans (Bulgaria-Pannonia) and Thrace-Macedonia in the west, to the Indus Valley in the east, making it the largest empire the world had yet seen. The empire collapsed in 330 BCE following the conquests of Alexander the Great. The area eventually regained influence under the Parthian Empire and rose to prominence once more after the establishment of the Sasanian dynasty (Neo-Persian empire) in 224 CE, under which Iran again became one of the leading powers in the world along with the Byzantine Empire for the next four centuries.

Manichaeism and Zoroastrianism were largely replaced after Rashidun Muslims invaded Persia in 633 CE, and conquered it by 651 CE. Iran thereafter played a vital role in the subsequent Islamic Golden Age, producing numerous influential scientists, scholars, artists, and thinkers. The emergence in 1501 of the Safavid dynasty, which promoted the Twelver school of thought as the official religion, marked one of the most important turning points in Iranian and Muslim history. It also culminated into tensions, which in 1514 led to the Battle of Chaldiran. Starting in 1736 under Nader Shah, Iran would once again reach high prominence, reaching its greatest territorial extent since the Sassanid Empire, and briefly possessing what was arguably the most powerful empire in the world. The Persian Constitutional Revolution of 1906 established the nation's first parliament, which operated within a constitutional monarchy. Following a coup d'état instigated by the UK and the US in 1953, Iran gradually became autocratic. Growing dissent against foreign influence and political repression culminated in the Iranian Revolution, which led to the establishment of an Islamic republic on 1 April 1979.

Tehran is the capital and largest city, serving as the cultural, commercial, and industrial centre of the nation. Iran is a major regional and middle power, exerting considerable influence in international energy security and the world economy through its large reserves of fossil fuels, which include the largest natural gas supply in the world and the fourth-largest proven petroleum reserves. It hosts Asia's fourth-largest number of UNESCO World Heritage Sites.

Iran is a founding member of the UN, NAM, OIC and OPEC. Its unique political system, based on the 1979 constitution, combines elements of a parliamentary democracy with a religious theocracy run by the country's clergy, wherein the Supreme Leader wields significant influence. A multicultural nation comprising numerous ethnic and linguistic groups, most inhabitants are Shi'ites, the Iranian rial is its currency, and Persian is the official language.

History of Iran

Early History in Iran

The earliest archaeological artifacts in Iran, like those excavated at the Kashafrud and Ganj Par sites, attest to a human presence in Iran since the Lower Paleolithic era. Neanderthal artifacts dating back to the Middle Paleolithic period have been found mainly in the Zagros region at sites such as Warwasi and Yafteh Cave. Early agricultural communities such as Chogha Golan in 10,000 BCE began to flourish in Iran along with settlements such as Chogha Bonut in 8000 BCE, as well as Susa and Chogha Mish developing in and around the Zagros region.

The emergence of Susa as a city is determined by C14 dating as early as 4395 BCE. There are dozens of pre-historic sites across the Iranian plateau pointing to the existence of ancient cultures and urban settlements in the fourth millennium BCE. During the Bronze age Iran was home to several civilisations such as Elam, Jiroft and Zayandeh Rud civilisations. Elam, the most prominent of these civilisations developed in the southwest of Iran alongside those in Mesopotamia. The development of writing in Elam in fourth millennium BCE paralleled that in Sumer. The Elamite kingdom continued its existence until the emergence of the Median and Achaemenid Empires.

Classical Era

During the second millennium BCE, Proto-Iranian tribes arrived in Iran from the Eurasian steppes, rivaling the native settlers of the country. As these tribes dispersed into the wider area of Greater Iran and beyond, the boundaries of modern Iran were dominated by the Persian, Parthian, and Median tribes. From the late 10th to late 7th centuries BCE, these Iranian peoples, together with the *pre Iranian* kingdoms, fell under the domination of the Assyrian Empire, based in northern Mesopotamia. Under king Cyaxares, the Medes and Persians entered into an alliance with Nabopolassar of Babylon, as well as the Scythians, Cimmerians, and Arameans, and together they attacked the Assyrian Empire. The civil war ravaged Assyrian Empire between 616 BCE and 605 BCE, thus freeing their respective peoples from three centuries of Assyrian rule. The unification of the Median tribes under a single ruler in 728 BCE led to the creation of a Median empire which, by 612 BCE, controlled the whole of Iran as well as eastern Anatolia.

In 550 BCE, Cyrus the Great from the state of Anshan took over the Median empire, and founded the Achaemenid empire by unifying other city states. The conquest of Media was a result of what is called the Persian revolt; the brouhaha was initially triggered by the actions of the Median ruler Astyages and quickly spread to other provinces as they allied with the Persians. Later conquests under Cyrus and his successors expanded the empire to include Lydia, Babylon, Egypt, and the lands to the west of the Indus and Oxus rivers. At its greatest extent, the empire included the modern territories of Iran, Iraq, Kuwait, Syria, Jordan, Israel, Palestine, Lebanon, all significant population centres of ancient Egypt as far west as Libya, Turkey, Thrace and Macedonia, much of the Black Sea coastal regions, Armenia, Georgia, Azerbaijan, much of Central Asia, Afghanistan, northern Saudi Arabia, Pakistan, and parts of Oman and the UAE, making it the first world empire. Conflict on the western borders began with the famous Greco-Persian Wars which continued through the first half of the 5th century BCE and ended with the Persian withdrawal from all of their European territories. The empire had a centralised, bureaucratic administration under the Emperor and a large professional army and civil services, inspiring similar developments in later empires.

In 334 BCE, Alexander the Great invaded the Achaemenid Empire, defeating the last Achaemenid Emperor Darius III at the Battle of Issus in 333 BCE. Following the premature death of Alexander, Iran came under the control of Hellenistic Seleucid Empire. In the middle of the 2nd century BCE, the Parthian Empire rose to become the main power in Iran and continued as a feudal monarchy for nearly five centuries until 224 CE, when it was succeeded by the Sassanid Empire. The Sassanids established an empire roughly within the frontiers achieved by the Achaemenids, with the capital at Ctesiphon, and were alongside the Byzantines the two most dominant powers in the world for nearly four centuries. Most of the period of the Parthian and Sassanid Empires were overshadowed by the Roman-Persian Wars, which raged on their western borders for over 700 years. These wars exhausted both Romans and Sassanids, which arguably led to the defeat of both at the hands of the invading Muslim Arabs.

Middle Ages (652–1501)

The prolonged Roman-Persian wars, as well as social conflict within the Empire opened the way for an Islamic invasion of Iran in the 7th century. Gundeshapur was the most important medical centre of the ancient world at the time of the Islamic conquest. Initially defeated by the Rashidun Caliphate, Iran later came under the rule of their successors the Ummayad and Abbasid Caliphates. The process of conversion of Iranians to Islam which followed was prolonged and gradual. Under the new Arab elite of the Rashidun and later Ummayad Caliphates Iranians, both Muslim (mawali) and non-Muslim (Dhimmi), were discriminated against, being excluded from government and military, and having to pay a special tax. In 750 the Abbasids succeeded in overthrowing the Ummayad Caliphate, mainly due to the support from dissatisfied Iranian mawali. The mawali formed the majority of the rebel army, which was led by the Iranian general Abu Muslim. After two centuries of Arab rule semi-independent and independent Iranian kingdoms (such as the Tahirids, Saffarids, Samanids and Buyids) began to appear on the fringes of the declining Abbasid Caliphate. By the Samanid era in the 9th and 10th centuries Iran's efforts to regain its independence had been well solidified.

The arrival of the Abbasid Caliphs saw a revival of Persian culture and influence, and a move away from Arabic culture. The role of the old Arab aristocracy was slowly replaced by a Persian bureaucracy.

The blossoming Persian literature, philosophy, medicine, and art became major elements in the forming of a Muslim civilization during the Islamic Golden Age. The Islamic Golden Age reached its peak in the 10th and 11th centuries, during which Persia was the main theatre of scientific activity. After the 10th century, Persian, alongside Arabic, was used for scientific, philosophical, historical, mathematical, musical, and medical works, as important Iranian writers such as Nasir al-Din al-Tusi, Avicenna, Qotb al-Din Shirazi, Naser Khusraw and Biruni made contributions to Persian scientific writing.

The cultural revival that began in the Abbasid period led to a resurfacing of Iranian national identity, and so earlier attempts of Arabization never succeeded in Iran. The Iranian Shuubiyah movement became a catalyst for Iranians to regain their independence in their relations with the Arab invaders. The most notable effect of the movement was the continuation of the Persian language attested to the epic poet Ferdowsi, now regarded as the most important figure in Persian literature.

The 10th century saw a mass migration of Turkic tribes from Central Asia into the Iranian plateau. Turkic tribesmen were first used in the Abbasid army as slave-warriors (Mamluks), replacing Persian and Arab elements within the army. As a result the Mamluks gained significant political power. In 999, large parts of Iran came briefly under the rule of the Ghaznavid dynasty, whose rulers were of Mamluk Turk origin, and longer subsequently under the Turkish Seljuk and Khwarezmian Empires. These Turks had been fully Persianised and had adopted Persian models of administration and rulership.

The result of the adoption and patronage of Persian culture by Turkish rulers was the development of a distinct Turko-Persian tradition.

In 1219–21 the Khwarezmian Empire suffered a devastating invasion by Genghis Khan's Mongol army. According to Steven R. Ward, "Mongol violence and depredations killed up to three-fourths of the population of the Iranian Plateau, possibly 10 to 15 million people. Some historians have estimated that Iran's population did not again reach its pre-Mongol levels until the mid-20th century." Following the fracture of the Mongol Empire in 1256 Hulagu Khan, Genghis Khan's grandson, established the Ilkhanate dynasty in Iran. In 1370 yet another conqueror, Timur, commonly known as Tamerlane in the West, followed Hulagu's example, establishing the Timurid Dynasty which lasted for another 156 years. In 1387, Timur ordered the complete massacre of Isfahan, reportedly killing 70,000 citizens. Hulagu, Timur and their successors soon came to adopt the ways and customs of the Persians, choosing to surround themselves with a culture that was distinctively Persian.

Dynasties (1501–1979)

At the start of the 1500s, Shah Ismail I established the Safavid Dynasty in western Persia and Azerbaijan. He subsequently extended his authority over all of Persia, and established intermittent Persian hegemony over vast nearby regions which would last for many centuries onwards. Ismail instigated a forced conversion from Sunni to Shi'a Islam. The rivalry between Safavid Persia and the Ottoman Empire led to numerous Ottoman–Persian Wars. The Safavid era peaked in the reign of the brilliant soldier, statesman and administrator Shah Abbas I (1587–1629), surpassing their Ottoman arch rivals in strength, and making the empire a leading hub in Western Eurasia for the sciences and arts. The Safavid era also saw the start of the creation of new layers in Persian society, composed of hundreds of thousands of ethnic Georgians, Circassians, Armenians, and other peoples of the Caucasus. Following a slow decline in the late 1600s and early 1700s by internal strife, royal intrigues, continuous wars between them and their Ottoman arch rivals, and foreign interference (most notably by the Russians) the Safavid dynasty was ended by Pashtun rebels who besieged Isfahan and defeated Soltan Hosein in 1722.

In 1729, an Iranian Khorasan chieftain and military genius, Nader Shah, successfully drove out, then conquered the Pashtun invaders.

During Nader Shah's reign, Iran reached its greatest extent since the Sassanian Empire, reestablishing Persian hegemony over all of the Caucasus, other major parts of West Asia, Central Asia and parts of South Asia, and briefly possessing what was arguably the most powerful empire in the world.

In 1738-39, he invaded India and sacked Delhi, bringing great loot back to Persia. Nader Shah's assassination sparked a brief period of civil war and turmoil, after which Karim Khan came to power in 1750, bringing a period of relative peace and prosperity.

Another civil war ensued after Karim Khan's death in 1779, out of which Aga Muhammad Khan emerged victorious, founding the Qajar Dynasty in 1794. In 1795, following the disobedience of their Georgian subjects and their alliance with the Russians, the Qajars sacked and ravaged Tblisi, and drove the Russians out of the entire Caucasus, reestablishing Persian suzerainty over the region. However Persian control was short-lived and the Russo-Persian War (1804–13) and the

Russo-Persian War (1826–28) resulted in large territorial losses for Peria but substantial gains for the Russian Empire which took over the Caucasus (modern Dagestan, Georgia, Armenia and Azerbaijan) as a result of the treaties of Gulistan and Turkmenchay. Apart from Agha Mohammad Khan rule, Qajar rule is characterised as a century of misrule.

Around 1.5 million people, or 20–25% of Persia's population, died as a result of the Great Persian Famine of 1870–1871.

Whilst resisting efforts to be colonised, Iran suffered in the 1800s as a result of Russian and British empire-building, known as 'The Great Game', losing much of its territory in the Russo-Persian and the Anglo-Persian Wars. A series of protests took place in response to the sale of concessions to foreigners by Nasser al-Din Shah and Mozaffar ad-Din Shah between 1872 and 1905, the last of which resulted in the Iranian Constitutional Revolution and establishment of Iran's first national parliament in 1906, which was abolished in 1908. The struggle continued until 1911, when Mohammad Ali was defeated and forced to abdicate. On the pretext of restoring order, the Russians occupied northern Iran in 1911. During World War I, the British occupied much of western Iran, not fully withdrawing until 1921.

Figure: *Mohammad Mosaddegh, democracy advocate and deposed Prime Minister of Iran*

In 1921, Reza Khan, Prime Minister of Iran and former general of the Persian Cossack Brigade, overthrew the Qajar Dynasty and became Shah. In 1941 he was forced to abdicate in favour of his son, Mohammad Reza Pahlavi, after Iran came under British and Russian occupation following the Anglo-Soviet invasion that established the Persian Corridor and would last until 1946.

In 1951 Mohammad Mosaddegh was elected prime minister. He became enormously popular in Iran after he nationalized Iran's petroleum industry and oil reserves. He was deposed in the 1953 Iranian coup d'état, an Anglo-American covert operation that marked the first time the US had overthrown a foreign government during the Cold War.

After the coup, the Shah became increasingly autocratic. Arbitrary arrests and torture by his secret police, SAVAK, were used to crush all forms of political opposition. Ayatollah Ruhollah Khomeini became an active critic of the Shah's White Revolution and publicly denounced the government. Khomeini was arrested and imprisoned for 18 months. After his release in 1964, Khomeini publicly criticized the United States government. The Shah sent him into exile. He went first to Turkey, then to Iraq and finally to France.

Due to the 1973 spike in oil prices Iran's economy was flooded with foreign currency which caused inflation. By 1974 Iran's economy was experiencing double digit inflation and despite many large projects to modernise the country corruption was rampant and caused large amounts of waste. By 1975 and 1976 an economic recession led to increased unemployment, especially among millions of young men who had migrated to Iran's cities looking for construction jobs during the boom years of the early 1970s. By 1977 many of these men opposed the shah's regime and began to organise and join protests against it.

After the Iranian Revolution (1979)

The Iranian Revolution, later known as the Islamic Revolution, began in January 1978 with the first major demonstrations against the Shah. After a year of strikes and demonstrations paralyzed the country and its economy the Shah fled the country and Ayatollah Ruhollah Khomeini returned from exile to Tehran in February 1979. A new government was formed and in April 1979 Iran officially became an Islamic Republic, after its establishment was supported in a referendum. A second referendum in December 1979 approved a theocratic constitution.

Almost immediately nationwide uprisings against the new regime began in Iranian Kurdistan, Khuzestan, Balochistan and other areas. Over the next several years these uprisings were subdued in a violent manner by the new Islamic government. The new government went about purging itself of the non-Islamist political opposition (e.g. although both nationalists and Marxists had initially joined with Islamists to overthrow the Shah, tens of thousands were executed by the Islamic regime afterward).

On March 8, 1979, coinciding with International Women's Day, many Iranian women demonstrated against perceived reductions to the status and rights of women, especially with regard to family law and mandatory veiling. The Iranian Cultural Revolution began in 1980 and universities were closed by the theocratic regime.

On 4 November 1979, a group of Iranian students seized the U.S. embassay and took 52 US citizens and embassy personnel hostage after the US refused to return the former Shah to Iran to face trial and execution. Attempts by the Jimmy Carter administration to negotiate for the release of the hostages and a failed rescue attempt helped force Carter out of office and brought Ronald Reagan to power. On Jimmy Carter's final day in office the last hostages were finally set free as a result of the Algiers Accords.

On 22 September 1980 the Iraqi army invaded Iranian Khuzestan, precipitating the Iran–Iraq War. Although Saddam Hussein's forces made several early advances, by 1982 the Iranian forces successfully managed to drive the Iraqi army back into Iraq. Despite receiving large amounts of foreign financial and military aid, all of Saddam's subsequent offencives were thrown back. The war continued until 1988, when Khomeini accepted a truce mediated by the UN. The total Iranian casualties in the war were estimated to be 123,220–160,000 KIA, 60,711 MIA and 11,000-16,000 civilians killed.

Following the Iran–Iraq War, President Akbar Hashemi Rafsanjani and his administration (1989-1997) concentrated on a pragmatic pro-business policy of rebuilding and strengthening the economy without making any dramatic break with the ideology of the revolution. Rafsanjani was succeeded by the moderate reformist Mohammad Khatami whose government (1997-2005) attempted, unsuccessfully, to make the country more free and democratic.

The 2005 presidential election brought the conservative populist candidate, Mahmoud Ahmadinejad, to power. During the 2009 Iranian presidential election the Interior Ministry announced incumbent president Ahmadinejad had won 62.63% of the vote, while Mir-Hossein Mousavi had come in second place with 33.75%. Allegations of large irregularities and fraud provoked the 2009–2010 Iranian election protests both within Iran and in major cites outside the country.

Hassan Rouhani was elected as President of Iran on 15 June 2013, defeating Mohammad Bagher Ghalibaf and four other candidates. The electoral victory of new Iranian President Hassan Rouhani has improved Iran's relations with other countries.

Government and Politics

The political system of the Islamic Republic is based on the 1979 Constitution, and comprises several intricately connected governing bodies. The Leader of the Revolution ("Supreme Leader") is responsible for delineation and supervision of the general policies of the Islamic Republic of Iran. The Supreme Leader is Commander-in-Chief of the armed forces, controls the military intelligence and security operations; and has sole power to declare war or peace. The heads of the judiciary, state radio and television networks, the commanders of the police and military forces and six of the twelve members of the Guardian Council are appointed by the Supreme Leader. The Assembly of Experts elects and dismisses the Supreme Leader on the basis of qualifications and popular esteem.

After the Supreme Leader, the Constitution defines the President of Iran as the highest state authority. The President is elected by universal suffrage for a term of four years and can only be re-elected for one term. Presidential candidates must be approved by the Guardian Council prior to running in order to ensure their allegiance to the ideals of the Islamic revolution.

The President is responsible for the implementation of the Constitution and for the exercise of executive powers, except for matters directly related to the Supreme Leader, who has the final say in all matters. The President appoints and supervises the Council of Ministers, coordinates government decisions, and selects government policies to be placed before the legislature. Eight Vice-Presidents serve under the President, as well as a cabinet of twenty two ministers, who must all be approved by the legislature.

The legislature of Iran (known in English as the Islamic Consultative Assembly) is a unicameral body. The Majlis of Iran comprises 290 members elected for four-year terms. The Majlis drafts legislation, ratifies international treaties, and approves the national budget. All Majlis candidates and all legislation from the assembly must be approved by the Guardian Council.

The Guardian Council comprises twelve jurists including six appointed by the Supreme Leader. The others are elected by the Parliament from among the jurists nominated by the Head of the Judiciary. The Council interprets the constitution and may veto Parliament. If a law is deemed incompatible with the constitution or Sharia (Islamic law), it is referred back to Parliament for revision. The Expediency Council has the authority to mediate disputes between Parliament and the Guardian Council, and serves as an advisory body to the Supreme Leader, making it one of the most powerful governing bodies in the country. Local city councils are elected by public vote to four-year terms in all cities and villages of Iran.

Law

The Supreme Leader appoints the head of Iran's judiciary, who in turn appoints the head of the Supreme Court and the chief public prosecutor. There are several types of courts including public courts that deal with civil and criminal cases, and revolutionary courts which deal with certain categories of offences, including crimes against national security. The decisions of the revolutionary courts are final and cannot be appealed. The Special Clerical Court handles crimes allegedly committed by clerics, although it has also taken on cases involving lay people. The Special Clerical Court functions independently of the regular judicial framework and is accountable only to the Supreme Leader. The Court's rulings are final and cannot be appealed. The Assembly of Experts, which meets for one week annually, comprises 86 "virtuous and learned" clerics elected by adult suffrage for eight-year terms. As with the presidential and parliamentary elections, the Guardian Council determines candidates' eligibility. The Assembly elects the Supreme Leader and has the constitutional authority to remove the Supreme Leader from power at any time. It has not challenged any of the Supreme Leader's decisions.

The state-owned Telecommunication Company of Iran handles telecommunications. The media of Iran is a mixture of private and state-owned, but books and movies must be approved by "The ministry of Ershaad" before being released to the public. Iran originally received access to the internet in 1993, and it has become enormously popular among the Iranian youth.

Foreign Relations

The Iranian government's officially stated goal is to establish a new world order based on world peace, global collective security and justice although the current Supreme Leader of Iran, Ali Khamenei, had stated that these terms should be understood in the context of the Shia Islamic belief system. Iran's foreign relations are based on two strategic principles: eliminating outside influences in the region and pursuing extensive diplomatic contacts with developing and non-aligned countries.

Until late 2013, the regime had publicly expressed its will to fight western culture and attack the USA and its allies (in particular Israel). In September 2013 the newly elected President, Hassan Rouhani, concluded a CNN interview by saying in English: "I would like to say to the American people: I bring peace and friendship from the Iranians to the Americans", although only three months earlier he had called for the death of the American people along with their army.

As of 2009 Iran maintained full diplomatic relations with 99 countries worldwide but not the U.S. or Israel (which Iran does not officially recognise). Iran is also a member of dozens of international organisations including the G-15, G-24, G-77, IAEA, IBRD, IDA, IDB, IFC, ILO, IMF, International Maritime Organisation, Interpol, OIC, OPEC, the United Nations, WHO, and currently has observer status at the World Trade Organisation.

Since 2005, Iran's nuclear program has become the subject of contention with the international community. Many countries have expressed concern that Iran's nuclear program could divert civilian nuclear technology into a weapons program. This has led the UN Security Council to impose sanctions against Iran which has further isolated Iran politically, economically and socially from the rest of the global community. Following the departure of Iranian President Mahmoud Ahmadinejad from power the 2013 Geneva Agreement was signed and provided for a temporary lifting of some sanctions but as of September 2014 a comprehensive agreement is still being negotiated.

Military

The Islamic Republic of Iran has two types of armed forces: the regular forces Islamic Republic of Iran Army, Islamic Republic of Iran Air Force, Islamic Republic of Iran Navy and the Revolutionary Guards, totaling about 545,000 active troops. Iran also has around 350,000 Reserve Force totaling around 900,000 trained troops. Iran has a paramilitary, volunteer militia force within the IRGC, called the Basij, which includes about 90,000 full-time, active-duty uniformed members. Up to 11 million men and women are members of the Basij who could potentially be called up for service; GlobalSecurity.org estimates Iran could mobilize "up to one million men". This would be among the largest troop mobilizations in the world. In 2007, Iran's military spending represented 2.6% of the GDP or $102 per capita, the lowest figure of the Persian Gulf nations. Iran's military doctrine is based on deterrence.

Since the Iranian Revolution, to overcome foreign embargo, Iran has developed its own military industry, produced its own tanks, armored personnel carriers, guided missiles, submarines, military vessels, guided missile destroyer, radar systems, helicopters and fighter planes. In recent years, official announcements have highlighted the development of weapons such as the Hoot, Kowsar, Zelzal, Fateh-110, Shahab-3 and Sejjil missiles, and a variety of unmanned aerial vehicles (UAVs). The Fajr-3 (MIRV) is currently Iran's most advanced ballistic missile, it is a liquid fuel missile with an undisclosed range which was developed and produced domestically.

Economy

Iran's economy is a mixture of central planning, state ownership of oil and other large enterprises, village agriculture, and small-scale private trading and service ventures. In 2011 GDP was $482.4 billion ($1.003 trillion at PPP), or $13,200 at PPP per capita. Iran is ranked as an upper-middle income economy by the World Bank. In the early 21st century the service sector contributed the largest percentage of the GDP, followed by industry (mining and manufacturing) and agriculture. The Central Bank of the Islamic Republic of Iran is responsible for developing and maintaining the Iranian rial, which serves as the country's currency. The government doesn't recognise trade unions other than the Islamic Labour Councils, which are subject to the approval of employers and the security services. The minimum wage in June 2013 was 487 million rials a month ($134). Unemployment has remained above 10% since 1997, and the unemployment rate for women is almost double that of the men.

In 2006, about 45% of the government's budget came from oil and natural gas revenues, and 31% came from taxes and fees. As of 2007, Iran had earned $70 billion in foreign exchange reserves mostly (80%) from crude oil exports. Iranian budget deficits have been a chronic problem, mostly due to large-scale state subsidies, that include foodstuffs and especially gasoline, totaling more than $84 billion in 2008 for the energy sector alone. In 2010, the economic reform plan was approved by parliament to cut subsidies gradually and replace them with targeted social assistance. The objective is to move towards free market prices in a 5-year period and increase productivity and social justice.

The administration continues to follow the market reform plans of the previous one and indicated that it will diversify Iran's oil-reliant economy. Iran has also developed a biotechnology, nanotechnology, and pharmaceuticals industry. However, nationalized industries such as the bonyads have often been managed badly, making them ineffective and uncompetitive with years. Currently, the government is trying to privatize these industries, and, despite successes, there are still several problems to be overcome, such as the lagging corruption in the public sector and lack of competitiveness. In 2010, Iran was ranked 69, out of 139 nations, in the Global Competitiveness Report.

Iran has leading manufacturing industries in the fields of car-manufacture and transportation, construction materials, home appliances, food and agricultural goods, armaments, pharmaceuticals, information technology, power and petrochemicals in the Middle East.

Economic sanctions against Iran, such as the embargo against Iranian crude oil, have affected the economy. Sanctions have led to a steep fall in the value of the rial, and as of April 2013 one US dollar is worth 36,000 rial, compared with 16,000 in early 2012.

Tourism

Although tourism declined significantly during the war with Iraq, it has subsequently recovered. About 1,659,000 foreign tourists visited Iran in 2004 and 2.3 million in 2009 mostly from Asian countries, including the republics of Central Asia, while about 10% came from the European Union and North America.

The most popular tourist destinations are Isfahan, Mashhad and Shiraz. In the early 2000s the industry faced serious limitations in infrastructure, communications, industry standards and personnel training. The majority of the 300,000 tourist visas granted in 2003 were obtained by Asian Muslims, who presumably intended to visit important pilgrimage sites in Mashhad and Qom. Several organised tours from Germany, France and other European countries come to Iran annually to visit archaeological sites and monuments. In 2003 Iran ranked 68th in tourism revenues worldwide. According to UNESCO and the deputy head of research for Iran Travel and Tourism Organisation (ITTO), Iran is rated among the "10 most touristic countries in the world". Domestic tourism in Iran is one of the largest in the world. Weak advertising, unstable regional conditions, a poor public image in some parts of the world, and absence of efficient planning schemes in the tourism sector have all hindered the growth of tourism.

Energy

Iran has the largest proved gas reserves in the world, with 33.6 trillion cubic metres. It also ranks fourth in oil reserves with an estimated 153,600,000,000 barrels. It is OPEC's 2nd largest oil exporter and is an energy superpower. In 2005, Iran spent US$4 billion on fuel imports, because of contraband and inefficient domestic use. Oil industry output averaged 4 million barrels per day (640,000 m^3/d) in 2005, compared with the peak of six million barrels per day reached in 1974. In the early years of the 2000s (decade), industry infrastructure was increasingly inefficient because of technological lags. Few exploratory wells were drilled in 2005.

In 2004, a large share of natural gas reserves in Iran were untapped. The addition of new hydroelectric stations and the streamlining of conventional coal and oil-fired stations increased installed capacity to 33,000 megawatts. Of that amount, about 75% was based on natural gas, 18% on oil, and 7% on hydroelectric power. In 2004, Iran opened its first wind-powered and geothermal plants, and the first solar thermal plant is to come online in 2009. Iran is the third country in the world to have developed GTL technology.

Demographic trends and intensified industrialization have caused electric power demand to grow by 8% per year. The government's goal of 53,000 megawatts of installed capacity by 2010 is to be reached by bringing on line new gas-fired plants and by adding hydroelectric, and nuclear power generating capacity. Iran's first nuclear power plant at Bushehr went online in 2011. It is the second Nuclear Power Plant that ever built in the Middle East after Metsamor Nuclear Power Plant in Armenia.

Saudi Arabia

Saudi Arabia, officially known as the Kingdom of Saudi Arabia (KSA), is the largest Arab state in Western Asia by land area (approximately 2,150,000 km^2 (830,000 sq mi), constituting the bulk of the Arabian Peninsula), and the second-largest in the Arab world after Algeria. It is bordered by Jordan and Iraq to the north, Kuwait to the northeast, Qatar, Bahrain and the United Arab Emirates to the east, Oman to the southeast, and Yemen in the south. It is the only nation with both a Red Sea coast and a Persian Gulf coast and much of its terrain consists of inhospitable desert.

Before the inception of the Kingdom of Saudi Arabia, modern-day Saudi Arabia consisted of four distinct regions: Hejaz, Najd and parts of Eastern Arabia (Al-Hasa) and Southern Arabia ('Asir). The Kingdom of Saudi Arabia was founded in 1932 by Ibn Saud; he united the four regions into a single state through a series of conquests beginning in 1902 with the capture of Riyadh, the ancestral home of his family, the House of Saud. The country has since been an absolute monarchy governed along Islamic lines, namely under the influence of Wahhabism. Saudi Arabia is sometimes called "the Land of the Two Holy Mosques" in reference to Al-Masjid al-Haram (in Mecca), and Al-Masjid an-Nabawi (in Medina), the two holiest places in Islam. The Kingdom has the total population of 28.7 million; 20 million Saudi nationals and 8 million foreigners.

Saudi Arabia is the world's dominant oil producer and exporter while it controls world's second largest hydrocarbon reserves. Backed by the energy reserves, the kingdom is categorized as a high income economy and is the only Arab country to be part of the G-20 major economies. Saudi Arabia has the least diversified economy in the GCC. Saudi Arabia has a high Human Development Index (HDI). Saudi Arabia is ruled by an "authoritarian regime" and is ranked as "Not Free" by Freedom House. It also has the fourth highest military expenditure in the world. It is an active member of Gulf Cooperation Council, Organisation of Islamic Cooperation and OPEC.

History

Before the Foundation of Saudi Arabia: In pre-Islamic times, apart from a small number of urban trading settlements (such as Mecca and Medina), most of what was to become Saudi Arabia was populated by nomadic tribal societies in the inhospitable desert. The Islamic prophet, Muhammad, was born in Mecca in about 571 A.D. In the early 7th century, Muhammad united the various tribes of the peninsula and created a single Islamic religious polity. Following his death in 632, his followers rapidly expanded the territory under Muslim rule beyond Arabia, conquering huge swathes of territory (from the Iberian Peninsula in west to modern day Pakistan in east) in a matter of decades. In so doing, Arabia soon became a politically peripheral region of the Muslim world as the focus shifted to the more developed conquered lands. From the 10th century to the early 20th century Mecca and Medina were under the control of a local Arab ruler known as the Sharif of Mecca, but at most times the Sharif owed allegiance to the ruler of one of the major Islamic empires based in Baghdad, Cairo or Istanbul. Most of the remainder of what became Saudi Arabia reverted to traditional tribal rule.

In the 16th century, the Ottomans added the Red Sea and Persian Gulf coast (the Hejaz, Asir and Al-Hasa) to the Empire and claimed suzerainty over the interior. One reason was to thwart Portuguese attempts to attack the Red Sea (hence the Hejaz) and the Indian Ocean. Ottoman degree of control over these lands varied over the next four centuries with the fluctuating strength or weakness of the Empire's central authority. The emergence of what was to become the Saudi royal family, known as the Al Saud, began in Nejd in central Arabia in 1744, when Muhammad bin Saud, founder of the dynasty, joined forces with the religious leader Muhammad ibn Abd al-Wahhab, founder of the Wahhabi movement, a strict puritanical form of Sunni Islam. This alliance formed in the 18th century provided the ideological impetus to Saudi expansion and remains the basis of Saudi Arabian dynastic rule today. The first "Saudi state" established in 1744 in the area around Riyadh, rapidly expanded and briefly controlled most of the present-day territory of Saudi Arabia, but was destroyed by 1818 by the Ottoman viceroy of Egypt, Mohammed Ali Pasha. A much smaller second "Saudi state", located mainly in Nejd, was established in 1824. Throughout the rest of the 19th century, the Al Saud contested control of the interior of what was to become Saudi Arabia with another Arabian ruling family, the Al Rashid. By 1891, the Al Rashid were victorious and the Al Saud were driven into exile in Kuwait where the younger son of Faisal bin Turki bin Abdullah Al Saud; Prince Abdul Rahman bin Faisal was greeted during the reign of Abdullah II Sabah II Al-Jaber I Al-Sabah.

At the beginning of the 20th century, the Ottoman Empire continued to control or have a suzerainty over most of the peninsula. Subject to this suzerainty, Arabia was ruled by a patchwork of tribal rulers, with the Sharif of Mecca having pre-eminence and ruling the Hejaz. In 1902, Abdul Rahman's son, Abdul Aziz—later to be known as Ibn Saud—recaptured control of Riyadh in Nejd during the reign of Mubarak Sabah II Al-Jaber I Al-Sabah bringing the Al Saud back to Nejd. Ibn Saud gained the support of the Ikhwan, a tribal army inspired by Wahhabism and led by Faisal Al-Dawish, and which had grown quickly after its foundation in 1912. With the aid of the Ikhwan, Ibn Saud captured Hasa from the Ottomans in 1913.

In 1916, with the encouragement and support of Britain (which was fighting the Ottomans in World War I), the Sharif of Mecca, Hussein bin Ali, led a pan-Arab revolt against the Ottoman Empire to create a united Arab state. Although the Arab Revolt of 1916 to 1918 failed in its objective, the Allied victory in World War I resulted in the end of Ottoman suzerainty and control in Arabia.

Ibn Saud avoided involvement in the Arab Revolt, and instead continued his struggle with the Al Rashid. Following the latter's final defeat, he took the title Sultan of Nejd in 1921. With the help of the Ikhwan, the Hejaz was conquered in 1924–25 and on 10 January 1926, Ibn Saud declared himself King of the Hejaz. A year later, he added the title of King of Nejd. For the next five years, he administered the two parts of his dual kingdom as separate units.

After the conquest of the Hejaz, the Ikhwan leadership's objective switched to expansion of the Wahhabist realm into the British protectorates of Transjordan, Iraq and Kuwait, and began raiding those territories. This met with Ibn Saud's opposition, as he recognised the danger of a direct conflict with the British. At the same time, the Ikhwan became disenchanted with Ibn Saud's domestic policies which appeared to favour modernisation and the increase in the number of non-Muslim foreigners in the country. As a result, they turned against Ibn Saud and, after a two-year struggle, were defeated in 1930 at the Battle of Sabilla, where their leaders were massacred. In 1932 the two kingdoms of the Hejaz and Nejd were united as the *Kingdom of Saudi Arabia.*

Post-Unification

The new kingdom was one of the poorest countries in the world, reliant on limited agriculture and pilgrimage revenues. However, in 1938, vast reserves of oil were discovered in the Al-Hasa region along the coast of the Persian Gulf, and full-scale development of the oil fields began in 1941 under the US-controlled Aramco (Arabian American Oil Company). Oil provided Saudi Arabia with economic prosperity and substantial political leverage internationally. Cultural life rapidly developed, primarily in the Hejaz, which was the centre for newspapers and radio. However, the large influx of foreigners to work in the oil industry increased the pre-existing propensity for xenophobia. At the same time, the government became increasingly wasteful and extravagant. By the 1950s this had led to large governmental deficits and excessive foreign borrowing.

King Saud succeeded to the throne on his father's death in 1953. However, an intense rivalry between the King and his half-brother, Prince Faisal emerged, fuelled by doubts in the royal family over Saud's competence. As a consequence, Saud was deposed in favour of Faisal in 1964. Saudi Arabia gained control of a proportion (20%) of Aramco in 1972, thereby decreasing US control over Saudi oil. In 1973, Saudi Arabia led an oil boycott against the Western countries that supported Israel in the Yom Kippur War against Egypt and Syria. Oil prices quadrupled. Faisal was assassinated in 1975 by his nephew, Prince Faisal bin Musaid and was succeeded by his half-brother King Khalid.

By 1976 Saudi Arabia had become the largest oil producer in the world. Khalid's reign saw economic and social development progress at an extremely rapid rate, transforming the infrastructure and educational system of the country; in foreign policy, close ties with the US were developed. In 1979, two events occurred which greatly concerned the government, and had a long-term influence on Saudi foreign and domestic policy. The first was the Iranian Islamic Revolution. It was feared that the country's Shi'ite minority in the Eastern Province (which is also the location of the oil fields) might rebel under the influence of their Iranian co-religionists. In fact, there were several anti-government uprisings in the region in 1979 and 1980.

The second event was the seizure of the Grand Mosque in Mecca by Islamist extremists. The militants involved were in part angered by what they considered to be the corruption and un-Islamic nature of the Saudi government. The government regained control of the mosque after 10 days and those captured were executed. Part of the response of the royal family was to enforce a much stricter observance of traditional religious and social norms in the country (for example, the closure of cinemas) and to give the Ulema a greater role in government. Neither entirely succeeded as Islamism continued to grow in strength.

Figure: *The Kingdom of Saudi Arabia after unification in 1932 In 1980, Saudi Arabia took full control of Aramco from the US.*

King Khalid died of a heart attack in June 1982, and was succeeded by his brother, King Fahd, who added the title "Custodian of the Two Holy Mosques" to his name in 1986. Fahd continued to develop close relations with the United States and increased the purchase of American and British military equipment. The vast wealth generated by oil revenues was beginning to have an even greater impact on Saudi society. It led to rapid modernisation, urbanization, mass public education and the creation of new media. This and the presence of increasingly large numbers of foreign workers greatly affected traditional Saudi norms and values. Although there was dramatic change in the social and economic life of the country, political power continued to be monopolized by the royal family leading to discontent among many Saudis who began to look for wider participation in government. In the 1980s, Saudi Arabia spent $25 billion in support of Saddam Hussein in the Iran–Iraq War. However, Saudi Arabia condemned the Iraqi invasion of Kuwait in 1990 and asked the US to intervene. King Fahd allowed American and coalition troops to be stationed in Saudi Arabia. He invited the Kuwaiti government and many of its citizens to stay in Saudi Arabia, but expelled citizens of Yemen and Jordan because of their governments' support of Iraq. In 1991, Saudi Arabian forces were involved both in bombing raids on Iraq and in the land invasion that helped to liberate Kuwait.

Saudi Arabia's relations with the West began to cause growing concern among some of the ulema and students of sharia law and was one of the issues that led to an increase in Islamic terrorism in Saudi Arabia, as well as Islamic terrorist attacks in Western countries by Saudi nationals. Osama bin Laden was a Saudi national (until stripped of his nationality in 1994). 15 of the 19 hijackers involved in 9/11 attacks on New York, Washington and Virginia were Saudi nationals. Many Saudis who did not support the Islamist terrorists were nevertheless deeply unhappy with the government's policies.

Islamism was not the only source of hostility to the government. Although now extremely wealthy, Saudi Arabia's economy was near stagnant. High taxes and a growth in unemployment have contributed to discontent, and has been reflected in a rise in civil unrest, and discontent with the royal family. In response, a number of limited "reforms" were initiated by King Fahd. In March 1992, he introduced the "Basic Law", which emphasised the duties and responsibilities of a ruler. In December 1993, the Consultative Council was inaugurated. It is composed of a chairman and 60 members—all chosen by the King. The King's intent was to respond to dissent while making as few actual changes in the status quo as possible. Fahd made it clear that he did not have democracy in mind: "A system based on elections is not consistent with our Islamic creed, which approves of government by consultation shûrâ."

In 1995, Fahd suffered a debilitating stroke, and the Crown Prince, Abdullah, assumed the role of *de facto* regent, taking on the day-to-day running of the country. However, his authority was hindered by conflict with Fahd's full brothers (known, with Fahd, as the "Sudairi Seven"). From the 1990s, signs of discontent continued and included, in 2003 and 2004, a series of bombings and armed violence in Riyadh, Jeddah, Yanbu and Khobar. In February–April 2005, the first-ever nationwide municipal elections were held in Saudi Arabia. Women were not allowed to take part in the poll. In 2005, King Fahd died and was succeeded by Abdullah, who continued the policy of minimum reform and clamping down on protests. The king introduced a number of economic reforms aimed at reducing the country's reliance on oil revenue: limited deregulation, encouragement of foreign investment, and privatization. In February 2009, Abdullah announced a series of governmental changes to the judiciary, armed forces, and various ministries to modernise these institutions including the replacement of senior appointees in the judiciary and the Mutaween (religious police) with more moderate individuals and the appointment of the country's first female deputy minister.

On 29 January 2011, hundreds of protesters gathered in the city of Jeddah in a rare display of criticism against the city's poor infrastructure after deadly floods swept through the city, killing eleven people. Police stopped the demonstration after about 15 minutes and arrested 30 to 50 people.

Since 2011, Saudi Arabia has been affected by its own *Arab Spring* protests. In response, King Abdullah announced on 22 February 2011 a series of benefits for citizens amounting to $36 billion, of which $10.7 billion was earmarked for housing. No political reforms were announced as part of the package, though some prisoners indicted for financial crimes were pardoned. On 18 March the same year, King Abdullah announced a package of $93 billion, which included 500,000 new homes to a cost of $67 billion, in addition to creating 60,000 new security jobs.

Although male-only municipal elections were held on 29 September 2011, Abdullah announced that women will be able to vote and be elected in the 2015 municipal elections, and also to be nominated to the Shura Council.

Politics

Saudi Arabia is an absolute monarchy. However, according to the Basic Law of Saudi Arabia adopted by royal decree in 1992, the king must comply with Sharia (Islamic law) and the Quran, while the Quran and the Sunnah (the traditions of Muhammad) are declared to be the country's constitution. No political parties or national elections are permitted. *The Economist* rates the Saudi government as the fifth most authoritarian government out of 167 rated in its 2012 Democracy Index, and Freedom House gives it its lowest "Not Free" rating, 7.0 ("1=best, 7=worst") for 2013.

In the absence of national elections and political parties, politics in Saudi Arabia takes place in two distinct arenas: within the royal family, the Al Saud, and between the royal family and the rest of Saudi society. Outside of the Al-Saud, participation in the political process is limited to a relatively small segment of the population and takes the form of the royal family consulting with the ulema, tribal sheikhs and members of important commercial families on major decisions. This process is not reported by the Saudi media.

By custom, all males of full age have a right to petition the king directly through the traditional tribal meeting known as the *majlis*. In many ways the approach to government differs little from the traditional system of tribal rule. Tribal identity remains strong and, outside of the royal family, political influence is frequently determined by tribal affiliation, with tribal sheikhs maintaining a considerable degree of influence over local and national events. As mentioned earlier, in recent years there have been limited steps to widen political participation such as the establishment of the Consultative Council in the early 1990s and the National Dialogue Forum in 2003.

The rule of the Al Saud faces political opposition from four sources: Sunni Islamist activism; liberal critics; the Shi'ite minority—particularly in the Eastern Province; and long-standing tribal and regionalist particularistic opponents (for example in the Hejaz). Of these, the Islamic activists have been the most prominent threat to the government and have in recent years perpetrated a number of violent or terrorist acts in the country. However, open protest against the government, even if peaceful, is not tolerated.

Saudi Arabia is the only country in the world which bans women from driving. On 25 September 2011, Saudi Arabia's King Abdullah has announced that women will have the right to stand and vote in future local elections and join the advisory Shura council as full members.

Monarchy and Royal Family

The king combines legislative, executive, and judicial functions and royal decrees form the basis of the country's legislation. The king is also the prime minister, and presides over the Council of Ministers (Majlis al-Wuzarâ¾), which comprises the first and second deputy prime ministers and other ministers.

The royal family dominates the political system. The family's vast numbers allow it to control most of the kingdom's important posts and to have an involvement and presence at all levels of government. The number of princes is estimated to be at least 7,000, with most power and influence being wielded by the 200 or so male descendants of Ibn

Saud. The key ministries are generally reserved for the royal family, as are the thirteen regional governorships. Long term political and government appointments have resulted in the creation of "power fiefdoms" for senior princes, such as those of King Abdullah, who had been Commander of the National Guard since 1963 (until 2010, when he appointed his son to replace him), former Crown Prince Sultan, Minister of Defence and Aviation from 1962 to his death in 2011, former crown Prince Nayef who was the Minister of Interior from 1975 to his death in 2012, Prince Saud who has been Minister of Foreign Affairs since 1975 and current Minister of Defence and Aviation Prince Salman, who was Governor of the Riyadh Province from 1962 to 2011.

The royal family is politically divided by factions based on clan loyalties, personal ambitions and ideological differences. The most powerful clan faction is known as the 'Sudairi Seven', comprising the late King Fahd and his full brothers and their descendants. Ideological divisions include issues over the speed and direction of reform, and whether the role of the ulema should be increased or reduced. There were divisions within the family over who should succeed to the throne after the accession or earlier death of Prince Sultan. When prince Sultan died before ascending to the throne on 21 October 2011, King Abdullah appointed Prince Nayef as crown prince. Prince Nayef also died before ascending to the throne in 2012.

The Saudi government and the royal family have often, over many years, been accused of corruption. In a country that is said to "belong" to the royal family and is named for them, the lines between state assets and the personal wealth of senior princes are blurred. The extent of corruption has been described as systemic and endemic, and its existence was acknowledged and defended by Prince Bandar bin Sultan (a senior member of the royal family) in an interview in 2001. Although corruption allegations have often been limited to broad undocumented accusations, specific allegations were made in 2007, when it was claimed that the British defence contractor BAE Systems had paid Prince Bandar US$2 billion in bribes relating to the Al-Yamamah arms deal. Prince Bandar denied the allegations. Investigations by both US and UK authorities resulted, in 2010, in plea bargain agreements with the company, by which it paid $447 million in fines but did not admit to bribery. Transparency International in its annual Corruption Perceptions Index for 2010 gave Saudi Arabia a score of 4.7 (on a scale from 0 to 10 where 0 is "highly corrupt" and 10 is "highly clean"). Saudi Arabia has undergone a process of political and social reform, such as to increase public transparency and good governance. However, there are still some areas that are prone to corruption, such as public procurement. The occurrence of irregular payments and bribes are still common representing potential difficulties for doing business in Saudi Arabia.

There has been mounting pressure to reform and modernise the royal family's rule, an agenda championed by King Abdullah both before and after his accession in 2005. The creation of the Consultative Council in the early 1990s did not satisfy demands for political participation, and, in 2003, an annual *National Dialogue Forum* was announced that would allow selected professionals and intellectuals to publicly debate current national issues, within certain prescribed parameters. In 2005, the first municipal elections were held. In 2007, the Allegiance Council was created to regulate the succession. In 2009, the king made significant personnel changes to the government by appointing reformers to key positions and the first woman to a ministerial post. However, the changes have been criticized as being too slow or merely cosmetic.

Al Ash-Sheikh and Role of the Ulema

Saudi Arabia is almost unique in giving the ulema (the body of Islamic religious leaders and jurists) a direct role in government, the only other example being Iran. The ulema have also been a key influence in major government decisions, for example the imposition of the oil embargo in 1973 and the invitation to foreign troops to Saudi Arabia in 1990. In addition, they have had a major role in the judicial and education systems and a monopoly of authority in the sphere of religious and social morals.

By the 1970s, as a result of oil wealth and the modernisation of the country initiated by King Faisal, important changes to Saudi society were under way and the power of the ulema was in decline. However, this changed following the seizure of the Grand Mosque in Mecca in 1979 by Islamist radicals. The government's response to the crisis included strengthening the ulema's powers and increasing their financial support: in particular, they were given greater control over the education system and allowed to enforce stricter observance of Wahhabi rules of moral and social behaviour. Since his accession to the throne in 2005, King Abdullah has taken steps to reduce the powers of the ulema, for instance transferring control over girls' education to the Ministry of Education.

The ulema have historically been led by the Al ash-Sheikh, the country's leading religious family. The Al ash-Sheikh are the descendants of Muhammad ibn Abd al-Wahhab, the 18th century founder of the Wahhabi form of Sunni Islam which is today dominant in Saudi Arabia. The family is second in prestige only to the Al Saud (the royal family) with whom they formed a "mutual support pact" and power-sharing arrangement nearly 300 years ago. The pact, which persists to this day, is based on the Al Saud maintaining the Al ash-Sheikh's authority in religious matters and upholding and propagating Wahhabi doctrine. In return, the Al ash-Sheikh support the Al Saud's political authority thereby using its religious-moral authority to legitimize the royal family's rule. Although the Al ash-Sheikh's domination of the ulema has diminished in recent decades, they still hold the most important religious posts and are closely linked to the Al Saud by a high degree of intermarriage.

Legal System

The primary source of law is the Islamic Sharia derived from the teachings of the Qu'ran and the Sunnah (the traditions of the Prophet). Saudi Arabia is unique among most modern Muslim states in that Sharia is not codified and there is no system of judicial precedent, giving judges the power to use independent legal reasoning to make a decision. Saudi judges tend to follow the principles of the Hanbali school of jurisprudence (or *fiqh*) found in pre-modern texts and noted for its literalist interpretation of the Qu'ran and hadith. Because the judge is empowered to disregard previous judgments (either his own or of other judges) and may apply his personal interpretation of Sharia to any particular case, divergent judgements arise even in apparently identical cases, making predictability of legal interpretation difficult. The Sharia court system constitutes the basic judiciary of Saudi Arabia and its judges (qadi) and lawyers form part of the ulema, the country's Islamic scholars.

Royal decrees are the other main source of law; but are referred to as *regulations* rather than *laws* because they are subordinate to the Sharia. Royal decrees supplement Sharia in areas such as labour, commercial and corporate law. Additionally, traditional tribal law and custom remain significant. Extra-Sharia government tribunals usually handle disputes relating to specific royal decrees. Final appeal from both Sharia courts and government tribunals is to the King and all courts and tribunals follow Sharia rules of evidence and procedure. The Saudi system of justice has been criticized for being slow, arcane, lacking in some of the safeguards of justice and unable to deal with the modern world.

Saudi justice has been criticized for "ultra-puritanical judges", being often harsh, (with beheading for the crime of witchcraft), but sometimes lenient, (for cases of rape or wife-beating), and slow, for example leaving thousands of abandoned women unable to secure a divorce. In 2007, King Abdullah issued royal decrees reforming the judiciary and creating a new court system, and, in 2009, the King made a number of significant changes to the judiciary's personnel at the most senior level by bringing in a younger generation.

Capital and physical punishments imposed by Saudi courts, such as beheading, stoning (to death), amputation and lashing, as well as the sheer number of executions have been strongly criticized. The death penalty can be imposed for a wide range of offences including murder, rape, armed robbery, repeated drug use, apostasy, adultery, witchcraft and sorcery and can be carried out by beheading with a sword, stoning or firing squad, followed by crucifixion. The 345 reported executions between 2007 and 2010 were all carried out by public beheading. The last reported execution for sorcery took place in September 2014.

Although repeated theft can be punishable by amputation of the right hand, only one instance of judicial amputation was reported between 2007 and 2010. Homosexual acts are punishable by flogging or death. Atheism or "calling into question the fundamentals of the Islamic religion on which this country is based" is considered a terrorist crime. Lashings are a common form of punishment and are often imposed for offences against religion and public morality such as drinking alcohol and neglect of prayer and fasting obligations.

Retaliatory punishments, or Qisas, are practised: for instance, an eye can be surgically removed at the insistence of a victim who lost his own eye. Families of someone unlawfully killed can choose between demanding the death penalty or granting clemency in return for a payment of diyya (blood money), by the perpetrator.

Human Rights

Western-based organisations such as Amnesty International and Human Rights Watch condemn both the Saudi criminal justice system and its severe punishments. There are no jury trials in Saudi Arabia and courts observe few formalities. Human Rights Watch, in a 2008 report, noted that a criminal procedure code had been introduced for the first time in 2002, but it lacked some basic protections and, in any case, had been routinely ignored by judges. Those arrested are often not informed of the crime of which they are accused or given access to a lawyer and are subject to abusive treatment and torture if they do not confess. At trial, there is a presumption of guilt and the accused is often unable to examine witnesses and evidence or present a legal defence. Most trials are held in secret. However, "ordinary Saudis", according to a BBC report, support the system and say that it maintains a low crime rate.

Saudi Arabia has long been criticized for its human rights record. Human rights issues that have attracted strong criticism include the extremely disadvantaged position of women, capital punishment for homosexuality, religious discrimination, the lack of religious freedom and the activities of the religious police. Between 1996 and 2000, Saudi Arabia acceded to four UN human rights conventions and, in 2004, the government approved the establishment of the National Society for Human Rights (NSHR), staffed by government employees, to monitor their implementation. To date, the activities of the NSHR have been limited and doubts remain over its neutrality and independence. Saudi Arabia remains one of the very few countries in the world not to accept the UN's Universal Declaration of Human Rights. In response to the continuing criticism of its human rights record, the Saudi government points to the special Islamic character of the country, and asserts that this justifies a different social and political order. The United States Commission on International Religious Freedom had unsuccessfully urged President Barack Obama to raise human rights concerns with King Abdullah on his March 2014 visit to the Kingdom especially the imprisonments of Sultan Hamid Marzooq al-Enezi, Saud Falih Awad al-Enezi, and Raif Badawi.

Foreign Relations

Saudi Arabia joined the UN in 1945 and is a founding member of the Arab League, Gulf Cooperation Council, Muslim World League, and the Organisation of the Islamic Conference (now the Organisation of Islamic Cooperation). It plays a prominent role in the International Monetary Fund and the World Bank, and in 2005 joined the World Trade Organisation. Saudi Arabia supports the intended formation of the Arab Customs Union in 2015 and an Arab common market by 2020, as announced at the 2009 Arab League summit. As a founding member of OPEC, its oil pricing policy has been generally to stabilize the world oil market and try to moderate sharp price movements so as to not jeopardise the Western economies.

Between the mid-1970s and 2002 Saudi Arabia expended over $70 billion in "overseas development aid". However, there is evidence that the vast majority was, in fact, spent on propagating and extending the influence of Wahhabism at the expense of other forms of Islam. There has been an intense debate over whether Saudi aid and Wahhabism has fomented extremism in recipient countries. The two main allegations are that, by its nature, Wahhabism encourages intolerance and promotes terrorism. Relations with the United States became strained following 9/11. American politicians and media accused the Saudi government of supporting terrorism and tolerating a *jihadist* culture. Indeed, Osama bin Laden and fifteen out of the nineteen 9/11 hijackers were from Saudi Arabia. According to former U.S. Secretary of State Hillary Clinton, "Saudi Arabia remains a critical financial support base for al-Qaida, the Taliban, LeT and other terrorist groups... Donors in Saudi Arabia constitute the most significant source of funding to Sunni terrorist groups worldwide." Former CIA director James Woolsey described it as "the soil in which Al-Qaeda and its sister terrorist organisations are flourishing." However, the Saudi government strenuously denies these claims or that it exports religious or cultural extremism.

In the Arab and Muslim worlds, Saudi Arabia is considered to be pro-Western and pro-American, and it is certainly a long-term ally of the United States. However, this and Saudi Arabia's role in the 1991 Persian Gulf War, particularly the stationing of U.S. troops on Saudi soil from 1991, prompted the development of a hostile Islamist response internally. As a result, Saudi Arabia has, to some extent, distanced itself from the U.S. and, for example, refused to support or to participate in the U.S.-led invasion of Iraq in 2003.

Recent years have seen increasing alarm within the Saudi monarchy over the rise of Iran's influence in the region, reflected in the reported private comments of King Abdullah urging the US to attack Iran and "cut off the head of the snake". The tentative rapprochement between the US and Iran that began in secret in 2011 was said to be feared by the Saudis, and, during the run up to the widely welcomed deal on Iran's nuclear programme that capped the first stage of US–Iranian détente, Robert Jordan, who was U.S. ambassador to Riyadh from 2001 to 2003, said "the Saudis' worst nightmare would be the [Obama] administration striking a grand bargain with Iran." A trip to Saudi by US President Barack Obama in 2014 included discussions of US–Iran relations, though these failed to resolve Riyadh's concerns.

Saudi Arabia has been seen as a moderating influence in the Arab-Israeli conflict, periodically putting forward a peace plan between Israel and the Palestinians and condemning Hezbollah. Following the Arab Spring Saudi Arabia offered asylum to deposed President Zine El Abidine Ben Ali of Tunisia and King Abdullah telephoned President Hosni Mubarak of Egypt (prior to his deposition) to offer his support. In early 2014 relations with Qatar became strained over its support for the Muslim Brotherhood, and Saudi Arabia's belief that Qatar was interfering in its affairs. In August 2014 both countries appeared to be exploring ways of ending the rift.

Military

Saudi Arabia has the highest percentage of military expenditure in the world, spending more than 10% of its GDP in its military. The Saudi military consists of the Royal Saudi Land Forces, the Royal Saudi Air Force, the Royal Saudi Navy, the Royal Saudi Air Defence, the Saudi Arabian National Guard (SANG, an independent military force), and paramilitary forces, totaling nearly 200,000 active-duty personnel. In 2005 the armed forces had the following personnel: the army, 75,000; the air force, 18,000; air defence, 16,000; the navy, 15,500 (including 3,000 marines); and the SANG had 75,000 active soldiers and 25,000 tribal levies. In addition, there is an Al Mukhabarat Al A'amah military intelligence service.

The kingdom has a long standing military relationship with Pakistan, it has long been speculated that Saudi Arabia secretly funded Pakistan's atomic bomb programme and seeks to purchase atomic weapons from Pakistan, in near future. The SANG is not a reserve but a fully operational front-line force, and originated out of Ibn Saud's tribal military-religious force, the Ikhwan. Its modern existence, however, is attributable to it being effectively Abdullah's private army since the 1960s and, unlike the rest of the armed forces, is independent of the Ministry of Defence and Aviation. The SANG has been a counterbalance to the Sudairi faction in the royal family: Prince Sultan, the Minister of Defence and Aviation, is one of the so-called 'Sudairi Seven' and controls the remainder of the armed forces.

Spending on defence and security has increased significantly since the mid-1990s and was about US$25.4 billion in 2005. Saudi Arabia ranks among the top 10 in the world in government spending for its military, representing about 7% of gross domestic product in 2005. Its modern high-technology arsenal eakes Saudi Arabaa among the world's most densely armed nations, with its military equipment being supplied primarily by the US, France and Britain. The United States sold more than $80 billion in military hardware between 1951 and 2006 to the Saudi military. On 20 October 2010, the U.S. State Department notified Congress of its intention to make the biggest arms sale in American history—of estimated $60.5 billion purchase by the Kingdom of Saudi Arabia. The package represents a considerable improvement in the offencive capability of the Saudi arab forces. This 2013 saw Saudi military spending climb to $67bn, overtaking that of the UK, France and Japan to place fourth globally.

The UK has also been a major supplier of military equipment to Saudi Arabia since 1965. Since 1985, the UK has supplied military aircraft—notably the Tornado and Eurofighter Typhoon combat aircraft—and other equipment as part of the long-term Al-Yamamah arms deal estimated to have been worth £43 billion by 2006 and thought to be worth a further £40 billion. In May 2012, British defence giant BAE signed a £1.9bn ($3bn) deal to supply Hawk trainer jets to Saudi Arabia.

Geography

Saudi Arabia occupies about 80% of the Arabian Peninsula, lying between latitudes 16° and 33° N, and longitudes 34° and 56° E. Because the country's southern borders with the United Arab Emirates and Oman are not precisely defined or marked, the exact size of the country remains unknown. The CIA World Factbook's estimate is 2,250,000 km^2 (868,730 sq mi) and lists Saudi Arabia as the world's 13th largest state.

Saudi Arabia's geography is dominated by the Arabian Desert and associated semi-desert and shrubland. It is, in fact, a number of linked deserts and includes the 647,500 km^2 (250,001 sq mi) Rub' al Khali ("Empty Quarter") in the southern part of the country, the world's largest contiguous sand desert. There are virtually no rivers or lakes in the country, but wadis are numerous. The few fertile areas are to be found in the alluvial deposits in wadis, basins, and oases. The main topographical feature is the central plateau which rises abruptly from the Red Sea and gradually descends into the Nejd and toward the Persian Gulf. On the Red Sea coast, there is a narrow coastal plain, known as the Tihamah parallel to which runs an imposing escarpment. The southwest province of Asir is mountainous, and contains the 3,133 m (10,279 ft) Mount Sawda, which is the highest point in the country.

Except for the southwestern province of Asir, Saudi Arabia has a desert climate with extremely high day-time temperatures and a sharp temperature drop at night. Average summer temperatures are around 113 °F (45 °C), but can be as high as 129 °F (54 °C). In the winter the temperature rarely drops below 32 °F (0 °C). In the spring and autumn the heat is temperate, temperatures average around 84 °F (29 °C). Annual rainfall is extremely low. The Asir region differs in that it is influenced by the Indian Ocean monsoons, usually occurring between October and March. An average of 300 mm (12 in) of rainfall occurs during this period, that is about 60% of the annual precipitation.

Animal life includes wolves, hyenas, mongooses, baboons, hares, sand rats, and jerboas. Larger animals such as gazelles, oryx, and leopards were relatively numerous until the 1950s, when hunting from motor vehicles reduced these animals almost to extinction. Birds include falcons (which are caught and trained for hunting), eagles, hawks, vultures, sand grouse and bulbuls. There are several species of snakes, many of which are venomous, and numerous types of lizards. There is a wide variety of marine life in the Persian Gulf. Domesticated animals include camels, sheep, goats, donkeys, and chickens. Reflecting the country's desert conditions, Saudi Arabia's plant life mostly consists of small herbs and shrubs requiring little water. There are a few small areas of grass and trees in southern Asir. The date palm (*Phoenix dactylifera*) is widespread.

Economy

Saudi Arabia's command economy is petroleum-based; roughly 75% of budget revenues and 90% of export earnings come from the oil industry. It is strongly dependent on foreign workers with about 80% of those employed in the private sector being non-Saudi. Among the challenges to Saudi economy include halting or reversing the decline in per capita income, improving education to prepare youth for the workforce and providing them with employment, diversifying the economy, stimulating the private sector and housing construction, diminishing corruption and inequality.

The oil industry comprises about 45% of Saudi Arabia's nominal gross domestic product, compared with 40% from the private sector. Saudi Arabia officially has about 260 billion barrels (4.1×10^{10} m^3) of oil reserves, comprising about one-fifth of the world's proven total petroleum reserves.

In the 1990s, Saudi Arabia experienced a significant contraction of oil revenues combined with a high rate of population growth. Per capita income fell from a high of $11,700 at the height of the oil boom in 1981 to $6,300 in 1998. Increases in oil prices since 2000 have helped boost per capita GDP to $17,000 in 2007 dollars, or about $7,400 adjusted for inflation. Taking into account the impact of the real oil price changes on the Kingdom's real gross domestic income, the real command-basis GDP was computed to be 330.381 billion 1999 USD in 2010. Oil price increases of 2008–2009 have triggered a second oil boom.

OPEC (the Organisation of Petroleum Exporting Countries) limits its members' oil production based on their "proven reserves." Saudi Arabia's published reserves have shown little change since 1980, with the main exception being an increase of about 100 billion barrels (1.6×10^{10} m^3) between 1987 and 1988. Matthew Simmons has suggested that Saudi Arabia is greatly exaggerating its reserves and may soon show production declines.

From 2003-2013 "several key services" were privatized — municipal water supply, electricity, telecommunications — and parts of education and health care, traffic control and car accident reporting were also privatized. According to Arab News columnist Abdel Aziz Aluwaisheg, "in almost every one of these areas, consumers have raised serious concerns about the performance of these privatized entities." The Tadawul All Share Index (TASI) of the Saudi stock exchange peaked at 16,712.64 in 2005, and closed at 8,535.60, at the end of 2013. In recent years, Saudi Arabia sought to join the World Trade Organisation. Negotiations have focused on the degree to which Saudi Arabia is willing to increase market access to foreign goods and services and the timeframe for becoming fully compliant with World Trade Organisation obligations. In April 2000, the government established the Saudi Arabian General Investment Authority to encourage foreign direct investment in Saudi Arabia. Saudi Arabia maintains a negative list of sectors in which foreign investment is prohibited, but the government plans to open some closed sectors such as telecommunications, insurance, and power transmission/distribution over time. As of November 2005, Saudi Arabia was officially approved to enter World Trade Organisation.

The government has also attempted to "Saudizing" the economy, replacing foreign workers with Saudi nationals with limited success.

Saudi Arabia plans to launch six "economic cities" (e.g. King Abdullah Economic City), to be completed by 2020, in an effort to diversify the economy and provide jobs. The King has announced that the per capita income is forecast to rise from $15,000 in 2006 to $33,500 in 2020. The cities will be spread around Saudi Arabia to promote diversification for each region and their economy, and the cities are projected to contribute $150 billion to the GDP.

Saudi also has a small gold mining sector in the Mahd adh Dhahab region, but Saudi Arabian stores suffered a significant decrease in gold sales in 2012.

Reporting of poverty remains a state taboo. In December 2011, days after the Arab Spring uprisings, the Saudi interior ministry detained reporter Feros Boqna and two colleagues and held them for almost two weeks for questioning after they uploaded a video on the topic to social networking site. Statistics on the issue are not available through the UN resources because the Saudi government does not issue poverty figures. Observers researching the issue prefer to stay anonymous because of the risk of being arrested. Three journalists: Feras Boqna, Hussam al-Drewesh and Khaled al-Rasheed were detained after posting 10-minute film 'Mal3ob 3alena', or 'We are being cheated' on Saudis living in poverty to social networking site. Authors of the video claim that 22% of Saudis are considered to be poor (2009) and 70% of Saudis do not own their houses.

Demographics

The population of Saudi Arabia as of July 2013 is estimated to be 26.9 million, including between 5.5 million and 10 million non-nationalized immigrants, Saudi population has grown rapidly since 1950 when it was estimated to be 3 million. The ethnic composition of Saudi citizens is 90% Arab and 10% Afro-Asian. Most Saudis live in Hejaz (35%), Najd (28%) and the Eastern Province (15%). Hejaz is the most populated region in Saudi Arabia.

The CIA Factbook estimated that as of 2013 foreign nationals living in Saudi Arabia made up about 21% of the population. Other sources report differing estimates. Indian: 1.3 million, Pakistani: 1.5 million, Egyptian: 900,000, Yemeni: 800,000, Bangladeshi: 500,000, Filipino: 500,000, Jordanian/Palestinian: 260,000, Indonesian: 250,000, Sri Lankan: 350,000, Sudanese: 250,000, Syrian: 100,000 and Turkish: 100,000. There are around 100,000 Westerners in Saudi Arabia, most of whom live in compounds or gated communities.

Saudi Arabia expelled 800,000 Yemenis in 1990 and 1991. An estimated 240,000 Palestinians are living in Saudi Arabia. They are not allowed to hold or even apply for Saudi citizenship, because of Arab League instructions barring the Arab states from granting them citizenship; the only other alternative for them is to marry a Saudi national. Palestinians are the sole foreign group that cannot benefit from a 2004 law passed by Saudi Arabia's Council of Ministers, which entitles expatriates of all nationalities who have resided in the kingdom for ten years to apply for citizenship with priority being given to holders of degrees in various scientific fields. The Articles 12.4 and 14.1 of the Executive Regulation of Saudi Citizenship System can be interpreted as requiring applicants to be Muslim. As recently as the early 1960s, Saudi Arabia's slave population was estimated at 300,000. Slavery was officially abolished in 1962.

In a 2011 news story, *Arab News* reported, "Nearly three million expatriate workers will have to leave the Kingdom in the next few years as the Labour Ministry has put a 20% ceiling on the country's guest workers." The Saudi–Yemen barrier was constructed by Saudi Arabia against an influx of illegal immigrants and against the smuggling of drugs and weapons. In November 2013, Saudi Arabia expelled thousands of illegal Ethiopians from the Kingdom. Various Human Rights entities have criticised Saudi Arabia's handling of the issue.

Languages

The official language of Saudi Arabia is Arabic. The three main regional variants spoken by Saudis are Hejazi Arabic (about 6 million speakers), Nejdi Arabic (about 8 million speakers) and Gulf Arabic (about 0.2 million speakers). Saudi Sign Language is the principal language of the deaf community. The large expatriate communities also speak their own languages, the most numerous being Tagalog (700,000), Rohingya (400,000), Urdu (380,000), and Egyptian Arabic (300,000).

Religion

There are about 25 million people who are Muslim, or 97% of the total population. However excluding foreign workers, about 100% of its population is Muslim. Data for Saudi Arabia comes primarily from general population surveys, which are less reliable than censuses or large-scale demographic and health surveys for estimating minority-majority ratios. About 85–90% of Saudis are Sunni, while Shias represent around 10–15% of the Muslim population. The official and dominant form of Sunni Islam in Saudi Arabia is commonly known as Wahhabism (a name which some of its proponents consider derogatory, preferring the term Salafism), founded in the Arabian Peninsula by Muhammad ibn Abd al-Wahhab in the eighteenth century, is often described as "puritanical", "intolerant", or "ultra-conservative". However, proponents consider that its teachings seek to purify the practice of Islam of any innovations or practices that deviate from the seventh-century teachings of Muhammad and his companions.

According to Human Rights Watch, the Shia minority face systematic discrimination from the Saudi government in education, the justice system and especially religious freedom. Shias also face discrimination in employment and restrictions are imposed on the public celebration of Shia festivals such as Ashura and on the Shia taking part in communal public worship.

In 2010, the U.S. State Department stated that in Saudi Arabia "freedom of religion is neither recognised nor protected under the law and is severely restricted in practice" and that "government policies continued to place severe restrictions on religious freedom". No faith other than Islam is permitted to be practiced, although there are nearly a million Christians—nearly all foreign workers—in Saudi Arabia. There are no churches or other non-Muslim houses of worship permitted in the country. Even private prayer services are forbidden in practice and the Saudi religious police reportedly regularly search the homes of Christians. Foreign workers have to observe Ramadan but are not allowed to celebrate Christmas or Easter. In 2007, Human Rights Watch requested that King Abdullah stop a campaign to round up and deport foreign followers of the Ahmadiyya faith.

Conversion by Muslims to another religion (apostasy) carries the death penalty, although there have been no confirmed reports of executions for apostasy in recent years. Proselytizing by non-Muslims is illegal, and the last Christian priest was expelled from Saudi Arabia in 1985. There are some Hindus and Buddhists in Saudi Arabia. Compensation in court cases discriminates against non-Muslims: once fault is determined, a Muslim receives all of the amount of compensation determined, a Jew or Christian half, and all others a sixteenth. Saudi Arabia has officially identified atheists as terrorists. The regulations place secular citizens who commit thought crimes in the same category as violent terrorist groups

Syria

Syria, officially the Syrian Arab Republic, is a country in Western Asia, bordering Lebanon and the Mediterranean Sea to the west, Turkey to the north, Iraq to the east, Jordan to the south, and Israel to the southwest. Its capital Damascus is among the oldest continuously-inhabited cities in the world. A country of fertile plains, high mountains, and deserts, it is home to diverse ethnic and religious groups, including the majority Arab population. Other ethnic groups include Armenians, Assyrians, Kurds, Circassians, Mhallami, Mandeans and Turks. Religious groups include Sunni, Christians, Alawite, Druze religion, Mandeanism and Yezidi. Sunni Arabs make up the largest population group in Syria.

In English, the name "Syria" was formerly synonymous with the Levant (known in Arabic as *al-Sham*) while the modern state encompasses the sites of several ancient kingdoms and empires, including the Eblan civilization of the 3rd millennium BC. In the Islamic era, Damascus was the seat of the Umayyad Caliphate and a provincial capital of the Mamluk Sultanate in Egypt.

The modern Syrian state was established after World War I as a French mandate, and represented the largest Arab state to emerge from the formerly Ottoman-ruled Arab Levant. It gained independence in April 1946, as a parliamentary republic. The post-independence period was tumultuous, and a large number of military coups and coup attempts shook the country in the period 1949–1971. Between 1958-61, Syria entered a brief union with Egypt, which was terminated by a military coup. The Arab Republic of Syria came into being in 1963, transforming from the Republic of Syria in the Ba'athist coup d'état. Syria was under Emergency Law from 1963 to 2011, effectively suspending most constitutional protections for citizens, and its system of government is considered to be non-democratic. Bashar al-Assad has been president since 2000 and was preceded by his father Hafez al-Assad, who was in office from 1970 to 2000.

Syria is a member of one international organisation other than the United Nations, the Non-Aligned Movement; it is currently suspended from the Arab League and the Organisation of Islamic Cooperation, and self-suspended from the Union for the Mediterranean. Since March 2011, Syria has been embroiled in an uprising against Assad and the Ba'athist regime as part of the Arab Spring, a crackdown which contributed to the Syrian Civil War and Syria becoming among the least peaceful countries in the world. The Syrian Interim Government was formed by the opposition umbrella group, the Syrian National Coalition, in March 2012. Representatives of this government were subsequently invited to take up Syria's seat at the Arab League.

History of Syria

Ancient Near East

Since approximately 10,000 BC, Syria (alongside Asia Minor and Mesopotamia) was one of centres of Neolithic culture (known as Pre-Pottery Neolithic A) where agriculture and cattle breeding appeared for the first time in the world. The following Neolithic period (PPNB) is represented by rectangular houses of Mureybet culture. At the time of the pre-pottery Neolithic, people used vessels made of stone, gyps and burnt lime (Vaisselle blanche). Finds of obsidian tools from Anatolia are evidences of early trade relations. Cities of Hamoukar and Emar played an important role during the late Neolithic and Bronze Age. Archaeologists have demonstrated that civilization in Syria was one of the most ancient on earth, perhaps only preceded by those of Mesopotamia.

Eblaites and Amorites

The earliest recorded indigenous civilization in the region was the Kingdom of Ebla near present-day Idlib, northern Syria. Ebla appears to have been founded around 3500 BC, and gradually built its fortune through trade with the Mesopotamian states of Sumer, Assyria and

Akkad, as well as with the Hurrian and Hattian peoples to the northwest, in Asia Minor. Gifts from Pharaohs, found during excavations, confirm Ebla's contact with Egypt.

One of the earliest *written texts* from Syria is a Cuneiform trading agreement between vizier Ibrium of Ebla and an ambiguous kingdom called Abarsal c. 2350 BC. Scholars believe the language of Ebla to be among the oldest known written Semitic languages after Akkadian, Recent classifications of the Eblaite language have shown that it was an East Semitic language, closely related to the Akkadian language of Mesopotamia.

Another early kingdom of Syria was Mari, which although speaking the same East Semitic language as Ebla, was a major rival for domination of the region.

From the 24th century BC, much of Syria outside of the regions controlled by Ebla and Mari came to be called the *Land of the Amurru* (Amorites) in the Mesopotamian annals of Sumer, Akkad and Assyria. The Northwest Semitic language of the Amorites is the earliest attested of the Canaanite languages. The Mesopotamians were disparaging of the semi-nomadic Amorites, regarding them as uncivilized barbarians.

Ebla was weakened by a long war with Mari, and Syria became part of the Mesopotamian Akkadian Empire (2335-2154 BC) after Sargon of Akkad and his grandson Naram-Sin's conquests ended the domination of Ebla, Mari and the Amorites over Syria from the latter half of the 24th century BC.

After the collapse of the Akkadian Empire in the 22nd century BC, some regions of eastern Syria were conquered into the Neo-Sumerian Empire during the late 22nd and early 21st century BC.

However the semi-nomadic Amorites emerged as the dominant force in most of Syria during the late 21st century BC, while Language Isolate speaking Hurrians from Asia Minor had settled the northern parts of the region, creating small kingdoms such as Urshu and Hassum. Mari reemerged during this period, now Amorite rule, and saw renewed prosperity.

The Amorite states of Qatna, Yamhad (modern Aleppo) dominated much of Syria for two centuries, and in 1809 BC, an Amorite king from northern Syria named Shamshi-Adad I usurped the throne of the Old Assyrian Empire from the Akkadian speaking Erishum II, thus giving the Amorites domination over the whole of The Levant, Mesopotamia, and swathes of Asia Minor. Mari was conquered by Assyria and Yamhad was also attacked, leading its king to enter into an alliance with the new state of Babylon and also Eshnunna against Assyria. In 1792 BC the Amorite king Hammurabi had come to the fore, building the minor town of Babylon into a major city and becoming the first to declare himself its king. Hammurabi then engaged in a series of wars of expansion, creating the short lived Babylonian Empire, and conquered Mari and much of eastern Syria, though retaining friendly relations with Yamhad. It is from his reign that southern Mesopotamia came to be known as Babylonia, although his empire soon collapsed after his death, and both Syria and Assyria shrugged off Babylonian rule.

Yamhad, with its capital of Halab, was described in the tablets of Mari as the mightiest state in the near east and as having more vassals than Hammurabi of Babylon. Yamhad imposed its authority over Alalakh, Qatna, the Hurrians states and the Euphrates Valley down to the borders with Babylon. The army of Yamhad campaigned as far away as Dçr on the border of Elam (modern Iran).

Ugarit also arose during this time, circa 1800 BC, close to modern Latakia. Ugaritic was a Semitic language loosely related to but distinct from the Canaanite languages, and developed the Ugaritic alphabet. the Ugarites kingdom survived until its destruction at the hands of the marauding Indo-European Sea Peoples in the 12th century BC. Yamhad was finally conquered and destroyed, along with Ebla, by the Indo-European Hittite Empire from Asia Minor circa 1600 BC.

From the end of the 17th century BC, Syria became a battle ground for various foreign empires, these being the Hittite Empire, Mitanni Empire, Egyptian Empire, Middle Assyrian Empire, and to a lesser degree Babylonia. The Egyptians initially occupied much of the south, while the Hittites, and the Mitanni, much of the north. However, the Middle Assyrian Empire (1366-1020 BC) eventually gained the upper hand, destroying the Mitanni Empire, forcing the Egyptians from the region, conquering huge swathes of territory from the Hittites, and stamping out Babylonian ambitions in the region. The Assyrians conquered as far as the Syrian and Phoenician coasts of the Mediterranean, and beyond into Cyprus.

Arameans and Phoenicians

Around the 14th century BC, various new Semitic peoples appeared in the area, such as the semi-nomadic Suteans who came into an unsuccessful conflict with Babylonia to the east, and the West Semitic speaking Arameans who subsumed the earlier Amorites. They too were subjugated by the Middle Assyrian Empire and the Hittite Empire for centuries. The Egyptians fought the Hittites for control over south western Syria; the fighting reached its zenith in 1274 BC with the Battle of Kadesh. The Egyptians and Hittites then made peace, both unable to gain the upper hand over the other, and both fearing the growing might of Assyria. The west remained part of the reduced Hittite empire until its destruction c. 1200 BC by the Phrygians, an Indo-European people who had entered Asia Minor from The Balkans. Eastern Syria had gradually became part of the Middle Assyrian Empire from the early 14th century BC, with the Assyrians having conquered these areas from the Hittites and the Mitanni-Hurrian empire. After the destruction of the remaining Hittite lands by the Phrygians in 1200 BC, the Assyrians also annexed much of the west, after first defeating and driving off Phrygian attempts on Syria. Assyria had reached the Mediterranean by the reign of Tiglath-Pileser I 1114–1076 BC.

However, in the late 11th century BC Assyria went into a *comparative decline* following a civil war, and was reduced to controlling only regions of north eastern Syria. This allowed the Aramean tribes to gradually gain control of much of the interior from Assyria, founding states such as Bit Bahiani, Aram-Damascus, Hamath, Aram-Rehob, Aram-Naharaim, and Luhuti. From this point, the region became known as Aramea or Aram. There was also a synthesis between the Semitic Arameans and the remnants of the Indo-European Hittites, with the founding of a number of Syro-Hittite states centred in north central Aram (Syria) and south central Asia Minor (modern Turkey), including Palistin, Carchemish and Sam'al.

A Canaanite group known as the Phoenicians came to dominate the coasts of Syria, (and also Lebanon and south west Turkey) from the 13th century BC, founding city states such as Berytus (Beirut), Tyre, Sidon (Siduna), Amrit, Simyra, Arwad, Paltos, Ramitha and Shuksi. From these coastal regions they eventually spread their influence throughout the Mediterranean, including building colonies in Malta, Sicily, the Iberian peninsula (modern Spain and Portugal), the coasts of North Africa, and most significantly, founding the major city state of Carthage (in modern Tunisia) in the 9th century BC which was much later to become the centre of a major empire, the Carthaginian Empire, rivaling the Roman Empire.

The Aramean, Syro-Hittite and Phoenician states of the Levant were however still subject to periodic attacks by Assyria during the 11th and 10th centuries BC, one of which reached the Mediterranean. In 935 BC the Assyrians once more began to expand outwards.

During this period Babylonia fell into decline, and the 11th century saw tribes of Arameans and Suteans migrating into Babylonia from

Syria. These were followed into Babylonia during the late 10th or early 9th century BC by another Levantine tribe, that of the Chaldeans.

Syria, and the entire Near East and beyond, then fell to the vast Neo Assyrian Empire (911 BC – 605 BC) which stretched from The Caucasus to Egypt and Arabia, and Cyprus to Persia. The Assyrians introduced Imperial Aramaic as the lingua franca of their empire, This language was to remain dominant in Syria and the entire Near East until after the Arab Islamic conquest in the 7th and 8th centuries AD, and was to be a vehicle for the spread of Christianity. The Assyrians named their colonies of Syria and Lebanon Eber-Nari.

It was during the 850's BC that the Arabs of the Arabian Peninsula and the Chaldean immigrants to Babylonia first appear in the pages of *written history*, as among those conquered by Shalmaneser III of Assyria.

After three centuries, Assyrian domination ended, the Assyrians greatly weakened themselves in a series of brutal internal civil wars, followed by an attacking coalition of their former subject peoples; the Medes, Babylonians, Chaldeans, Persians, Scythians and Cimmerians. During the fall of Assyria, the Scythians ravaged and plundered much of Syria. The last stand of the Assyrian army was at the by then Assyrian populated city of Carchemish in northern Syria in 605 BC.

The Assyrian Empire was followed by the short lived Neo-Babylonian Empire (605 BC – 539 BC). During this period, Syria became a battle ground between Babylonia and another former Assyrian colony, that of Egypt. The Babylonians, like their Assyrian relations, were victorious over Egypt.

Classical Antiquity

The Achaemenid Persians took Syria from Babylonia as part of their hegemony of Southwest Asia in 539 BC. The Persians, having spent four centuries under Assyrian rule, retained Imperial Aramaic as the language of the Achaemenid Empire (539 BC- 33O BC), and also the Assyrian name of the satrapy of Aram/Syria Eber-Nari.

Syria was conquered by the Greek Macedonian Empire, ruled by Alexander the Great circa 330 BC, and consequently became Coele-Syria province of the Greek Seleucid Empire (323 BC – 64 BC).

It was the Greeks who introduced the name "Syria" to the region. Originally an Indo-European corruption of "Assyria" in northern Mesopotamia, the Greeks used this term not only to describe Assyria itself but the lands to the west which had for centuries been under Assyrian dominion. Thus in the Greco-Roman world both the Arameans of Syria and the Assyrians of Mesopotamia to the east were referred to as "Syrians" or "Syriacs", despite these being distinct peoples in their own right, a confusion which would continue into the modern world.

Palmyra, a rich and sometimes powerful native Aramean kingdom arose in northern Syria in the 4th century BC, independent of the Greeks. Eventually parts of southern Seleucid Syria were taken by Judean Hasmoneans upon the slow disintegration of the Hellenistic Empire.

Syria briefly came under Armenian control from 83 BC, with the conquests of Tigranes the Great, who was welcomed as a savior from the Seleucids and Romans by its people. The Armenians retained control of Syria for two decades before being driven out by the Romans.

Pompey the Great of the Roman Empire, who captured Antioch in 64 BC, turning Syria into a Roman province. Palmyra again remained largely independent, and in the late 3rd century AD it became the centre of the short lived Palmyrene Empire, which briefly conquered Egypt, Syria, Palestine, much of Asia Minor, Judah and Lebanon, before being finally brought under Roman control in 273 AD.

The northern Mesopotamian Assyrian kingdom of Adiabene controlled areas of north east Syria between 10 AD and 117 AD, before it was conquered by Rome.

The Aramaic language has been found as far afield as Hadrians Wall in Ancient Britain, with inscriptions written by Assyrian and Aramean soldiers of the Roman Empire.

Control of Syria eventually passed from the Romans to the Byzantines, with the split in the Roman Empire.

The largely Aramaic speaking population of Syria during the heyday of the Byzantine empire was probably not exceeded again until the 19th century. Prior to the *Arab Islamic Conquest* in the 7th century AD, the bulk of the population were Arameans, but Syria was also home to Greek and Roman ruling classes, Assyrians still dwelt in the north east, Phoenicians along the coasts, and Jewish and Armenian communities was also extant in major cities, with Nabateans and *pre-Islamic* Arabs such as the Lakhmids and Ghassanids dwelling in the deserts of southern Syria. Syriac Christianity had taken hold as the major religion, although others still followed Judaism, Mithraism, Manicheanism, Greco-Roman Religion, Canaanite Religion and Mesopotamian Religion. Syria's large and prosperous population made Syria one of the most important of the Roman and Byzantine provinces, particularly during the 2nd and 3rd centuries (AD).

The Roman Emperor Alexander Severus, who was emperor from 222 to 235, was an Aramean from Syria. His cousin Elagabalus, who was emperor from 218 to 222, was also from Syria and his family held hereditary rights to the high priesthood of the Aramean sun god El-Gabal at Emesa (modern Homs) in Syria. Another Roman emperor who was a Syrian was Philip the Arab (Marcus Julius Philippus), emperor from 244 to 249.

Syria is significant in the history of Christianity; Saulus of Tarsus, better known as the Apostle Paul, was converted on the Road to Damascus and emerged as a significant figure in the Christian Church at Antioch in ancient Syria, from which he left on many of his missionary journeys. (Acts 9:1–43)

Middle Ages

During Muhammad's Era

Muhammad's first interaction with the people and tribes of Syria was during the Invasion of Dumatul Jandal in July 626 where he ordered his followers to Invade Duma, because Muhammad received intelligence that some tribes there were involved in highway robbery and preparing to attack Medina itself.

William Montgomery Watt claims that this was the most significant expedition Muhammad ordered at the time, even though it received little notice in the primary sources. Duma was 500 miles from Medina, and Watt says that there was no immediate threat to Muhammad, other than the possibility that his communications to Syria and supplies to Medina being interrupted.

Watt says "It is tempting to suppose that Muhammad was already envisaging something of the expansion which took place after his death", and that the rapid march of his troops must have "impressed all those who heard of it".

William Muir also believes that the expedition was important as Muhammad followed by 1000 men reached the confines of Syria, where distant tribes had now learnt his name, while the political horizon of Muhammad was extended.

Islamic Syria (Al-Sham)

By AD 640, Syria was conquered by the Arab Rashidun army led by Khalid ibn al-Walid. In the mid-7th century, the Umayyad dynasty, then rulers of the empire, placed the capital of the empire in Damascus. The country's power declined during later Umayyad rule; due mainly to totalitarianism, corruption and the resulting revolutions. The

Umayyad dynasty was then overthrown in 750 by the Abbasid dynasty, which moved the capital of empire to Baghdad.

Arabic – made official under Umayyad rule – became the dominant language, replacing Greek and Aramaic of the Byzantine era. In 887, the Egypt-based Tulunids annexed Syria from the Abbasids, and were later replaced by once the Egypt-based Ikhshidids and still later by the Hamdanids originating in Aleppo founded by Sayf al-Dawla.

Crusaders, Ayubids, Mamluks and Nizaris

Sections of Syria were held by French, English, Italian and German overlords between 1098 and 1189 AD during the Crusades and were known collectively as the Crusader states among which the primary one in Syria was the Principality of Antioch. The coastal mountainous region was also occupied in part by the Nizari Ismailis, the so-called Assassins, who had intermittent confrontations and truces with the Crusader States. Later in history when "the Nizaris faced renewed Frankish hostilities, they received timely assistance from the Ayyubids."

After a century of Seljuk rule, Syria was largely conquered (1175–1185) by the Kurdish warlord Saladin, founder of the Ayyubid dynasty of Egypt. Aleppo fell to the Mongols of Hulegu in January 1260, and Damascus in March, but then Hulegu was forced to break off his attack to return to China to deal with a succession dispute.

A few months later, the Mamluks arrived with an army from Egypt and defeated the Mongols in the Battle of Ain Jalut in Galilee. The Mamluk leader, Baibars, made Damascus a provincial capital. When he died, power was taken by Qalawun. In the meantime, an emir named Sunqur al-Ashqar had tried to declare himself ruler of Damascus, but he was defeated by Qalawun on 21 June 1280, and fled to northern Syria. Al-Ashqar, who had married a Mongol woman, appealed for help from the Mongols. The Mongols of the Ilkhanate took the city, but Qalawun persuaded Al-Ashqar to join him, and they fought against the Mongols on 29 October 1281, in the Second Battle of Homs, which was won by the Mamluks.

In 1400, the Muslim Turco-Mongol conqueror Timur Lenk (Tamurlane) invaded Syria, sacked Aleppo and captured Damascus after defeating the Mamluk army. The city's inhabitants were massacred, except for the artisans, who were deported to Samarkand Timur-Lenk also conducted specific massacres of the Aramean and Assyrian Christian populations, greatly reducing their numbers. By the end of the 15th century, the discovery of a sea route from Europe to the Far East ended the need for an overland trade route through Syria.

Ottoman Syria

Syrian Women, 1683: In 1516, the Ottoman Empire invaded the Mamluk Sultanate of Egypt, conquering Syria, and incorporating it into its empire. The Ottoman system was not burdensome to Syrians because the Turks respected Arabic as the language of the Koran, and accepted the mantle of defenders of the faith. Damascus was made the major entrepot for Mecca, and as such it acquired a holy character to Muslims, because of the beneficial results of the countless pilgrims who passed through on the hajj, the pilgrimage to Mecca.

Ottoman administration followed a system that led to peaceful coexistence. Each ethno-religious minority – Arab Shia Muslim, Arab Sunni Muslim, Aramean-Syriac Orthodox, Greek Orthodox, Maronite Christians, Assyrian Christians, Armenians, Kurds and Jewish – constituted a millet. The religious heads of each community administered all personal status laws and performed certain civil functions as well. In 1831, Ibrahim Pasha of Egypt renounced his loyalty to the Empire and overran Ottoman Syria, capturing Damascus. His short-term rule over the domain attempted to change the demographics and social structure of the region: he brought thousands of Egyptian villagers to populate the plains of Southern Syria, rebuilt Jaffa and settled it with veteran Egyptian soldiers aiming to turn it into a regional capital, and he crushed peasant and Druze rebellions and deported non-loyal tribesmen. By 1840, however, he had to surrender the area back to the Ottomans.

From 1864, Tanzimat reforms were applied on Ottoman Syria, carving out the provinces (vilayets) of Aleppo, Zor, Beirut and Damascus Vilayet; Mutasarrifate of Mount Lebanon was created, as well, and soon after the Mutasarrifate of Jerusalem was given a separate status.

During World War I the Ottoman Empire entered the conflict on the side of Germany and the Austro-Hungarian Empire. It ultimately suffered defeat and loss of control of the entire Near East to the British Empire and French Empire. During the conflict, genocide against indigenous Christian peoples was carried out by the Ottomans and their allies in the form of the Armenian Genocide and Assyrian Genocide, of which Deir ez-Zor, in Ottoman Syria, was the final destination of these death marches. In the midst of World War I, two Allied diplomats (Frenchman François Georges-Picot and Briton Mark Sykes) secretly agreed on the post-war division of the Ottoman Empire into respective zones of influence in the Sykes-Picot Agreement of 1916. Initially, the two territories were separated by a border that ran in an almost straight line from Jordan to Iran. However, the discovery of oil in the region of Mosul just before the end of the war led to yet another negotiation with France in 1918 to cede this region to 'Zone B', or the British zone of influence. This border was later recognised internationally when Syria became a League of Nations mandate in 1920 and has not changed to date.

French Mandate

In 1920, a short-lived independent Kingdom of Syria was established under Faisal I of the Hashemite family. However, his rule over Syria ended after only a few months, following the Battle of Maysalun. French troops occupied Syria later that year after the San Remo conference proposed that the League of Nations put Syria under a French mandate.

In 1925, Sultan al-Atrash led a revolt that broke out in the Druze Mountain and spread to engulf the whole of Syria and parts of Lebanon. Al-Atrash won several battles against the French, notably the Battle of al-Kafr on 21 July 1925, the Battle of al-Mazraa on 2–3 August 1925, and the battles of Salkhad, al-Musayfirah and Suwayda. France sent thousands of troops from Morocco and Senegal, leading the French to regain many cities, although resistance lasted until the spring of 1927. The French sentenced Sultan al-Atrash to death, but he had escaped with the rebels to Transjordan and was eventually pardoned. He returned to Syria in 1937 after the signing of the Syrian-French Treaty.

Syria and France negotiated a treaty of independence in September 1936, and Hashim al-Atassi was the first president to be elected under the first incarnation of the modern republic of Syria. However, the treaty never came into force because the French Legislature refused to ratify it. With the fall of France in 1940 during World War II, Syria came under the control of Vichy France until the British and Free French occupied the country in the Syria-Lebanon campaign in July 1941. Continuing pressure from Syrian nationalists and the British forced the French to evacuate their troops in April 1946, leaving the country in the hands of a republican government that had been formed during the mandate.

Independent Syrian Republic

Upheaval dominated Syrian politics from independence through the late 1960s. On May 1948, Syrian forces invaded Palestine, together with other Arab states, and immediately attacked Jewish settlements. Their president, Shukri al-Quwwatli instructed his troops in the front, "to destroy the Zionists". The Invasion purpose was prevention of the establishment of the State of Israel. Defeat in this war was one of several trigger factors for the March 1949 Syrian coup d'état by Col. Husni al-Za'im, described as the first military overthrow of the Arab World since the start of the Second World War. This was soon followed by another overthrow, by Col. Sami al-Hinnawi, who was himself quickly deposed by Col. Adib Shishakli, all within the same year.

Shishakli eventually abolished multipartism altogether, but was himself overthrown in a 1954 coup and the parliamentary system was restored. However, by this time, power was increasingly concentrated in the military and security establishment. The weakness of Parliamentary institutions and the mismanagement of the economy led to unrest and the influence of Nasserism and other ideologies. There was fertile ground for various Arab nationalist, Syrian nationalist, and socialist movements, which represented disaffected elements of society. Notably included were religious minorities, who demanded radical reform.

In November 1956, as a direct result of the Suez Crisis, Syria signed a pact with the Soviet Union. This gave a foothold for Communist influence within the government in exchange for military equipment. Turkey then became worried about this increase in the strength of Syrian military technology, as it seemed feasible that Syria might attempt to retake Ýskenderun. Only heated debates in the United Nations lessened the threat of war.

On 1 February 1958, Syrian President Shukri al-Quwatli and Egypt's Nasser announced the merging of Egypt and Syria, creating the United Arab Republic, and all Syrian political parties, as well as the communists therein, ceased overt activities. Meanwhile, a group of Syrian Ba'athist officers, alarmed by the party's poor position and the increasing fragility of the union, decided to form a secret Military Committee; its initial members were Lieutenant-Colonel Muhammad Umran, Major Salah Jadid and Captain Hafez al-Assad. When Syria seceded on 28 September 1961, the ensuing instability culminated in the 8 March 1963 coup. The takeover was engineered by members of the Arab Socialist Ba'ath Party, led by Michel Aflaq and Salah al-Din al-Bitar. The new cabinet was dominated by Ba'ath members.

Ba'athist Syria

On 23 February 1966, the Military Committee carried out an intra-party overthrow, imprisoned President Amin Hafiz and designated a regionalist, civilian Ba'ath government on 1 March. Although Nureddin al-Atassi became the formal head of state, Salah Jadid was Syria's effective ruler from 1966 until 1970. The coup led to a split within the original pan-Arab Ba'ath Party: one Iraqi-led ba'ath movement (ruled

Iraq from 1968 to 2003) and one Syrian-led ba'ath movement was established. In the first part of 1967 a low-key state of war existed between Syria and Israel. Conflict over Israeli cultivation of land in the Demilitarized Zone led to 7 April prewar aerial clashes between Israel and Syria. After Israel launched a preemptive strike on Egypt to begin the Six-Day War, Syria joined the war and attacked against Israel as well. In the final days of the war, Israel turned its attention to Syria, capturing two-thirds of the Golan Heights in under 48 hours. The defeat caused a split between Jadid and Assad over what steps to take next.

Disagreement developed between Jadid, who controlled the party apparatus, and Assad, who controlled the military. The 1970 retreat of Syrian forces sent to aid the PLO during the "Black September" hostilities with Jordan reflected this disagreement. The power struggle culminated in the November 1970 Corrective Movement, a bloodless military overthrow that installed Hafez al-Assad as the strongman of the government.

On 6 October 1973, Syria and Egypt initiated the Yom Kippur War against Israel. The Israel Defence Forces reversed the initial Syrian gains and pushed deeper into Syrian territory.

In early 1976, Syria entered Lebanon, beginning the thirty-year Syrian military occupation. Over the following 15 years of civil war, Syria fought for control over Lebanon, and attempted to stop Israel from taking over in southern Lebanon, through extensive use of proxy militias. Syria then remained in Lebanon until 2005.

In the late 1970s, an Islamist uprising by the Muslim Brotherhood was aimed against the government. Islamists attacked civilians and off-duty military personnel, leading security forces to also kill civilians in retaliatory strikes. The uprising had reached its climax in the 1982 Hama massacre, when some 10,000 – 40,000 people were killed by regular Syrian Army troops.

In a major shift in relations with both other Arab states and the Western world, Syria participated in the US-led Gulf War against Saddam Hussein. Syria participated in the multilateral Madrid Conference of 1991, and during the 1990s engaged in negotiations with Israel. These negotiations failed, and there have been no further direct Syrian-Israeli talks since President Hafez al-Assad's meeting with then President Bill Clinton in Geneva in March 2000.

Hafez al-Assad died on 10 June 2000. His son, Bashar al-Assad, was elected President in an election in which he ran unopposed. His election saw the birth of the Damascus Spring and hopes of reform, but by autumn 2001 the authorities had suppressed the movement, imprisoning some of its leading intellectuals. Instead, reforms have been limited to some market reforms.

On 5 October 2003, Israel bombed a site near Damascus, claiming it was a terrorist training facility for members of Islamic Jihad. In March 2004, Syrian Kurds and Arabs clashed in the northeastern city of al-Qamishli. Signs of rioting were seen in the towns of Qameshli and Hassakeh. In 2005, Syria ended its occupation of Lebanon. On 6 September 2007, Israeli jet fighters carried out Operation Orchard against a suspected nuclear reactor under construction by North Korean technicians.

The ongoing Syrian civil war was inspired by the Arab Spring Revolutions. It began in 2011 as a chain of peaceful protests, followed by a crackdown by the Syrian Army. In July 2011, army defectors declared the formation of the Free Syrian Army and began forming fighting units. The opposition is dominated by Sunni Muslims, whereas the leading government figures are Alawites. According to various sources, including the United Nations, up to 100,000 people have been killed, including 11,000 children. To escape the violence, over 2.1 million Syrian refugees have fled to neighbouring countries of Jordan, Iraq, Lebanon, and Turkey. An estimated 450,000 Syrian Christians have fled their homes. As the civil war has dragged on, there have been worries that the country could become fragmented and cease to function as a state.

Politics and Government

Syria is formally a unitary republic. The constitution adopted in 2012 effectively transformed Syria into a semi-presidential republic due to the constitutional right for individuals to be elected which do not form part of the National Progressive Front. The President is Head of State and the Prime Minister is Head of Government. The legislature, the Peoples Council is the body responsible for passing laws, approving government appropriations and debating policy. In the event of a vote of no confidence by a simple majority, the Prime Minister is required to tender the resignation of their government to the President.

The executive branch consists of the president, two vice presidents, the prime minister, and the Council of Ministers (cabinet). The constitution requires the president to be a Muslim but does not make Islam the state religion.

The constitution gives the president the right to appoint ministers, to declare war and state of emergency, to issue laws (which, except in the case of emergency, require ratification by the People's Council), to declare amnesty, to amend the constitution, and to appoint civil servants and military personnel. According to the 2012 constitution, the president is elected by Syrian citizens in a direct election.

Syria's legislative branch is the unicameral People's Council. Under the previous constitution, Syria did not hold multi-party elections for the legislature, with two-thirds of the seats automatically allocated to the ruling coalition. On 7 May 2012, Syria held its first elections in which parties outside the ruling coalition could take part. Seven new political parties took part in the elections, of which Popular Front for Change and Liberation was the largest opposition party. The armed anti-government rebels, however, chose not to field candidates and called on their supporters to boycott the elections.

The President is currently the Regional Secretary of the Ba'ath party in Syria and leader of the National Progressive Front governing coalition. Outside of the coalition are 14 illegal Kurdish political parties.

Syria's judicial branches include the Supreme Constitutional Court, the High Judicial Council, the Court of Cassation, and the State Security Courts. Islamic jurisprudence is a main source of legislation and Syria's judicial system has elements of Ottoman, French, and Islamic laws. Syria has three levels of courts: courts of first instance, courts of appeals, and the constitutional court, the highest tribunal. Religious courts handle questions of personal and family law. The Supreme State Security Court (SSSC) was abolished by President Bashar al-Assad by legislative decree No. 53 on 21 April 2011.

The Personal Status Law 59 of 1953 (amended by Law 34 of 1975) is essentially a codified sharia. Article 3(2) of the 1973 constitution declares Islamic jurisprudence a main source of legislation. The Code of Personal Status is applied to Muslims by sharia courts.

As a result of the ongoing civil war, various alternative governments were formed, including the Syrian Interim Government, the Democratic Union Party and localised regions governed by sharia law. Representatives of the Syrian Interim government were invited to take up Syria's seat at the Arab League on 28 March 2013 and was recognised as the "sole representative of the Syrian people" by several nations including the United States, United Kingdom and France.

Human Rights

The situation for human rights in Syria has long been a significant concern among independent organisations such as Human Rights Watch, who in 2010 referred to the country's record as "among the worst in the world." The US State Department funded Freedom House ranked Syria "Not Free" in its annual Freedom in the World survey.

The authorities are accused of arresting democracy and human rights activists, censoring websites, detaining bloggers, and imposing travel bans. Arbitrary detention, torture, and disappearances are widespread. Although Syria's constitution guarantees gender equality, critics say that personal statutes laws and the penal code discriminate against women and girls. Moreover, it also grants leniency for so-called 'Honour killing'. As of 9 November 2011 during the uprising against President Bashar al-Assad, the United Nations reported that of the over 3500 total deaths, over 250 deaths were children as young as 2 years old, and that boys as young as 11 years old have been gang raped by security services officers. People opposing President Assad's rule claim that more than 200, mostly civilians, were massacred and about 300 injured in Hama in shelling by the Government forces on 12 July 2012.

In August 2013 the government was suspected of using chemical weapons against its civilians. US Secretary of State John Kerry said it was "undeniable" that chemical weapons had been used in the country and that President Bashar al-Assad's forces had committed a "moral obscenity" against his own people. "Make no mistake," Kerry said. "President Obama believes there must be accountability for those who would use the world's most heinous weapon against the world's most vulnerable people. Nothing today is more serious, and nothing is receiving more serious scrutiny".

The Emergency Law, effectively suspending most constitutional protections, was in effect from 1963 until 21 April 2011. It was justified by the government in the light of the continuing war with Israel over the Golan Heights.

In August 2014, UN Human Rights chief Navi Pillay criticized the international community over its "paralysis" in dealing with the more than 3-year old civil war gripping the country, which by April 30, 2014 had resulted in 191,369 deaths with war crimes, according to Pillay, being committed with total impunity on all sides in the conflict. Minority Alawites and Christians are being increasingly targeted by Islamists and other groups fighting in the Syrian civil war.

Military

The President of Syria is commander in chief of the Syrian armed forces, comprising some 400,000 troops upon mobilization. The military is a conscripted force; males serve in the military upon reaching the age of 18. The obligatory military service period is being decreased over time, in 2005 from two and a half years to two years, in 2008 to 21 months and in 2011 to year and a half. About 20,000 Syrian soldiers were deployed in Lebanon until 27 April 2005, when the last of Syria's troops left the country after three decades.

The breakup of the Soviet Union—long the principal source of training, material, and credit for the Syrian forces—may have slowed Syria's ability to acquire modern military equipment. It has an arsenal of surface-to-surface missiles. In the early 1990s, Scud-C missiles with a 500-kilometre range were procured from North Korea, and Scud-D, with a range of up to 700 kilometres, is allegedly being developed by Syria with the help of North Korea and Iran, according to Zisser.

Syria received significant financial aid from Persian Gulf Arab states as a result of its participation in the Persian Gulf War, with a sizable portion of these funds earmarked for military spending.

Foreign Relations

Ensuring national security, increasing influence among its Arab neighbours, and securing the return of the Golan Heights, are the primary goals of President Bashar al-Assad's foreign policy. At many points in its history, Syria has seen virulent tension with its geographically cultural neighbours, such as Turkey, Israel, Iraq, and Lebanon. Syria enjoyed an improvement in relations with several of the states in its region in the 21st century, prior to the Arab Spring and the Syrian civil war.

Since the ongoing civil war of 2011, and associated killings and human rights abuses, Syria has been increasingly isolated from the countries in the region, and the wider international community. Diplomatic relations have been severed with several countries including: Britain, Canada, France, Italy, Germany, Tunisia, Egypt, Libya, the United States, Belgium, Spain, and the Gulf States.

From the Arab league, Syria continues to maintain diplomatic relations with Algeria, Egypt, Iraq, Lebanon, Sudan and Yemen. Syria's violence against civilians has also seen it suspended from the Arab League and the Organisation of Islamic Cooperation in 2012. Syria continues to foster good relations with her traditional allies, Iran, China, Venezuela and Russia, who are among the few countries which have supported the Syrian government in its conflict with the Syrian opposition.

Syria considers the Hatay Province of Turkey as part of its own territory.

Israel unilaterally annexed the Golan Heights in 1981, although the Syrian government continues to demand the return of this territory.

The Syrian occupation of Lebanon began in 1976 as a result of the civil war and ended in April 2006 in response to domestic and international pressure after the assassination of former Lebanese Prime Minister, Rafik Hariri.

Syria is included in the European Union's European Neighbourhood Policy (ENP) which aims at bringing the EU and its neighbours closer.

Economy

Syria is classified by the World Bank as a "lower middle income country." Syria remains dependent on the oil and agriculture sectors. The oil sector provides about 40% of export earnings. In addition, proven offshore expeditions have indicated that large sums of oil exist on the Mediterranean Sea floor between Syria and Cyprus. The agriculture sector contributes to about 20% of GDP and 20% of employment. Oil reserves are expected to decrease in the coming years and Syria has already become a net oil importer. Since the civil war began, the economy shrank by 35%, and the Syrian pound has fallen to one-sixth of its prewar value. The government increasingly relies on credit from Iran, Russia and China.

The economy is highly regulated by the government, which has increased subsidies and tightened trade controls to assuage protesters and protect foreign currency reserves. Long-run economic constraints include foreign trade barriers, declining oil production, high unemployment, rising budget deficits, and increasing pressure on water supplies caused by heavy use in agriculture, rapid population growth, industrial expansion, and water pollution. The UNDP announced in 2005 that 30% of the Syrian population lives in poverty and 11.4% live below the subsistence level.

Syria's main exports include crude oil, refined products, raw cotton, clothing, fruits, and grains. The bulk of Syrian imports are raw materials essential for industry, vehicles, agricultural equipment, and heavy machinery. Earnings from oil exports as well as remittances from Syrian workers are the government's most important sources of foreign exchange.

Syria's share in global exports has eroded gradually since 2001. The real per capita GDP growth was just 2.5% per year in the 2000–2008 period. Unemployment is high at above 10%. Poverty rates have increased from 11% in 2004 to 12.3% in 2007.

Political instability poses a significant threat to future economic development. Foreign investment is constrained by violence, government restrictions, economic sanctions, and international isolation. Syria's economy also remains hobbled by state bureaucracy, falling oil production, rising budget deficits, and inflation.

Prior to the civil war in 2011, the government hoped to attract new investment in the tourism, natural gas, and service sectors to diversify its economy and reduce its dependence on oil and agriculture. The government began to institute economic reforms aimed at liberalizing most markets, but those reforms were slow and ad hoc, and have been completely reversed since the outbreak of conflict in 2011.

As of 2012, because of the ongoing Syrian civil war, the value of Syria's overall exports has been slashed by two-thirds, from the figure of US$12 billion in 2010 to only US$4 billion in 2012. Syria's GDP declined by over 3% in 2011, and is expected to further decline by 20% in 2012.

As of 2012, Syria's oil and tourism industries in particular have been devastated, with US$5 billion lost to the ongoing conflict of the civil war. Reconstruction needed because of the ongoing civil war will cost as much as US$10 billion. Sanctions have sapped the government's finance. US and European Union bans on oil imports, which went into effect in 2012, are estimated to cost Syria about $400 million a month.

Revenues from tourism have dropped dramatically, with hotel occupancy rates falling from 90% before the war to less than 15% in May 2012. Around 40% of all employees in the tourism sector have lost their jobs since the beginning of the war.

Petroleum Industry

Syria has produced heavy-grade oil from fields located in the northeast since the late 1960s. In the early 1980s, light-grade, low-sulphur oil was discovered near Deir ez-Zor in eastern Syria. Syria's rate of oil production has decreased dramatically from a peak close to 600,000 barrels per day (95,000 m^3/d) (bpd) in 1995 down to less than 140,000 bbl/d (22,000 m^3/d) in 2012.

Syria exported roughly 200,000 bbl/d (32,000 m^3/d) in 2005, and oil still accounts for a majority of the country's export income. Syria also produces 22 million cubic metres of gas per day, with estimated reserves around 8.5 trillion cubic feet (240 km^3). While the government has begun to work with international energy companies in the hopes of eventually becoming a gas exporter, all gas currently produced is consumed domestically.

Prior to the uprising, more than 90% of Syrian oil exports were to EU countries, with the remainder going to Turkey. Oil and gas revenues constituted around 20% of total GDP and 25% of total government revenue.

Expressway M5 Near Al-Rastan

Transport

Syria has three international airports (Damascus, Aleppo and Lattakia), which serve as hubs for Syrian Air and are also served by a variety of foreign carriers.

The majority of Syrian cargo is carried by Chemins de Fer Syriens (the Syrian railway company), which links up with Turkish State Railways (the Turkish counterpart). For a relatively underdeveloped country, Syria's railway infrastructure is well maintained with many express services and modern trains.

The road network in the Syria is 69,873 km long including 1,103 km of expressways, the country also have 900 km of navigable but not economically significant Waterways.

Syrians are an overall indigenous Levantine people, closely related to their immediate neighbours, like Lebanese people, Palestinians, Israelis, Iraqis, Maltese and Jordanians. Syria has a population of approximately 17,951,639 (2014 est.) Syrian Arabs, together with some 500,000 Palestinian Arabs, make up roughly 74% of the population (if Syriac Christians are excluded).

The indigenous Christian Syriac-Aramean people and Assyrians are numbered around 400,000 people, with the Syriac-Aramaic group living all over the country, particularly in major urban centres, while the Assyrians mainly reside in the north and northeast (Homs, Aleppo, Qamishli, Hasakah). Many (particularly the Assyrian group) still retain several Akkadian infused Neo-Aramaic dialects as spoken and written languages, while a small number of Syriac-Arameans still retain Western Aramaic.

The second largest ethnic group in Syria are The Kurds. They constitute about 9% of the population, or approximately 2 million people. Most Kurds reside in the northeastern corner of Syria and most speak the Kurmanji variant of the Kurdish language.

Syria is also a home to several other ethnic groups mainly the Turkmens (number around 500,000–1,000,000), Circassians (number some 100,000), Greeks, Jews, and Armenians (number approximately 100,000), most arrived during the Armenian Genocide. Syria holds the

7th largest Armenian population in the world. They are mainly gathered in Aleppo, Qamishli, Damascus and Kesab.

The largest concentration of the Syrian diaspora outside the Arab world is in Brazil, which has millions of people of Arab and other Near Eastern ancestries. Brazil is the first country in the Americas to offer humanitarian visas to Syrian refugees. The majority of Arab Argentines are from either Lebanese or Syrian background.

Religion

Sunni Arabs account for 59–60% of the population, most Kurds (9%) and Turkomen (3%) are Sunni, while 13% are Shia (Alawite, Twelvers, and Ismailis combined), 10% Christian (the majority Antiochian Orthodox, the rest including Greek Catholic, Assyrian Church of the East, Armenian Orthodox, Protestants and other denominations), and 3% Druze. Druze number around 500,000, and concentrate mainly in the southern area of Jabal al-Druze.

President Bashar al-Assad's family is Alawite and Alawites dominate the government of Syria and hold key military positions.

Christians (2.5 million), a sizable number of whom are found among Syria's population of Palestinian refugees, are divided into several groups. Chalcedonian Antiochian Orthodox make up 35.7% of the Christian population; the Catholics (Melkite, Armenian Catholic, Syriac Catholic, Maronite, Chaldean Catholic and Latin) make up 26.2%; the Armenian Apostolic Church 10.9%, the Syriac Orthodox make up 22.4%; Assyrian Church of the East and several smaller Christian denominations account the remainder. Many Christian monasteries also exist. Many Christian Syrians belong to a high socio-economic class.

Languages

Arabic is the official language. Several modern Arabic dialects are used in everyday life, most notably Levantine in the west and Mesopotamian in the northeast. Kurdish (in its Kurmanji form) is widely spoken in the Kurdish regions of Syria. Armenian and Turkish (South Azeri dialect) are spoken among the Armenian and Turkmen minorities.

Aramaic was the lingua franca of the region before the advent of Arabic, and is still spoken among Assyrians, and Classical Syriac is still used as the liturgical language of various Syriac Christian denominations. Most remarkably, Western Neo-Aramaic is still spoken in the village of Ma'loula as well as two neighbouring villages, 35 miles (56 km) northeast of Damascus. Many educated Syrians also speak English and French.

Turkey

Turkey, officially the Republic of Turkey, is a contiguous transcontinental parliamentary republic largely located in Western Asia with the smaller portion of Eastern Thrace in Southeastern Europe. Turkey is bordered by eight countries: Bulgaria to the northwest; Greece to the west; Georgia to the northeast; Armenia, Iran and the Azerbaijani exclave of Nakhchivan to the east; and Iraq and Syria to the southeast. The Mediterranean Sea is to the south; the Aegean Sea to the west; and the Black Sea to the north. The Sea of Marmara, the Bosphorus and the Dardanelles (which together form the Turkish Straits) demarcate the boundary between Thrace and Anatolia; they also separate Europe and Asia. Turkey's location at the crossroads of Europe and Asia makes it a country of significant geostrategic importance.

Turkey has been inhabited since the paleolithic age, including various Ancient Anatolian civilizations, Aeolian and Ionian Greeks, Thracians and Persians. After Alexander the Great's conquest, the area was Hellenized, which continued with the Roman rule and the transition into the Byzantine Empire. The Seljuk Turks began migrating into the area in the 11th century, starting the process of Turkification, which was greatly accelerated by the Seljuk victory over the Byzantines at the Battle of Manzikert in 1071. The Seljuk Sultanate of Rûm ruled Anatolia until the Mongol invasion in 1243, upon which it disintegrated into several small Turkish beyliks.

Starting from the late 13th century, the Ottomans united Anatolia and created an empire encompassing much of Southeastern Europe, Western Asia and North Africa, becoming a major power in Eurasia and Africa during the early modern period. The empire reached the peak of its power between the 15th and 17th centuries, especially during the reign of Suleiman the Magnificent (r. 1520–1566). After the second Ottoman siege of Vienna in 1683 and the end of the Great Turkish War in 1699, the Ottoman Empire entered a long period of decline. The Tanzimat reforms of the 19th century, which aimed to modernise the Ottoman state, proved to be inadequate in most fields, and failed to stop the dissolution of the empire. The Ottoman Empire entered World War I (1914–1918) on the side of the Central Powers and was ultimately defeated. During the war, major atrocities were committed by the Ottoman government against the Armenians, Assyrians and Pontic Greeks. Following WWI, the huge conglomeration of territories and peoples that formerly comprised the Ottoman Empire was divided into several new states. The Turkish War of Independence (1919–1922), initiated by Mustafa Kemal Atatürk and his colleagues in Anatolia, resulted in the establishment of the modern Republic of Turkey in 1923, with Atatürk as its first president.

Turkey is a democratic, secular, unitary, constitutional republic with a diverse cultural heritage. The country's official language is Turkish, a Turkic language spoken natively by approximately 85% of the population. About 70-75% of the population are ethnic Turks and about 25-30% of the population consists of legally (per the Treaty of Lausanne) recognised (Armenians, Greeks and Jews) and unrecognised (Kurds, Circassians, Albanians, Bosniaks, Georgians, etc.) minorities. The vast majority of the population is Muslim. Turkey is a member of the UN, NATO, OECD, OSCE, OIC and the G-20. After becoming one of the first members of the Council of Europe in 1949, Turkey became an associate member of the EEC in 1963, joined the EU Customs Union in 1995 and started full membership negotiations with the European Union in 2005. Turkey's growing economy and diplomatic initiatives have led to its recognition as a regional power.

History of Turkey

Prehistory of Anatolia and Eastern Thrace

The Anatolian peninsula, comprising most of modern Turkey, is one of the oldest permanently settled regions in the world. Various Ancient Anatolian populations have lived in Anatolia, beginning with the Neolithic period until conquest of Alexander the Great. Many of these peoples spoke the Anatolian languages, a branch of the larger Indo-European language family. In fact, given the antiquity of the Indo-European Hittite and Luwian languages, some scholars have proposed Anatolia as the hypothetical centre from which the Indo-European languages radiated. The European part of Turkey, called Eastern Thrace, has also been inhabited since forty thousand years ago, and is known to have been in the Neolithic era by about 6000 B.C. with its inhabitants starting the practice of agriculture.

Göbekli Tepe is the site of the oldest known man-made religious structure, a temple dating to 10,000 BC, while Çatalhöyük is a very large Neolithic and Chalcolithic settlement in southern Anatolia, which existed from approximately 7500 BCE to 5700 BCE. It is the largest and best-preserved Neolithic site found to date and in July 2012 was inscribed as a UNESCO World Heritage Site. The settlement of Troy started in the Neolithic Age and continued into the Iron Age.

The earliest recorded inhabitants of Anatolia were the Hattians and Hurrians, non-Indo-European peoples who inhabited central and eastern Anatolia, respectively, as early as ca. 2300 BC. Indo-European Hittites came to Anatolia and gradually absorbed the Hattians and Hurrians ca. 2000–1700 BC. The first major empire in the area was founded by the Hittites, from the 18th through the 13th century BC. The Assyrians conquered and settled parts of southeastern Turkey as early as 1950 BC until the year 612 BC. Urartu re-emerged in Assyrian inscriptions in the 9th century BC as a powerful northern rival of Assyria.

Following the collapse of the Hittite empire c. 1180 BC, the Phrygians, an Indo-European people, achieved ascendancy in Anatolia until their kingdom was destroyed by the Cimmerians in the 7th century BC. Starting from 714 BC, Urartu shared the same fate and dissolved in 590 BC. The most powerful of Phrygia's successor states were Lydia, Caria and Lycia.

Antiquity and Byzantine Period

Starting around 1200 BC, the coast of Anatolia was heavily settled by Aeolian and Ionian Greeks. Numerous important cities were founded by these colonists, such as Miletus, Ephesus, Smyrna and Byzantium, the latter founded by Greek colonists from Megara in 657 BC. The first state that was called Armenia by neighbouring peoples was the state of the Armenian Orontid dynasty, which included parts of eastern Turkey beginning in the 6th century BC. In Northwest Turkey, the most significant tribal group in Thrace was the Odyrisians, founded by Teres I.

Anatolia was conquered by the Persian Achaemenid Empire during the 6th and 5th centuries BC and later fell to Alexander the Great in 334 BC, which led to increasing cultural homogeneity and Hellenization in the area. Following Alexander's death in 323 BC, Anatolia was subsequently divided into a number of small Hellenistic kingdoms, all of which became part of the Roman Republic by the mid-1st century BC. The process of Hellenization that began with Alexander's conquest accelerated under Roman rule, and by the early centuries AD the local Anatolian languages and cultures had become extinct, being largely replaced by ancient Greek language and culture.

In 324, Constantine I chose Byzantium to be the new capital of the Roman Empire, renaming it New Rome. Following the death of Theodosius I in 395 and the permanent division of the Roman Empire between his two sons, the city, which would popularly come to be known as Constantinople became the capital of the Eastern Roman Empire. This, which would later be branded by historians as the Byzantine Empire, ruled most of the territory of what is today Turkey until the Late Middle Ages.

The Seljuks and the Ottoman Empire

The *House of Seljuk* was a branch of the *Kýnýk* Oðuz Turks who resided on the periphery of the Muslim world, in the Yabghu Khaganate of the Oðuz confederacy, to the north of the Caspian and Aral Seas, in the 9th century. In the 10th century, the Seljuks started migrating from their ancestral homeland into Persia, which became the administrative core of the Great Seljuk Empire.

In the latter half of the 11th century, the Seljuks began penetrating into the eastern regions of Anatolia. In 1071, the Seljuk Turks defeated the Byzantines at the Battle of Manzikert, starting Turkification of the area; the Turkish language and Islam were introduced to Anatolia and gradually spread over the region and the slow transition from a predominantly Christian and Greek-speaking Anatolia to a predominantly Muslim and Turkish-speaking one was underway.

In 1243, the Seljuk armies were defeated by the Mongols, causing the Seljuk Empire's power to slowly disintegrate. In its wake, one of the Turkish principalities governed by Osman I would, over the next 200 years, evolve into the Ottoman Empire, expanding throughout Anatolia, the Balkans, the Levant and North Africa. In 1453, the Ottomans completed their conquest of the Byzantine Empire by capturing its capital, Constantinople.

In 1514, Sultan Selim I (1512–1520) successfully expanded the Empire's southern and eastern borders by defeating Shah Ismail I of the Safavid dynasty in the Battle of Chaldiran. In 1517, Selim I expanded Ottoman rule into Algeria and Egypt, and created a naval presence in the Red Sea. Subsequently, a competition started between the Ottoman and Portuguese empires to become the dominant sea power in the Indian Ocean, with a number of naval battles in the Red Sea, the Arabian Sea and the Persian Gulf. The Portuguese presence in the Indian Ocean was perceived as a threat for the Ottoman monopoly over the ancient trading routes between East Asia and Western Europe (later collectively named the Silk Road). This important monopoly was increasingly compromised following the discovery of a sea route around Africa by Portuguese explorer Bartolomeu Dias in 1488, which had a considerable impact on the Ottoman economy.

The Ottoman Empire's power and prestige peaked in the 16th and 17th centuries, particularly during the reign of Suleiman the Magnificent. The empire was often at odds with the Holy Roman Empire in its steady advance towards Central Europe through the Balkans and the southern part of the Polish-Lithuanian Commonwealth. At sea, the Ottoman Navy contended with several Holy Leagues (composed primarily of Habsburg Spain, the Republic of Genoa, the Republic of Venice, the Knights of St. John, the Papal States, the Grand Duchy of Tuscany and the Duchy of Savoy) for control of the Mediterranean Sea. In the east, the Ottomans were occasionally at war with Safavid Persia over conflicts stemming from territorial disputes or religious differences between the 16th and 18th centuries.

From the beginning of the 19th century onwards, the Ottoman Empire began to decline. As it gradually shrank in size, military power and wealth, many Balkan Muslims migrated to the Empire's heartland in Anatolia, along with the Circassians fleeing the Russian conquest of the Caucasus. The decline of the Ottoman Empire led to a rise in nationalist sentiment among the various subject peoples, leading to increased ethnic tensions which occasionally burst into violence, such as the Hamidian massacres of Armenians.

The Ottoman Empire entered World War I on the side of the Central Powers and was ultimately defeated. During the war, the empire's Armenians were deported from Eastern Anatolia to Syria as part of the Armenian Genocide. As a result, an estimated 1,500,000 Armenians were killed. The Turkish government denies that there was an Armenian Genocide and claims that Armenians were only relocated from the eastern war zone. Large-scale massacres were also committed against the empire's other minority groups such as the Greeks and Assyrians. Following the Armistice of Mudros on 30 October 1918, the victorious Allied Powers sought to partition the Ottoman state through the 1920 Treaty of Sèvres.

Republic of Turkey

Figure: *Mustafa Kemal Atatürk, founder and first President of the Republic of Turkey.*

The occupation of Constantinople and Smyrna by the Allies in the aftermath of World War I prompted the establishment of the Turkish National Movement. Under the leadership of Mustafa Kemal Pasha, a military commander who had distinguished himself during the Battle of Gallipoli, the Turkish War of Independence was waged with the aim of revoking the terms of the Treaty of Sèvres.

By 18 September 1922, the occupying armies were expelled, and the Ankara-based Turkish regime, which declared itself the legitimate government of the country in April 1920, started to formalize the legal transition from the old Ottoman into the new Republican political system. On 1 November, the newly founded parliament formally abolished the Sultanate, thus ending 623 years of monarchical Ottoman rule. The Treaty of Lausanne of 24 July 1923 led to the international recognition of the sovereignty of the newly formed "Republic of Turkey" as the continuing state of the Ottoman Empire, and the republic was officially proclaimed on 29 October 1923 in Ankara, the country's new capital. The Lausanne treaty stipulated a population exchange between Greece and Turkey, whereby 1.1 million Greeks left Turkey for Greece in exchange for 380,000 Muslims transferred from Greece to Turkey.

Mustafa Kemal became the republic's first President and subsequently introduced many radical reforms with the aim of transforming the old Ottoman-Turkish state into a new secular republic. With the Surname Law of 1934, the Turkish Parliament bestowed upon Mustafa Kemal the honorific surname "Atatürk" (*Father of the Turks*).

Turkey remained neutral during most of World War II, but entered the closing stages of the war on the side of the Allies on 23 February 1945. On 26 June 1945, Turkey became a charter member of the United Nations. Difficulties faced by Greece after the war in quelling a communist rebellion, along with demands by the Soviet Union for military bases in the Turkish Straits, prompted the United States to declare the Truman Doctrine in 1947. The doctrine enunciated American intentions to guarantee the security of Turkey and Greece, and resulted in large-scale U.S. military and economic support. Both countries were included in the Marshall Plan and OEEC for rebuilding European economies in 1948, and subsequently became founding members of the OECD in 1961.

After participating with the United Nations forces in the Korean War, Turkey joined NATO in 1952, becoming a bulwark against Soviet expansion into the Mediterranean. Following a decade of Cypriot intercommunal violence and the coup in Cyprus on 15 July 1974 staged by the EOKA B paramilitary organisation, which overthrew President

Makarios and installed the pro-Enosis (union with Greece) Nikos Sampson as dictator, Turkey invaded Cyprus on 20 July 1974. Nine years later the Turkish Republic of Northern Cyprus, which is recognised only by Turkey, was established.

The single-party period ended in 1945. It was followed by a tumultuous transition to multiparty democracy over the next few decades, which was interrupted by military coups d'état in 1960, 1971, and 1980, as well as a military memorandum in 1997. In 1984, the PKK, a Kurdish separatist group, began an insurgency campaign against the Turkish government, which to date has claimed over 40,000 lives. Peace talks are ongoing. Since the liberalization of the Turkish economy during the 1980s, the country has enjoyed stronger economic growth and greater political stability. In 2013, widespread protests erupted in many Turkish provinces, sparked by a plan to demolish Gezi Park but growing into general anti-government dissent.

Administrative Divisions

Turkey has a unitary structure in terms of administration and this aspect is one of the most important factors shaping the Turkish public administration. When three powers (executive, legislature and judiciary) are taken into account as the main functions of the state, local administrations do not have almost any power. In other words, there are not units called "states" in Turkey and the provinces and cities come after the central administration. Local administrations were established to provide services in place and the government is represented by the governors and city governors. Besides the governors and the city governors, other senior public officials are also appointed by the central government rather than to be appointed by mayors or elected by constituents.

Turkey is subdivided into 81 provinces for administrative purposes. Each province is divided into districts, for a total of 923 districts.

Turkey is also subdivided into 7 regions and 21 subregions for geographic, demographic and economic purposes; this does not refer to an administrative division.

Politics

Turkey is a parliamentary representative democracy. Since its foundation as a republic in 1923, Turkey has developed a strong tradition of secularism. Turkey's constitution governs the legal framework of the country. It sets out the main principles of government and establishes Turkey as a unitary centralized state. The President of the Republic is the head of state and has a largely ceremonial role.

The president is elected for a five-year term by direct elections and Recep Tayyip Erdoðan is first president elected by direct voting.

Executive power is exercised by the Prime Minister and the Council of Ministers which make up the government, while the legislative power is vested in the unicameral parliament, the Grand National Assembly of Turkey. The judiciary is independent of the executive and the legislature, and the Constitutional Court is charged with ruling on the conformity of laws and decrees with the constitution. The Council of State is the tribunal of last resort for administrative cases, and the High Court of Appeals for all others.

The prime minister is elected by the parliament through a vote of confidence in the government and is most often the head of the party having the most seats in parliament. The prime minister is Ahmet Davutoðlu who is also the leader of the Justice and Development Party (AKP) since 27 August 2014.

Universal suffrage for both sexes has been applied throughout Turkey since 1933, and every Turkish citizen who has turned 18 years of age has the right to vote. There are 550 members of parliament who are elected for a four-year term by a party-list proportional representation system from 85 electoral districts. The Constitutional Court can strip the public financing of political parties that it deems anti-secular or separatist, or ban their existence altogether. The electoral threshold is 10% of the votes.

Supporters of Atatürk's reforms are called Kemalists, as distinguished from Islamists, representing two extremes on a continuum of beliefs about the proper role of religion in public life. The Kemalist position generally combines a kind of democracy with a laicist constitution and westernised secular lifestyle, while supporting state intervention in the economy, education, and other public services. Since the 1980s, a rise in income inequality and class distinction has given rise to Islamic populism, a movement that in theory supports obligation to authority, communal solidarity and social justice, though what that entails in practice is often contested.

Human rights in Turkey have been the subject of some controversy and international condemnation. Between 1998 and 2008 the European Court of Human Rights made more than 1,600 judgements against Turkey for human rights violations, particularly regarding the right to life, and freedom from torture. Other issues, such as Kurdish rights, women's rights, and press freedom, have also attracted controversy. Turkey's human rights record continues to be a significant obstacle to future membership of the EU. According to the Committee to Protect

Journalists, the AKP government has waged one of the world's biggest crackdowns on press freedoms. A large number of journalists have been arrested using charges of "terrorism" and "anti-state activities" such as the Ergenekon and Balyoz cases, while thousands have been investigated on charges such as "denigrating Turkishness" or "insulting Islam" in an effort to sow self-censorship. In 2012, the CPJ identified 76 jailed journalists in Turkey, including 61 directly held for their published work, more than in Iran, Eritrea or China. A former U.S. State Department spokesman, Philip J. Crowley, said that the United States had "broad concerns about trends involving intimidation of journalists in Turkey."

Law

Turkey has a legal system which has been wholly integrated with the system of continental Europe. For instance, the Turkish Civil Law has been modified by incorporating elements mainly of the Swiss Civil Code, the Code of Obligations and the German Commercial Code. The Administrative Law bears similarities with its French counterpart, and the Penal Code with its Italian counterpart.

Turkey has adopted the principle of the separation of powers. In line with this principle, judicial power is exercised by independent courts on behalf of the Turkish nation. The independence and organisation of the courts, the security of the tenure of judges and public prosecutors, the profession of judges and prosecutors, the supervision of judges and public prosecutors, the military courts and their organisation, and the powers and duties of the high courts are regulated by the Turkish Constitution.

According to Article 142 of the Turkish Constitution, the organisation, duties and jurisdiction of the courts, their functions and the trial procedures are regulated by law. In line with the aforementioned article of the Turkish Constitution and related laws, the court system in Turkey can be classified under three main categories; which are the Judicial Courts, Administrative Courts and Military Courts. Each category includes first instance courts and high courts. In addition, the Court of Jurisdictional Disputes rules on cases that cannot be classified readily as falling within the purview of one court system.

Law enforcement in Turkey is carried out by several departments (such as the General Directorate of Security and Gendarmerie General Command) and agencies, all acting under the command of the Prime Minister of Turkey or mostly the Minister of Internal Affairs. According to figures released by the Justice Ministry, there are 100,000 people in Turkish prisons as of November 2008, a doubling since 2000.

Foreign Relations

Turkey is a founding member of the United Nations (1945), the OECD (1961), the OIC (1969), the OSCE (1973), the ECO (1985), the BSEC (1992), the D-8 (1997) and the G-20 major economies (1999). Turkey was a member of the United Nations Security Council in 1951–1952, 1954–1955, 1961 and 2009-2010. In September 2013, Turkey became a member of the Asia Cooperation Dialogue (ACD).

In line with its traditional Western orientation, relations with Europe have always been a central part of Turkish foreign policy. Turkey became one of the first members of the Council of Europe in 1949, applied for associate membership of the EEC (predecessor of the European Union) in 1959 and became an associate member in 1963. After decades of political negotiations, Turkey applied for full membership of the EEC in 1987, became an associate member of the Western European Union in 1992, joined the EU Customs Union in 1995 and has been in formal accession negotiations with the EU since 2005. Today, EU membership is considered as a state policy and a strategic target by Turkey. Turkey's support for Northern Cyprus in the Cyprus dispute complicates Turkey's relations with the EU and remains a major stumbling block to the country's EU accession bid.

The other defining aspect of Turkey's foreign policy is the country's strategic alliance with the United States. The common threat posed by the Soviet Union during the Cold War led to Turkey's membership of NATO in 1952, ensuring close bilateral relations with Washington. Subsequently Turkey benefited from the United States' political, economic and diplomatic support, including in key issues such as the country's bid to join the European Union. In the post–Cold War environment, Turkey's geostrategic importance shifted towards its proximity to the Middle East, the Caucasus and the Balkans.

The independence of the Turkic states of the Soviet Union in 1991, with which Turkey shares a common cultural and linguistic heritage, allowed Turkey to extend its economic and political relations deep into Central Asia, thus enabling the completion of a multi-billion-dollar oil and natural gas pipeline from Baku in Azerbaijan to the port of Ceyhan in Turkey. The Baku–Tbilisi–Ceyhan pipeline forms part of Turkey's foreign policy strategy to become an energy conduit to the West. However Turkey's border with Armenia, a state in the Caucasus, was closed by Turkey in support of Azerbaijan during the Nagorno-Karabakh War and remains closed.

Under the AK Party government, Turkey's influence has grown in the formerly Ottoman territories of the Middle East and the Balkans, based on the "strategic depth" doctrine (a terminology that was coined by Ahmet Davutoðlu for defining Turkey's increased engagement in regional foreign policy issues), also called Neo-Ottomanism. Following the Arab Spring in December 2010 and the choices made by the AK Party for supporting certain political opposition groups in the affected countries, this policy has led to tensions with some Arab states, such as Turkey's neighbour Syria since the start of the Syrian civil war, and with Egypt after the ousting of President Mohamed Morsi. As of 2014, Turkey doesn't have an ambassador in Syria, Egypt and Israel (diplomatic relations with the latter country were severed after its bombing raids on the Gaza Strip.) This has left Turkey with few allies in the East Mediterranean (where rich natural gas fields have recently been discovered), and is in sharp contrast with the original goals that were set by the Foreign Minister (currently Prime Minister) Ahmet Davutoðlu in his "zero problems with neighbours" foreign policy doctrine.

Turkey has maintained forces in international missions under the United Nations and NATO since 1950, including peacekeeping missions in Somalia and former Yugoslavia, and support to coalition forces in the First Gulf War. Turkey maintains 36,000 troops in Northern Cyprus, though their presence is controversial, and assists Iraqi Kurdistan with security. Turkey has had troops deployed in Afghanistan as part of the United States stabilization force and the UN-authorized, NATO-commanded International Security Assistance Force (ISAF) since 2001. Since 2003, Turkey contributes military personnel to Eurocorps and takes part in the EU Battlegroups.

Military

The Turkish Armed Forces consists of the Land Forces, the Naval Forces and the Air Force. The Gendarmerie and the Coast Guard operate as parts of the Ministry of Internal Affairs in peacetime, although they are subordinated to the Army and Navy Commands respectively in wartime, during which they have both internal law enforcement and military functions.

The Chief of the General Staff is appointed by the President and is responsible to the Prime Minister. The Council of Ministers is responsible to the Parliament for matters of national security and the adequate preparation of the armed forces to defend the country. However, the authority to declare war and to deploy the Turkish Armed Forces to foreign countries or to allow foreign armed forces to be stationed in Turkey rests solely with the Parliament.

Turkey has the second largest standing armed force in NATO, after the US Armed Forces, with an estimated strength of 495,000 deployable forces, according to a 2011 NATO estimate. Turkey is one of five NATO member states which are part of the nuclear sharing policy of the alliance, together with Belgium, Germany, Italy, and the Netherlands. A total of 90 B61 nuclear bombs are hosted at the Incirlik Air Base, 40 of which are allocated for use by the Turkish Air Force in case of a nuclear conflict, but their use requires the approval of NATO.

Every fit male Turkish citizen otherwise not barred is required to serve in the military for a period ranging from three weeks to a year, dependent on education and job location. Turkey does not recognise conscientious objection and does not offer a civilian alternative to military service.

Geography

Turkey is a transcontinental Eurasian country. Asian Turkey, which includes 97% of the country, is separated from European Turkey by the Bosphorus, the Sea of Marmara, and the Dardanelles. European Turkey comprises 3% of the country.

The territory of Turkey is more than 1,600 kilometres (1,000 mi) long and 800 km (500 mi) wide, with a roughly rectangular shape. It lies between latitudes 35° and 43° N, and longitudes 25° and 45° E. Turkey's area, including lakes, occupies 783,562 square kilometres (300,948 sq mi), of which 755,688 square kilometres (291,773 sq mi) are in Southwest Asia and 23,764 square kilometres (9,174 sq mi) in Europe. Turkey is the world's 37th-largest country in terms of area. The country is encircled by seas on three sides: the Aegean Sea to the west, the Black Sea to the north and the Mediterranean to the south. Turkey also contains the Sea of Marmara in the northwest.

The European section of Turkey, East Thrace, forms the borders of Turkey with Greece and Bulgaria. The Asian part of the country, Anatolia, consists of a high central plateau with narrow coastal plains, between the Köroðlu and Pontic mountain ranges to the north and the Taurus Mountains to the south. Eastern Turkey has a more mountainous landscape and is home to the sources of rivers such as the Euphrates, Tigris and Aras, and contains Mount Ararat, Turkey's highest point at 5,137 metres (16,854 ft), and Lake Van, the largest lake in the country.

Turkey is divided into seven census regions: Marmara, Aegean, Black Sea, Central Anatolia, Eastern Anatolia, Southeastern Anatolia and the Mediterranean. The uneven north Anatolian terrain running along the Black Sea resembles a long, narrow belt. This region comprises approximately one-sixth of Turkey's total land area. As a general trend, the inland Anatolian plateau becomes increasingly rugged as it progresses eastward.

Turkey's varied landscapes are the product of complex earth movements that have shaped the region over thousands of years and still manifest themselves in fairly frequent earthquakes and occasional volcanic eruptions. The Bosphorus and the Dardanelles owe their existence to the fault lines running through Turkey that led to the creation of the Black Sea. There is an earthquake fault line across the north of the country from west to east, along which a major earthquake occurred in 1999.

Economy

Turkey has the world's 17th largest GDP by PPP and 17th largest nominal GDP. The country is among the founding members of the OECD and the G-20 major economies.

The EU – Turkey Customs Union in 1995 led to an extensive liberalization of tariff rates, and forms one of the most important pillars of Turkey's foreign trade policy. Turkey's exports were $143.5 billion in 2011 and they reached $163 billion in 2012 (main export partners in 2012: Germany 8.6%, Iraq 7.1%, Iran 6.5%, UK 5.7%, UAE 5.4%). However, larger imports which amounted to $229 billion in 2012 threatened the balance of trade (main import partners in 2012: Russia 11.3%, Germany 9%, China 9%, USA 6%, Italy 5.6%).

Turkey has a large automotive industry, which produced over a million motor vehicles in 2012, ranking as the 16th largest producer in the world. Turkish shipbuilding exports were worth US$1.2 billion in 2011. The major export markets are Malta, Marshall Islands, Panama and the United Kingdom. Turkish shipyards have 15 floating docks of different sizes and one dry dock. Tuzla, Yalova, and Ýzmit have developed into dynamic shipbuilding centres. In 2011, there were 70 active shipyards in Turkey, with another 56 being built. Turkish shipyards are highly regarded both for the production of chemical and oil tankers up to 10,000 dwt and also for their mega yachts.

Turkish brands like Beko and Vestel are among the largest producers of consumer electronics and home appliances in Europe, and invest a substantial amount of funds for research and development in new technologies related to these fields.

Other key sectors of the Turkish economy are banking, construction, home appliances, electronics, textiles, oil refining, petrochemical products, food, mining, iron and steel, and machine industry. In 2010, the agricultural sector accounted for 9% of GDP, while the industrial sector accounted for 26% and the services sector for 65%. However, agriculture still accounted for a quarter of employment. In 2004, it was estimated that 46% of total disposable income was received by the top 20% of income earners, while the lowest 20% received only 6%. The rate of female employment in Turkey was 30% in 2012, the lowest among all OECD countries.

Foreign direct investment (FDI) was $8.3 billion in 2012, a figure expected to rise to $15 billion in 2013. In 2012, Fitch Group upgraded Turkey's credit rating to investment grade after an 18-year gap; this was followed by a ratings upgrade by Moody's in May 2013, as the service lifted Turkey's government bond ratings to the lowest investment grade Baa3.

In the early years of the 21st century, the chronically high inflation was brought under control; this led to the launch of a new currency, the Turkish new lira in 2005, to cement the acquisition of the economic reforms and erase the vestiges of an unstable economy. In 2009, the new Turkish lira was renamed back to the Turkish lira, with the introduction of new banknotes and coins. As a result of continuing economic reforms, inflation dropped to 8% in 2005, and the unemployment rate to 10%.

History

During the first six decades of the republic, between 1923 and 1983, Turkey generally adhered to a quasi-statist approach with strict government planning of the budget and government-imposed limitations over private sector participation, foreign trade, flow of foreign currency, and foreign direct investment. However in 1983 Prime Minister Turgut Özal initiated a series of reforms designed to shift the economy from a statist, insulated system to a more private-sector, market-based model.

The reforms, combined with unprecedented amounts of funding from foreign loans, spurred rapid economic growth; but this growth was punctuated by sharp recessions and financial crises in 1994, 1999 (following the earthquake of that year), and 2001; resulting in an average of 4% GDP growth per annum between 1981 and 2003. Lack of additional fiscal reforms, combined with large and growing public sector deficits and widespread corruption, resulted in high inflation, a weak banking sector and increased macroeconomic volatility. Since the economic crisis of 2001 and the reforms initiated by the finance minister of the time, Kemal Dervi°, inflation has fallen to single-digit numbers, investor confidence and foreign investment have soared, and unemployment has fallen.

Turkey has gradually opened up its markets through economic reforms by reducing government controls on foreign trade and investment and the privatization of publicly owned industries, and the liberalization of many sectors to private and foreign participation has continued amid political debate. The public debt to GDP ratio peaked at 75.9% during the recession of 2001, falling to an estimated 26.9% by 2013.

The real GDP growth rate from 2002 to 2007 averaged 6.8% annually, which made Turkey one of the fastest growing economies in the world during that period. However, growth slowed to 1% in 2008, and in 2009 the Turkish economy was affected by the global financial crisis, with a recession of 5%. The economy was estimated to have returned to 8% growth in 2010. According to Eurostat data, Turkish GDP per capita adjusted by purchasing power standard stood at 52% of the EU average in 2011.

Infrastructure

In 2013 there were 98 airports in Turkey, including 22 international airports. As of 2014, Istanbul Atatürk Airport is the 13th busiest airport in the world, serving 31,833,324 passengers between January and July 2014, according to Airports Council International. The new (third) international airport of Istanbul is planned to be the largest airport in the world, with a capacity to serve 150 million passengers per annum. Turkish Airlines, flag carrier of Turkey since 1933, was selected by Skytrax as Europe's best airline for four consecutive years in 2011, 2012, 2013 and 2014. With 254 destinations worldwide, Turkish Airlines is the fourth largest carrier in the world by number of destinations as of 2014.

As of 2014, the country has a roadway network of 65,623 kilometres (40,776 mi). The total length of the rail network was 10,991 km in 2008, including 2,133 km of electrified and 457 km of high-speed track. The Turkish State Railways started building high-speed rail lines in 2003. The Ankara-Konya line became operational in 2011 while the Ankara-Istanbul line entered service in 2014.

In 2008, 7,555 kilometres (4,694 mi) of natural gas pipelines and 3,636 kilometres (2,259 mi) of petroleum pipelines spanned the country's territory. The Baku-Tbilisi-Ceyhan pipeline, the second longest oil pipeline in the world, was inaugurated on May 10, 2005.

In 2013, the energy consumption was 240 billion kilowatt hours. As Turkey imported 72% of its energy in 2013, the government decided to invest in nuclear power to reduce imports. Three nuclear power stations are to be built by 2023. Turkey has the fifth highest direct utilisation and capacity of geothermal power in the world. Turkey is a partner country of the EU INOGATE energy programme.

Turkey's first nuclear power plants are expected to be built in Mersin's Akkuyu district on the Mediterranean coast; in Sinop's Ýnceburun district on the Black Sea coast; and in Kýrklareli's Ýðneada district on the Black Sea coast. Turkey has the fifth highest direct utilisation and capacity of geothermal power in the world. Turkey is a partner country of the EU INOGATE energy programme, which has four key topics: enhancing energy security, convergence of member state energy markets on the basis of EU internal energy market principles, supporting sustainable energy development, and attracting investment for energy projects of common and regional interest.

Science and Technology

TÜBÝTAK is the leading agency for developing science, technology and innovation policies in Turkey. TÜBA is an autonomous scholarly society acting to promote scientific activities in Turkey. TAEK is the official nuclear energy institution of Turkey. Its objectives include academic research in nuclear energy, and the development and implementation of peaceful nuclear tools.

Turkish government companies for research and development in military technologies include Turkish Aerospace Industries, Aselsan, Havelsan, Roketsan, MKE, among others. Turkish Satellite Assembly, Integration and Test Centre (UMET) is a spacecraft production and testing facility owned by the Ministry of National Defence and operated by the Turkish Aerospace Industries (TAI). The Turkish Space Launch System (UFS) is a project to develop the satellite launch capability of Turkey. It consists of the construction of a spaceport, the development of satellite launch vehicles as well as the establishment of remote earth stations.

Religion

Turkey is a secular state with no official state religion; the Turkish Constitution provides for freedom of religion and conscience. The role of religion has been a controversial debate over the years since the formation of Islamist parties. For many decades, the wearing of the hijab was banned in schools and government buildings because it was viewed as a symbol of political Islam. However, the ban was lifted from universities in 2011, from government buildings in 2013, and from schools in 2014.

Islam is the dominant religion of Turkey with 99.8% of the population being registered as Muslim. while some sources give a little lower estimate of 96.4%, with the most popular sect being the Hanafite school of Sunni Islam. The highest Islamic religious authority is the Presidency of Religious Affairs (Turkish: *Diyanet Ýþleri Baþkanlýðý*), it interprets the Hanafi school of law, and is responsible for regulating the operation of the country's 80,000 registered mosques and employing local and provincial imams. Academics suggest the Alevi population may be from 15 to 20 million. and according to Aksiyon magazine, the number of Shiite Twelvers (excluding Alevis) is 3 million (4.2%). There are also some Sufi Muslims. Roughly 2% are non-denominational Muslims.

The percentage of non-Muslims in Turkey fell from 19% in 1914 to 2.5% in 1927, due to events which had a significant impact on the country's demographical structure, such as the Armenian Genocide, the population exchange between Greece and Turkey, and the emigration of non-Muslims (such as Levantines, Greeks, Armenians, Jews, etc.) to foreign countries (mostly in Europe and the Americas) that actually began in the late 19th century and gained pace in the first quarter of the 20th century, especially during World War I and after the Turkish War of Independence. Today there are more than 120,000 people of different Christian denominations, representing less than 0.2% of Turkey's population, including an estimated 80,000 Oriental Orthodox, 35,000 Roman Catholics, 18,000 Antiochian Greeks, 5,000 Greek Orthodox and smaller numbers of Protestants. Currently there are 236 churches open for worship in Turkey. The Eastern Orthodox Church has been headquartered in Istanbul since the 4th century.

There are about 26,000 people who are Jewish, the vast majority of whom are Sephardi. There have been Jewish communities in Asia Minor since at least the 5th century BCE and many Spanish and Portuguese Jews expelled from Spain were welcomed into the Ottoman Empire in the late 15th century, twenty centuries later. Despite emigration during the 20th century, modern-day Turkey continues to have a small Jewish population.

Education

The Ministry of National Education is responsible for pre-tertiary education. This is compulsory and lasts twelve years: four years each of primary school, middle school and high school. Less than half of 25-

34 year old Turks have completed at least upper secondary education, compared with an OECD average of over 80%. Basic education in Turkey is considered to lag behind other OECD countries, with significant differences between high and low performers. Turkey is ranked 32nd out of 34 in the OECD's PISA study. Access to high-quality school heavily depends on the performance in the secondary school entrance exams, to the point that some students begin taking private tutoring classes when they are 10 years old. The overall adult literacy rate in 2011 was 94.1%, 97.9% for males and 90.3% for females.

By 2011, there were 166 universities in Turkey. Entry to higher education depends on the Student Selection Examination (ÖSS). In 2008, the quota of admitted students was 600,000, compared to 1,700,000 who took the ÖSS exam in 2007. Except for the Open Education Faculty (Turkish: *Açýköðretim Fakültesi*) at Anadolu University, entrance is regulated by the national ÖSS examination, after which high school graduates are assigned to universities according to their performance. According to the 2012–2013 Times Higher Education World University Rankings, the top university in Turkey is Middle East Technical University (in the 201–225 rank range), followed by Bilkent University and Koç University (both in the 226–250 range), Istanbul Technical University and Boðaziçi University (in the 276-300 bracket).

Healthcare

Health care in Turkey used to be dominated by a centralized state system run by the Ministry of Health. In 2003, the government introduced a sweeping health reform programme aimed at increasing the ratio of private to state health provision and making healthcare available to a larger share of the population. Turkish Statistical Institute announced that 76.3 billion TL was spent for healthcare in 2012; 79.6% of which was covered by the Social Security Institution and 15.4% of which was paid directly by the patients. In 2012, there were 29,960 medical institutions in Turkey, and on average one doctor per 583 people and 2.65 beds per 1000 people.

Life expectancy stands at 71.1 years for men and 75.3 years for women, with an overall average of 73.2 years for the populace as a whole.

The first three groups of diseases that cause death, respectively; Diseases of the circulatory system (39.8%), cancer (21.3%), respiratory diseases (9.8%)

Culture

Turkey has a very diverse culture that is a blend of various elements of the Oðuz Turkic, Anatolian, Ottoman (which was itself a continuation of both Greco-Roman and Islamic cultures) and Western culture and traditions, which started with the Westernisation of the Ottoman Empire and still continues today.

This mix originally began as a result of the encounter of Turks and their culture with those of the peoples who were in their path during their migration from Central Asia to the West. Turkish culture is a product of efforts to be a "modern" Western state, while maintaining traditional religious and historical values.

United Arab Emirates

The United Arab Emirates, sometimes simply called the Emirates or the UAE, is a country located in the southeast end of the Arabian Peninsula on the Persian Gulf, bordering Oman to the east and Saudi Arabia to the south, as well as sharing sea borders with Qatar and Iran. In 2013, the UAE's total population was 9.2 million, of which 1.4 million are Emirati citizens and 7.8 million are expatriates from around the world. Established on 2 December 1971, the country is a federation of seven emirates (equivalent to principalities).

Each emirate is governed by a hereditary ruler who jointly form the Federal Supreme Council, the highest legislative and executive body in the country. One of the rulers is selected as the President of the United Arab Emirates.

The constituent emirates are Abu Dhabi (which serves as the capital), Ajman, Dubai, Fujairah, Ras al-Khaimah, Sharjah, and Umm al-Quwain. Islam is the official religion of the UAE, and Arabic is the official language.

Its most populous city, Dubai, has emerged as a business hub and a global city. The UAE's oil reserves are the seventh-largest in the world, while its natural gas reserves are the world's seventeenth-largest. The late Sheikh Zayed, ruler of Abu Dhabi and the first President of the UAE, oversaw the development of the Emirates and steered oil revenues into healthcare, education and infrastructure.

The UAE's economy is the most diversified in the Gulf Cooperation Council, with Dubai in particular developing into a global hub for tourism, retail, and finance. Nevertheless, the country remains extremely reliant on petroleum and natural gas; more than 85% of the economy was based on the oil exports in 2009, while oil exports accounted for 77% of the state budget in 2011.

The UAE's rapid economic growth and rising international profile have led some analysts to identify it as a middle power.

History

Ancient History

The earliest known human habitation in the UAE dated from 5500 BC, but finds of flint tools could date the first human habitation of the UAE's western coast to 130,000 years ago. At this early stage, there is proof of interaction with the outside world, particularly with civilizations to the northwest in Mesopotamia.

These contacts persisted and became wide-ranging, probably motivated by trade in copper from the Hajar Mountains, which commenced around 3000 BC. In 637, Julfar (today Ra's al-Khaimah) was used as a staging post for the Islamic invasion of Sassanian Iran. From the second century AD, a movement of tribes along the North East along the southern coast of Arabia took place, with groups of the Azdite Qahtani (or Yamani) and Quda'ah occupying the areas south west of the Hajar Mountains while Sassanid groups dominated the Eastern or Batinah coast. With the Persian coast known as Al Bahreyn, the interior oasis town of Al Ain was known as Tu'am and became an important staging post of the trade routes to the interior from the east coast.

The earliest Christian site in the UAE was first discovered in the 1990s, an extensive monastic complex on what is now known as Sir Bani Yas Island and which dates back to the 7th century. Thought to be Nestorian and built in 600 AD, the church appears to have been abandoned peacefully in 750 AD. It forms a rare physical link to a legacy of Christianity which is thought to have spread across the peninsula from 50-350 AD following trade routes. Certainly, by the 5th century, Oman had a bishop named John - the last bishop of Oman being Etienne, in 676 AD.

The spread of Islam to the North Eastern tip of the Arabian Peninsula is thought to have followed directly from a letter sent by the Prophet Muhammad to the rulers of Oman in 630 AD, nine years after the hijrah, led to a group of rulers travelling to Medina, converting to Islam and subsequently driving a successful uprising against the unpopular Sassanids, who dominated the Northern coasts at the time.

Following the death of the Prophet, the new Islamic communities south of the Persian Gulf threatened to disintegrate, with insurrections against the Muslim leaders. The Caliph Abu Bakr sent an army from Medina which completed its reconquest of the territory (the Ridda Wars) with the bloody battle of Dibba in which 10,000 lives are thought to have been lost.

17th Century-19th Century

The harsh nature of the territory, dominated by arid desert, gravel plains and mountain, led to the emergence of the 'versatile tribesman', nomadic groups who subsisted thanks to a variety of economic activities, including animal husbandry, agriculture and hunting. The seasonal movements of these groups led both to frequent clashes between groups but also the establishment of seasonal and semi-seasonal settlements and centres. These formed tribal groupings whose names are still carried by modern Emiratis, including the Bani Yas and Al Bu Falah of Abu Dhabi, Al Ain, Liwa and the Al Bahrayn coast, the Dhawahir, Awamir and Manasir of the interior, the Sharqiyin of the east coast and the Qawasim to the North.

By the 17th century, the Bani Yas confederation was the dominant force in most of the area now known as Abu Dhabi.

The Portuguese maintained an influence over the coastal settlements, building forts in the wake of the bloody 16th century conquests of coastal communities by Albuquerque and the Portuguese commanders who followed him - particularly on the east coast at Muscat, Sohar and Khor Fakkan.

The southern coast of the Persian Gulf was known to the British as the "Pirate Coast", as boats of the Al Qawasim (Al Qasimi) federation based in the area harassed British-flagged shipping from the 17th century into the 19th. British expeditions to protect the Indian trade from raiders at Ras al-Khaimah led to campaigns against that headquarters and other harbours along the coast in 1809 and subsequently 1819. The following year, Britain and a number of local rulers signed a treaty to combat piracy along the Persian Gulf coast, giving rise to the term Trucial States, which came to define the status of the coastal emirates. Further treaties were signed in 1843 and 1853.

Primarily in reaction to the ambitions of other European countries, namely France and Russia, the British and the Trucial Sheikhdoms established closer bonds in an 1892 treaty, similar to treaties entered into by the British with other Persian Gulf principalities. The sheikhs agreed not to dispose of any territory except to the British and not to enter into relationships with any foreign government other than the British without its consent. In return, the British promised to protect the Trucial Coast from all aggression by sea and to help in case of land attack. This treaty, the Exclusive Agreement, was signed by the Rulers of Abu Dhabi, Dubai, Sharjah, Ajman, Ras Al Khaimah and Umm Al Quwain between 6 and 8 March 1892. It was subsequently ratified by the Viceroy of India and the British Government in London. British maritime policing meant that pearling fleets could operate in relative security. However, the British prohibition of the slave trade meant an important source of income was lost to some sheikhs and merchants. The charge of piracy is disputed by modern Emirati historians, including the current Ruler of Sharjah in his 1986 book 'The Myth of Arab Piracy in the Gulf'.

British Rule, Oil Industry

During the 19th and early 20th centuries, the pearling industry thrived, providing both income and employment to the people of the Persian Gulf. The First World War had a severe impact on the industry, but it was the economic depression of the late 1920s and early 1930s, coupled with the Japanese invention of the cultured pearl, that wiped out the trade. The remnants of the trade eventually faded away shortly after the Second World War, when the newly independent Government of India imposed heavy taxation on pearls imported from the Arab states of the Persian Gulf. The decline of pearling resulted in extreme economic hardship in the trucial states.

The British set up a development office that helped in some small developments in the emirates. The seven sheikhs of the emirates then decided to form a council to coordinate matters between them and took over the development office. In 1952, they formed the Trucial States Council, and appointed Adi Bitar, Sheikh Rashid's legal advisor, as Secretary General and Legal Advisor to the Council. The council was terminated once the United Arab Emirates was formed. The tribal nature of society and the lack of definition of borders between emirates frequently led to disputes, settled either through mediation or, more rarely, force. The Trucial Oman Scouts was a small military force used by the British to keep the peace.

In 1955, the United Kingdom sided with Abu Dhabi in the latter's dispute with Oman over the Buraimi Oasis, another territory to the south. A 1974 agreement between Abu Dhabi and Saudi Arabia would have settled the Abu Dhabi-Saudi border dispute; however, the agreement has yet to be ratified by the UAE government and is not recognised by the Saudi government. The UAE's border with Oman was ratified in 2008.

The development of the oil industry in the 1960s transformed the fortunes of Abu Dhabi and later Dubai. Sheikh Zayed bin Sultan Al Nahyan became ruler of Abu Dhabi in 1966 and embarked on a massive modernisation drive. The British started losing their oil investments and contracts to U.S. oil exploration and production companies.

In 1922 the British government secured undertakings from the trucial rulers not to sign concessions with foreign companies. Aware of the potential for the development of natural resources such as oil, following finds in Persia (from 1908) and Mesopotamia (from 1927), a British-led oil company, the Iraq Petroleum Company (IPC) showed an interest in the region. The Anglo-Persian Oil Company (APOC, later to become British Petroleum, or BP), had a 23.75 percent share in IPC. From 1935, onshore concessions to explore for oil were agreed with local rulers, with APOC signing the first one on behalf of Petroleum Concessions Ltd (PCL), an associate company of IPC. APOC was prevented from developing the region alone because of the restrictions of the Red Line Agreement, which required it to operate through IPC. A number of options between PCL and the trucial rulers were signed, providing useful revenue for communities experiencing poverty following the collapse of the pearl trade.

However, the wealth of oil which the rulers could see from the revenues accruing to surrounding countries such as Iran, Bahrain, Kuwait, Qatar and Saudi Arabia remained elusive. The first bore holes in Abu Dhabi were drilled by IPC's operating company, Petroleum Development (Trucial Coast) Ltd (PDTC) at Ras Sadr in 1950, with a 13,000 feet deep bore hole taking a year to drill and turning out dry, at the tremendous cost at the time of £1 million.

In 1953, a subsidiary of BP, D'Arcy Exploration Ltd, obtained an offshore concession from the ruler of Abu Dhabi. BP joined with Compagnie Française des Pétroles (later Total) to form operating companies, Abu Dhabi Marine Areas Ltd (ADMA) and Dubai Marine Areas Ltd (DUMA). A number of undersea oil surveys were carried out, including one led by the famous marine explorer, Jacques Cousteau. In 1958, a floating platform rig was towed from Hamburg, Germany, and positioned over the Umm Shaif pearl bed, in Abu Dhabi waters, where drilling began. In March, it struck oil in the Upper Thamama, a rock formation that would provide many valuable oil finds. This was the first commercial discovery of the Trucial Coast, leading to the first exports of oil in 1962. ADMA made further offshore discoveries at Zakum and elsewhere, and other companies made commercial finds such as the Fateh oilfield off Dubai, and the Mubarak field off Sharjah (shared with Iran).

Meanwhile, PDTC had continued its onshore exploration activities, drilling five more bore holes that were also dry, but on 27 October 1960, the company discovered oil in commercial quantities at the Murban No. 3 well on the coast near Tarif. In 1962, PDTC became the Abu Dhabi Petroleum Company.

As oil revenues increased, the ruler of Abu Dhabi, Zayed bin Sultan Al Nahyan, undertook a massive construction program, building schools, housing, hospitals and roads. When Dubai's oil exports commenced in 1969, Sheikh Rashid bin Saeed Al Maktoum, the ruler of Dubai, was able to invest the revenues from the limited reserves found to spark the diversification drive that would create the modern global city of Dubai.

Independence (1971)

By 1966 it had become clear the British government could no longer afford to administer and protect what is now the United Arab Emirates. British MPs debated the preparedness of the Royal Navy to defend the trucial sheikhdoms. Secretary of State for Defence Denis Healey reported that the British Armed Forces were seriously overstretched and in some respects dangerously under-equipped to defend the trucial sheikhdoms. On 24 January 1968, British Prime Minister Harold Wilson announced the government's decision, reaffirmed in March 1971 by Prime Minister Edward Heath to end the treaty relationships with the seven Trucial sheikhdoms that had been, together with Bahrain and Qatar, under British protection. Days after the announcement, the ruler of Abu Dhabi Sheikh Zayed bin Sultan Al Nahyan, fearing vulnerability, tried to persuade the British to honour the protection treaties by offering to pay the full costs of keeping the British Armed Forces in the Emirates. The British Labour government rejected the offer. After Labour MP Goronwy Roberts informed Sheikh Zayed of the news of British withdrawal, the nine Persian Gulf sheikhdoms attempted to form a union of Arab emirates, but by mid-1971 they were still unable to agree on terms of union even though the British treaty relationship was to expire in December of that year.

Bahrain became independent in August, and Qatar in September 1971. When the British-Trucial Sheikhdoms treaty expired on 1 December 1971, they became fully independent. The rulers of Abu Dhabi and Dubai decided to form a union between their two emirates independently, prepare a constitution, then call the rulers of the other five emirates to a meeting and offer them the opportunity to join. It was also agreed between the two that the constitution be written by 2 December 1971. On that date, at the Dubai Guesthouse Palace, four other emirates agreed to enter into a union called the United Arab Emirates. Bahrain and Qatar declined their invitations to join the union. Ras al-Khaimah joined later, in early 1972. In February 1972, the Federal National Council (FNC) was created; it was a 40 member consultative body appointed by the seven rulers. The UAE joined the Arab League in

1971. It was a founding member of the Gulf Cooperation Council in May 1981, with Abu Dhabi hosting the first summit. UAE forces joined the allies against Iraq after the invasion of Kuwait in 1990.

After Independence

The UAE supported military operations from the US and other Coalition nations that are engaged in the war against the Taliban in Afghanistan (2001) and Saddam Hussein in Iraq (2003) as well as operations supporting the Global War on Terror for the Horn of Africa at Al Dhafra Air Base located outside of Abu Dhabi. The air base also supported Allied operations during the 1991 Persian Gulf War and Operation Northern Watch.

The country had already signed a military defence agreement with the U.S. in 1994 and one with France in 1995. In January 2008, France and the UAE signed a deal allowing France to set up a permanent military base in the emirate of Abu Dhabi. The UAE joined international military operations in Libya in March 2011.

On 2 November 2004, the UAE's first president, Sheikh Zayed bin Sultan Al Nahyan, died. His eldest son, Sheikh Khalifa bin Zayed Al Nahyan, succeeded as Emir of Abu Dhabi. In accordance with the constitution, the UAE's Supreme Council of Rulers elected Khalifa as president. Sheikh Mohammed bin Zayed Al Nahyan succeeded Khalifa as Crown Prince of Abu Dhabi. In January 2006, Sheikh Maktoum bin Rashid Al Maktoum, the prime minister of the UAE and the ruler of Dubai, died, and the crown prince Sheikh Mohammed bin Rashid Al Maktoum assumed both roles.

The first-ever national elections were held in the UAE on 16 December 2006. A small number of hand-picked voters chose half of the members of the Federal National Council—which is an advisory body. Largely unaffected by the Arab Spring turmoil, the government has nonetheless clamped down on Internet activism. In April 2011, five activists who signed an online petition calling for reforms were imprisoned. They were pardoned and released in November. Since March 2012 more than 60 activists (later showed evidence of being moved by Iran to create chaos) have been detained without charge (at the time) – some of them supporters of the Islah Islamic group. A member of the ruling family in Ras al-Khaimah was put under house arrest in April 2012 after calling for political openness. Mindful of the protests in nearby Bahrain, in November 2012 the UAE outlawed online mockery of its own government or attempts to organise public protests through social media.

Geography

The United Arab Emirates is situated in Southwest Asia, bordering the Gulf of Oman and the Persian Gulf, between Oman and Saudi Arabia; it is in a strategic location along southern approaches to the Strait of Hormuz, a vital transit point for world crude oil.

The UAE lies between 22°30' and 26°10' north latitude and between 51° and 56°252 east longitude. It shares a 530-kilometre border with Saudi Arabia on the west, south, and southeast, and a 450-kilometre border with Oman on the southeast and northeast. The land border with Qatar in the Khawr al Udayd area is about nineteen kilometres (12 miles) in the northwest; however, it is a source of ongoing dispute. Following Britain's military departure from UAE in 1971, and its establishment as a new state, the UAE laid claim to islands resulting in disputes with Iran that remain unresolved. UAE also disputes claim on other islands against the neighbouring state of Qatar. The largest emirate, Abu Dhabi, accounts for 87% of the UAE's total area (67,340 square kilometres (26,000 sq mi)). The smallest emirate, Ajman, encompasses only 259 km^2 (100 sq mi).

The UAE coast stretches for more than 650 km (404 mi) along the southern shore of the Persian Gulf. Most of the coast consists of salt pans that extend far inland. The largest natural harbor is at Dubai, although other ports have been dredged at Abu Dhabi, Sharjah, and elsewhere. Numerous islands are found in the Persian Gulf, and the ownership of some of them has been the subject of international disputes with both Iran and Qatar. The smaller islands, as well as many coral reefs and shifting sandbars, are a menace to navigation. Strong tides and occasional windstorms further complicate ship movements near the shore. The UAE also has a stretch of the Al Bâþinah coast of the Gulf of Oman, although the Musandam Peninsula, the very tip of Arabia by the Strait of Hormuz is an exclave of Oman separated by the UAE.

South and west of Abu Dhabi, vast, rolling sand dunes merge into the Rub al-Khali (Empty Quarter) of Saudi Arabia. The desert area of Abu Dhabi includes two important oases with adequate underground water for permanent settlements and cultivation. The extensive Liwa Oasis is in the south near the undefined border with Saudi Arabia. About 100 km (62 mi) to the northeast of Liwa is the Al-Buraimi oasis, which extends on both sides of the Abu Dhabi-Oman border. Lake Zakher is a man-made lake near the border with Oman.

Prior to withdrawing from the area in 1971, Britain delineated the internal borders among the seven emirates in order to preempt territorial disputes that might hamper formation of the federation. In general, the rulers of the emirates accepted the British intervention, but in the case of boundary disputes between Abu Dhabi and Dubai, and also between Dubai and Sharjah, conflicting claims were not resolved until after the UAE became independent. The most complicated borders were in the Al-Hajar al-Gharbi Mountains, where five of the emirates contested jurisdiction over more than a dozen enclaves.

Flora and Fauna

The oases grow date palms, acacia and eucalyptus trees. In the desert, the flora is very sparse and consists of grasses and thorn bushes. The indigenous fauna had come close to extinction because of intensive hunting, which has led to a conservation program on Bani Yas Island initiated by Sheikh Zayed bin Sultan Al Nahyan in the 1970s, resulting in the survival of, for example, Arabian oryx and leopards. Coastal fish and mammals consist mainly of mackerel, perch, and tuna, as well as sharks and whales.

Climate

The climate of the U.A.E is subtropical-arid with hot summers and warm winters. The hottest months are July and August, when average maximum temperatures reach above 45 °C (113 °F) on the coastal plain. In the Al Hajar Mountains, temperatures are considerably lower, a result of increased elevation. Average minimum temperatures in January and February are between 10 and 14 °C (50 and 57 °F). During the late summer months, a humid southeastern wind known as Sharqi (i.e. "Easterner") makes the coastal region especially unpleasant. The average annual rainfall in the coastal area is less than 120 mm (4.7 in), but in some mountainous areas annual rainfall often reaches 350 mm (13.8 in). Rain in the coastal region falls in short, torrential bursts during the summer months, sometimes resulting in floods in ordinarily dry wadi beds. The region is prone to occasional, violent dust storms, which can severely reduce visibility. The Jebel Jais mountain cluster in Ras al-Khaimah has experienced snow only twice since records began.

Law

The UAE is ruled by the federal court system. There are three main branches within the court structure: civil, criminal and Sharia law.

Sharia Law

The UAE's judicial system is derived from the civil law system and Sharia law. The court system consists of civil courts and Sharia courts. According to Human Rights Watch, UAE's criminal and civil courts apply elements of Sharia law, codified into its criminal code and family law, in a way which discriminates against women.

Flogging is a legal punishment for criminal offences such as adultery, premarital sex, drug abuse and prostitution. In all emirates except Dubai, flogging is legal with sentences ranging from 80 to 200 lashes. Between 2007 and 2013, many people were sentenced to 100 lashes. In Abu Dhabi, people have been sentenced to 80 lashes for kissing in public. Moreover in 2010 and 2012, several Muslims were sentenced to 80 lashes for alcohol consumption. An Estonian soldier in 2004 was sentenced to 40 lashes for being drunk. In some cases, people have been sentenced to 60 lashes for illicit sex. Under UAE law, premarital sex is punishable by 100 lashes.

Stoning is a legal form of judicial punishment in the UAE. In 2006, an expatriate was sentenced to death by stoning for committing adultery. Between 2009 and 2013, several people were sentenced to death by stoning. In May 2014, an Asian housemaid was sentenced to death by stoning in Abu Dhabi.

Sharia law dictates the personal status law, which regulate matters such as marriage, divorce and child custody. The Sharia-based personal status law is applied to Muslims and sometimes non-Muslims. Non-Muslim expatriates are liable to Sharia rulings on marriage, divorce and child custody. Sharia courts have exclusive jurisdiction to hear family disputes, including matters involving divorce, inheritances, child custody, child abuse and guardianship of minors. Sharia courts may also hear appeals of certain criminal cases including rape, robbery, driving under the influence of alcohol and related crimes.

Apostasy is a crime punishable by death in the UAE. UAE incorporates hudud crimes of Sharia into its Penal Code – apostasy being one of them. Article 1 and Article 66 of UAE's Penal Code requires hudud crimes to be punished with the death penalty, therefore apostasy is punishable by death in the UAE.

Emirati women must receive permission from male guardian to remarry. The requirement is derived from Sharia, and has been federal law since 2005. In all emirates, it is illegal for Muslim women to marry non-Muslims. In the UAE, a marriage union between a Muslim woman and non-Muslim man is punishable by law, since it is considered a form of "fornication".

Kissing in public is illegal and can result in deportation. Expats in Dubai have been deported for kissing in public. In Abu Dhabi, people have been sentenced to 80 lashes for kissing in public.

Homosexuality is illegal: the death penalty is one of the punishments for homosexuality. Article 80 of the Abu Dhabi Penal Code makes sodomy punishable with imprisonment of up to 14 years, while article 177 of the Penal Code of Dubai imposes imprisonment of up to 10 years on consensual sodomy.

Amputation is a legal punishment in the UAE due to the Sharia courts. Article 1 of the Federal Penal Code states that "provisions of the Islamic Law shall apply to the crimes of doctrinal punishment, punitive punishment and blood money." The Federal Penal Code repealed only those provisions within the penal codes of individual emirates which are contradictory to the Federal Penal Code. Hence, both are enforceable simultaneously.

During the month of Ramadan, it is illegal to publicly eat, drink, or smoke between sunrise and sunset. Exceptions are made for pregnant women and children. The law applies to both Muslims and non-Muslims, and failure to comply may result in arrest.

Human Rights

The treatment of migrant workers in the UAE has been likened to "modern-day slavery". Migrant workers are excluded from the UAE's collective labour rights, hence migrants are vulnerable to forced labour. Migrant workers in the UAE are not allowed to join trade unions. Moreover, migrant workers are banned from going on strike. Dozens of workers were deported in 2014 for going on strike. As migrant workers do not have the right to join a trade union or go on strike, they don't have the means to denounce the exploitation they suffer. Those who protest risk prison and deportation. The International Trade Union Confederation has called on the United Nations to investigate evidence that thousands of migrant workers in the UAE are treated as slave labour.

Human Rights Watch have drawn attention to the mistreatment of migrant workers who have been turned into debt-ridden *de facto* indentured servants following their arrival in the UAE. Confiscation of passports, although illegal, occurs on a large scale, primarily from unskilled or semi-skilled employees. Labourers often toil in intense heat with temperatures reaching 40–50 degrees Celsius in the cities in August. Although attempts have been made since 2009 to enforce a midday break rule, these are frequently flouted. Those labourers who do receive a midday break often have no suitable place to rest and tend to seek relief in bus or taxi stands and gardens. Initiatives taken have brought about a huge impact on the conditions of the labourers.

According to Human Rights Watch, migrant workers in Dubai live in "inhumane" conditions.

Flogging and stoning are legal punishments in the UAE. The UAE has not ratified the UN Convention on the elimination of cruel, degrading and inhuman torture. Some laws continue to discriminate Emirati women. Emirati women must receive permission from a "male guardian" to remarry. The requirement is derived from Sharia law, and has been federal law since 2005. Some women in UAE are victims of Sharia-derived judicial punishments such as flogging and stoning.

In 2007, the UAE government attempted to cover up information on the rape of Alexander Robert, a 15 year old French-Swiss national, by three Emirati locals, one of whose HIV-positive status was hidden by Emirati authorities for several months.

In April 2009, a video tape of torture smuggled out of the UAE showed Sheikh Issa bin Zayed Al Nahyan torturing a man (Mohammed Shah Poor) with whips, electric cattle prods, wooden planks with protruding nails and running him over repeatedly with a car. In December 2009 Issa appeared in court and proclaimed his innocence. The trial ended on 10 January 2010, when Issa was cleared of the torture of Mohammed Shah Poor. Human Rights Watch criticised the trial and called on the government to establish an independent body to investigate allegations of abuse by UAE security personnel and other persons of authority.

The US State Department has expressed concern over the verdict and said all members of Emirati society "must stand equal before the law" and called for a careful review of the decision to ensure that the demands of justice are fully met in this case.

Rape victims are often criminalized in the UAE. The Emirates Centre for Human Rights expressed concern over Dubai's criminalization of rape victims. In Dubai, a woman who reports being raped can be sentenced to over a year of time in prison for "engaging in extramarital relations" if there is no evidence that she was raped. The Emirates Centre for Human Rights states that "Until laws are reformed, victims of sexual violence in the UAE will continue to suffer," referring to a case in July 2013 in which a 24 year old Norwegian woman, Marte Dalelv, reported an alleged rape to the police and received a prison sentence for "perjury, consensual extramarital sex and alcohol consumption".

In 2012, Dubai police subjected three British citizens to beatings and electric shocks after arresting them on drugs charges. The British

Prime Minister, David Cameron, expressed "concern" over the case and raised it with the UAE President, Sheikh Khalifa bin Zayed Al Nahyan, during his 2013 state visit to the UK. The three men – Grant Cameron (no relation to the British PM), Suneet Jeerh, and Karl Williams – were pardoned and released in July 2013.

The annual Freedom House report on Freedom in the World has listed the United Arab Emirates as "Not Free" every year since 1999 (the first year for which records are available on their website). Freedom House have also condemned the UAE for imprisoning human rights defenders.

In its 2013 Annual Report, Amnesty International drew attention to the United Arab Emirates' poor record on a number of human rights issues. They highlighted the government's restrictive approach to freedom of speech and assembly, their use of arbitrary arrest and torture, and UAE's significant use of the death penalty.

In July 2013, a video was uploaded onto social networking sites, depicting a local driver hitting an expatriate worker, following a road related incident. Using part of his head gear, the local driver whips the expatriate and also taunts him, before other passers-by intervene. A short while later, Dubai police announced that the person who filmed the video had been taken into custody. It was also revealed that the local driver was a senior UAE government official. Later in 2013, police arrested a US citizen and some UAE citizens, in connection with a parody video which allegedly portrayed Dubai and its residents in a bad light. The video was shot in areas of Satwa, Dubai and featured gangs learning how to fight using simple weapons, including shoes, the aghal, etc.

UAE has organisations promoting human rights, such as the Dubai Women's and Children's Foundation, Ewaa in Abu Dhabi, Human Rights Care Department in Dubai and the Social Support Centre in Abu Dhabi . The issue of sexual abuse among female domestic servants is another area of concern, particularly given that domestic servants are not covered by the UAE labour law of 1980 or the draft labour law of 2007. Worker protests have been suppressed and protesters imprisoned without due process. Dubai police opened designated departments in all emirate police stations that are mandated to protect the human rights of victims and perpetrators of crime.

UAE has escaped most of the effects of the Arab Spring; however, many UAE citizens were jailed and/or tortured because they heavily criticized the government system. There were also foreign nationals who had their residency in the country revoked. Human Rights Watch criticized the forced exile of UAE activist Ahmed Abdul Khaleq, calling the action an "unlawful expulsion" motivated by the government's desire to stifle dissent. Amnesty International issued a statement that "Ahmed Abdul Khaleq should never have been forced to leave the country and this event sets alarm bells ringing regarding the fate of others held in the UAE in connection with alleged plots against state security".

Politic

The United Arab Emirates is a federation of hereditary absolute monarchies. It is governed by a Federal Supreme Council made up of the seven emirs of Abu Dhabi, Ajman, Fujairah, Sharjah, Dubai, Ras al-Khaimah and Umm al-Qaiwain. All responsibilities not granted to the national government are reserved to the emirates. A percentage of revenues from each emirate is allocated to the UAE's central budget.

Although elected by the Supreme Council, the presidency and prime ministership are essentially hereditary: The emir of Abu Dhabi holds the presidency, and the emir of Dubai is prime minister. All prime ministers but one have served concurrently as vice president. Sheikh Zayed bin Sultan Al Nahyan was the UAE's president from the nation's founding until his death on 2 November 2004. On the following day the Federal Supreme Council elected his son, Sheikh Khalifa bin Zayed Al Nahyan, to the post. Abu Dhabi's crown prince, Mohammed bin Zayed Al Nahyan, is the heir apparent.

The UAE convened a half-elected Federal National Council in 2006. The FNC consists of 40 members drawn from all the emirates. Half are appointed by the rulers of the constituent emirates, and the other half are indirectly elected to serve two-year terms. However, the FNC is restricted to a largely consultative role. The UAE e-government is the extension of the UAE Federal Government in its electronic form.

The UAE is frequently described as an "autocracy". According to the *New York Times*, the UAE is "an autocracy with the sheen of a progressive, modern state". The UAE ranks poorly in freedom indices measuring civil liberties and political rights. The UAE is annually ranked as "Not Free" in Freedom House's annual Freedom in the World report, which measures civil liberties and political rights. The UAE also ranks poorly in the annual Reporters without Borders' Press Freedom Index.

Relations

The UAE has extensive diplomatic and commercial relations with other countries. It plays a significant role in OPEC and the UN, and is one of the founding members of the Gulf Cooperation Council (GCC). The UAE was one of only three countries to recognise the Taliban as Afghanistan's legitimate government (Pakistan and Saudi Arabia were the other two countries). The UAE maintained diplomatic relations with the Taliban until the September 11 attacks in 2001. The UAE has long maintained close relations with Egypt and remains the biggest investor in that country from the rest of the Arab world. Pakistan had been first country to formally recognise the UAE upon its formation and continues to be one of its major economic and trading partners; about 400,000 Pakistani expatriates are employed in the UAE.

The UAE spends more than any other country in the world to influence U.S. policy and shape domestic debate, and it pays former high-level government officials who worked with it to carry out its agenda within the U.S. The largest expatriate presence in the UAE is Indian. Following British withdrawal from the UAE in 1971 and the establishment of the UAE as a state, the UAE disputed rights to a number of islands in the Persian Gulf against Iran. The UAE went so far as to bring the matter to the United Nations, but the case was dismissed. The dispute has not significantly impacted relations because of the large Iranian community presence and strong economic ties.

In its dispute with the USA and Israel, Iran has repeatedly threatened to close the strait at the mouth of the Persian Gulf, a vital oil-trade route. Therefore, in July 2012, the UAE began operating a key overland oil pipeline which bypasses the Strait of Hormuz in order to mitigate any consequences of an Iranian shut-off.

Commercially, the UK and Germany are the UAE's largest export markets and bilateral relations have long been close as a large number of their nationals reside in the UAE. Diplomatic relations between UAE and Japan were established as early as UAE's independence in December 1971. The two countries had always enjoyed friendly ties and trade between each other. Exports from the UAE to Japan include crude oil and natural gas and imports from Japan to UAE include cars and electric items.

Military

France and the United States have played the most strategically significant roles with defence cooperation agreements and military material provision. The UAE discussed with France the possibility of a purchase of 60 Rafale fighter aircraft in January 2013. The UAE helped the U.S. launch its first air offencive against Islamic State targets in Syria.

Political Divisions

The United Arab Emirates is divided into seven emirates. Dubai is the most populated Emirate with 35.6% of the UAE population. The Emirate of Abu Dhabi has a further 31.2%, meaning that over two-thirds of the UAE population live in either Abu Dhabi or Dubai.

Abu Dhabi has an area of 67,340 square kilometres (26,000 square miles), which is 86.7% of the country's total area, excluding the islands. It has a coastline extending for more than 400 km (249 mi) and is divided for administrative purposes into three major regions. The Emirate of Dubai extends along the Persian Gulf coast of the UAE for approximately 72 km (45 mi). Dubai has an area of 3,885 square kilometres (1,500 square miles), which is equivalent to 5% of the country's total area, excluding the islands. The Emirate of Sharjah extends along approximately 16 km (10 mi) of the UAE's Persian Gulf coastline and for more than 80 km (50 mi) into the interior. The northern emirates which include Fujairah, Ajman, Ras al-Khaimah, and Umm al-Qaiwain all have a total area of 3,881 km^2. There are two areas under joint control. One is jointly controlled by Oman and Ajman, the other by Fujairah and Sharjah.

There is an Omani exclave surrounded by UAE territory, known as Wadi Madha. It is located halfway between the Musandam peninsula and the rest of Oman in the Emirate of Sharjah. It covers approximately 75 square kilometres (29 square miles) and the boundary was settled in 1589. The north-east corner of Madha is closest to the Khor Fakkan-Fujairah road, barely 10 metres (33 ft) away. Within the Omani exclave of Madha, is a UAE exclave called Nahwa, also belonging to the Emirate of Sharjah. It is about 8 kilometres (5 mi) on a dirt track west of the town of New Madha. It consists of about forty houses with its own clinic and telephone exchange.

Economy

UAE has the second largest economy in the GCC (after Saudi Arabia), with a gross domestic product (GDP) of $377 billion (AED1.38 trillion) in 2012. Since independence in 1971, UAE's economy has grown by nearly 231 times to AED1.45 trillion in 2013. The non-oil trade has grown to AED1.2 trillion, a growth by around 28 times from 1981 to 2012. In 2011, UAE is ranked as the 14th best nation in the world for doing business based on its economy and regulatory environment, ranked by the Doing Business 2011 Report published by the World Bank Group

Figure: *Burj Khalifa*

Although UAE has the most diversified economy in the GCC, the UAE's economy remains extremely reliant on oil. With the exception of Dubai, most of the UAE is dependent on oil revenues. Petroleum and natural gas continue to play a central role in the economy, especially in Abu Dhabi. More than 85% of the UAE's economy was based on the oil exports in 2009. While Abu Dhabi and other UAE emirates have remained relatively conservative in their approach to diversification, Dubai, which has far smaller oil reserves, was bolder in its diversification policy. In 2011, oil exports accounted for 77% of the UAE's state budget.

Dubai suffered from a significant economic crisis in 2007-2010 and was bailed out by Abu Dhabi's oil wealth. Dubai's current prosperity has been attributed to Abu Dhabi's petrodollars. Dubai is currently in extreme debt. The GDP growth rate for 2010 was 3.20%. Consumer price index inflation in the April 2008 — April 2009 year was 1.9%. The national debt as of June 2009 was $142 billion. In 2009, its GDP, as measured by purchasing power parity, stood at US$ 400.4 billion. With a population of just under 900,000 Abu Dhabi was labeled "The richest city in the world" by a CNN article.

UAE law does not allow trade unions to exist. The right to collective bargaining and the right to strike are not recognised, and the Ministry of Labour has the power to force workers to go back to work. Migrant workers who participate in a strike can have their work permits cancelled and be deported. Consequently, there are very few anti-discrimination laws in relation to labour issues, with Emiratis – other

GCC Arabs – getting preference when it comes to employment, even though they show scant regard for work and learning on the job.

The UAE's economy, particularly that of Dubai, was badly hit by the financial crisis of 2007–2010. In 2009, the country's economy shrank by 4.00% and the property sector and construction went into decline. As the epicentre of the crisis, Dubai was bailed out by Abu Dhabi, with the latter's petrodollars continuing to offer relief. Dubai nonetheless remains in extreme debt.

However, tourism, trade and the retail sector have remained buoyant and the UAE's overseas investments are expected to support its full economic recovery. Concern remains about the property sector. Property prices in Dubai fell dramatically when Dubai World, the government construction company, sought to delay a debt payment. The economy is depending on foreign labour force and Emerisation is only showing few positive effects which was found out in studies from Paul Dyer and Natasha Ridge from Dubai School of Government, Ingo Forstenlechner from United Arab Emirates University, Kasim Randaree from the British University of Dubai and Paul Knoglinger from the FHWien.

The UAE has been spending billions of dollars on infrastructure. These developments are particularly evident in the larger emirates of Abu Dhabi and Dubai. The northern emirates are rapidly following suit, providing major incentives for developers of residential and commercial property.

Dubai International Airport was the Busiest airport in the world by international passenger traffic from January to May 2013, overtaking London Heathrow. As roads in the western and southern regions are still relatively undeveloped, residents prevalently use airplanes as the main or alternative mode of transportation. A 1,200 km (750 mi) country-wide national railway is under construction which will connect all the major cities and ports. The Dubai Metro is the first urban train network in the Arabian Peninsula. The major ports of the United Arab Emirates are Khalifa Port, Zayed Port, Port Jebel Ali, Port Rashid, Port Khalid, Port Saeed, and Port Khor Fakkan.

The UAE is served by two telecommunications operators, Etisalat and Emirates Integrated Telecommunications Company ("du"). Etisalat operated a monopoly until du launched mobile services in February 2007. Internet subscribers are expected to increase from 0.904 million in 2007 to 2.66 million in 2012. The authorities filter websites for religious, political and sexual content.

Demographics

The demographics of the UAE are extremely diverse. In 2010, the UAE's population was estimated to be 8,264,070, of whom only 13% were UAE nationals or Emiratis, while the majority of the population were expatriates. The country's net migration rate stands at 13.6, one of the world's highest. Under Article 8 of UAE Federal Law no. 17, an expatriate can apply for UAE citizenship after residing in the country for 20 years, providing that person has never been convicted of a crime and can speak fluent Arabic.

There are 1.4 million Emirati citizens. With a male/female sex ratio of 2.2 for the total population and 2.75 for the 15–65 age group, the UAE's gender imbalance is second highest in the world after Qatar.

In 2009, Emirati citizens accounted for 17% of the total population; South Asian (Indian, Sri Lankan, Pakistani, Bangladeshi) constituted the largest group, making up 58% of the total; other Asians made up 17% while Western expatriates were 8% of the total population.

There is a growing presence of Europeans in the UAE. Western expatriates, from Europe, Australia, Northern America and Latin America make up 500,000 of the UAE population. The UAE has also attracted a small number of expatriates from countries in Europe, North America, Africa, Asia, and Oceania. More than 100,000 British nationals live in the country. The rest of the population were from other Arab states.

The average life expectancy is 77 years (2014). About 88% of the population of the United Arab Emirates is urban.

Religion

Islam is the largest and the official state religion of the UAE. The government follows a policy of tolerance toward other religions and rarely interferes in the activities of non-Muslims. By the same token, non-Muslims are expected to avoid interfering in Islamic religious matters or the Islamic upbringing of Muslims.

The government imposes restrictions on spreading other religions through any form of media as it is considered a form of proselytizing. There are approximately 31 churches throughout the country, one Hindu temple in the region of Bur Dubai, one Sikh Gurudwara in Jebel Ali and also a Buddhist temple in Al Garhoud.

Based on the Ministry of Economy census in 2005, 76% of the total population was Muslim, 9% Christian, and 15% other (mainly Hindu). Census figures do not take into account the many "temporary" visitors and workers while also counting Baha'is and Druze as Muslim. Among Emirati citizens, 85% are Sunni Muslim, while Shi'a Muslims are 15%, mostly concentrated in the emirates of Sharjah and Dubai. Omani immigrants are mostly Ibadi, while Sufi influences exist too.

People of all faiths or no faith are given equal protection under the country's constitution and laws.

Languages

Arabic is the national language of the United Arab Emirates. The Gulf dialect of Arabic is spoken natively by the Emirati people. As a British colony until 1971 and being a hub for commerce, English is the primary *lingua franca* in the UAE. As such, a knowledge of the language is a requirement when applying for most of the jobs in the UAE. Other widely used languages are Persian, Nepali, Bengali, Hindi-Urdu, Balochi, Pashto, Tagalog and Malayalam. Additionally, there are small Somali, Malay, Mandarin and Japanese speaking communities.

Culture

Arab descendants of the Bani Yas, Al Nahyan and Al Maktoum families in Abu Dhabi and Dubai represent the Emirati leadership. Al Qawasim have also played a vital role in the history of the UAE.

Emirati culture is based on Arabian culture and has been heavily influenced by Persian culture. Arabian and Persian inspired architecture is part of the expression of the local Emirati identity. Persian influence on Emirati culture is noticeably visible in traditional Emirati architecture and folk arts. For example, the "barjeel" has become an identifying mark of traditional Emirati architecture and is attributed to Persian influence. Certain folk dances, such as "al-habban", are originally Persian. Local Emirati culture has also been influenced by the cultures of East Africa and India.

The United Arab Emirates has a diverse society. Major holidays in Dubai include *Eid al Fitr*, which marks the end of *Ramadan*, and National Day (2 December), which marks the formation of the United Arab Emirates.

Emirati males prefer to wear a kandura, an ankle-length white tunic woven from wool or cotton, and Emirati women wear an abaya, a black over-garment that covers most parts of the body. The campaign UAE Dress Code aims to educate the expat population on modest Islamic dressing and its sensitivity to Emirati population. Each of the seven semiautonomous emirates has its own rules about attire. Dubai is the most liberal in that regard while Ras al-Khaimah is the most strict.

Ancient Emirati poetry was strongly influenced by the 8th-century Arab scholar Al Khalil bin Ahmed. The earliest known poet in the UAE is Ibn Majid, born between 1432 and 1437 in Ras Al-Khaimah. The most famous Emirati writers were Mubarak Al Oqaili (1880–1954), Salem bin Ali al Owais (1887–1959) and Ahmed bin Sulayem (1905–1976). Three other poets from Sharjah, known as the Hirah group, are observed to have been heavily influenced by the Apollo and romantic poets. The Sharjah International Book Fair is the oldest and largest in the country.

The list of museums in the United Arab Emirates includes some of regional repute, most famously Sharjah with its Heritage District containing 17 museums, which in 1998 was the Cultural Capital of the Arab World. In Dubai, the area of Al Quoz has attracted a number of art galleries as well as museums such as the Salsali Private Museum. Abu Dhabi has established a culture district on Saadiyat Island. There, six grand projects are planned, including the Guggenheim Abu Dhabi and the Louvre Abu Dhabi. Dubai also plans to build a Kunsthal museum and a district for galleries and artists.

Emirati culture is a part of the culture of Eastern Arabia. Liwa is a type of music and dance performed mainly in communities that contain descendants of Bantu peoples from the African Great Lakes region. The Dubai Desert Rock Festival is also another major festival consisting of heavy metal and rock artists. The cinema of the United Arab Emirates is minimal but expanding.

The Media of the United Arab Emirates plays an important role in the region. Dubai Media City and two four 54, Abu Dhabi's media zone, were set up to attract key players. The UAE is home to major pan-Arab broadcasters, including the Middle East Broadcasting Centre and Orbit Showtime Network. On 25 September 2007 Sheikh Mohammed bin Rashid Al Maktoum decreed that journalists can no longer be prosecuted or imprisoned for reasons relating to their work. At the same time, the UAE has made it illegal to disseminate online material that can threaten "public order". Criticism of the Royal family or government procedures is not allowed. Prison terms have been given to those who "deride or damage" the reputation of the state and "display contempt" for religion.

Education

The education system through secondary level is monitored by the Ministry of Education in all emirates except Abu Dhabi, where it falls under the authority of the Abu Dhabi Education Council. It consists of primary schools, middle schools and high schools. The public schools are government-funded and the curriculum is created to match the United Arab Emirates development's goals and values. The medium of instruction in the public school is Arabic with emphasis on English as a second language. There are also many private schools which are internationally accredited. Public schools in the country are free for citizens of the UAE, while the fees for private schools vary.

The higher education system is monitored by the Ministry of Higher Education. The ministry also is responsible for admitting students to its undergraduate institutions.

The literacy rate in 2007 was 91%. Thousands of nationals are pursuing formal learning at 86 adult education centres spread across the country.

The UAE has shown a strong interest in improving education and research. Enterprises include the establishment of the CERT Research Centres and the Masdar Institute of Science and Technology and Institute for Enterprise Development.

According to the QS Rankings, the top-ranking universities in the country are the United Arab Emirates University (421–430th worldwide), the American University of Sharjah (431–440th) and University of Sharjah (3046th).

Bibliography

Ahmad, Feroz: *The Making of Modern Turkey*, Routledge, London, 1993.

Akhtar, Salman: *The Crescent and the Couch: Cross-Currents Between Islam and Psychoanalysis*, Rowman & Littlefield, United States, 2008.

Al-Rasheed, Madawi: *A History of Saudi Arabia*, Cambridge University Press, New York, 2010.

Andrew, Mango Atatürk: *The Biography of the Founder of Modern Turkey*, Overlook Press, New York, 2002.

Barlas, Dilek: *Statism and Diplomacy in Turkey: Economic and Foreign Policy Strategies in an Uncertain World, 1929–1939*, Brill Academic Publishers, New York, 1998.

Bowman, Alan K.: *Egypt after the Pharaohs 332 BC – AD 642,* University of California Press, Berkeley, 1996.

Cleveland, William L.: *A History of the Modern Middle East*, Westview Press, Boulder, Colorado, 2004.

Clogg, Richard: *A Concise History of Greece*, Cambridge University Press, New York, 2002.

Commins, David: *The Wahhabi Mission and Saudi Arabia*, I.B. Tauris, London, 2006.

Donald Quataert: *The Ottoman Empire, 1700-1922*, Cambridge University Press, New York, 2005.

Edward J. Erickson: *Defeat in Detail: The Ottoman Army in the Balkans, 1912–1913*, Praeger, New York, 2003.

El-Daly, Okasha: *Egyptology: The Missing Millennium*, UCL Press, London, 2005.

Gerd, Nonneman: *Analyzing Middle East foreign policies and the relationship with Europe*, Routledge, New York, 2005 .

Hanioglu, M. Suekrue: *Atatürk: An Intellectual Biography*, Princeton University Press, New Jersey and Woodstock, 2011.

Helms, Christine Moss: *The Cohesion of Saudi Arabia*, The Johns Hopkins University Press, Baltimore, 1981.

Jesse Ferris: *Nasser's Gamble: How Intervention in Yemen Caused the Six-Day War and the Decline of Egyptian Power*, Princeton University Press, US., 2013.

Kevin Shillington: *Encyclopedia of African History*, Michigan University Press, 2005.

Kinross, Patrick: *The Ottoman Centuries: The Rise and Fall of the Turkish Empire*, Morrow, New York, 1979.

Kinross, Patrick: *Atatürk: The Rebirth of a Nation*, Phoenix Press, London, 2003.

Laitin, David D.: *Hegemony and culture: politics and religious change among the Yoruba*, University of Chicago Press, v.

Landau, Jacob M.: *Atatürk and the Modernization of Turkey*, Westview Press, Boulder, Colorado, 1983.

Majid, Khadduri: *War and peace in the law of Islam*, Phoenix Press, London, 2006.

Midant-Reynes, Béatrix: *The Prehistory of Egypt: From the First Egyptians to the First Kings*, Oxford, Blackwell Publishers, 2008.

Navaro-Yashin, Yael: *Faces of the State: Secularism and Public Life in Turkey*, Princeton University Press, 2002.

Richard C. Hall, *The Balkan Wars 1912–1913: Prelude to the First World War*, Routledge, 2002.

Saikal, Amin; Schnabel, Albrecht: *Democratization in the Middle East: Experiences, Struggles, Challenges*, United Nations University Press, Tokyo, 2003.

Samir, A. Mutawi: *Jordan in the 1967 War*, Cambridge University Press, London, 2002.

Shaw, Stanford Jay; Shaw, Ezel Kural: *History of the Ottoman Empire and Modern Turkey*, Cambridge University Press, Cambridge; New York, 1976.

Stanwick, Paul Edmond: *Portraits of the Ptolemies: Greek kings as Egyptian pharaohs*, University of Texas Press, Austin, 2003.

Suberu, Rotimi T.: *Federalism and Ethnic Conflict in Nigeria*, US Institute of Peace Press, 2001.

Troeller, Gary: *The Birth of Saudi Arabia: Britain and the Rise of the House of Sa'ud*, Routledge, London, 1976.

Vatikiotis, P.J.: *The history of modern Egypt: from Muhammad Ali to Mubarak*, Weidenfeld and Nicolson, London, 1991.

Yapp, Malcolm: *The Making of the Modern Near East, 1792–1923*, Longman, New York, 1987.

Zürcher, Erik Jan: *Turkey: A Modern History*, I.B. Tauris, London, 2004.

Index

❑❑❑